THE MacARTHUR NEW TESTAMENT COMMENTARY

LUKE 11-17

John MacArthur

MOODY PUBLISHERS/CHICAGO

Cover Design: Smartt Guys design

Library of Congress Cataloging-in-Publication Data

MacArthur, John
    Luke 11-17 / John MacArthur.
        p. cm.— (The MacArthur New Testament commentary)
    Includes bibliographical references and indexes.
    ISBN 978-0-8024-0873-0
    1. Bible. N. T. Luke XI-XVII—Commentaries. I. Title. II. Title: Luke eleven-seventeen.

BS2595.53.M33 2013
226.4`077—dc22

2013021035

We hope you enjoy this book from Moody Publishers. Our goal is to provide high-quality, thought-provoking books and products that connect truth to your real needs and challenges. For more information on other books and products written and produced from a biblical perspective, go to www.moodypublishers.com or write to:

Moody Publishers
820 N. LaSalle Boulevard
Chicago, IL 60610

7 9 10 8 6

Printed in the United States of America

Dedicated to Albert Mohler,
a treasured friend and trustworthy voice of clarity
in confusing times. I love his unapologetic commitment
to the authority of Scripture, courageous leadership, untiring zeal,
and faithful devotion to the truth – written and incarnate.
He is that rare combination of intrepid intellectualism and
passionate love for the Lord (not merely academic curiosity)
who, by his influence, has galvanized
a generation of preachers who share his convictions.

Contents

CHAPTER	PAGE
Preface	vii
1. Jesus' Pattern for Every Prayer—Part 1: Teach Us to Pray (Luke 11:1–2*a*)	1
2. Jesus' Pattern for Every Prayer—Part 2: God's Person (Luke 11:2*b,c*)	9
3. Jesus' Pattern for Every Prayer—Part 3: God's Purpose (Luke 11:2*d*)	19
4. Jesus' Pattern for Every Prayer—Part 4: God's Provision (Luke 11:3–4)	31
5. Jesus' Pattern for Every Prayer—Part 5: God's Promise (Luke 11:5–13)	49
6. The Vilification of Jesus (Luke 11:14–23)	59
7. The Danger of Moral Reformation (Luke 11:24–28)	69
8. Judgment on a Wicked Generation (Luke 11:29–36)	79
9. Characteristics of False Religionists (Luke 11:37–54)	93
10. A Certain Cure for Hypocrisy (Luke 12:1–12)	111

11.	The Rich Fool (Luke 12:13–21)	127
12.	Anxiety-Free Living (Luke 12:22–34)	137
13.	Anticipating Christ's Return (Luke 12:35–48)	149
14.	The Tragedy of Wasted Opportunity (Luke 12:49–59)	167
15.	Living on Borrowed Time (Luke 13:1–9)	179
16.	Christ Creates Conflict in the Synagogue (Luke 13:10–17)	193
17.	The Increasing Influence of the Kingdom (Luke 13:18–21)	205
18.	Are Just a Few Being Saved? (Luke 13:22–30)	215
19.	Who Really Killed Jesus? (Luke 13:31–33)	225
20.	Divine Compassion for Those Deserving Condemnation (Luke 13:34–35)	235
21.	Confronting Hypocritical False Teachers (Luke 14:1–14)	253
22.	An Invitation to God's Great Banquet (Luke 14:15–24)	267
23.	The Extreme Nature of True Discipleship (Luke 14:25–35)	277
24.	Heaven's Joy: Recovering the Lost (Luke 15:1–10)	291
25.	The Tale of Two Sons (Luke 15:11–32)	303
26.	Investing Earthly Finances with an Eternal Focus (Luke 16:1–13)	331
27.	Why False Teachers Mock the Truth (Luke 16:14–18)	341
28.	A Testimony of One Surprised to Be in Hell (Luke 16:19–31)	355
29.	Four Hallmarks of Humility (Luke 17:1–10)	373
30.	Ten Men Healed; One Man Saved (Luke 17:11–19)	387
31.	The Invisible Kingdom of God (Luke 17:20–21)	397
32.	Seven Characteristics of the King's Coming (Luke 17:22–37)	407
	Bibliography	421
	Index of Greek Words and Phrases	423
	Index of Scripture	424
	Index of Subjects	437

Preface

It continues to be a rewarding, divine communion for me to preach expositionally through the New Testament. My goal is always to have deep fellowship with the Lord in the understanding of His Word and out of that experience to explain to His people what a passage means. In the words of Nehemiah 8:8, I strive "to give the sense" of it so they may truly hear God speak and, in so doing, may respond to Him.

Obviously, God's people need to understand Him, which demands knowing His Word of Truth (2 Tim. 2:15) and allowing that Word to dwell in them richly (Col. 3:16). The dominant thrust of my ministry, therefore, is to help make God's living Word alive to His people. It is a refreshing adventure.

This New Testament commentary series reflects this objective of explaining and applying Scripture. Some commentaries are primarily linguistic, others are mostly theological, and some are mainly homiletical. This one is basically explanatory, or expository. It is not linguistically technical but deals with linguistics when that seems helpful to proper interpretation. It is not theologically expansive but focuses on the major doctrines in each text and how they relate to the whole of Scripture. It is not primarily homiletical, although each unit of thought is generally treated as one chapter, with a clear outline and logical flow of thought. Most truths are illustrated and applied with other Scripture. After establishing the context of a passage, I have tried to follow closely the writer's development and reasoning.

My prayer is that each reader will fully understand what the Holy Spirit is saying through this part of His Word, so that His revelation may lodge in the mind of believers and bring greater obedience and faithfulness—to the glory of our great God.

Jesus' Pattern for Every Prayer—Part 1: Teach Us to Pray (Luke 11:1–2a)

It happened that while Jesus was praying in a certain place, after He had finished, one of His disciples said to Him, "Lord, teach us to pray just as John also taught his disciples." And He said to them, "When you pray, say:" (11:1–2a)

On the importance of prayer in the Christian life, the notable Puritan pastor Thomas Brooks wrote,

> The power of religion and godliness lives, thrives, or dies, as closet [private] prayer lives, thrives, or dies. Godliness never rises to a higher pitch than when men keep closest to their closets.

> Private prayer is that privy [secret] key of heaven that unlocks all the treasures of glory to the soul. The best riches and the sweetest mercies God usually gives to his people when they are in their closets upon their knees ... the graces of the saints are enlivened, and cherished, and strengthened by the sweet secret influences which their souls fall under when they are in their closet-communion with God. (*The Secret Key to Heaven* [Reprint; Edinburgh: Banner of Truth, 2006], xiv, 44)

Prayer is more than merely an occasional duty; it is a way of life. The New Testament commands believers to "keep watching and praying" (Matt. 26:41); "that at all times they ought to pray" (Luke 18:1); to be "devoted to prayer" (Rom. 12:12); to "pray at all times" (Eph. 6:18); to "devote [themselves] to prayer" (Col. 4:2); to "in everything by prayer and supplication with thanksgiving let [their] requests be made known to God" (Phil. 4:6); and to "pray without ceasing" (1 Thess. 5:17).

Old Testament saints believed that God heard their prayers. In Psalm 65:2 David addressed God as "You who hear prayer," while Solomon wrote that God "hears the prayer of the righteous" (Prov. 15:29). Not only does He hear the prayers of His people, He also delights in hearing them (Prov. 15:8). But those prayers must be from a pure heart (Job 16:17; Ps. 17:1; Prov. 28:9), because God will not hear the prayers of those who harbor sin in their heart (Ps. 66:18; Isa. 1:15), and must also reflect trust in Him (1 Chron. 5:20).

The Old Testament records, for example, the prayers of Abraham for Abimelech (Gen. 20:7, 17), Isaac for Rebekah (Gen. 25:21), Moses for Israel after the people rebelled against God in the wilderness (Num. 14:13–19), Hannah for a son (1 Sam. 1:10–12), David in response to the promise of the Davidic covenant (2 Sam. 7:18–29), Solomon at the dedication of the temple (1 Kings 8:22–53), Elijah for the resurrection of a widow's son (1 Kings 17:21), Elisha for the resurrection of a Shunnamite woman's son (2 Kings 4:33), Hezekiah in response to an Assyrian invasion (2 Kings 19:15–19), and for healing (2 Kings 20:2–3), David and Manasseh for personal forgiveness (Ps. 51; 2 Chron. 33:11–13), Jonah for personal deliverance (Jon. 2:1–9), and Ezra (Ezra 9:5–15), Nehemiah (Neh. 1:4–11), and Daniel (Dan. 9:1–19) for forgiveness and deliverance for the nation of Israel.

The New Testament records the prayers of Anna (Luke 2:37), the apostles (Acts 1:14; 6:6 [cf. 6:4]), the early church (Acts 1:24; 2:42; 4:23–31; 12:5, 12; 13:3), Peter and John (Acts 8:14–15), Peter (Acts 9:40; 11:5), Paul (Acts 9:11; 16:25 [with Silas]; 20:36; 21:5; 28:8; Rom. 1:10; 10:1; 2 Cor. 13:7, 9; Eph. 1:16–23; 3:14–21; Phil. 1:4, 9–11; Col. 1:3, 9–12; 1 Thess. 1:2; 3:10; 2 Thess. 1:11; 2 Tim. 1:3; Philem. 4), and John (3 John 2).

But the supreme example of prayer in all of Scripture is drawn from the Lord Jesus Christ. Prayer permeated our Lord's earthly ministry from beginning to end. He prayed at His baptism (Luke 3:21), during His first preaching tour (Mark 1:35; Luke 5:16), before choosing the Twelve (Luke 6:12–13), before feeding the five thousand (Matt. 14:19), after feeding the five thousand (Matt. 14:23), before feeding the four thousand (Matt. 15:36), before Peter's confession of Him as the Christ (Luke 9:18), at the transfiguration (Luke 9:28–29), for some children who had been brought to Him (Matt. 19:13), after the return of the seventy (Luke 10:21), before raising Lazarus from the dead (John 11:41–42), as He faced the reality of the cross (John 12:28), at the Last Supper (Matt. 26:26–27), for Peter (Luke 22:31–32), in Gethsemane (Matt. 26:36–44), from the cross (Matt. 27:46; Luke 23:34, 46), with the disciples He encountered on the road to Emmaus (Luke 24:30), at the ascension (Luke 24:50–51) and, supremely, in His high priestly prayer in John 17. It comes as no surprise, then, that this passage finds **Jesus . . . praying in a certain** unnamed **place** somewhere in Judea.

Luke's account of this model prayer is an abbreviated version of the one recorded by Matthew (6:9–13), though the two prayers were given on different occasions. The one in Matthew's gospel was in Galilee; the one recorded by Luke occurred several months later in Judea. Undoubtedly both prayers reflect teaching repeated frequently by Jesus to His followers throughout His earthly ministry. For the sake of completeness, the elements noted by Matthew but omitted by Luke will be included in the exposition of this prayer in the chapters that follow.

This prayer is Jesus' vehicle for teaching the disciples (and all believers) the essential structure and required features of prayer. The elements in His prayer emphasize the overarching reason for prayer, as will be seen. This overview may be divided into two sections: the disciples' request that Jesus teach them to pray, and the Lord's response.

THE DISCIPLES' REQUEST

after He had finished, one of His disciples said to Him, "Lord, teach us to pray just as John also taught his disciples." (11:1*b*)

While Jesus frequently sought solitude when He prayed (cf. 5:16; Matt. 14:23; Mark 1:35), on this occasion some of His disciples were present. When the Lord had **finished** praying **one of His disciples,** no doubt speaking for the rest, **said to Him, "Lord, teach us to pray."** Given both the Old Testament's emphasis on prayer and their familiarity with it, this request seems somewhat surprising. But it reflects the sad reality that at that time in their history, tradition and ceremony had replaced the knowledge of Scripture so that true prayer had largely been lost to the Jewish people. The disciples' request for instruction in prayer also reveals that what they had come to be familiar with regarding prayer was not what God wanted. The prayer they heard Jesus pray was radically different from the traditional, customary prayers they were used to in their synagogues from the scribes, Pharisees, and rabbis.

Jesus noted that contrast in Matthew 6, where He indicted the phony, hypocritical religion of the scribes and Pharisees. "When you pray," He warned His hearers, "you are not to be like the hypocrites; for they love to stand and pray in the synagogues and on the street corners so that they may be seen by men. Truly I say to you, they have their reward in full" (v. 5). Those prayers were focused on putting on a show of piosity for the people who were watching, not on honoring and glorifying God. Instead of showy, ostentatious, public prayers, Jesus instructed His followers, "When you pray, go into your inner room, close your door and pray to your Father who is in secret, and your Father who sees what is done in secret will reward you" (v. 6). Many Jewish prayers were marked by the ritualistic, meaningless, empty, vain repetition that characterized pagan prayers. But Jesus declared, "When you are praying, do not use meaningless repetition as the Gentiles do, for they suppose that they will be heard for their many words" (v. 7).

That **John** the Baptist had **also taught his disciples** to pray (cf. Luke 5:33) also prompted the Lord's disciples to ask Him to teach them. They were acquainted with John's disciples (cf. 7:18–24), and wanted the same kind of instruction from Jesus that John had given his followers. It is reasonable to assume that since John was not a part of the religious establishment, he had maintained a pure, uncorrupted approach to prayer in keeping with that of Old Testament saints.

THE LORD'S RESPONSE

And He said to them, "When you pray, say:" (*2b*)

The disciples had not requested that Jesus teach them a prayer to recite, but how to pray. He responded by giving them a prayer that, while it is recited and even sung, is not intended for merely that. Having warned against meaningless repetition in prayer (Matt. 6:7), Jesus would hardly have given His followers a prayer to recite mechanically. Nor is there any record in the New Testament of anyone subsequently reciting this prayer. Far from being merely another ritual prayer, it is a skeleton or framework for all prayer. As such, it is of great practical value, as the Puritan pastor and theologian Thomas Watson noted:

> There is a double benefit arising from framing our petitions suitably to this prayer. 1. Hereby error in prayer is prevented. It is not easy to write wrong after this copy; we cannot easily err when we have our pattern before us. 2. Hereby mercies requested are obtained; for the apostle assures us that God will hear us when we pray "according to his will." 1 John v. 14. And sure we pray according to his will when we pray according to the pattern he has set us. (*Body of Divinity* [Reprint; Grand Rapids: Baker, 1979], 400–401)

This prayer reflects the elements of prayer found in the Old Testament. There was a sense in which God was unapproachable, symbolized by the veil separating the Holy of Holies from the rest of the temple, and the prohibition against touching Mt. Sinai when God appeared (Ex. 19:12). Yet while the people could not enter directly into God's presence, they were invited to approach Him in prayer. "In my distress" David said, "I called upon the Lord, and cried to my God for help; He heard my voice out of His temple, and my cry for help before Him came into His ears" (Ps. 18:6). In Psalm 145:18 he added, "The Lord is near to all who call upon Him, to all who call upon Him in truth." In Psalm 50:15 God invited His people to "Call upon Me in the day of trouble; I shall rescue you, and you will honor Me," and in 91:15 He promised, "He will call upon Me, and I will answer him; I will be with him in trouble; I will rescue him and honor him."

Prayers in the Old Testament were characterized by several elements. First, they were marked by adoration, love, and praise, as the passion of the heart flowed out from the lips (Pss. 7:17; 22:23, 26; 34:1).

Second, they reflected an attitude of gratefulness and thanksgiving for God's blessings and provision (Pss. 9:1; 30:4; 33:2; 50:14, 23; Isa. 12:1; Dan. 2:23; Jon. 2:9), Third, they recognized God's holiness (Ps. 22:3), acknowledging His transcendent glory. Fourth, they manifested a heartfelt desire to obey God (Ps. 119:5, 8, 17, 34, 88, 134), which resulted in confession of sin (Ps. 51) when there was disobedience. Fifth, instead of focusing exclusively on the needs of individuals, Old Testament prayers also expressed the needs of the nation as a whole (Ex. 33:13, 16; Deut. 26:15). Sixth, prayer in the Old Testament also involved perseverance, such as that exemplified by Moses, who interceded on behalf of the people for forty days after the incident of the golden calf (Deut. 9:18, 25). Finally, prayers were offered in humility (2 Chron. 7:14; Ezra 8:21; Ps. 10:17). Those same elements are in view in Jesus' prayer, as He reestablished the divine pattern that had largely been lost in Israel.

This rich, multifaceted template may be approached in several ways. It unfolds the various relationships between the believer and God: Father and child ("Our Father"), Holy One and worshiper ("hallowed be Your name"), Ruler and subject ("Your kingdom come"), Master and servant ("Your will be done"), Savior and sinner ("forgive us our debts"), and Guide and pilgrim ("do not lead us into temptation"). It also defines the proper attitudes for prayer: unselfishness ("our"), intimacy ("Father"), reverence ("hallowed be Your name"), loyalty ("Your kingdom come"), submissiveness ("Your will be done"), dependence ("give us this day our daily bread"), penitence ("forgive us our debts"), humility ("do not lead us into temptation"), and confident, triumphant joy ("Yours is the kingdom and the power and the glory forever").

Focusing on God's glory, Jesus ignored non-essential elements such as the posture of prayer. Scripture records people praying in every conceivable position: standing (Gen. 24:12–14; 1 Sam. 1:26), sitting (Judg. 21:2–3; 2 Sam. 7:18; 1 Kings 19:4), kneeling (1 Kings 8:54; Ezra 9:5; Dan. 6:10), bowing (Ex. 34:8–9), lying face down (Ezek. 9:8; Matt. 26:39), with uplifted hands (Ps. 28:2; 1 Tim. 2:8), looking up (John 11:41; 17:1), and looking down (Luke 18:13).

Nor is there any particular location that prayers must be offered, though Jesus did suggest a private place (Matt. 6:6) rather than a pretentious public display. Still, the men of Judah prayed in the midst of battle

(2 Chron. 13:14); Elijah prayed in a cave (1 Kings 19:9–10); Jesus prayed in the garden of Gethsemane (Matt. 26:36–44), in the wilderness (Mark 1:35; Luke 5:16), on a mountain, (Luke 6:12), and on the cross (Luke 23:33–34); the early church prayed in a house (Acts 1:14, 24; 12:12); Peter prayed on a housetop (Acts 10:9); Paul and Silas prayed in jail (Acts 16:25); Paul prayed on a beach (Acts 21:5) and in the temple (Acts 22:17); Hezekiah prayed in bed (Isa. 38:2); and Jonah prayed in the stomach of a fish (Jon. 2:1–9).

Nor did Jesus specify any particular time to pray. Scripture records people praying in the early morning before dawn (Mark 1:35), in the morning after sunrise (Pss. 5:3; 88:13), three times a day (Dan. 6:10 [morning, noon, and evening; Ps. 55:17]), at noon (Acts 10:9), in the afternoon (Acts 3:1), in the evening (1 Kings 18:36), during the night (Pss. 4:4; Luke 6:12), at midnight (Acts 16:25), all day long (Ps. 86:3), and day and night (Neh. 1:6; Luke 2:37; 1 Thess. 3:10; 1 Tim. 5:5); in short, believers are to pray at all times (Luke 18:1; Eph. 6:18), continually (Acts 1:14), and unceasingly (1 Thess. 5:17).

The Lord also did not mandate one particular attitude for prayer. On the one hand, some approached God with an attitude of sadness, grief, even despair. Daniel prayed wearing sackcloth, a manifestation of sorrow (Dan. 9:3); a repentant tax collector beat his breast, a sign of remorse, while praying (Luke 18:13); Hannah "wept bitterly" as she prayed (1 Sam. 1:9–11), as did David (Ps. 39:12); appalled by Israel's defeat at Ai following Achan's sin, Joshua and the elders of Israel put dust on their heads and tore their clothes when they sought the Lord in prayer (Josh. 7:6–7); after the devastating catastrophes that hit him "Job arose and tore his robe and shaved his head, and he fell to the ground and worshiped" (Job 1:20); Moses (Deut. 9:18–19), Nehemiah (Neh. 1:4), Anna (Luke 2:37), the leaders of the church at Antioch (Acts 13:1–3), and Paul and Barnabas (Acts 14:23) fasted and prayed; Jesus, "in the days of His flesh,... offered up both prayers and supplications with loud crying and tears to the One able to save Him from death, and He was heard because of His piety" (Heb. 5:7; cf. Luke 22:44); David exhorted the people, "Pour out your heart before Him; God is a refuge for us" (Ps. 62:8).

On the other hand, prayer can be offered with an attitude of joy. Paul wrote to the Philippians that he was "always offering prayer with joy in my every prayer for you all" (Phil. 1:4); 1 Samuel 2:1 records that "Hannah prayed and said, 'My heart exults in the Lord; my horn is exalted in the Lord, my mouth speaks boldly against my enemies, because I rejoice in Your salvation'"; David declared, "My mouth offers praises with joyful lips" (Ps. 63:5; cf. 71:23; 84:2; 92:4); Psalm 66:1 exhorts, "Shout joyfully to God, all the earth"; in Psalm 95:1–2 the psalmist exhorted, "O come, let us sing for joy to the Lord, let us shout joyfully to the rock of our salvation. Let us come before His presence with thanksgiving, let us shout joyfully to Him with psalms" (cf. 98:4–6; 100:1–2).

The petitions in the first half of this model for prayer focus on God's glory, those in the second half on man's need. Yet in reality the entire prayer is God-centered, since He glorifies Himself by providing for man's needs. Prayer arises from the Word of God (cf. Dan. 9:2–3) and has as its ultimate goal the glory of God. It is not an attempt to change the will of God, still less does it attempt to manipulate Him to gain one's greedy, selfish desires, as the "Health and Wealth" movement falsely teaches. True prayer puts God in His rightful place of sovereign authority and willingly, joyfully subordinates itself to His purposes. As Thomas Brooks noted, "Such prayers never reach the ear of God, nor delight the heart of God, nor shall ever be lodged in the bosom of God, that are not directed to the glory of God" (*Secret Key*, 235). Everything in Christ's model prayer is in reality a rehearsal of what God has affirmed to be true, concerning both His person and His promises. Prayer seeks God's glory and aligns itself with the promises He has made in Scripture.

All of the petitions affirm the supremacy of God. "Father" acknowledges Him as the source of all blessing; "hallowed be Your name" as sacred; "Your kingdom come" as sovereign; "Your will be done" as superior, "give us each day our daily bread" as supporter; "forgive us our sins" as savior, and "lead us not into temptation" as shelter.

This opening section of chapter 11 focuses on the importance of prayer. Verses 1–4 contain the Lord's instruction on prayer, verses 5–8 reveal God's eagerness to hear prayer, verses 9–10 teach the certainty that God will answer prayer, and verses 11–13 express God's desire to give the best to those who pray. All of those rich truths will be the subject of the next several chapters of this volume.

Jesus' Pattern for Every Prayer—Part 2: God's Person
(Luke 11:2*b*, *c*)

2

Father, hallowed be Your name. (11:2*b, c*)

As it does all aspects of spiritual truth, false religion twists and distorts the true meaning of prayer. Some religions address prayer to false gods, or false misrepresentations of the true God. Others prescribe prayers to be recited ritually as one means of earning salvation. In other religions introspective meditation or the mechanical chanting of mantras—sometimes multiplied by writing them on a prayer wheel—takes the place of prayer. All prayer in false religions is addressed to gods who do not exist, and is therefore useless. It becomes nothing but a form of self-help, focusing on the needs, hopes, and aspirations of the one who prays in a vain hope for some supernatural aid.

Even some who profess to worship the God of the Bible think they can use prayer as a means of selfish gain. The Word Faith movement —known also as Positive Confession, Name It and Claim It, and the Prosperity Gospel—unabashedly proclaims the lying notion that the purpose of prayer is for the release of physical, financial, and material blessings.

As the title of a book by one of the movement's leaders proclaims, following the Word Faith principles will teach you "How to Write Your Own Ticket with God."

The god of the Word Faith movement is a false god, not the true God, the sovereign Lord of heaven and earth (Matt. 11:25; Luke 10:21; Acts 17:24). This false god, say these deceivers, is bound by the law of faith that governs the spiritual realm, just as the law of gravity does the physical universe. Using the law or principle of faith, people can compel God to respond in whatever way they determine. Further, this false teaching claims that He is dependent on human faith and human words to accomplish His work. "Word-faithers" are, as their teachers with shocking hubris blasphemously assert, "little gods." That satanically inspired (Gen. 3:5) lie removes any need for genuine, submissive prayer for God to act, since people's own words supposedly have the power to bring them whatever they selfishly desire. (I critique the Word Faith movement in my book *Charismatic Chaos* [Grand Rapids: Zondervan, 1992]; see also D. R. McConnell, *A Different Gospel* [Peabody, Mass.: Hendrickson, 1988].)

But the true and living God is not an impersonal force or principle, nor can He be manipulated by egocentric people, especially greedy ones. He is the "God and Father of our Lord Jesus Christ" (Rom. 15:6; 2 Cor. 1:3; Eph. 1:3), who has "established His throne in the heavens, and His sovereignty rules over all" (Ps. 103:19; cf. 115:3). Far from being dependent on weak, sinful people, "Whatever the Lord pleases, He does, in heaven and in earth, in the seas and in all deeps" (Ps. 135:6; cf. Isa. 43:13; 46:10; Dan. 4:35; Eph. 1:11). God rebuked those who would recreate Him in their own image, declaring to them, "You thought that I was just like you" (Ps. 50:21).

The fundamental error in all wrong thinking about prayer is that it is primarily for people to get what they want. In reality, it is the unfathomable privilege of communing with the sovereign God of the universe; of living in constant awareness of the One who is equally and perfectly aware of us. True prayer brings believers into the presence of God to submit to His will and see His glory on display in His answers.

Jesus specifically taught that prayer is to display God's glory when He promised, "Whatever you ask in My name, that will I do, so that the Father may be glorified" (John 14:13). Consistent with that principle, the Lord's model prayer focuses on God, revealing His paternity ("Father"), priority ("hallowed be Your name"), program ("Your kingdom come"), plan ("Your will be done"), provision ("give us each day our daily bread"), pardon ("forgive us our sins"), and protection ("lead us not into temptation"). The first two truths, which focus on the person of God, are the subject of this chapter. Viewing God both as Father and as sacred preserves the balance between His transcendence and His immanence, between His compassionate love and His majestic glory, and between intimacy with Him and reverence for Him.

GOD AS FATHER

Father, (11:2*b*)

The first word in Jesus' prayer marks it as profoundly different from the Jewish prayers of that day. God is seldom referred to as Father in the Old Testament, and then only in a national sense to refer to Israel as a whole (Deut. 32:6; 1 Chron. 29:10; Ps. 68:5; Isa. 63:16; 64:8; Jer. 3:4, 19; 31:9; Mal. 1:6; 2:10), or its king (1 Sam. 8:7). Nowhere in the Old Testament is God addressed as Father in a personal prayer, which would have been considered presumptuous. For Jesus to address God as Father (as He always did except on the cross [Luke 23:34]), and to instruct His followers to do so was revolutionary and shocking.

One of the things that agitated Israel's apostate religious leaders the most was Christ's referring to God as His Father (e.g., Matt. 7:21; 10:32–33; 12:50; 16:17; Luke 22:29; John 8:54; 10:29). They correctly understood Jesus' statement, "My Father is working until now, and I Myself am working" (John 5:17) to be nothing less than a claim to full deity and absolute equality with God the Father. Because of that claim "the Jews were seeking all the more to kill Him, because He not only was breaking the Sabbath, but also was calling God His own Father, making Himself equal with God" (v. 18).

But not only did Jesus call God His Father, He also declared Him to be the Father of all those who are in Christ. In the Sermon on the Mount Jesus said to the disciples, "Your Father knows what you need before you ask Him" (Matt. 6:8; cf. vv. 15, 18). In Mark 11:25 He exhorted,

"Whenever you stand praying, forgive, if you have anything against any-one, so that your Father who is in heaven will also forgive you your trans-gressions.""Stop clinging to Me," Jesus said to Mary Magdalene after the resurrection, "for I have not yet ascended to the Father; but go to My brethren and say to them, 'I ascend to My Father and your Father, and My God and your God'" (John 20:17).

The Greek word translated **Father** is *patēr*, but the Aramaic (the language commonly spoken by the Jewish people) term was *abba* (cf. Mark 14:36; Rom. 8:15; Gal. 4:6). *Abba* was an intimate term used by chil-dren, and was often one of the first words a young child learned to say. It emphasizes that prayer involves intimacy with God. Believers have the privilege of entering the presence of the Creator and sovereign King of the universe and addressing Him on tender, intimate terms. Addressing God as Father affirms that believers live in God's eternal family and are partakers of His divine nature (2 Peter 1:4). Though sinners (1 John 1:8), they are nonetheless His beloved and redeemed children, to whom He has granted eternal life (John 3:15, 16, 36; 5:24; 6:40, 47; 10:28; 17:2; 1 John 5:11–12).

It should be noted that the possessive phrase "our Father" (Matt. 6:9), referring to true believers, is the deathblow to the false teaching of the universal fatherhood of God and brotherhood of man. God is the father of everyone in the sense that He created them (Acts 17:29), but not in a relational sense. Jesus made that truth clear when He said to the unbelieving Jews, "If God were your Father, you would love Me …You are of your father the devil" (John 8:42, 44). Only those who have received Jesus through saving faith are given "the right to become children of God" (John 1:12). Paul contrasted the "children of the flesh" with the "chil-dren of God" (Rom. 9:8) and the "children of the bondwoman [unbeliev-ers]" with the children of the "free woman [believers]" (Gal. 4:22–31), while the apostle John differentiated between "the children of God and the children of the devil" (1 John 3:10).

The fatherhood of God is the foundation of all prayer. His chil-dren are invited to enter His presence and "in everything by prayer and supplication with thanksgiving let [their] requests be made known to God" (Phil. 4:6). The best people without Christ cannot call God their Father, nor can they expect Him to hear their prayers. But the worst sinners, redeemed through Jesus Christ, become His children. To them Jesus made the staggering promise, "Ask, and it will be given to you; seek, and you will find; knock, and it will be opened to you. For everyone who asks receives, and he who seeks finds, and to him who knocks it will be opened" (Matt. 7:7–8). In the illustration of how fathers treat their children that follows, Jesus made it clear that the promise applies only to God's children:

> Or what man is there among you who, when his son asks for a loaf, will give him a stone? Or if he asks for a fish, he will not give him a snake, will he? If you then, being evil, know how to give good gifts to your children, how much more will your Father who is in heaven give what is good to those who ask Him! (vv. 9–11)

The fatherhood of God settles several key issues. First, it settles the matter of fear. The true and living God is a God of love (Deut. 23:5; Mic. 7:18; Zeph. 3:17; John 3:16; Rom. 5:8; Gal. 2:20; 2 Thess. 2:16; Titus 3:4), mercy (Ps. 86:15; 145:8; Luke 1:72; 6:36; Eph. 2:4; James 5:11; 1 Peter 1:3), grace (Ex. 34:6; Pss. 86:15; 103:8; 116:5; 145:8; Jer. 3:12; 1 Peter 5:10), compassion (Deut. 4:31; Neh. 9:19, 27, 28, 31; Pss. 111:4; 112:4; 116:5; Lam. 3:22; Dan. 9:18; Joel 2:13; Jon. 4:2), and kindness (Rom. 2:4; 11:22; Titus 3:4). No such god exists in false religions; those gods are in reality demons impersonating gods (Deut. 32:17), and no demon would manifest such a fatherly, loving, compassionate, tender-hearted attitude. To come to know the true God is to be freed from the slavish fear associated with the worship of false gods; it is to approach the one who will have compassion on them just as a father has on his children (Ps. 103:13).

Second, the fatherhood of God settles the matter of hope. The world lives in hopeless despair, alleviated only by self-deception that will ultimately fail (Job 8:13; 11:20; 27:8; Prov. 11:7; Eph. 2:12; 1 Thess. 4:13). But the hope that is anchored in God will never fail (Prov. 23:18; 24:14; Jer. 29:11; Rom. 5:2; 2 Thess. 2:16), because it is grounded in the believers' union with Jesus Christ (Col. 1:27), guarded in heaven (Col. 1:5), and granted by the God of hope (Rom. 15:13).

Third, the fatherhood of God settles the matter of loneliness—not the momentary absence of other people's company, but the cosmic loneliness that results from denying that God exists. Describing that loneliness

James W. Sire notes that if God does not exist, "We have been thrown up by an impersonal universe. The moment a self-conscious, self-determining being appears on the scene, that person asks the big question: What is the meaning of all this? What is the purpose of the cosmos? But the person's own creator—the impersonal forces of bedrock matter—cannot respond" (*The Universe Next Door* [Downers Grove, Ill. InterVarsity, 1988], 102). But God does exist, is a refuge for His children (Ps. 46:1), and is with them always (Ps. 139:7–12; Matt. 28:20).

Finally, the fatherhood of God settles the matter of resources. "My God," wrote the apostle Paul, "will supply all your needs according to His riches in glory in Christ Jesus" (Phil. 4:19). Since our Father is in heaven, He is above all circumstances and beyond all limitations of time and space. His power is unlimited, His grace measureless, and His treasure house of benedictions boundless. The many blessings God graciously grants His children include instruction (Pss. 25:12; 32:8; 94:12), comfort (Ps. 23:4; 2 Cor. 1:3–4), correction (Heb. 12:6), protection from Satan's assaults (John 17:15; 2 Thess. 3:3; 1 John 5:18), access to Him through prayer (Heb. 4:16), provision for all their needs (Pss. 34:10; 84:11; Phil. 4:19), and an inheritance that includes all the blessings of salvation (Matt. 19:29; 25:34; Eph. 1:11; Col. 1:12; 3:24; Heb. 1:14; 1 Peter 1:4).

GOD AS SACRED

hallowed be Your name. (11:2c)

The reality that Christians have an intimate relationship with their heavenly Father does not mean that they can treat Him with flippant, irreverent lack of respect. "A son honors his father," God reminded wayward Israel, "...then if I am a father, where is My honor?" (Mal. 1:6). Understanding that God is sacred provides a necessary balance to viewing Him as Father. It guards against abusing the intimacy believers have with Him.

This first petition in the Lord's model prayer stresses the point made earlier in this chapter that prayer is primarily for God's glory. Every request must be subordinated to and in harmony with that goal. Selfishness has no place in prayer; God does not exist to fulfill people's whims, but to glorify Himself. Prayer acknowledges God's declaration, "I am the Lord, that is My name; I will not give My glory to another" (Isa. 42:8; cf. 48:11). Therefore when believers approach Him they must seek to "ascribe to the Lord the glory due to His name" (Ps. 29:2; cf. 66:1–4), desiring to see "the whole earth ... filled with His glory" (Ps. 72:19). Like the psalmist they pray, "Not to us, O Lord, not to us, but to Your name give glory" (Ps. 115:1). Even their requests for His help are ultimately for the glory of His name (Pss. 79:9; 106:47).

Hallowed translates a form of the verb *hagiazō*, which means to set something apart as holy. It is related to the terms *doxazō* ("glorify"), *eulogeō* ("bless" or "praise"), and *hupsoō* ("lift up" or "exalt"). In this context, it means to acknowledge that God's name deserves to be differentiated from and set above all that is created. God is supremely separate from what He made, exists in a different sphere, and has knowledge and wisdom far beyond our own. To hallow His name is to believe that God is who He has revealed Himself to be on the pages of Scripture (cf. Heb. 11:6) and to live a God-conscious life. It is to set His name apart from everything common, profane, earthly, human, and temporal, just as the Sabbath was to be kept holy by being treated differently than the other six days (Ex. 20:8–11); to hold His matchless name in reverence and awe; to honor God as unique and above everyone else; and to esteem, prize, honor, revere, and adore Him as infinitely holy.

At Meribah in the wilderness, Moses disobeyed God by striking a rock to bring water instead of speaking to it as the Lord had commanded him. For that act of disobedience he was forbidden to enter the promised land "because," God told him, "you have not believed Me, to treat Me as holy in the sight of the sons of Israel, therefore you shall not bring this assembly into the land which I have given them" (Num. 20:12). In contrast the Lord Jesus Christ, anticipating the cross with its sin-bearing and separation from the Father, said, "Now My soul has become troubled; and what shall I say, 'Father, save Me from this hour'? But for this purpose I came to this hour" (John 12:27). Then, affirming that God's glory was more important than the suffering He would endure, Jesus prayed, "Father, glorify Your name" (v. 28). He was willing to endure the cross so that God's holy wrath against sin, His justice, His grace, and His mercy might be put on display.

Living a life that hallows God begins in the heart. Using a form of the word translated **hallowed** in this passage, Peter exhorted believers to "sanctify Christ as Lord in [their] hearts" (1 Peter 3:15). It involves a constant awareness of God's presence, a truth that David expressed when he wrote, "I have set the Lord continually before me" (Ps. 16:8). Most significantly, a life that hallows the name of God is inevitably marked by obedience in all aspects of life. As Paul exhorted the Corinthians, "Whether, then, you eat or drink or whatever you do, do all to the glory of God" (1 Cor. 10:31). When believers' lives conform to God's will the unbelieving world will "see [their] good works, and glorify [their] Father who is in heaven" (Matt. 5:16). They also hallow God's name by confessing it (Matt. 10:32), trusting it (Ps. 33:21), refusing to profane it (Lev. 18:21; cf. Ex. 20:7), loving it (Ps. 119:132), and honoring it (Ps. 96:8).

God's **name** is much more than merely a title; it refers to all that He is, including His nature, attributes, and character. In response to Moses' plea, "I pray You, show me Your glory!" (Ex. 33:18) God promised, "I Myself will make all My goodness pass before you, and will proclaim the name of the Lord before you" (v. 19). In fulfillment of that promise God declared some of His attributes to Moses:

> Then the Lord passed by in front of him and proclaimed, "The Lord, the Lord God, compassionate and gracious, slow to anger, and abounding in lovingkindness and truth; who keeps lovingkindness for thousands, who forgives iniquity, transgression and sin; yet He will by no means leave the guilty unpunished, visiting the iniquity of fathers on the children and on the grandchildren to the third and fourth generations." (Ex. 34:6–7)

Throughout Scripture God's name is equated with His person. When David declared that he would "sing praise to the name of the Lord Most High" (Ps. 7:17; cf. 113:1; 135:1; 148:5) he was not referring to a title, but to the person who bears it. Conversely, when the nations are said to "fear the name of the Lord" (Ps. 102:15), it is God's majestic being that is in view. When the Lord Jesus Christ said to the Father in His high-priestly prayer, "I have manifested Your name to the men whom You gave Me out of the world" (John 17:6), He meant that He had revealed God's true nature to them. Understanding God's name is a prerequisite to trusting

Him. In Psalm 9:10 David said to God, "Those who know Your name will put their trust in You."

The names of God revealed in Scripture identify the range of His glorious attributes. Elohim, the plural name of the triune God, describes Him as the Creator (Gen. 1:1); El-elyon (God Most High) as the sovereign ruler of the universe (Gen. 14:22); I AM as the eternally existing one (Ex. 3:13–14; cf. John 8:58); Jehovah-jireh (The Lord Will Provide) as the one who meets the needs of His children (Gen. 22:14); Jehovah-nissi (The Lord is My Banner) as the King under whom His people march (Ex. 17:15); Jehovah-ropheka (The Lord your healer) as the one who cares for their physical needs (Ex. 15:26). He is Jehovah-shalom (The Lord is Peace [Judg. 6:24]); Jehovah-roi (the Lord our Shepherd [Ps. 23:1]); Jehovah-tsidkenu (The Lord our Righteousness [Jer. 23:6]); Jehovah-sabaoth (the Lord of Hosts [1 Sam. 1:3]); Jehovah-meqaddeskem (the Lord who sanctifies you [Ex. 31:13]), and, supremely, "the God and Father of our Lord Jesus Christ" (Rom. 15:6)—God incarnate who perfectly reveals Him (John 1:18; 14:9).

The Bible also lists many names and titles that unfold the nature of the Lord Jesus Christ. He is called the Amen (Rev. 3:14; cf. 2 Cor. 1:20), the Alpha and the Omega (Rev. 22:13), the Advocate (1 John 2:1), the Apostle (Heb. 3:1), the Author and Perfecter of faith (Heb. 12:2), the Beginning (source, origin) of the creation of God (Rev. 3:14), the Branch (Jer. 23:5), the Bread of Life (John 6:35), the Author of salvation (Heb. 2:10), the Cornerstone (Eph. 2:20), the Consolation of Israel (Luke 2:25), the Counselor (Isa. 9:6), the Sunrise from on high (Luke 1:78), the Deliverer (Rom. 11:26), the Door of the sheep (John 10:7), God blessed forever (Rom. 9:5), Eternal Father (Isa. 9:6), the Faithful witness (Rev. 1:5), the First and the Last (Rev. 1:17), the Firstborn (preeminent one) from the dead (Rev. 1:5) and over all creation (Col. 1:15), the Forerunner (Heb. 6:20), the Good Shepherd (John 10:11), the Great High Priest (Heb. 4:14), the Guardian of souls (1 Peter 2:25), the Head of the church (Col. 1:18), the Holy One of God (John 6:69), I AM (John 8:58), Immanuel (Isa. 7:14), the King of Israel (John 1:49; cf. Zech. 9:9), King of kings and Lord of lords (1 Tim. 6:15), the last Adam (1 Cor. 15:45), the Lamb of God (John 1:29), the Light of the world (John 8:12), the Lion of the tribe of Judah (Rev. 5:5), Lord (John 13:13), the Lord of glory (1 Cor. 2:8), the Mediator (1 Tim. 2:5), the Messenger of the covenant (Mal. 3:1), the Messiah (John 1:41), the Mighty God (Isa. 9:6), the Morning Star (Rev. 22:16), the Only Begotten (unique one) from the Father (John 1:14), our Passover (1 Cor. 5:7), the Prince of life (Acts 3:15), the Prince of Peace (Isa. 9:6), the Resurrection and the Life (John 11:25), the Righteous One (Acts 7:52), the Rock (1 Cor. 10:4), the Root and Descendant of David (Rev. 22:16), the Root of Jesse (Isa. 11:10), the Ruler in Israel (Mic. 5:2; Matt. 2:6), the Ruler of the kings of the earth (Rev. 1:5), Savior (Luke 2:11; Titus 1:4), Servant (Isa. 42:1), Shiloh (Gen. 49:10), Son of the Blessed One (Mark 14:61), Son of David (Matt. 12:23; 21:9), Son of God (Luke 1:35), Son of the Most High (Luke 1:32), the Sun of Righteousness (Mal. 4:2), the True God (1 John 5:20), the True Vine (John 15:1), the Way, the Truth, and the Life (John 14:6), the Word (John 1:1, 14), the Word of God (Rev. 19:13), and the Word of Life (1 John 1:1).

True prayer begins, therefore, with a proper understanding of God. Emphasizing the importance of the correct thinking about Him from which true, God-honoring prayer flows A. W. Tozer wrote,

> We must think worthily of God. It is morally imperative that we purge from our minds all ignoble concepts of the Deity and let Him be the God in our minds that He is in His universe. . . . That God exists for Himself and man for the glory of God is the emphatic teaching of the Bible. The high honor of God is first in heaven as it must yet be in earth. (*The Knowledge of the Holy* [New York: Harper & Row, 1961], 42)

Such thinking and praying must begin, as the example of the Lord Jesus Christ in this passage reveals, with recognizing God as our sacred Father.

Jesus' Pattern for Every Prayer—Part 3: God's Purpose (Luke 11:2*d*)

3

Your kingdom come (11:2*d*)

Ever since the fall the human race has been in rebellion against God. Most people from earliest childhood mistakenly believe that they can set the direction for their lives, determine their own destiny, decide their own future, and chart their own life course. That is especially true in today's narcissistic, self-exalting, ego-mad culture. The nineteenth-century English poet William Ernest Henley captured the essence of this defiant, man-centered view in his famous poem "Invictus":

> Out of the night that covers me,
> Black as the Pit from pole to pole,
> I thank whatever gods may be
> For my unconquerable soul.
>
> In the fell clutch of circumstance,
> I have not winced nor cried aloud;
> Under the bludgeonings of chance
> My head is bloody, but unbowed.

Beyond this place of wrath and tears
Looms but the Horror of the shade,
And yet the menace of the years
Finds, and shall find, me unafraid.

It matters not how strait the gate,
How charged with punishments the scroll.
I am the master of my fate;
I am the captain of my soul.

Even Israel frequently chose to defy God's authority and the Old Testament chronicles the nation's long history of rebellion. "You have been rebellious against the Lord from the day I knew you," Moses told the people (Deut. 9:24). Later he added, "I know your rebellion and your stubbornness; behold, while I am still alive with you today, you have been rebellious against the Lord; how much more, then, after my death?" (Deut. 31:27). Israel's subsequent history showed that Moses' fear was justified. Looking back at the cause of Israel's exile to Babylon, Nehemiah acknowledged to God that Israel "became disobedient and rebelled against You, and cast Your law behind their backs" (Neh. 9:26). The Psalms frequently lament Israel's rebellion against God, especially Psalm 78. Verse 8 describes the exodus generation as "a stubborn and rebellious generation"; despite all of God's provision for them in the wilderness (vv. 11–16) "they still continued to sin against Him, to rebel against the Most High in the desert" (v. 17; cf. vv. 40, 56; 106:7). Psalms 5:10 and 107:11 also describe those who rebelled against God. Isaiah denounced Israel as "a rebellious people, false sons, sons who refuse to listen to the instruction of the Lord (Isa. 30:9; cf. 3:8; 65:2). Israel's rebellion had devastating consequences. Because "they rebelled and grieved His Holy Spirit; therefore He turned Himself to become their enemy, He fought against them" (Isa. 63:10). Through the prophet Jeremiah, God Himself declared of Israel, "This people has a stubborn and rebellious heart" (Jer. 5:23). He told Ezekiel, "Son of man, I am sending you to the sons of Israel, to a rebellious people who have rebelled against Me; they and their fathers have transgressed against Me to this very day" (Ezek. 2:3; cf. 5:6; 20:13; Hos. 7:13; 8:1). Repeatedly in Ezekiel God referred to Israel as a "rebellious house" (2:5, 6, 8; 3:26, 27; 12:3, 9, 25; 17:12; 24:3). In his passionate intercessory prayer for his people, Daniel also acknowledged that Israel had consistently revolted against God (Dan. 9:5,9).

Revolt is inherent in the very definition of sin, the essence of which, the apostle John wrote, is "lawlessness" (1 John 3:4). Paul paired lawlessness with rebellion (1 Tim. 1:9), and described the future antichrist, the ultimate rebel against God, as the "man of lawlessness" (2 Thess. 2:3).

But to come to Christ savingly is to forsake one's pretended autonomy from God and acknowledge that He sets the course for our lives. It is to forsake self-centered living and replace selfishness with submission. In salvation the sinner bows the knee to the lordship of Jesus Christ, submitting to Him as King and acknowledging His absolute, sovereign authority (see the discussion below). One day "at the name of Jesus every knee will bow, of those who are in heaven and on earth and under the earth, and ... every tongue will confess that Jesus Christ is Lord, to the glory of God the Father" (Phil. 2:10–11), as God sovereignly determined: "I will surely tell of the decree of the Lord: He said to Me, 'You are My Son, today I have begotten You. Ask of Me, and I will surely give the nations as Your inheritance, and the very ends of the earth as Your possession'" (Ps. 2:7–8).

The two petitions discussed in this chapter, one from Luke's account and the other from Matthew's, focus on God's plan. Both acknowledge that all history is inevitably, inexorably moving toward the reign of Jesus Christ, and each expresses a strong desire for that to be realized. The nineteenth-century English hymn writer Frances Ridley Havergal expressed the cry of the believer's heart in her hymn, "Thou Art Coming, O My Saviour":

> Oh the joy to see Thee reigning,
> Thee, my own beloved Lord!
> Every tongue Thy Name confessing,
> Worship, honor, glory, blessing,
> Brought to Thee with glad accord;
> Thee, my Master and my Friend,
> Vindicated and enthroned:
> Unto earth's remotest end
> Glorified, adored, and owned.

These next two petitions in our Lord's model prayer introduce God as sovereign, and supreme.

GOD AS SOVEREIGN

Your kingdom come (11:2*d*)

There have been a multitude of states, empires, and nations throughout human history, but spiritually there are only two kingdoms: the kingdom of God and the kingdom of Satan (cf. Col. 1:13). All the kingdoms of this world are currently part of Satan's domain of darkness. In the future, however, "The kingdom of the world [will] become the kingdom of our Lord and of His Christ; and He will reign forever and ever" (Rev. 11:15). Having been "rescued ... from the domain of darkness, and transferred ... to the kingdom of His beloved Son" (Col. 1:13), believers have as their highest goal the advancement of that kingdom. They do not love the kingdom of this world (1 John 2:15), but as Paul wrote they "keep seeking the things above, where Christ is, seated at the right hand of God" (Col. 3:1; cf. Matt. 6:33; Phil. 3:20).

Basileia (**kingdom**), which can also mean "rule," or "reign," refers to a sovereign realm. It is used most frequently in the New Testament to refer to the kingdom of God (called the kingdom of heaven in Matthew's gospel), as it does here. Combined with the imperative form of the verb *erchomai,* this petition could be translated, "Your kingdom, let it happen"; "let it actually take place"; or "let it actually come." To see God's kingdom triumphant and His rule manifest on earth is the believer's desire and prayer.

The word **Your** indicates that the kingdom of which Jesus was speaking is the one ruled by His Father. Earthly powers, such as Egypt, Assyria, Babylon, Medo-Persia, Greece, Rome and, in more modern times, Nazi Germany and Soviet Russia, and every other nation rise and fall (cf. Acts 14:16). Nations have their moment in the sun, but as their power grows, so does their pride, and sin brings about their fall. "Righteousness exalts a nation," wrote Solomon, "but sin is a disgrace to any people" (Prov. 14:34). God sovereignly determines the nations' extent and duration. Daniel declared to the Babylonian king Belshazzar, "God has numbered your kingdom and put an end to it" (Dan. 5:26), while Paul proclaimed to the Greek philosophers in Athens that God "made from one man every nation of mankind to live on all the face of the earth, having determined their appointed times and the boundaries of their habitation" (Acts 17:26).

The sovereign rule of God was the context of all the teaching and preaching of the Lord Jesus Christ. At the outset of His ministry "Jesus began to preach and say, 'Repent, for the kingdom of heaven is at hand'" (Matt. 4:17). In Luke 4:43 He said, "I must preach the kingdom of God ... for I was sent for this purpose" (cf. 8:1). The kingdom of God continued to be the theme of His instruction to the apostles even after His resurrection, when He "appear[ed] to them over a period of forty days and [spoke to them] of the things concerning the kingdom of God" (Acts 1:3).

Jesus spoke of the kingdom in three dimensions. First, He referred to it as existing in the past. In Matthew 8:11 He spoke of the patriarchs Abraham, Isaac, and Jacob as already being in the kingdom.

Second, Jesus spoke of the kingdom as present. In Luke 17:21 He told the Pharisees, "The kingdom of God is in your midst"; earlier the Lord had commanded the seventy to proclaim to the people, "The kingdom of God has come near to you" (Luke 10:9; cf. v. 11). He replied to the Pharisees' blasphemous allegation that He cast out demons through the power of Satan by saying to them, "If I cast out demons by the Spirit of God, then the kingdom of God has come upon you" (Matt. 12:28). The Jewish people, and their leaders in particular, failed to recognize the presence of the kingdom, since they were not looking for a spiritual kingdom, but rather a political, social, military, and economic one. The kingdom was a reality, but unbelief blinded their eyes so that they could not see it.

But although the kingdom continues to be present today as the living God rules the hearts of the penitent who trust in Him, there is also a future, unique form of it. Jesus told the disciples in the Upper Room, "Truly I say to you, I will never again drink of the fruit of the vine until that day when I drink it new in the kingdom of God" (Mark 14:25). At the sheep and goat judgment "the King will say to those on His right [the sheep], 'Come, you who are blessed of My Father, inherit the kingdom prepared for you from the foundation of the world'" (Matt. 25:34), but for those who reject Him "there will be weeping and gnashing of teeth when [they] see Abraham and Isaac and Jacob and all the prophets in the kingdom of God, but [they themselves] being thrown out. And they will come from east and west and from north and south, and will recline at the table in the kingdom of God" (Luke 13:28–29). This refers to our

Lord's millennial reign on earth (Rev. 20:1–6).

By way of further distinction, two aspects of the kingdom of God may be noted. The universal kingdom encompasses God's rule over the entire universe. As the Creator, He is sovereign over His creation. Psalm 29:10 says that "the Lord sat as King forever," while Revelation 15:3 addresses Him as "King of the nations." Psalm 103:19 adds, "The Lord has established His throne in the heavens, and His sovereignty rules over all." In 1 Chronicles 29:11–12 David prayed,

> Yours, O Lord, is the greatness and the power and the glory and the victory and the majesty, indeed everything that is in the heavens and the earth; Yours is the dominion, O Lord, and You exalt Yourself as head over all. Both riches and honor come from You, and You rule over all, and in Your hand is power and might; and it lies in Your hand to make great and to strengthen everyone.

The universal kingdom is eternal, providential, supernatural, and efficacious. Authority over it has been delegated to the Lord Jesus Christ, whom God employed to create (Col. 1:16) and sustain it (Heb. 1:1–3).

But the universal kingdom is not in view here. There is no need to pray for it to advance, since it is eternal, comprehensive, and absolute. This petition asks instead that the redemptive kingdom, the sphere of salvation, the supernatural realm of believing people, advance. It does so in three ways.

First, through salvation; the redemptive kingdom grows one redeemed soul at a time. It is not a visible, earthly structure, nor can it be identified with any nation, denomination, or organization; it is the realm of souls ruled by Christ. The request "Your kingdom come" is first of all a missionary prayer, in which the petitioner submits his or her will, ambitions, plans, goals, and concerns to the life priority of advancing God's redemptive kingdom by seeing sinners converted. "First of all, then," Paul instructed Timothy, "I urge that entreaties and prayers, petitions and thanksgivings, be made on behalf of all men" (1 Tim. 2:1), because God "desires all men to be saved and to come to the knowledge of the truth" (v. 4). The prayer of the believing heart is that people would "repent, for the kingdom of heaven is at hand" (Matt. 4:17; cf. 3:2). All else is secondary (cf. Matt. 6:33).

Contrary to much popular teaching today, entrance to the kingdom is not easy. Nor should we expect it to be; after all, the price of redemption was the sacrifice of God's dear Son. Those who would enter His kingdom must force their way in (Luke 16:16)—not through meritorious good works that earn salvation, but through the self-denial that characterizes the truly penitent (Luke 9:23–24). Far from merely uttering a glib prayer and then continuing to live as they choose, those who would enter the kingdom must go through the narrow gate, jettisoning their baggage of good deeds, self-will, and selfish desires, none of which will fit through the turnstile at the entrance to the narrow way (Matt. 7:13–14). In words that are jarringly discordant with today's man-centered gospel of self-fulfillment and easy believism, Jesus bluntly declared that following Him demands complete self-denial and total surrender to His lordship:

> If anyone wishes to come after Me, he must deny himself, and take up his cross daily and follow Me. (Luke 9:23)

> If anyone comes to Me, and does not hate his own father and mother and wife and children and brothers and sisters, yes, and even his own life, he cannot be My disciple. (Luke 14:26)

> Whoever does not carry his own cross and come after Me cannot be My disciple. (Luke 14:27)

> So then, none of you can be My disciple who does not give up all his own possessions. (Luke 14:33)

> Not everyone who says to Me, "Lord, Lord," will enter the kingdom of heaven, but he who does the will of My Father who is in heaven will enter. (Matt. 7:21)

> Why do you call Me, "Lord, Lord," and do not do what I say? (Luke 6:46)

> If you love Me, you will keep My commandments. (John 14:15)

> He who has My commandments and keeps them is the one who loves Me. (John 14:21)

> If anyone loves Me, he will keep My word. (John 14:23)

> He who does not love Me does not keep My words. (John 14:24)

> You are My friends if you do what I command you. (John 15:14)

In His parables, Jesus likened those who enter the kingdom to a man who finds treasure in a field, or a merchant who finds a priceless pearl, and sells everything he owns to buy it (Matt. 13:44–46). (I discuss the high cost and infinite value of entering the kingdom by following Jesus in *Hard to Believe* [Nashville: Thomas Nelson, 2003].)

Second, the redemptive kingdom comes not only through salvation, but also through sanctification. The kingdom progresses when people come in repentance and faith to Christ, and also when those who are His increasingly grow and submit to His lordship. The writer of the familiar hymn "Lead Me to Calvary" expressed the heart cry of every believer in this regard:

> King of my life, I crown Thee now,
> Thine shall the glory be.

The kingdom advances when its subjects see an increase of "righteousness and peace and joy in the Holy Spirit" (Rom. 14:17) in their lives.

Finally, the kingdom will consummate in the second coming of the King to establish His promised earthly millennial kingdom. To pray, "Your kingdom come" reflects a joyful, expectant desire for that glorious event to take place. Paul exclaimed in 1 Corinthians 16:22 "Maranatha," an Aramaic expression that means, "O Lord, come." Near the end of the book of Revelation John wrote, "Come, Lord Jesus" (Rev. 22:20). In their lives as well as their prayers, those who love the Lord Jesus Christ are always "looking for and hastening [eagerly desiring] the coming of the day of God" (2 Peter 3:12). John described the coming of the kingdom in Revelation 20:1–6:

> Then I saw an angel coming down from heaven, holding the key of the abyss and a great chain in his hand. And he laid hold of the dragon, the serpent of old, who is the devil and Satan, and bound him for a thousand years; and he threw him into the abyss, and shut it and sealed it over him, so that he would not deceive the nations any longer, until the thousand years were completed; after these things he must be released for a short time. Then I saw thrones, and they sat on them, and judgment was given to them. And I saw the souls of those who had been beheaded because of their testimony of Jesus and because of the word of God, and those who had not worshiped the beast or his image, and had

not received the mark on their forehead and on their hand; and they came to life and reigned with Christ for a thousand years. The rest of the dead did not come to life until the thousand years were completed. This is the first resurrection. Blessed and holy is the one who has a part in the first resurrection; over these the second death has no power, but they will be priests of God and of Christ and will reign with Him for a thousand years.

To pray for the coming of the kingdom is to pray for the salvation of sinners, the sanctification of believers, and the second coming in glory of the Savior.

GOD AS SUPREME

This concept derives from the petition that follows the request, "Your kingdom come" in Matthew's account: "Your will be done, on earth as it is in heaven" (Matt. 6:10). Honoring the Father's person and desiring to see His kingdom advance requires an inseparable concern for His will to be done. The Christian's desire and prayer is that God's will, which is always done perfectly and completely in heaven, would be done on earth as well. This petition is the expression of a heart that seeks God's glory and wants what He wants; it is an expression of worship.

During His earthly ministry, the Lord Jesus Christ perfectly carried out the Father's will. In Gethsemane, anticipating his forthcoming sin-bearing and separation from the Father, He cried out, "My Father, if it is possible, let this cup pass from Me; yet not as I will, but as You will" (Matt. 26:39). In Mark 3:35 He said, "Whoever does the will of God, he is My brother and sister and mother." The Lord told His disciples, "My food is to do the will of Him who sent Me and to accomplish His work" (John 4:34), while in John 6:38 He said to the crowd, "I have come down from heaven, not to do My own will, but the will of Him who sent Me."

Ultimately, all things will resolve in accordance with God's eternal purpose, which was established before the world began. Paul ex-pressed that truth when he told the Ephesians that God "works all things after the counsel of His will" (Eph. 1:11). But most of what happens in this evil, fallen, sin-cursed world is contrary to God's purpose. A proper understanding of the will of God reveals why that tragic reality is perfectly consistent with His absolute sovereignty. Theologians distinguish between three aspects of God's will, as R. C. Sproul helpfully notes:

> When we speak about God's will we do so in at least three different ways. The broader concept is known as God's *decretive, sovereign,* or *hidden will.* By this, theologians refer to the will of God by which He sovereignly ordains everything that comes to pass. Because God is sovereign and His will can never be frustrated, we can be sure that nothing happens over which He is not in control....
>
> Though God's sovereign will is often hidden from us until after it comes to pass, there is one aspect of His will that is plain to us—His *preceptive* will. Here God reveals His will through His holy law.... This aspect of God's will is revealed in His Word as well as in our conscience, by which God has written His moral law upon our heart.... We have the power or ability to thwart the preceptive will of God, though never the right to do so....
>
> The third way the Bible speaks of the will of God is with respect to God's *will of disposition.* This will describes God's attitude. It defines what is pleasing to Him. For example, God takes no delight in the death of the wicked, yet he most surely wills or decrees the death of the wicked. God's ultimate delight is in His own holiness and righteousness. When He judges the world, He delights in the vindication of His own righteousness and justice, yet He is not gleeful in a vindictive sense toward those who receive His judgment. God is pleased when we find our pleasure in obedience. He is sorely displeased when we are disobedient. (*Essential Truths of the Christian Faith* [Wheaton, Ill.: Tyndale, 1992], 67–68. Italics in original.)

The petition for His will to be done especially considers that third feature, His will of disposition. Their heavenly preoccupation (cf. Col. 3:1–2) motivates Christians to pray that God's will be carried out by obedience so that He may be honored by the testimony of the faithful.

There are several wrong views of God's will that must be avoided. First, some manifest an attitude of bitter resentment. They acknowledge that what God wills is inevitably going to come to pass whether they like it or not. Therefore, they reason, it is useless to resist. Such people take a fatalistic, deterministic view of God's will, and are angry at Him because of it. The medieval Persian poet Omar Khayyam expressed this view in his poem "The Rubaiyat":

> But helpless Pieces of the Game He plays
> Upon this Chequer-board of Nights and Days;
> Hither and thither moves, and checks, and slays,
> And one by one back in the Closet lays.
>
> The Ball no question makes of Ayes and Noes,
> But Here or There as strikes the Player goes;
> And He that toss'd you down into the Field,
> He knows about it all–He knows–HE knows!

Others pray with a sort of passive resignation. They are not angry with God, but their prayers reflect a sort of gray acceptance; a weary, tired, listless resignation that whatever is going to happen will happen. Such people pray very little and with no assurance that their prayers will have any impact. They go through the motions because it is their duty, but they lack the passionate heart that cries out to God and believes He will answer.

Even the early church fell prey to this attitude. When Peter was imprisoned by Herod, who had just executed the apostle James, John's brother, the believers gathered to pray to God on his behalf (Acts 12:5). An angel miraculously released Peter from prison and he came to the house where they were praying. When a servant girl who had answered his knock at the gate excitedly told them that Peter was outside, they scoffed and "said to her, 'You are out of your mind!' But she kept insisting that it was so. They kept saying, 'It is his angel'" (v. 15). Despite their fervency, they really had not expected God to answer their prayers; hence their reluctance to accept that He had.

A third wrong attitude in prayer might be termed theological reservation. Some Christians take such an extreme view of God's sovereignty that it paralyzes their prayers. Since God will inevitably carry out His will, they reason, there is really nothing to pray for. This view overlooks the explicit teaching of the Lord Jesus Christ, who told "a parable to show that at all times [people] ought to pray and not to lose heart" (Luke 18:1). That parable spoke of an unjust judge, who finally gave legal protection to a desperate widow because she kept hounding him (vv. 2–5). Driving home his point "the Lord said, 'Hear what the unrighteous judge said; now, will not God bring about justice for His elect who cry to Him day and night, and will He delay long over them? I tell you that He will bring about justice for them quickly'" (vv. 6–8). This view also ignores the reality that "the effective prayer of a righteous man can accomplish much" (James 5:16)—a truth borne out by the numerous answers to prayer recorded in Scripture (see the examples listed in chapter 1 of this volume). Failure to pray is disobedience to the explicit commands of the Bible (e.g., Rom. 12:12; Eph. 6:18; Phil. 4:6; Col. 4:2; 1 Thess. 5:17).

Nothing will destroy passion and effectiveness in prayer more than bitter anger, a defeatist attitude, or aberrant theology. In contrast to those wrong attitudes about prayer, true prayer manifests an attitude of rebellion. It rebels with holy indignation against everything that is contrary to God's will. Jesus Himself rebelled against the terrible consequences of sin, which would result in His being made sin on behalf of the redeemed (2 Cor. 5:21) when He prayed in Gethsemane. In response, God strengthened Him to carry out His divine plan and purpose. Peter, James, and John, however, failed to heed the Lord's command to them, "Keep watching and praying that you may not enter into temptation; the spirit is willing, but the flesh is weak" (Matt. 26:41). As a result, when their time of trial and temptation came, they were defeated. Matthew 26:56 records that "all the disciples left Him and fled," while Peter even denied that he knew Him (vv. 58–75). They forgot the example of their Lord who, as noted in chapter 1 of this volume, prayed before all the great events of His life.

To pray for God's will to be done is to refuse to be resigned to the sinful status quo. It is to wake up and stop sleeping, fainting, or losing heart. It is to recognize that there is a cosmic war going on between the kingdom of God and the kingdom of Satan, and to refuse to strike a truce with the forces of evil. True prayer focuses on God. It acknowledges His sovereign right to refuse any request that is not in keeping with His perfect will, as was the case with Paul (2 Cor. 12:7–10). In every circumstance the believer's prayer is to be that God's name be honored by His kingdom being advanced, and that by His will being done.

Jesus' Pattern for Every Prayer—Part 4: God's Provision (Luke 11:3–4)

4

Give us each day our daily bread. And forgive us our sins, for we ourselves also forgive everyone who is indebted to us. And lead us not into temptation. (11:3–4)

Verse 3 marks a turning point in this profound prayer, given by the Lord Jesus Christ to teach believers how to pray. The prayer divides logically and spiritually into two sequential sections. The first three petitions, "Father, hallowed be Your name," "Your kingdom come," and "Your will be done," concern God and His glory. The second three requests, "give us each day our daily bread," "forgive us our sins," and "lead us not into temptation," focus on man's most basic, fundamental needs. The order of the two groups of requests indicates that God's person and purposes must always be given the supreme place. Only then does everything else fit into its proper place; only when acknowledging God as Father, Holy One, King, and Master can believers establish the foundation on which they ask Him for provision, pardon, and protection. True prayer, praying in the Spirit (Eph. 6:18), acknowledges that God's glory is primary and supreme, so that above all else He is to be exalted and worshiped.

The final three requests implore God to glorify Himself by sup-plying believers' most basic needs. Thus, although the focus in the prayer shifts to those needs, the overall emphasis on God's glory remains. This prayer, like all prayer, is neither selfish nor man-centered. The goal of the first three petitions is not to give God glory in exchange for His indulging people's greed. They are not an attempt to manipulate God and force His hand, as if they were coins to put in the celestial vending machine to get what is desired.

These final three petitions also glorify God by highlighting His compassion, grace, and love. Far from being brash demands on God like those the Word Faith movement blasphemously makes (see the discus-sion of the Word Faith movement in chapter 2 of this volume), they express humble dependence on God to supply what is needed for the well-being of His children. The plural pronouns "us," "we," and "ourselves" in these three requests further distance them from any selfish, greedy inten-tions. These last three petitions reveal God as supporter, savior, and shelter.

GOD AS SUPPORTER

Give us each day our daily bread. (11:3)

The substance of this request, **bread,** encompasses all the basic temporal requirements of life, such as food, housing, clothing, health care, and perhaps even government that provides peace and order in society (cf. Rom. 13:1–4). It focuses on the staples necessary to maintain life, and is far from a greedy demand for luxuries. This petition is funda-mental, because unless the Lord sustains believers' physical lives, they cannot in this world advance His kingdom, do His will, or honor and glo-rify His name.

In an Old Testament counterpart to this petition, Agur made the following wise request to God:

> Two things I asked of You, do not refuse me before I die: keep deception and lies far from me, give me neither poverty nor riches; feed me with

> the food that is my portion, that I not be full and deny You and say, "Who is the Lord?" Or that I not be in want and steal, and profane the name of my God. (Prov. 30:7–9)

His prayer was that God would deliver him from two extremes: poverty, which might tempt him to steal, and excessive riches, which might tempt him to arrogantly deny his dependence on the Lord. Instead, Agur asked that God in His wisdom would portion out to him what was appropriate.

The amazing reality is that the infinite, transcendent creator and ruler of the universe cares about the needs of the humblest of His children. He is not only concerned with great, world-shaking events such as creation, the flood, judgment, the earthly millennial kingdom, and the new heaven and the new earth, but also that His people have food, clothing, shelter, and the other mundane, yet essential things of life. The Lord Jesus Christ taught that truth in the Sermon on the Mount:

> For this reason I say to you, do not be worried about your life, as to what you will eat or what you will drink; nor for your body, as to what you will put on. Is not life more than food, and the body more than clothing? Look at the birds of the air, that they do not sow, nor reap nor gather into barns, and yet your heavenly Father feeds them. Are you not worth much more than they? And who of you by being worried can add a single hour to his life? And why are you worried about clothing? Observe how the lilies of the field grow; they do not toil nor do they spin, yet I say to you that not even Solomon in all his glory clothed himself like one of these. But if God so clothes the grass of the field, which is alive today and tomorrow is thrown into the furnace, will He not much more clothe you? You of little faith! Do not worry then, saying, "What will we eat?" or "What will we drink?" or "What will we wear for clothing?" For the Gentiles eagerly seek all these things; for your heavenly Father knows that you need all these things. But seek first His kingdom and His righteousness, and all these things will be added to you. (Matt. 6:25–33)

Worrying about the physical needs of this life—food, drink, clothing—is the height of sinful folly for believers. The same God who feeds the birds and spectacularly clothes the plants in the field will certainly provide for His children, who are of far greater value. In light of that, Christians are not to worry about life's necessities like the unbelieving world does. Their priority, set forth by Jesus, is to seek God's kingdom and righteousness.

As the creator and sustainer of the universe, God is the source and provider of everything, especially in relation to His children. Since He has promised to meet all their needs, they can confidently cast all their anxiety on Him, knowing that He cares for them (1 Peter 5:7). "Ask, and it will be given to you," Jesus declared; "seek, and you will find; knock, and it will be opened to you. For everyone who asks receives, and he who seeks finds, and to him who knocks it will be opened" (Matt. 7:7–8). The Lord then illustrated God's promise to provide for the needs of His people:

> What man is there among you who, when his son asks for a loaf, will give him a stone? Or if he asks for a fish, he will not give him a snake, will he? If you then, being evil, know how to give good gifts to your children, how much more will your Father who is in heaven give what is good to those who ask Him! (vv. 9–11)

Human fathers provide for their children; how much more will God do so for His, since He has "created [food] to be gratefully shared in by those who believe and know the truth" (1 Tim. 4:3)?

The variety of food in the world is staggering. The Bible mentions grains such as wheat, barley, beans, lentils, millet and spelt (Ezek. 4:9), bread (Gen. 18:5–6); nuts (Gen. 43:11); cucumbers, melons, leeks, onions, garlic (Num. 11:5); bitter herbs (Ex. 12:8); mint, dill, cummin (Matt. 23:23); sweet cane (Jer. 6:20); salt (Job 6:6); fruit (Ezek. 25:4); grapes (Num. 13:23); raisins (1 Sam. 25:18); figs, pomegranates (Num. 20:5); apples (Prov. 25:11); honey (1 Sam. 14:27); eggs (Luke 11:12); oxen, sheep, cattle (1 Sam. 14:32); goats (Deut. 14:4); game animals (Deut. 14:5); fish (Matt. 14:19); birds, including partridge (1 Sam. 26:20); quail (Num. 11:31–33); and others, with a few specific exceptions (cf. Deut. 14:11–18); certain kinds of insects (Lev. 11:22); and dairy products, such as milk from cows (1 Sam. 6:7); camels (Gen. 32:15); and sheep (1 Cor. 9:7); butter (Prov. 30:33); cheese (1 Sam. 17:18); and curds (Judg. 5:25).

All of that variety reflects God's generosity and goodness, even to unbelievers in common grace. To pray for one's daily bread is to grate fully acknowledge God as its source, and to fail to do so is the height of ingratitude, as the notable Puritan Thomas Watson wrote:

> If all be a gift, see the odious ingratitude of men who sin against their giver! God feeds them, and they fight against him; he gives them bread, and they give him affronts. How unworthy is this! Should we not cry shame of him who had a friend always feeding him with money, and

yet he should betray and injure him? Thus ungratefully do sinners deal with God; they not only forget his mercies, but abuse them. "When I had fed them to the full, they then committed adultery." Jer. v. 7. Oh, how horrid it is to sin against a bountiful God!—to strike the hands that relieve us! . . . They are like Absalom, who as soon as David his father kissed him, plotted treason against him. 2 Sam. xv. 10. They are like the mule who kicks the dam after she has given it milk. Those who sin against their giver, and abuse God's royal favours, the mercies of God will come in as witnesses against them. . . .

If God gives us all, let his giving excite us to thanksgiving. He is the founder and donor of all our blessings, and should have all our acknowledgments. . . . All our gifts come from God, and to him must all our praises return. (*A Body of Divinity* [Reprint: Grand Rapids: Baker, 1979], 542)

The supplication, **give,** reflects a child-like trust in the Father's care. The basis for asking for life's necessities is the confidence that God will provide them for His children. David, no stranger to trouble and trials, expressed that confidence when he declared, "I have been young and now I am old, yet I have not seen the righteous forsaken or his descendants begging bread" (Ps. 37:25). Earlier in that psalm he wrote, "The Lord knows the days of the blameless, and their inheritance will be forever. They will not be ashamed in the time of evil, and in the days of famine they will have abundance" (vv. 18–19), while in Psalm 33:18–19 the psalmist added, "Behold, the eye of the Lord is on those who fear Him, on those who hope for His lovingkindness, to deliver their soul from death and to keep them alive in famine." Job 5:17–20 also conveys God's deliverance of His people from the scourge of famine:

Behold, how happy is the man whom God reproves, so do not despise the discipline of the Almighty. For He inflicts pain, and gives relief; He wounds, and His hands also heal. From six troubles He will deliver you, even in seven evil will not touch you. In famine He will redeem you from death, and in war from the power of the sword.

Proverbs 10:3 echoes that truth, promising that "the Lord will not allow the righteous to hunger."

God's provision for the community of believers can impact the society in which they live. Christianity's influence in contemporary secular, godless, humanistic, pluralistic America is far less than when the nation was founded. Nevertheless the residue of those Christian roots has given America a perspective on the value and dignity of man not shared by cultures that have not been exposed to the Bible's influence. The humanitarian and philanthropic concern for human life and well-being that, though fading, still influences American society is largely unknown in such cultures. Famine and starvation often results not from lack of natural resources, but from lack of spiritual resources and the resulting indifference to human suffering.

Praying for the necessities of life no more precludes believers' responsibility to work and earn a living than praying for the salvation of the lost precludes evangelism. Paul made that principle clear when he reminded the Christians in Thessalonica,

> For even when we were with you, we used to give you this order: if any-one is not willing to work, then he is not to eat, either. For we hear that some among you are leading an undisciplined life, doing no work at all, but acting like busybodies. Now such persons we command and exhort in the Lord Jesus Christ to work in quiet fashion and eat their own bread. (2 Thess. 3:10–12)

Nor does the general principle that God provides for the physical needs of His own guarantee that there will not be exceptions; even some of the Old Testament heroes of the faith were destitute, afflicted, and ill-treated (Heb. 11:37). Some believers may even die of exposure or starva-tion. But until their time to die comes, those who remain faithful to the Lord will experience His care for them, as in answer to their prayers He provides **each day** what they require to sustain their lives.

GOD AS SAVIOR

And forgive us our sins, for we ourselves also forgive everyone who is indebted to us. (11:4*a*)

This request goes beyond the need for the things that sustain physical life to the far more significant need for that which provides spiri-tual life. Forgiveness is the greatest need of every person, since unfor-given sins expose the soul irremediably to divine judgment and the certainty of eternal punishment. That the Lord Jesus Christ, God incarnate, tells us to pray, **forgive us our sins,** reveals that God is eager to forgive (cf. Ps. 86:5). This petition assumes not only that people need forgiveness, but also that God grants it.

The deadly problem facing all men is sin (Rom. 3:23), the only cure is forgiveness (Col. 1:14), and only God, the one offended by sin (Ps. 51:4), can forgive it (Luke 5:21). Those are the central realities of the Christian gospel.

The inescapable problem all people face is that their **sins** have left them estranged from God and doomed to eternal punishment in hell. "Your iniquities have made a separation between you and your God," Isaiah wrote, "and your sins have hidden His face from you so that He does not hear" (Isa. 59:2). The problem is universal, for as Solomon acknowledged, "There is no man who does not sin" (1 Kings 8:46). In Proverbs 20:9 he asked, "Who can say, 'I have cleansed my heart, I am pure from my sin?'"; then he answered his own rhetorical question in Ecclesiastes 7:20: "Indeed, there is not a righteous man on earth who continually does good and who never sins." The apostle Paul agreed with Solomon, arguing that "there is none righteous, not even one" (Rom. 3:10), since "all have sinned and fall short of the glory of God" (Rom. 3:23).

Sin infects every baby born into the world (Ps. 51:5). It is the current monarch of the world, ruling the heart of every man, woman, and child. Sin contaminates every person at every level—mind, will, affections, emotions, and conduct. Its degenerative power makes people susceptible to disease, illness, injury, sorrow, and death. Sin is the culprit in every broken marriage, every disrupted home, every shattered relationship, every argument, battle, and war. Because of sin the unregenerate are spiritually dead (Eph. 2:1), targets of God's wrath (v. 3), cut off from Him and without hope (v. 12).

The dilemma for sinners is twofold. On the one hand, God cannot simply overlook sin or be indifferent to it. His justice, righteousness, and holiness demand that every sin ever committed be punished. The God who condemns those who justify the wicked (Prov. 17:15; cf. 24:24) cannot Himself turn a blind eye to sin. Thus in Exodus 23:7 the Lord declared, "I will not acquit the guilty." Nahum's prophecy states unequivocally that "the Lord will by no means leave the guilty unpunished" (Nah. 1:3), while Paul wrote that "the wrath of God is revealed from heaven against all ungodliness and unrighteousness of men who suppress the truth in unrighteousness" (Rom. 1:18). God is not the friend of unrepentant sinners; He is their enemy. Psalm 5:5 warns that God "hate[s] all who do iniquity," while Psalm 7:11 notes that "God is angry with the wicked every day" (NKJV).

On the other hand, sinners are unable to extricate themselves from their dilemma, as the picturesque language of Jeremiah 13:23 indicates: "Can the Ethiopian change his skin or the leopard his spots? Then you also can do good who are accustomed to doing evil." The unregenerate are dead in their sins (Eph. 2:1), spiritually blind (John 12:40), deceived by Satan (2 Cor. 4:4) and "held captive by him to do his will" (2 Tim. 2:26), enslaved by sin (John 8:34; Rom. 6:6, 16–20), alienated from God and hostile to Him (Col. 1:21), unable to understand spiritual truth (1 Cor. 2:14); in short, utterly helpless to redeem themselves (Rom. 5:6).

The various New Testament words used to describe sin paint a grim portrait of its heinousness. The word translated **sins** is the plural form of *hamartia*, the basic meaning of which is "to miss the mark." Sin is any failure to meet God's standard, as defined by the Lord in Matthew 5:48: "Therefore you are to be perfect, as your heavenly Father is perfect" (cf. Lev. 11:44–45). Only God is good (Mark 10:18).

A second New Testament word for sin is *parabasis*, which means "to step across," or "overstep." Sin crosses the line between right and wrong; it oversteps the bounds of God's law and crosses the barrier into forbidden territory whether in thought, word, or deed.

Another word for sin that appears in the New Testament is *anomia*, which is translated "lawlessness" (cf. 1 John 3:4). Sin is the primary act of the proud, selfish sinner who, seeking to go his own way, rebels against God and breaks His law.

Paraptōma ("transgression," "trespass") means "to take a false step," "to slip," "to stumble," or "to fall." The word likens sin to a lack of the self-control necessary to stand up. To sin is to be out of control; to be swept away by impulse or passion. It highlights the sinner's impotence and inability to keep God's law.

A fifth word, *opheilēma*, describes an obligation or a debt. It is used in Matthew 6:12 to refer to believers' sin against God, and the verb form in verse 4 of this passage to speak of others' transgressions against them. By causing people to miss the mark, cross the line, act lawlessly, and lose self-control, sin puts them in debt to God. It defrauds Him of the righteousness and obedience that He is due.

To confess one's sins is to acknowledge sin in all of its facets. Proud religious sinners, like the people in Jesus' home village of Nazareth (Luke 4:28–30), reject the reality that they are guilty sinners who owe God an unpayable debt because they are not good. But the humblest of men, acutely aware of their sin and guilt, are eager to repent and confess their condition and need of forgiveness. In Psalm 51 David poured out his soul in contrition, penitence, and confession. After witnessing Jesus perform an amazing miracle that revealed His deity, Peter cried out, "Go away from me Lord, for I am a sinful man, O Lord!" (Luke 5:8). The repentant tax collector in Jesus' parable "was beating his breast, saying, 'God, be merciful to me, the sinner!'" (Luke 18:13).

Because the unregenerate are proud and blind to the reality both of their sin and the availability of forgiveness, it is necessary for the Holy Spirit to "convict the world concerning sin and righteousness and judgment" (John 16:8). He awakens sinners to the reality of their desperate plight and God's gracious offer of forgiveness. Recognizing their wretched, sinful condition, they make the confession of their sins apart from which there is no salvation. Confession then becomes a way of life; in fact, the apostle John defines Christians as those who are continually confessing their sins (1 John 1:9).

The only solution to the problem of sin is God's gracious provision of forgiveness. Forgiveness is God's passing by or overlooking believers' sins, ceasing to be angry with them; but rather loving them, and showing them compassion (Mic. 7:18–19), wiping the record of their sins (Isa. 43:25; 44:22), forgetting their sins (Heb. 8:12; 10:17), and not counting their sins against them (2 Cor. 5:19). The Bible pictures God's forgiveness of sins as purging them like washing scarlet wool until it is white as snow (Isa. 1:18), casting them behind His back (Isa. 38:17), hiding them behind a thick cloud (Isa. 44:22), removing them "as far [away] as the east is from the west" (Ps. 103:12), trampling them under foot, and burying them in the depths of the sea (Mic. 7:19).

The forgiveness in view in this petition is initially the judicial forgiveness granted by God at salvation. As noted above, God cannot simply ignore or overlook sin. The critical question, then, is how can He "be just and the justifier" of sinners (Rom. 3:26), since His justice and holiness demand full punishment for every sin?

The answer lies in comprehending the doctrine of substitutionary atonement. God placed all of believers' sins on the Lord Jesus Christ and then punished Him for them. In the simple yet profound words of 2 Corinthians 5:21, "He [God] made Him [Christ] who knew no sin to be sin on our behalf, so that we might become the righteousness of God in Him." Peter wrote, "He Himself bore our sins in His body on the cross, so that we might die to sin and live to righteousness" (1 Peter 2:24). Isaiah predicted that Messiah would die for the sins of His people when he wrote, "All of us like sheep have gone astray, each of us has turned to his own way; but the Lord has caused the iniquity of us all to fall on Him" (Isa. 53:6). On the night before His death Jesus said to the disciples, "This is My blood of the covenant, which is poured out for many for forgiveness of sins" (Matt. 26:28). In Ephesians 1:7 Paul wrote, "In Him [Christ] we have redemption through His blood, the forgiveness of our trespasses, according to the riches of His grace." To the Colossians he wrote,

> When you were dead in your transgressions and the uncircumcision of your flesh, He made you alive together with Him, having forgiven us all our transgressions, having canceled out the certificate of debt consisting of decrees against us, which was hostile to us; and He has taken it out of the way, having nailed it to the cross. (Col. 2:13–14)

God "did not spare His own Son, but delivered Him over for us all" (Rom. 8:32). The writer of Hebrews also emphasized that Christ was a sacrifice for the sins of His people (cf. Heb. 10:10–18).

By satisfying God's justice by complete payment of the penalty, the work of Christ on the cross provided complete, irreversible, and permanent forgiveness for every sin of all who put their faith in Him, who are all for whom He died. This judicial forgiveness has been available since the fall; the sins of the Old Testament saints who believed what God had revealed to them were forgiven on the basis of Christ's future sacrifice. Both Paul (Rom. 4:3) and James (James 2:23) wrote that Abraham was justified and received forgiveness for his sin through his trust in God's revelation. Of that forgiveness David wrote, "How blessed is he whose transgression is forgiven, whose sin is covered! How blessed is the man to whom the Lord does not impute iniquity" (Ps. 32:1; cf. 103:3; 130:3–4; Jer. 33:8).

The question naturally arises as to why the Lord commands us, whose sins have already been forgiven, to ask the Father for forgiveness. The answer lies in grasping a second aspect of forgiveness, relational forgiveness. While believers' sins—past, present, and future—were forgiven at the point of salvation, they nevertheless still sin. Those sins do not change the declaration by the "Judge of all the earth" (Gen. 18:25) that Christians are just and righteous because their sins were paid for by the death of Christ. But they do affect their relationship with God, whose "eyes are too pure to approve evil," and who "can not look on wickedness with favor" (Hab. 1:13).

David's penitent prayer in Psalm 51 illustrates this principle. His terrible sin with Bathsheba did not cause him to lose his salvation; in fact, in verse 14 David addressed God as "the God of my salvation." It did, however, disrupt his communion with God, causing him to cry out, "Restore to me the joy of Your salvation" (v. 12). He did not ask for his salvation to be restored, but rather for his relationship with God to be restored so his joy would return.

John 13 presents another illustration of relational forgiveness. In an example of humble service, Jesus began washing the disciples' feet. But when He came to Peter, he objected and said to Jesus, "Lord, do You wash my feet?" (v. 6). It did not seem proper and fitting to Peter that the Lord of the universe should perform a task reserved for the most menial of slaves. Even after Jesus explained that Peter would understand later the meaning of His act, Peter was adamant. "Never shall You wash my feet!" he exclaimed. Only when Jesus answered him, "If I do not wash you, you have no part with Me" (v. 8) did Peter consent. In typical fashion, he then went overboard in the other direction and enthusiastically said to Jesus, "Lord, then wash not only my feet, but also my hands and my head" (v. 9). The Lord replied, "He who has bathed needs only to wash his feet, but is completely clean; and you are clean, but not all of you" (v. 10). In Christ's analogy the apostles (except for the traitor Judas Iscariot) had been totally cleansed of their sin at salvation, an experience that did not need to be repeated. All they needed was to have their feet cleaned, symbolizing the confession and daily cleansing of those sins that disrupt fellowship with God.

Unlike the other petitions in this prayer, this one has a prerequisite: **for we ourselves also forgive everyone who is indebted to us.** An unforgiving Christian is a contradiction in terms. Those who come to God seeking relational forgiveness will find it only if they forgive those who have wronged them. The Lord gave this prerequisite because bitterness can easily reign supreme in the human heart. People hold grudges —sometimes for a lifetime—and are prone to seeking vengeance. Relationships that fall apart do so ultimately because one or both parties involved are unwilling to forgive. The world is filled with bitter, angry people. Vengeance is considered a virtue, and those who seek it are heroes. The result is shattered marriages, broken relationships, gang warfare, crime, and lawsuits. Some psychologists argue that it is unhealthy to forgive, that it is healthy and normal to lash back at those who hurt us and give them what they deserve. That, they insist, makes the angry person feel better.

But the price of unforgiveness is actually extremely high. Rather than make someone feel better, unforgiveness imprisons people in their past and makes those they refuse to forgive their jailers. Those who refuse to forgive continually pick at an open wound, never allowing it to heal. Having chosen to embrace hate, they become tortured prisoners of the offense and the offender. Such behavior is foolish, lacks common sense, and is self-destructive. It consumes unforgiving people's lives, robs them of their well-being, and deprives them of happiness and joy.

Forgiveness, on the other hand, is a virtuous, noble, liberating, and loving act. But the more profound and compelling reason to forgive others is that doing so allows one to receive relational forgiveness from God. Unforgiveness is presented by the Lord Jesus Christ as the sin that blocks temporal forgiveness (cf. Matt. 6:12, 14–15). Both uses of **forgive** in this passage translate forms of the Greek verb *aphiēmi*, which can be translated "send away," "abandon," "leave behind," or "dismiss." Perhaps the synonym that best reflects its use in this passage is "to hurl." Just as God figuratively hurled believers' sins into the depths of the sea at salvation (Mic. 7:19), so also must believers hurl away the sins of others and not hold on to them. Only then will the Lord forgive the sins that disrupt their relationship with

Him. (I discuss the importance of forgiveness in my book *The Freedom and Power of Forgiveness* [Wheaton, Ill.: Crossway, 1998].)

While the most important reason to forgive others is to enjoy our relationship with God, there are at least nine other reasons to do so.

First, forgiveness is the most God-like thing believers can do; nothing is more divine than to forgive. The father's eager forgiveness of his wayward son in the Lord's parable illustrates God's gracious willingness to forgive repentant sinners (Luke 15:20–32; cf. Ps. 86:5; Isa. 55:7; Dan. 9:9). That provides a pattern for believers to imitate. "Be kind to one another," Paul wrote in Ephesians 4:32, "tender-hearted, forgiving each other, just as God in Christ also has forgiven you" (cf. Matt. 5:44–45; Col. 3:13).

Second, failing to forgive violates the sixth commandment, "You shall not murder" (Ex. 20:13). It is not murder alone that is forbidden, but also the lack of forgiveness that makes one a murderer in the heart. In Matthew 5:21–22 Jesus taught that the Old Testament prohibition against murder also included being angry with someone (cf. 1 John 3:15), which presupposes a lack of forgiveness toward them.

Third, whoever offends a Christian has offended God more. David committed adultery with Bathsheba, then had her husband Uriah murdered in a brutal attempt to cover up his sin. Yet when he poured out his heart in confession, he acknowledged to God, "Against You, You only, I have sinned and done what is evil in Your sight" (Ps. 51:4). If God, the most holy and the most offended, forgives an offense, how much more so must those who are the least holy and least offended?

Fourth, it is only reasonable that those forgiven the greater sins by God forgive the lesser offenses against them. This and the next two points are taken from a parable the Lord gave to teach the importance of forgiveness (Matt. 18:23–35). The parable was prompted by Peter's question, "Lord, how often shall my brother sin against me and I forgive him? Up to seven times?" (v. 21). The rabbis, based on several verses in the book of Amos (1:3, 6, 9, 11), taught that God forgave three times, then judged for the fourth offense. They taught that people should forgive no more than the three times they assumed God forgives. Knowing that Jesus had called His followers to a higher standard (cf. Matt. 5:20), Peter magnanimously was willing to forgive seven times—more than double the rabbinic prescription. Shockingly, Jesus replied, "I do not say to you, up to seven times, but up to seventy times seven" (v. 22), or 490 times. On another occasion Jesus made a similar statement:"Be on your guard! If your brother sins, rebuke him; and if he repents, forgive him. And if he sins against you seven times a day, and returns to you seven times, saying,'I repent,' forgive him" (Luke 17:4). In other words, forgiveness is to be unlimited.

Jesus then told a story involving a high-ranking slave (probably a provincial governor charged with collecting taxes).This man was guilty of embezzlement, and owed the king a staggering, unpayable debt (v. 24; the word translated "ten thousand" was the largest word for a number in the Greek language and signifies an incalculable amount).Since he was not able to repay the money he had embezzled, the king ordered him and his family to be sold into slavery to recoup as much of the money he had been defrauded of as possible (v.25).

In desperation,"the slave fell to the ground and prostrated himself before him,saying,'Have patience with me and I will repay you everything'" (v. 26). Of course, he could do no such thing; his debt was far beyond his ability to ever repay.Incredibly,"the lord of that slave felt compassion and released him and forgave him the debt" (v.27).Here is a marvelous picture of salvation by grace, in which God forgives sinners who owe Him an eternally unpayable debt because of their sin.

But what happened next was even more shocking. Leaving the king's presence,"that slave went out and found one of his fellow slaves who owed him a hundred denarii; and he seized him and began to choke him, saying,'Pay back what you owe'" (v. 28).This was a debt that could have been repaid, since it only amounted to about three months' wages for an average laborer.The man made the same plea to him that he had just made to the king (v. 29). But unlike the king, who had graciously forgiven him, "he was unwilling and went and threw him in prison until he should pay back what was owed" (v.30).

His response was absurd, incomprehensible. How could one who had just been forgiven a staggering, incalculable debt refuse to forgive one who owed him a trivial amount? But that is the Lord's point. Those freely and fully forgiven of the unpayable debt they owe God have no right to have a vengeful, bitter, unforgiving attitude over the trivial offenses committed against them by others.Believers who manifest such an attitude have not yet been humbled by the magnitude of their own salvation.

Fifth, the one who is unforgiving will forfeit the fellowship of other Christians. Verse 31 records that "when his fellow slaves saw what had happened, they were deeply grieved and came and reported to their lord all that had happened." Having witnessed the man who had been forgiven so much refuse to forgive his fellow slave, the other slaves reported him to the king. This pictures church discipline, where the unforgiving sinner, having alienated himself from the fellowship of other Christians, is turned over to the Lord for discipline (cf. 1 Cor. 5).

Sixth, failure to forgive results in divine chastening. After summoning the unforgiving man into his presence, the king sternly rebuked him:

> "You wicked slave, I forgave you all that debt because you pleaded with me. Should you not also have had mercy on your fellow slave, in the same way that I had mercy on you?" And his lord, moved with anger, handed him over to the torturers until he should repay all that was owed him. (vv. 32–34)

Although believers who sin by failing to forgive others will not lose their salvation, neither will they escape being disciplined by the Lord. The use of the strong word "torturers" indicates the painful nature of that chastening. It may involve loss of joy, peace, assurance of salvation, usefulness in service, and result in conflict, stress, hardship, difficulty, and trouble. The Lord Jesus Christ commanded His followers, "Be merciful, just as your Father is merciful" (Luke 6:36; cf. Matt. 5:7), while James warned that "judgment will be merciless to one who has shown no mercy" (James 2:13; cf. Matt. 7:2).

Seventh, failure to forgive renders a person unfit for worship. In the Sermon on the Mount Jesus said, "Therefore if you are presenting your offering at the altar, and there remember that your brother has something against you, leave your offering there before the altar and go; first be reconciled to your brother, and then come and present your offering" (Matt. 5:23–24). When a believer is aware of a conflict with or a lack of forgiveness toward another person, the situation needs to be resolved before coming to worship God. Reconciliation precedes worship, which is not acceptable when sin is harbored in the heart (Ps. 66:18; Prov. 15:8).

Eighth, failure to forgive usurps the authority of God. It is to presumptuously take the sword of divine judgment out of His hand and wield it for oneself—which Scripture explicitly forbids. "Never take your own revenge, beloved," wrote Paul, "but leave room for the wrath of God, for it is written, 'Vengeance is Mine, I will repay,' says the Lord" (Rom. 12:19). Refusing to forgive takes from God His right to retaliate against sin and places it in the hands of those who are not qualified to do so. Only God has the perfect understanding of the offenses against believers; only He has the ultimate authority, is impartial, perfectly wise and good, and always acts in pure holiness.

Finally, the offenses against believers are the trials that perfect them. James wrote, "Consider it all joy, my brethren, when you encounter various trials, knowing that the testing of your faith produces endurance. And let endurance have its perfect result, so that you may be perfect and complete, lacking in nothing" (James 1:2–4). Peter encouraged suffering believers to remember that "after [they] have suffered for a little while, the God of all grace, who called [them] to His eternal glory in Christ, will Himself perfect, confirm, strengthen and establish [them]" (1 Peter 5:10; cf. 2:19–21). Paul was "content with weaknesses, with insults, with distresses, with persecutions, with difficulties, for Christ's sake; for when [he was] weak, then [he was] strong" (2 Cor. 12:10).

Viewing the offenses of others against us as God's means of perfecting us puts them in a different light, and enables us to follow the example of Christ, "who committed no sin, nor was any deceit found in His mouth; and while being reviled, He did not revile in return; while suffering, He uttered no threats, but kept entrusting Himself to Him who judges righteously" (1 Peter 2:22–23). Christ's embracing of unjust suffering resulted in the greatest triumph in history, His sacrificial death on the cross (v. 24).

GOD AS SHELTER

And lead us not into temptation. (11:4*b*)

At first glance, this request seems puzzling. Since God does not tempt anyone (James 1:13), to ask Him not to do what He has already promised never to do seems superfluous. But in reality, this shows again the parallel realities of divine sovereignty and human responsibility. God does His will, not apart from us, but through our obedience and prayers. There are, then, two perfectly legitimate reasons why the Lord included this petition.

First, it reflects the believer's humble sense of weakness, knowing that the evil, fallen world is inevitably a hostile, dangerous environment. There are physical dangers from volcanoes, earthquakes, fires, floods, accidents, disease, terrorism, and crime. In the intellectual realm believers face unfair judgments, laws and regulations, and the influence of an increasingly narcissistic, self-centered culture dominated by pride and greed. From the spiritual world come assaults on believers' faith from postmodern relativism, humanism, evolution, false religions, and other manifestations of earthly, natural, demonic wisdom (James 3:15), all of which the Bible calls "doctrines of demons" (1 Tim. 4:1). Even the church is riddled with false teaching, worldliness, compromise, lack of knowledge of biblical truth, and waning zeal for God. Most deadly of all are the assaults from Satan, who blinds men to the truth (2 Cor. 4:4), tempts them to sin (1 Cor. 7:5; Eph. 4:27; 6:11; 1 Thess. 3:5); and "prowls around like a roaring lion, seeking someone to devour" (1 Peter 5:8).

With deadly dangers all about them and the fallen nature still in them, it is only natural for believers to cry out to God for protection as David did: "My eyes are toward You, O God, the Lord; in You I take refuge; do not leave me defenseless" (Ps. 141:8; cf. 18:30; 46:1; 62:8; 91:2; 94:22; 2 Sam. 22:3; Prov. 18:10; 30:5). Jesus made that same request for His own in His high-priestly prayer when He asked the Father to "keep them from the evil one" (John 17:15). In the Sermon on the Mount, the Lord taught believers to make that same request for deliverance from evil (Matt. 6:13).

But there is a second sense in which this petition may be understood. It is an appeal to God not to allow the inevitable tests and trials of life to become temptations that would prove overpowering. *Peirasmos* (**temptation**) is a neutral word with no inherent moral connotation. God does not tempt anyone to do evil, but He does permit tests to come into the lives of believers, as He did to Job (Job 23:10), Abraham (Heb. 11:17–19), Paul (2 Cor. 12:7–10), and Jesus (Heb. 5:8), as part of the process of strengthening and maturing them (Deut. 13:3; 1 Peter 1:6–7; 5:10). How believers respond to those tests determines whether they remain perfecting trials that bring spiritual growth, or become debilitating temptations that overwhelm them and lead them into sin.

The basis for this request is God's promise, expressed in 1 Corinthians 10:13, that He will never allow a temptation that is stronger than believers can bear. Those He permits are common to all people, and He will provide a way to escape being led into sin by them. People fall into sin not because they are overpowered by Satan and the demons, or because they were trapped with no way out. As James explained, "Each one is tempted when he is carried away and enticed by his own lust. Then when lust has conceived, it gives birth to sin; and when sin is accomplished, it brings forth death" (James 1:14–15).

In these three brief sentences Jesus masterfully encompassed all of life's most basic needs:

> Our whole life is found there in those three petitions, and that is what makes this prayer so utterly amazing. In such a small compass our Lord has covered the whole life of the believer in every respect. Our physical needs, our mental needs and, of course, our spiritual needs are included. The body is remembered, the soul is remembered, the spirit is remembered....We cannot fail to be impressed by the all-inclusiveness of these petitions. That does not mean that we should never enter into details; we must, we are taught to do so. We are taught to bring our life in detail to God in prayer; but here we have only the great headings. Our Lord gives us these and we fill in the details, but it is important for us to be sure that all our petitions should belong under one or other of the headings. (D. Martyn Lloyd-Jones, *Studies in the Sermon on the Mount* [Grand Rapids: Eerdmans, 1974], 2:67–68)

Jesus' Pattern for Every Prayer—Part 5: God's Promise (Luke 11:5–13)

5

Then He said to them, "Suppose one of you has a friend, and goes to him at midnight and says to him, 'Friend, lend me three loaves; for a friend of mine has come to me from a journey, and I have nothing to set before him'; and from inside he answers and says, 'Do not bother me; the door has already been shut and my children and I are in bed; I cannot get up and give you anything.' I tell you, even though he will not get up and give him anything because he is his friend, yet because of his persistence he will get up and give him as much as he needs. So I say to you, ask, and it will be given to you; seek, and you will find; knock, and it will be opened to you. For everyone who asks, receives; and he who seeks, finds; and to him who knocks, it will be opened. Now suppose one of you fathers is asked by his son for a fish; he will not give him a snake instead of a fish, will he? Or if he is asked for an egg, he will not give him a scorpion, will he? If you then, being evil, know how to give good gifts to your children, how much more will your heavenly Father give the Holy Spirit to those who ask Him?" (11:5–13)

A.W. Tozer opened his classic work on the attributes of God with the following astute and penetrating observations:

> What comes into our minds when we think about God is the most important thing about us.
>
> The history of mankind will probably show that no people has ever risen above its religion, and man's spiritual history will positively demonstrate that no religion has ever been greater than its idea of God. Worship is pure or base as the worshiper entertains high or low thoughts of God.
>
> For this reason the gravest question before the church is always God Himself, and the most portentous fact about any man is not what he at a given time may say or do, but what he in his deep heart conceives God to be like. We tend by a secret law of the soul to move toward our mental image of God....
>
> Were we able to extract from any man a complete answer to the question, "what comes into your mind when you think about God?" we might predict with certainty the spiritual future of that man....
>
> A right conception of God is basic not only to systematic theology but to practical Christian living as well. It is to worship what the foundation is to the temple; where it is inadequate or out of plumb the whole structure must sooner or later collapse. I believe there is scarcely an error in doctrine or a failure in applying Christian ethics that cannot be traced finally to imperfect and ignoble thoughts about God. (*The Knowledge of the Holy* [New York: Harper & Row, 1961], 9, 10)

There is no clearer, more definitive benchmark of a person's spiritual maturity than his or her view of God. The apostle John described the most spiritually mature individuals, the "fathers," as those who "know Him who has been from the beginning" (1 John 2:13, 14). Paul wrote that his supreme goal was to know the Lord Jesus Christ (Phil. 3:10; cf. v. 8).

To be spiritually mature is to understand that God is eternal, omnipotent, holy, unchangeable, omniscient, omnipresent, majestic, and transcendent, above and beyond and outside of all contingencies in the universe He created. It is to know that He is sovereign, bringing to pass the perfect plan He ordained from the beginning. Humbled by God's declaration of His power and sovereignty Job acknowledged, "I know that You can do all things, and that no purpose of Yours can be thwarted"

(Job 42:2), because "the counsel of the Lord stands forever, the plans of His heart from generation to generation" (Ps. 33:11). "Many plans are in a man's heart," said Solomon, "but the counsel of the Lord will stand" (Prov. 19:21). In Isaiah 46:9–10 the Lord declared, "I am God, and there is no other; I am God, and there is no one like Me, declaring the end from the beginning, and from ancient times things which have not been done, saying, 'My purpose will be established, and I will accomplish all My good pleasure'" (cf. 14:24; 43:13). In Acts 1:7 Jesus told the disciples that God has absolute, sovereign control over all the events of history, while the early church affirmed that even the murder of the Lord Jesus Christ, history's most heinous act, was under God's sovereign control: "For truly in this city there were gathered together against Your holy servant Jesus, whom You anointed, both Herod and Pontius Pilate, along with the Gentiles and the peoples of Israel, to do whatever Your hand and Your purpose predestined to occur" (Acts 4:27–28). In Ephesians 1:11 Paul affirmed that God "works all things after the counsel of His will."

In light of God's sovereign control of events and the inevitable outworking of His purpose and plan, the question arises as to whether believers' prayers change anything. And since He is omniscient, God does not need more information, nor is He surprised by circumstances. Going to Him in prayer therefore seems to be little more than an unnecessary expression. But having a correct view of God's nature and purposes does not squelch prayer; the Lord Jesus Christ, God incarnate, prayed to the Father (e.g., Matt. 26:39–44; Luke 10:21; John 11:41–42; 17:1–26), gave model prayers to teach believers to pray (Matt. 6:9–13; Luke 11:1–4), and commanded them to pray (Luke 18:1). God's words addressed to Israel in Jeremiah 29 also make it clear that His sovereign purposes do not negate prayer. In verse 11 He said, "For I know the plans that I have for you ... plans for welfare and not for calamity to give you a future and a hope." Still, in verse 12 He added, "You will call upon Me and come and pray to Me, and I will listen to you."

The first chapter of Nehemiah finds Israel in exile (v. 1). After hearing a report that Jerusalem was in ruins (vv. 2–3), Nehemiah "sat down and wept and mourned for days; and ... was fasting and praying before the God of heaven" (v. 4). That Nehemiah understood and accepted God's sovereign control of events is evident from verse 5, where he referred to God as the "Lord God of heaven, the great and awesome God, who preserves the covenant and lovingkindness for those who love Him and keep His commandments." Yet understanding that truth did not keep Nehemiah from imploring God to take note of His people's desperate situation: "Let Your ear now be attentive and Your eyes open to hear the prayer of Your servant which I am praying before You now, day and night, on behalf of the sons of Israel Your servants" (v.6).

The psalms record numerous pleas for God to hear and answer prayer:

> Hear a just cause, O Lord, give heed to my cry; give ear to my prayer, which is not from deceitful lips. (17:1)

> Hear, O Lord, when I cry with my voice, and be gracious to me and answer me. (27:7)

> Give ear to my prayer, O God; and do not hide Yourself from my supplication. Give heed to me and answer me; I am restless in my complaint and am surely distracted. (55:1–2)

> Hear my cry, O God; give heed to my prayer. (61:1)

> Hear my prayer, O Lord! And let my cry for help come to You. Do not hide Your face from me in the day of my distress; incline Your ear to me; in the day when I call answer me quickly. (102:1–2)

> Hear my prayer, O Lord, give ear to my supplications! Answer me in Your faithfulness, in Your righteousness! (143:1. See also 4:1; 5:1–3; 39:12; 54:2; 69:13; 84:8; 86:1, 6; 88:2, 13; 142:1–2)

In addition, Psalm 65:2 addresses God as "You who hear prayer" (cf. 77:1; 145:19).

But if prayer does not change God's mind or plans, or give Him information He lacks, what purpose does it serve? The answer to that question lies in understanding that God not only ordains the ends He purposes to accomplish, but also the means to those ends. For example the Old Testament predicted that Jesus would be born in Bethlehem (Mic. 5:2), but God used the decree of the pagan Roman emperor Augustus Caesar as a means of fulfilling His plan (Luke 2:1–4). Similarly, God used both the hostile Jews and the Romans as the means of carrying out His plan that Christ would be the sacrifice for the sins of His people (Acts

2:22–23). Because it is a God-ordained means to accomplish His purposes, "The effective prayer of a righteous man can accomplish much" (James 5:16).

In this passage Jesus encourages believers to pray boldly. It may be divided into four sections: the parable, the promise, the principle, and the premise.

THE PARABLE

Then He said to them, "Suppose one of you has a friend, and goes to him at midnight and says to him, 'Friend, lend me three loaves; for a friend of mine has come to me from a journey, and I have nothing to set before him'; and from inside he answers and says, 'Do not bother me; the door has already been shut and my children and I are in bed; I cannot get up and give you anything.' I tell you, even though he will not get up and give him anything because he is his friend, yet because of his persistence he will get up and give him as much as he needs. (11:5–8)

Jesus illustrated the importance of boldness in prayer in a story unforgettable for its clarity and touch of humor. **He said to** those whom He had addressed his teaching on prayer (vv. 1–4), **Suppose one of you has a friend.** *Philos* (**friend**) refers to anyone held in affection, in this case a neighbor. In Israel, as throughout the ancient world, people were dependent on their neighbors. There were no grocery or convenience stores, or restaurants, nor did most people have large stockpiles of food. A man went to his neighbor at **midnight,** obviously not a normal time for a visit. In that day no one was up at that hour, since there was no TV, radio, or internet. Most people went to bed shortly after nightfall, since they were awake and working shortly after sunrise. Arriving at his friend's house he called out to him, **Friend** (a sensible greeting considering that he had come uninvited at a most inopportune time), **lend me three loaves.** These were not loaves in the modern sense, but the typical flat bread.

The man's friend no doubt did not appreciate being awakened

in the middle of the night for what seemingly was not an emergency. After all the first man had not been robbed, his wife was not having a baby, and no one had been injured or taken ill. But there was more to it than his seeking a midnight snack; there was an emergency, not a physical one, but a social one. As he went on to explain, **A friend of mine has come to me from a journey.** Travelling at night was not unusual during hot weather, and another friend had just arrived at his house. The traveler would have been hungry after his journey, and at this late hour, the man had **nothing to set before him** to eat. Since hospitality was an important social duty in the ancient world (Gen. 19:8), and particularly in Israel (cf. Gen. 18:1–8), he faced a difficult dilemma. Either he could be a poor host to his guest by letting him go hungry, or a poor neighbor to his friend by waking him up in the middle of the night. He chose the latter.

The predictable response **from** his neighbor **inside** the house was, **Do not bother me; the door has already been shut and my children and I are in bed; I cannot get up and give you anything.** Doors were often made of wood and iron, and opening one could be noisy enough to wake the entire household. As was customary in the typical one-room houses of the time, the man's **children** were **in bed** with him (families often slept on one large mat), so by getting out of bed he would disturb the entire family. He therefore refused to **get up** and **give** his friend **anything.**

Skipping any further dialogue, the Lord jumped straight to the point of the story: **I tell you, even though he will not get up and give him anything because he is his friend, yet because of his persistence he will get up and give him as much as he needs.** Despite the initial rebuff, the man stubbornly refused to give up. In the end, his friend realized that the ongoing dialogue was going to awaken his children anyway (along with everyone else living nearby). So **even though he** would **not get up and give him anything because he** was **his friend, yet because of his persistence he** finally got **up and** gave **him as much as he** needed. **Persistence** (*anaideia*) means "shamelessness," "insolence," "audacity," "boldness"; today his behavior might be characterized by the Yiddish term "chutzpah." His shameless persistence succeeded where friendship failed, and the food he needed was set before the guest.

THE PROMISE

So I say to you, ask, and it will be given to you; seek, and you will find; knock, and it will be opened to you. For everyone who asks, receives; and he who seeks, finds; and to him who knocks, it will be opened. (11:9–10)

The parable illustrates an incredible promise. The use of the personal pronoun in addition to the first person form of the verb in the Lord's statement **I say to you** adds emphasis. As God incarnate, the Lord Jesus Christ speaks with the voice of absolute divine authority. Using three present tense imperative verbs, the Lord commands believers to boldly, aggressively storm the gates of heaven. The three verbs, **ask, seek,** and **knock** are progressively more intense, and each one repeats the promise: to those who **ask . . . it will be given;** those who **seek . . . will find;** those who **knock . . . will** find heaven's doors **opened to** them. Jesus then repeated this amazing promise so there would be no mistaking His meaning: **For everyone who asks, receives; and he who seeks, finds; and to him who knocks, it will be opened.**

This promise is not a blank check granting people whatever they wish, since it has already been qualified by the Lord's teaching in verses 2–4 that God is the focus of all true prayer. James struck this same balance between boldness in prayer and selfish greed. In James 4:2 he rebuked his readers for failing to pray boldly: "You do not have because you do not ask." But then he went on to warn, "You ask and do not receive, because you ask with wrong motives, so that you may spend it on your pleasures" (v. 3). Those who pray with a proper, God-centered focus will receive what they desire, but the selfish requests of the greedy will not be granted.

THE PRINCIPLE

Now suppose one of you fathers is asked by his son for a fish; he will not give him a snake instead of a fish, will he? Or if he is asked for an egg, he will not give him a scorpion, will he? (11:11–12)

The parable illustrates the promise and that promise in turn rests on a principle. That principle is couched in the common Jewish pattern of reasoning from the lesser to the greater. It raises the level of the discussion from friendship to fatherhood; if a person would respond to a bold request from a friend, how much more so would a father respond to his children?

Jesus introduced the principle by posing two hypothetical questions to His audience. **Suppose one of you fathers is asked by his son for a fish,** He said. Children, of course, can be expected to ask their fathers for what they need. They understand that the relationship between them and their father is one of love, care, responsibility, and affection. That gives them the confidence that they will receive what they ask for. Therefore if a father **is asked by his son for a fish; he will not give him a snake instead of a fish, will he?** No normal father would mock his child's hunger by giving him a deadly snake instead of the fish he requested. Nor **if he is asked for an egg** would he **give him a scorpion**—another unsavory and dangerous creature—or an inedible stone instead of bread (Matt. 7:9).

The obvious answer to Christ's questions is no, because of the principle that fathers take care of their children and meet their needs. Knowing their heavenly Father's care for them and commitment to meet their needs, believers can confidently ask Him for all that they need. Unlike the false gods of pagan religions, God is loving, approachable, and generous.

THE PREMISE

If you then, being evil, know how to give good gifts to your children, how much more will your heavenly Father give the Holy Spirit to those who ask Him? (11:13)

This premise, expressed in the form of a comparison, is the foundation upon which the whole discussion rests. Christ's opening words, **If you then, being evil,** express the biblical doctrine of total or radical depravity. Even His true followers, those who had embraced Him as Lord, Savior, and Messiah, were still **evil** (*ponēros*; "bad," "wicked," "worthless";

also used as a title for Satan [Matt. 13:19, 38; John 17:15; Eph. 6:16; 2 Thess. 3:3; 1 John 2:13, 14; 3:12; 5:18, 19]). Significantly, the Lord did not say that they do evil, but rather that they are evil. Though they are redeemed and forgiven, sin remains a powerful operative principle in believers (Rom. 7:14–25). Yet despite being evil, human fathers still **know how to give good gifts to** their **children.** It is natural for even unbelievers to love their children, be kind to them, and provide for their needs. The image of God in that sense in people, though warped and scarred by the fall, is nonetheless still present.

The contrasting phrase **how much more** is the key to the Lord's point. Reasoning from the lesser to the greater, if human fathers who are sinners, who love imperfectly, and often lack the wisdom to know what is best for their children lovingly provide for them, how much more will God, who is absolutely holy, loves perfectly (cf. John 13:1), and has infinite wisdom give what is best to His children. As the psalmist wrote, "No good thing does He withhold from those who walk uprightly" (Ps. 84:11; cf. 34:9–10; Matt. 6:33; Phil. 4:19).

Then Jesus concluded His point by promising that believers' **heavenly Father** will **give the Holy Spirit to those who ask Him.** This is an intriguing statement, which differs from the Lord's teaching of this same truth on a different occasion, as recorded in Matthew 7:11. There He spoke of the Father giving what is good; here He expanded that and spoke of God's giving the Spirit, who is the source of all goodness and blessing, to live within every believer.

To those who ask for a gift, He gives the giver; to those who ask for an effect, He gives the cause; to those who ask for a product He gives the source; to those seeking comfort He gives the comforter (Acts 9:31); to those seeking power He gives the source of power (Acts 1:8); to those seeking help He gives the helper (John 14:26); to those seeking truth He gives the Spirit of truth (John 16:13); to those seeking "love, joy, peace, patience, kindness, goodness, faithfulness, gentleness, self-control" (Gal. 5:22–23) He gives the producer of all those things. The indwelling Holy Spirit (Rom. 8:9, 11; 1 Cor. 6:19; 2 Tim. 1:14) is the source of every good thing in the Christian's life (Eph. 3:20).

Though the New Testament would bring more complete revelation concerning the person and ministry of the Holy Spirit, the Jews of

Jesus' day were familiar with the Old Testament revelation concerning Him. They understood that He was involved in the creation (Gen. 1:2; cf. Job 33:4). Further, they knew that the Holy Spirit was associated with the coming of the Messiah (Isa. 61:1–3; cf. Joel 2:28–29, which was partially fulfilled on the Day of Pentecost [Acts 2:16–21]). They also understood that Messiah would send the Spirit to regenerate (Titus 3:5) and indwell those who put their faith in Him (Ezek. 36:25–27; cf. John 7:38–39; 14:16–17, 25–26; Titus 3:5).

The Holy Spirit is the cause of every truly good thing in the life of a Christian. He convicts unbelieving sinners, enabling them to be aware of and repent of their sin (John 16:8). They enter God's kingdom of salvation by being born of the Spirit (John 3:5–8) in regeneration (Titus 3:5) and confessing Jesus as Lord through the Spirit (1 Cor. 12:3). It is through the Holy Spirit that they receive the knowledge of God (1 Cor. 2:11–12)—knowledge not understood by the unregenerate (v. 14). The Spirit frees believers from the law of sin and death (Rom. 8:2; 2 Cor. 3:17) and seals them for eternal life (Eph. 1:13; 4:30). They are baptized with the Spirit, placing them in the church, the body of Christ (1 Cor. 12:13), indwelt by the Spirit (Rom. 8:9, 11; 1 Cor. 6:19; 2 Tim. 1:14), and filled (controlled, empowered by) with the Spirit (Eph. 5:18). The Holy Spirit empowers believers for evangelism (Acts 1:8), intercedes for them (Rom. 8:26), sanctifies them (1 Cor. 6:11), makes them progressively more like Christ (2 Cor. 3:18), pours out God's love into their hearts (Rom. 5:5), and gives them hope (Rom. 15:13).

Bold, confident prayer results in communion with God and all the rich blessings of His goodness as believers experience the reality that He "is able to do far more abundantly beyond all that we ask or think, according to the power that works within us" (Eph. 3:20).

The Vilification of Jesus (Luke 11:14–23)

6

And He was casting out a demon, and it was mute; when the demon had gone out, the mute man spoke; and the crowds were amazed. But some of them said, "He casts out demons by Beelzebul, the ruler of the demons." Others, to test Him, were demanding of Him a sign from heaven. But He knew their thoughts and said to them, "Any kingdom divided against itself is laid waste; and a house divided against itself falls. If Satan also is divided against himself, how will his kingdom stand? For you say that I cast out demons by Beelzebul. And if I by Beelzebul cast out demons, by whom do your sons cast them out? So they will be your judges. But if I cast out demons by the finger of God, then the kingdom of God has come upon you. When a strong man, fully armed, guards his own house, his possessions are undisturbed. But when someone stronger than he attacks him and overpowers him, he takes away from him all his armor on which he had relied and distributes his plunder. He who is not with Me is against Me; and he who does not gather with Me, scatters. (11:14–23)

Most people today view truth not as black and white, but rather as consisting of thousands of shades of gray. The countless philosophies, theories, ideas, and religions in the world today are seen as competing with equal validity and none is absolute and exclusively true. The popular ultimate truth is that there is no absolute truth. What is true for one is not necessarily true for others. Tolerance and diversity dominate in a society where pride reigns supreme.

Nothing could be further from reality. In fact, the entire human race may be precisely divided into two absolute categories, which the Lord Jesus Christ enumerated in verse 23 when He declared, "He who is not with Me is against Me; and he who does not gather with Me, scatters" (cf. 9:50). There are only two groups of people: those who are with Christ and those who are against Him; those who are God's, and those who are Satan's; those who are in the kingdom of light, and those who are in the kingdom of darkness; those who are righteous and those who are unrighteous; the "saints" and the "ain'ts". Everyone lives and dies in one of those two groups, which have distinct and opposite eternal consequences.

In the war between God and Satan, between heaven and hell, between good and evil, and between truth and error, no one is neutral. Those who do not believe in Jesus Christ, receive Him, follow Him with all their heart, and seek to advance His kingdom are as much in partnership with the devil as those who openly worship Satan. It is not necessary to overtly oppose Christ by attacking His deity, word, character, gospel, or church to be against Him; it is enough merely not to make a decision regarding Him. Ignoring Jesus, or espousing what C. S. Lewis described in his book *Mere Christianity* as "patronizing nonsense" about Him being merely a great moral teacher, but not God incarnate, is a decision against His person, work, word, and kingdom. There is no third option. Either Jesus was a blasphemer, or those who reject Him are.

In his narrative of Christ's life and ministry, Luke has presented convincing, irrefutable evidence that Jesus is the Messiah and Son of God, describing His power over the kingdom of darkness, disease, sin, and death, and recording His preaching of the kingdom of God. In the final months leading up to the cross, Jesus, the twelve, the seventy, and others of His faithful disciples, were proclaiming His kingdom throughout Judea. The Lord's words in verse 23 mark a definitive moment in His

Judean ministry. The facts about Him were clear; the evidence was in and called for a decision.

By this time, however, that decision had largely been made, and was for the leaders and the nation a decision to reject Jesus. As the opposition to Him intensified, Jesus became more confrontational, addressing strong words of judgment and warning to those who had rejected Him (e.g., 11:29, 42–52; 12:1, 13–15, 49, 58–59; 13:5–9, 15, 24–25, 34–35). The tragic reality was that many people had believed the leaders' conclusion that Jesus was from hell, not heaven, and sent by Satan, not God. The incident reported in this passage was but one of many examples of that blasphemous lie gaining popularity. Luke records the crowd's accusation, and the Lord's response.

THE ACCUSATION

And He was casting out a demon, and it was mute; when the demon had gone out, the mute man spoke; and the crowds were amazed. But some of them said, "He casts out demons by Beelzebul, the ruler of the demons." Others, to test Him, were demanding of Him a sign from heaven. (11:14–16)

Though it might appear that this incident is the same one recorded in Matthew 12:22–30 and Mark 3:20–30, that one occurred in Galilee about a year earlier. It is better to view Luke's account as an event that took place during the Lord's Judean ministry (which Luke has beginning in 9:51). Further, Matthew notes that the demon-possessed man was also blind (12:22)—a detail that Luke the physician (Col. 4:14), with his attention to medical details, would not likely have omitted. The similarity in the two accounts reflects the widespread propagation of the Jewish leaders' blasphemous claim that Jesus performed miracles by Satan's power (cf. Matt. 12:24; Mark 3:22; John 7:20; 8:48; 10:20).

What triggered the confrontation between Jesus and His opponents in the crowd was His **casting out a demon.** This was a common occurrence during the Lord's earthly ministry (cf. Luke 4:33–35, 41; 8:27–37; 9:37–42; 13:32), as well as the ministries of the twelve apostles (9:1) and the seventy evangelists (10:17). This particular demon had made its victim **mute,** and likely deaf as well (cf. Mark 9:25). After **the demon had gone out** at the Lord's command, **the mute man spoke; and the crowds,** as was frequently the case (cf. Matt. 9:33; 12:22–23; Mark 1:27; 5:20), **were amazed.**

But some of them, propagandists spreading the lies of the Jewish leaders in Jerusalem, were quick to offer their slanderous, false explanation of the Lord's miraculous power. They began muttering, **"He casts out demons by Beelzebul, the ruler of the demons."** The same lie that had been spread in Galilee was now heard in Judea as well. Since it was impossible even for His enemies to deny that Christ's miracles occurred (cf. John 11:47), they sought instead to attack the source and assign them to demonic power. Not content merely to claim that Jesus received His power from an ordinary demon (cf. John 7:20; 8:48, 52; 10:20), they charged Him with being empowered **by Beelzebul,** a Jewish name for **the ruler of the demons,** Satan. That name, which means "lord of the flies," is a disdainful corruption of Baal-Zebul ("prince Baal," or "exalted lord"), the chief god of the Philistine city of Ekron (2 Kings 1:2–3, 6, 16). It was the worst name they could think of with which to associate Jesus.

Their use of that derogatory name couched their blasphemy in the vilest possible manner. They called the highest and most holy one the lowest and most evil; they called the one who was pure good pure evil; they called God the devil; perfect holiness wickedness; truth incarnate a liar, and branded the Son of God a servant of Satan. Their accusation was ridiculous, but it was also ominous, since in the earlier incident recorded by Matthew, Jesus solemnly warned that those who made it were guilty of blaspheming the Holy Spirit (Matt. 12:31–32). Because those who committed it rejected God's full revelation about Jesus Christ, that sin was unpardonable and left them unredeemable (cf. Heb. 6:4–6).

Despite the heinousness of the sin involved, there is a sense of pathos in this scene. For centuries the Jewish people had waited eagerly for God's covenant promise to be fulfilled in the coming of the Messiah. Jewish women hoped to be the mother of the Messiah; Jewish fathers longed for their children to experience Messiah's kingdom. The Lord Jesus Christ had by this time given a full manifestation of Himself, leaving no room for doubt that He was Israel's long-awaited Messiah. But after all the evidence was in, the people followed their leaders' conclusion that Jesus was a false messiah from hell. Soon they would scream for His blood before a Roman governor in the ultimate manifestation of hatred and rejection (John 19:1–16).

Caught up in the mocking and disdain **others, to test Him, were demanding of Him a sign from heaven.** These were not honest truth seekers, gathering information by which to make a decision, but blaspheming rejecters. They taunted Jesus, derisively demanding that He falsify their absurd charge that He was in league with the devil by performing a spectacular miracle. Because the mighty works He had already done were conclusive proof that He was the Messiah and Son of God (John 10:25), Jesus refused their request. As He said to them in Luke 11:29, "This generation is a wicked generation; it seeks for a sign, and yet no sign will be given to it but the sign of Jonah."

THE RESPONSE

But He knew their thoughts and said to them, "Any kingdom divided against itself is laid waste; and a house divided against itself falls. If Satan also is divided against himself, how will his kingdom stand? For you say that I cast out demons by Beelzebul. And if I by Beelzebul cast out demons, by whom do your sons cast them out? So they will be your judges. But if I cast out demons by the finger of God, then the kingdom of God has come upon you. When a strong man, fully armed, guards his own house, his possessions are undisturbed. But when someone stronger than he attacks him and overpowers him, he takes away from him all his armor on which he had relied and distributes his plunder. He who is not with Me is against Me; and he who does not gather with Me, scatters. (11:17–23)

The Lord graciously and calmly responded to His opponents' attack on Him by pointing out that their conclusion lacked rationality, integrity, and spirituality.

BLASPHEMY AGAINST JESUS CHRIST LACKS RATIONALITY

But He knew their thoughts and said to them, "Any kingdom divided against itself is laid waste; and a house divided against itself falls. If Satan also is divided against himself, how will his kingdom stand? For you say that I cast out demons by Beelzebul. (11:17–18)

Their whisperings may have been hidden from the Lord's ears, but not from His omniscience, since **He knew their thoughts** (cf. Luke 5:22; 6:8; 7:39–47; John 2:25). Their thought processes, purposes, and intents were transparent to Jesus, and He knew that those thoughts were sinful, blasphemous, and damning. He had every right at this point to abandon them to their unbelief and its inevitable eternal doom. Yet He reached out to them again in mercy, exposing the irrationality of their damning false conclusion.

The Lord's point, which He made using two illustrations, was simple and obvious. It is an axiomatic truth that **any kingdom divided against itself is laid waste.** No one would dispute the reality that a kingdom engaged in a civil war would self-destruct. That **a house divided against itself falls** is equally indisputable. In light of those self-evident realities Christ's question, **If Satan also is divided against himself, how will his kingdom stand?** exposes the absurdity of their accusation.

Inconsistencies often appear in the strategies of the kingdom of darkness, since evil is inherently inconsistent, demons operate independently, and Satan is not omniscient, omnipresent, or omnipotent. He may also allow his servants to pretend to cast out demons as part of their cover as angels of light (cf. 2 Cor. 11:14–15). But Satan's goal is to destroy God's kingdom, not his own, and his kingdom is unified in that evil intent. Therefore to argue that he would empower Jesus to cast out demons on an unprecedented scale and thereby destroy his own kingdom is ridiculous. Yet that is precisely what the Lord's opponents were doing by claiming that He **cast out demons by Beelzebul.** Since that option is irrational and untenable, the only alternative is that Jesus cast out demons by God's power.

BLASPHEMY AGAINST JESUS CHRIST LACKS INTEGRITY

And if I by Beelzebul cast out demons, by whom do your sons cast them out? So they will be your judges. (11:19)

For the sake of argument, Jesus granted their point. Assuming that He was, as they claimed, using the power of **Beelzebul** (Satan) to **cast out demons,** the Lord then asked, **By whom do your sons** (i.e., rabbis, scribes, Pharisees, and their associates) **cast them out?** The Jews uncritically assumed that their useless exorcists were doing the work of God. Acts 19 records a typical failed attempt by some would-be Jewish exorcists to cast out a demon at Ephesus. Impressed by the miraculous power displayed by the apostle Paul (vv. 11–12), they decided to add the name of Jesus to their repertoire. But the consequences were disastrous:

> Some of the Jewish exorcists, who went from place to place, attempted to name over those who had the evil spirits the name of the Lord Jesus, saying, "I adjure you by Jesus whom Paul preaches." Seven sons of one Sceva, a Jewish chief priest, were doing this. And the evil spirit answered and said to them, "I recognize Jesus, and I know about Paul, but who are you?" And the man, in whom was the evil spirit, leaped on them and subdued all of them and overpowered them, so that they fled out of that house naked and wounded. (vv. 13–16)

The Lord's question exposed their inconsistency, hypocrisy, and lack of integrity. If casting out demons proved someone was in league with Satan, then why were they not suspicious of their own exorcists? How could they not apply the same standards to their failures as they did to Jesus' successes? By insisting that their own exorcists' ineffective attempts to cast out demons were from God, while rejecting Jesus' uniformly effective exorcisms as being from Satan, they were in effect making Satan more powerful than God.

BLASPHEMY AGAINST JESUS CHRIST LACKS SPIRITUALITY

But if I cast out demons by the finger of God, then the kingdom of God has come upon you. When a strong man, fully armed, guards his own house, his possessions are undisturbed. But when someone

stronger than he attacks him and overpowers him, he takes away from him all his armor on which he had relied and distributes his plunder. He who is not with Me is against Me; and he who does not gather with Me, scatters. (11:20–23)

Jesus' opponents' irrationality and lack of integrity invalidated their false conclusion regarding Him and showed that He cast out demons by the power of God, not Satan. The Lord then drew the inescapable conclusion from that reality. **If I cast out demons by the finger of God,** He declared, **then the kingdom of God has come upon you.** They were face-to-face with the **kingdom of God** because they were in the presence of the king. But instead of accepting and worshiping Jesus, they committed the severest form of blasphemy possible by calling Him an agent of Satan. By so doing, they revealed themselves to be spiritually dead. They considered themselves to be the enlightened religious elite. Yet they were so lost, sinful, self-righteous, and hard-hearted that they failed to discern that **the kingdom of God** had **come upon** them. In reality they, not Jesus, were agents of Satan (John 8:44; 2 Cor. 4:4).

Jesus' use of the phrase **finger of God** to describe the divine power by which He cast out demons brought the whole drama into historical focus. In a dramatic scene leading up to Israel's exodus from Egypt, God through Moses confronted Pharaoh's false magicians. Using their trickery, they were able to replicate several of the miracles. But when Moses struck the dust with his staff and produced swarms of gnats, they were unable to duplicate it, and were forced to acknowledge, "This is the finger of God" (Ex. 8:19; cf. 31:18; Deut. 9:10; Dan. 5:5). But while those pagan magicians acknowledged God's power when they saw it, the ultra-religious Jewish leaders rejected God's power exhibited by the Lord Jesus Christ. Nothing could more clearly demonstrate their condition of spiritual death.

The Lord then gave a simple analogy to reinforce the truth that He was empowered by God, not Satan. In this analogy Satan is pictured as a **strong man** who, **fully armed, guards his own house** and keeps **his possessions** (the souls in his kingdom) **undisturbed.** But Jesus is the one who is stronger **than he** and **attacks him and overpowers him, takes away from him all his armor on which he had relied,**

and distributes his plunder. Satan and his demon hosts are powerless to keep the Lord Jesus Christ from rescuing souls from the kingdom of darkness. He had clearly demonstrated that power by healing the sickness and disease that resulted from Satan's leading the human race into sin, conquering death, thereby rendering "powerless him who had the power of death, that is, the devil" (Heb. 2:14), casting out demons, and forgiving sin—something Satan has neither the power nor the inclination to do—thereby transferring lost sinners from Satan's kingdom to God's (Col. 1:13–14). No one but God could so thoroughly "destroy the works of the devil" (1 John 3:8).

Jesus then concluded with a powerful final appeal and warning: **He who is not with Me is against Me; and he who does not gather with Me, scatters.** As noted earlier in this chapter, everyone falls into one of those two categories: they are either with Christ, or against Him. No one is neutral; no one is a disinterested bystander. In light of their irrationality and hypocrisy, Jesus challenged His opponents to rethink their conclusion regarding Him.

That same challenge faces every person. The complete record of the evidence in the inspired Gospels that Jesus is the Son of God and Messiah is more conclusive even than the experience of those who were there during Christ's life. He is either God incarnate or the greatest blasphemer who ever lived. He either speaks for God or for Satan. To reject the irrefutable evidence concerning Him; to follow instead a satanic false teacher, guru, mystic, or false prophet, is to side with those who openly blaspheme Him, and be worthy of eternal damnation in hell.

But there is hope for those who are with Him and not against Him; who embrace Jesus as Lord and Savior. He offers salvation as a free gift to those who cultivate their hearts to receive it through a proper fear of judgment and hell, humility, brokenness and contrition, and repentance. To such people the Lord addresses the wonderful promise, "Come to Me, all who are weary and heavy-laden, and I will give you rest. Take My yoke upon you and learn from Me, for I am gentle and humble in heart, and you will find rest for your souls. For My yoke is easy and My burden is light" (Matt. 11:28–30).

The Danger of Moral Reformation (Luke 11:24–28)

7

When the unclean spirit goes out of a man, it passes through waterless places seeking rest, and not finding any, it says, 'I will return to my house from which I came.' And when it comes, it finds it swept and put in order. Then it goes and takes along seven other spirits more evil than itself, and they go in and live there; and the last state of that man becomes worse than the first." While Jesus was saying these things, one of the women in the crowd raised her voice and said to Him, "Blessed is the womb that bore You and the breasts at which You nursed." But He said, "On the contrary, blessed are those who hear the word of God and observe it." (11:24–28)

In recent decades there has been increasing distress among Christians about the rampant moral corruption in society. Concern for the influence of this tolerance and advocacy of sin on present and subsequent generations, has led to efforts by the church to effect moral change through political activism, media exposure, and social pressure groups. Many evangelicals view promoting Judeo-Christian values, teaching morality to schoolchildren, and politicking the nation back to moral living as a priority for believers. Since such societal morality is also on the agenda of apostate Protestantism, Roman Catholicism, Judaism, Islam, Mormonism, and even some atheists, the church becomes trapped in compromising and ungodly alliances that undermine the clarity of the gospel.

True Christians rightly decried the abandonment of the saving gospel for the social gospel by the liberal mainline denominations in the previous century. Yet the emphasis among current professing believers on restoring public morality amounts to nothing more than a form of neo-liberalism. Once again the saving gospel of the Lord Jesus Christ is being set aside in favor of a different, non-saving message. Albert Mohler defines moralism as "the belief that the Gospel can be reduced to improvements in behavior" ("Why Moralism Is Not the Gospel—And Why So Many Christians Think It Is" [http://www.albertmohler.com/2009/09/03/why-moralism-is-not-the-gospel-and-why-so-many-christians-think-it-is/; accessed 26 Apr 2011]). It is a false gospel and hence under the condemnation of God (Gal. 1:8–9). Dr. Mohler goes on to note that

> Moralism . . . promises the favor of God and the satisfaction of God's righteousness to sinners if they will only behave and commit themselves to moral improvement . . . we sin against Christ and we misrepresent the Gospel when we suggest to sinners that what God demands of them is moral improvement in accordance with the Law. (ibid.)

He then concludes by noting the sharp contrast between the saving gospel and moralism: "Moralism produces sinners who are (potentially) better behaved. The Gospel of Christ transforms sinners into the adopted sons and daughters of God" (ibid.).

For the church of Jesus Christ to promote moralism is to obscure its true calling. As I wrote in my book *Why Government Can't Save You,*

> God simply is not calling us to wage a culture war that would seek to transform our countries into "Christian nations." To devote all, or even most, of our time, energy, money, and strategy to putting a façade of morality on the world or the appearance of "rightness" over our governmental and political institutions is to badly misunderstand our roles as Christians in a spiritually lost world. (Nashville: Word Publishing, 2000, 13)

The church's mandate is clear. It has been entrusted with the saving message of reconciliation, and commanded to proclaim the truth that sinners can be restored to union with God through Christ:

> Now all these things are from God, who reconciled us to Himself through Christ and gave us the ministry of reconciliation, namely, that God was in Christ reconciling the world to Himself, not counting their trespasses against them, and He has committed to us the word of reconciliation. Therefore, we are ambassadors for Christ, as though God were making an appeal through us; we beg you on behalf of Christ, be reconciled to God. (2 Cor. 5:18–20)

Moralism was never the message of the Lord Jesus Christ, the Old Testament prophets, or the New Testament apostles. On the contrary, Jesus reserved His most scathing denunciations for the outwardly moral scribes and Pharisees, characterizing them as hypocrites, destined for eternal punishment in hell (Matt. 23; Luke 11:37–54). He pronounced judgment and damnation on the most outwardly moral society in the world (Matt. 23:33; Luke 20:45–21:6). Jesus further declared that He had come to call sinners, not the self-righteous, to repentance (Luke 5:32). The prophets likened the righteousness produced by moralism to "a filthy garment" (Isa. 64:6) and challenged people not to change their outward behavior but to be transformed on the inside (Joel 2:12–13) and repent of their sins (Jer. 36:3; Ezek. 18:30–32). The apostle Paul cautioned that "by the works of the Law no flesh will be justified in His sight" (Rom. 3:20) and reminded those who would pursue moralism that "if righteousness comes through the Law, then Christ died needlessly" (Gal. 2:21; cf. 3:21–22).

Improving a nation's morality, like bodily discipline, does have the limited temporal value of making life safer and more peaceful. But making a society more moral will not and cannot bring God's blessing, which comes only from true godliness (1 Tim. 4:8). A more outwardly moral society will not escape the same divine judgment that falls on perverted killers, any more than Pharisaic Judaism in Jesus' time escaped the devastating judgment of God in A.D. 70 and the eternal hell that followed. There is only one reality that God blesses—penitent saving faith in and love for His Son, the Lord Jesus Christ. That is not to say, of course, that Christians should not at all times hate evil and in all places oppose wickedness in every form. The issue is whether we are to carry out that effort by pursuing societal moralism through human effort, or by preaching personal salvation through the power of God.

The church's ill-conceived efforts to promote cultural morality are fraught with numerous dangers, some of which may be briefly summarized.

First, as already noted, the pursuit of cultural morality is outside the church's divine commission, which is to "Go therefore and make disciples of all the nations, baptizing them in the name of the Father and the Son and the Holy Spirit" (Matt. 28:19). By focusing its efforts on moralism, the church depletes its resources and diminishes its power.

Second, by doing so it wastes immense amounts of time, money, and resources trying to make people become what they cannot be apart from salvation (cf. Jer. 13:23). That violates the principle Paul laid down in Ephesians 5:16 when he commanded his readers to be continually "making the most of [their] time, because the days are evil."

Third, the pursuit of cultural morality is doomed to inevitable failure. No one can be truly righteous and moral before God apart from the transforming work of the Holy Spirit through the gospel (cf. Rom. 3:10–12). Since "the heart is deceitful above all things, and desperately wicked" (Jer. 17:9 NKJV), failing to change it will merely redirect sin. If some sins become illegal, people will pursue other sins, or do the ones they want to do secretly.

Fourth, the pursuit of cultural morality misunderstands the nature of the kingdom of God, which Jesus said in John 18:36 "is not of this world." There is no connection between a national entity and the kingdom of God, and nothing that fallen men can do to alter societies' behavior has any impact on God's purposes in redemption.

Fifth, the pursuit of cultural morality attempts to bring about moral change apart from the gospel. But that is impossible, because those who are accustomed to doing evil cannot do good (Jer. 13:23).

Sixth, the pursuit of cultural morality divorces morality from theology. Many involved in that pursuit demonstrate an ignorance of essential theological truths about God, His Word, and His holy law. Their efforts to bring about morality thus lack the highest motive, which is to honor and glorify God from a transformed heart (1 Cor. 10:31).

Seventh, the pursuit of cultural morality fails to understand correctly the references to salt and light in Matthew 5:13–14. The Lord's imagery does not refer to moral influence, but rather to gospel influence by word spoken and the power of holy living. Believers are light when they proclaim the truth of the gospel both with their words and their lives. They are salt in the sense that their virtuous and godly lives are a preservative against evil.

Eighth, the pursuit of cultural morality has no New Testament model to pattern itself after except that of the Pharisees. But as noted above, Jesus reserved His strongest rebuke for them because their outward morality merely masked their dominating inward corruption (cf. Matt. 23:25; Luke 11:39).

Ninth, the pursuit of cultural morality creates unholy unions with unbelievers and enemies of the gospel, which the Bible forbids (2 Cor. 6:14). Further, it leads to inclusivism, stretching the boundaries of the kingdom of God to embrace people who are not in Christ.

Tenth, those pursuing cultural morality are selective as to the sins they oppose. They attack sins such as homosexuality, pedophilia, abortion, and pornography, while largely ignoring other sins such as divorce, adultery, materialism, and pride. Most important, the emphasis on morality ignores the severest sin of all—failing to obey "the great and foremost commandment" (Matt. 22:38), which is, "You shall love the Lord your God with all your heart, and with all your soul, and with all your mind" (v. 37). Love the Lord Christ, Paul said, or be damned (1 Cor. 16:22).

Eleventh, the pursuit of cultural morality fails to understand the true nature of spiritual warfare. To attempt to change laws through political action is not spiritual warfare, which Paul defined as "destroying speculations and every lofty thing raised up against the knowledge of God, and . . . taking every thought captive to the obedience of Christ" (2 Cor. 10:5) by smashing the fortresses of human ideologies with the truth of God (v. 4). Those who think wrongly about God, Christ, and themselves must be confronted with the truth of the gospel, which alone is "the power of God for salvation to everyone who believes" (Rom. 1:16). True spiritual warfare is not political or social activism. It is a battle for the minds and eternal souls of lost sinners, seeking to see them turn from error to gospel truth.

Twelfth, pursuing cultural morality cultivates hostility toward those whom the church is commanded to reach with the gospel of love. They become enemies instead of the mission field. Unbelievers are not the enemy, but captives of the ultimate enemy, Satan (2 Tim. 2:26).

Thirteenth, pursuing cultural morality brings persecution and hatred of Christians for the wrong reasons. People calling themselves Christians are vilified by the world not for the name of Christ (cf. 1 Peter 4:14), but for their political views and disdain toward wicked unbelievers.

Fourteenth, the pursuit of cultural morality reverses the divine order by making morality the power for salvation. But morality does not produce salvation; salvation produces genuine morality.

Finally, the pursuit of cultural morality fails to understand the wrath of God, which Romans 1:18–32 discloses "is revealed from heaven against all ungodliness and unrighteousness of men who suppress the truth in unrighteousness" (v. 18). As a result God judged them by giving them over to sexual immorality (v. 24), including homosexuality (vv. 26–27), and to a twisted, reprobate, useless mind (v. 28). The rampant sin evident in the world is evidence of the wrath of God, which cannot be overturned by political or social activism. When this judgment from heaven comes, no one can stop it or change it.

Moralism, however, is not merely a disaster for the church, but also results in eternal tragedy for individuals:

> By trying to establish Christian values through earthly methods, we risk creating a false sense of morality. Forcing people to adopt our biblical standards of morality only brings superficial change and hides the real issue—sin and their need for rebirth in Jesus Christ. When people of this world face God's judgment, their "traditional Christian values" won't matter at all—only how they responded to Jesus Christ. That's why pursuing outward change at the expense of inward transformation is both a nearsighted and deadly choice. (*Why Government Can't Save You*, ix)

In this passage the Lord Jesus Christ told a parable (virtually identical to one He had told several months earlier in Galilee [Matt. 12:43–45]) that vividly illustrates the grave danger of moral reformation without regeneration. Jesus had closed His defense against the false, blasphemous accusations of the Jewish religious leaders in the previous section by warning, "He who is not with Me is against Me; and he who does not gather with Me, scatters" (11:23). In this next section He addressed the question of what it means to be with Him by contrasting reformation with transformation.

REFORMATION

When the unclean spirit goes out of a man, it passes through waterless places seeking rest, and not finding any, it says, 'I will return to my house from which I came.' And when it comes, it finds it swept and put in order. Then it goes and takes along seven other spirits more evil than itself, and they go in and live there; and the last state of that man becomes worse than the first." (11:24–26)

On the surface, this was a very religious **man,** one who had out-wardly cleaned up his life. His former wretched conduct had made him a comfortable haven for an **unclean spirit** (a common New Testament term for demons stressing their evil, impure natures; cf. Matt. 10:1; 12:43; Mark 1:23, 26, 27; 3:11, 30; 5:2, 8, 13; 7:25; 9:25; Luke 4:36; 6:18; Acts 5:16; 8:7). It may be that the demon went **out of** this **man** because his re-formed moral behavior made him no longer a suitable host for the demon's purposes. It may also have departed temporarily to validate the phony exorcisms of the Jewish exorcists (cf. 11:19).

Having left the man, the demon passed **through waterless places seeking rest.** Since they are spirit beings, demons do not wander in deserts in need of water; the Lord's language metaphorically depicts the demon existing aimlessly in the spirit realm. Demons do their diaboli-cal work in this world through people, and not to have a person to work through is the equivalent for a demon of being in a barren situation.

After wandering for a time but **not finding any** other person to indwell, the demon decided, **'I will return to my house from which I came.'** The description of the man as the demon's **house** indicates that this demon lived in him, not merely that the man was under its influ-ence. The man's legalistic effort at self-reformation, however, was no last-ing protection. When the demon returned, it found the man's heart **swept, put in order,** and unoccupied (cf. Matt. 12:44). Therein lies the fatal weakness of moralistic, legalistic efforts at self-reformation. The problem with the moral person's heart is that while it may be superficially cleaned up and put in order, it is a void. It is devoid of the true spiritual power of righteousness that comes only to the redeemed through the regenerating work of the Holy Spirit.

Mere external, superficial efforts at self-reformation only leave people in a more dangerous position, since those efforts foster the damning delusion that they are on a secure footing, protected from calamity and pleasing to God. That perspective was evident in this man's life. The spiritual vacuum in his heart created by his moralistic effort to clean up his life left him vulnerable to even more severe demonic oppression than before. Not only did the original demon return, but it also brought with it **seven other spirits more evil than itself.** They, too, were able to enter the man's empty heart **and live there** (*katoikeō*, which suggests a permanent indwelling). The end result of his moralism was that **the last state of that man** became **worse than the first.** He was like those of whom Peter wrote, "If, after they have escaped the defilements of the world by the knowledge of the Lord and Savior Jesus Christ, they are again entangled in them and are overcome, the last state has become worse for them than the first" (2 Peter 2:20). He was even more infested with the agents of hell after his attempt to reform himself morally than before that effort. Morality and religion are seductive and deadly. Although they lack any power to change the heart, they produce the soul-numbing deception that all is well with God. But those who believe in their own righteousness are not redeemable, are havens for demons, and receive no lasting benefit from their pursuit of reformation apart from regeneration.

TRANSFORMATION

While Jesus was saying these things, one of the women in the crowd raised her voice and said to Him, "Blessed is the womb that bore You and the breasts at which You nursed." But He said, "On the contrary, blessed are those who hear the word of God and observe it." (11:27–28)

This brief incident illustrates the true spiritual transformation that marks those who are with Christ (11:23). As the Lord **was saying these things, one of the women in the crowd raised her voice and said to Him, "Blessed is the womb that bore You and the breasts at which You nursed."** That proverbial saying was the ultimate commendation, "since a mother was valued in the accomplishments of her son" (Darrell L. Bock, *Luke 9:51–24:53*, Baker Exegetical Commentary on the New Testament [Grand Rapids: Baker, 1996], 1094). It suggests that she was open to believing that Jesus was the Messiah.

Her statement was correct, but not complete. The Lord's polite response challenged her to go beyond merely commending Him. **"On the contrary,** He told her, **"blessed are those who hear the word of God and observe it."** This statement is reminiscent of the one Jesus made in Luke 8:21: "My mother and My brothers are these who hear the word of God and do it." It is not enough merely to attempt to be moral. One must be regenerated so as to be a true follower of Christ who is first and foremost obedient to divine revelation; to be a doer, not merely a hearer, of the word of God (James 1:22); to not only hear Christ's words, but act on them (Matt. 7:24); to demonstrate one's love for Jesus by obeying Him (John 14:15, 21, 23; 15:10). First John 3:23–24 expresses the essence of what it means to be a true follower of the Lord Jesus Christ: "This is His commandment, that we believe in the name of His Son Jesus Christ, and love one another, just as He commanded us. The one who keeps His commandments abides in Him, and He in him."

The pursuit of moralism is doomed to failure, since "those who are in the flesh cannot please God" (Rom. 8:8; cf. Gal. 5:17). It is only through the transforming power of regeneration that sinners can become new creatures (2 Cor. 5:17) and be characterized by loving obedience that pleases God (2 Cor. 5:9; Eph. 5:10; Col. 1:10; 1 John 3:22). For the church to ignore that reality is to hide the light of gospel truth God has called it to shine forth in this sin-darkened world (Matt. 5:14; Phil. 2:15) and abandon its mission to turn sinners from the darkness of sin to the light of salvation (Acts 26:18).

Judgment on a Wicked Generation
(Luke 11:29–36)

8

As the crowds were increasing, He began to say, "This generation is a wicked generation; it seeks for a sign, and yet no sign will be given to it but the sign of Jonah. For just as Jonah became a sign to the Ninevites, so will the Son of Man be to this generation. The Queen of the South will rise up with the men of this generation at the judgment and condemn them, because she came from the ends of the earth to hear the wisdom of Solomon; and behold, something greater than Solomon is here. The men of Nineveh will stand up with this generation at the judgment and condemn it, because they repented at the preaching of Jonah; and behold, something greater than Jonah is here. No one, after lighting a lamp, puts it away in a cellar nor under a basket, but on the lamp-stand, so that those who enter may see the light. The eye is the lamp of your body; when your eye is clear, your whole body also is full of light; but when it is bad, your body also is full of darkness. Then watch out that the light in you is not darkness. If therefore your whole body is full of light, with no dark part in it, it will

be wholly illumined, as when the lamp illumines you with its rays." (11:29–36)

Throughout His ministry the Lord Jesus Christ faced hostility and opposition, primarily from the Jewish religious sect leaders; the scribes, Pharisees, and Sadducees. The Sadducees especially were outraged when, at the outset of His public ministry, Jesus attacked the temple by halting and dismantling their corrupt business operation (John 2:13–22). He would do the same thing again at the close of His life (Luke 19:45–48), so that the two attacks bracket His public ministry. But there were far more private and positive acts by Jesus for which they hated Him. For example, when the Lord forgave the sins of a paralyzed man, they accused Him of blasphemy (Luke 5:21). When He mingled with the dregs of Jewish society at a banquet, they were shocked (Luke 5:29–32). After Jesus healed a sick man on the Sabbath, they sought to kill Him (John 5:18). When He defended His disciples' breaking of their man-made Sabbath regulations by declaring Himself to be Lord of the Sabbath, they were furious (Luke 6:5). Yet another violation of their Sabbath restrictions, Christ's healing of a man with a crippled hand, further incensed them (Luke 6:6–11). The scribes and Pharisees also confronted Jesus when His disciples violated the frivolous rabbinic traditions by failing to observe the ritual washings before eating a meal (Matt. 15:1–2; cf. Luke 11:37–38). The Lord's powerful teaching in the temple, exposing their apostate theology, prompted the desperate authorities to try unsuccessfully to arrest Him (John 7:28–49), and then to accuse Him of lying about Himself (John 8:13). They contemptuously called Him a demon-possessed Samaritan (John 8:48, 52), and then attempted to stone Him when He asserted His deity (John 8:58–59; cf. 10:30–33). The Jewish leaders hated Jesus most of all because He exposed their true condition, revealing them to be hypocrites, displeasing to God, damaging to the people who followed them, and headed for eternal judgment.

Their hostility toward Jesus reached its apex early in His ministry when they decided to murder Him. That commitment ascended in fervor after He raised Lazarus from the dead, as demonstrated when

> The chief priests and the Pharisees convened a council, and were saying, "What are we doing? For this man is performing many signs. If we let Him go on like this, all men will believe in Him, and the Romans will come and take away both our place and our nation. But one of them, Caiaphas, who was high priest that year, said to them, "You know nothing at all, nor do you take into account that it is expedient for you that one man die for the people, and that the whole nation not perish." Now he did not say this on his own initiative, but being high priest that year, he prophesied that Jesus was going to die for the nation, and not for the nation only, but in order that He might also gather together into one the children of God who are scattered abroad. So from that day on they planned together to kill Him. (John 11:47–53)

The apostate religious leaders had long been mounting their case. In Galilee they had accused Him of doing His miracles through the power of Satan (Matt. 12:24). Several months later in Judea they repeated that false and blasphemous claim (see the exposition of 11:14–16 in chapter 6 of this volume). In response, Jesus' words to the leaders became largely judgmental toward them and all who followed their lead (see for example vv. 29, 42–52; 12:1, 13–15, 49, 58–59; 13:1–9, 15, 24–25, 34–35), though interspersed with offers of grace, mercy, and salvation to repentant sinners.

This passage is a fitting conclusion to Jesus' conversation with the scribes and Pharisees that began in verse 15. Implicit in their demand that He perform a sign (v. 16) was the allegation that Jesus had not given them enough evidence. Perversely, they placed the blame for their sin-induced spiritual darkness on Him, arguing that He had not given them enough light to see the truth. Supposedly, the sign they demanded would give them the proof they needed that Jesus was from God instead of Satan.

But the issue was not lack of light but lack of sight. The light was everywhere. It shone brilliantly in the unmatched miracles Jesus performed (John 15:24; cf. 5:36; 10:25, 38; 14:11) and the unparalleled teaching He gave (cf. Matt. 7:28; John 7:46). Nothing more profoundly reveals the wickedness of those who rejected Him than the reality that the light was everywhere, yet they refused to see it.

In this passage the Lord pronounced judgment on the willfully blind who rejected the Light of the world (John 8:12; 9:5). These verses reveal the reality of judgment, and the reason for judgment.

THE REALITY OF JUDGMENT

As the crowds were increasing, He began to say, "This generation is a wicked generation; it seeks for a sign, and yet no sign will be given to it but the sign of Jonah. For just as Jonah became a sign to the Ninevites, so will the Son of Man be to this generation. The Queen of the South will rise up with the men of this generation at the judgment and condemn them, because she came from the ends of the earth to hear the wisdom of Solomon; and behold, something greater than Solomon is here. The men of Nineveh will stand up with this generation at the judgment and condemn it, because they repented at the preaching of Jonah; and behold, something greater than Jonah is here. (11:29–32)

The Lord brought home the reality of judgment by making a final statement, giving a final sign, and declaring a final sentence.

THE FINAL STATEMENT

As the crowds were increasing, He began to say, "This generation is a wicked generation; it seeks for a sign, (11:29*a*)

Luke notes that Jesus made this statement **as the crowds were increasing** (cf. 12:1). The phrase **He began to say** indicates that this was something that He repeatedly said (cf. Matt. 12:34, 39; 16:4; Mark 8:38). The more people that collected around Him the more apparent it became that that **generation** was a **wicked** one. The use of *genea* (**generation**) indicates that Jesus was referring to the majority of people in Israel at that time; what was true of the Galileans (cf. 9:41) was also true of the Judeans.

That Jesus characterized the people of Israel as wicked is shocking. After all, He was not speaking of idol-worshiping pagans, or godless lawbreakers. The generation He referred to was, by normal human standards, extremely moral, religious, and God-conscious. The Jewish people were fanatically devoted to keeping the law of God and observing their religious traditions, as Paul's life before his conversion illustrates (cf. Acts

22:3; Gal. 1:14). But though they outwardly appeared to be righteous, inwardly they were filled with wickedness (11:39; Matt. 23:25–28). In that state, they were in more danger than those who were openly immoral. Devoutly religious people, confident that their self-righteousness has earned them favor with God, are self-satisfied. The gospel message that people are wretched sinners (Eph. 2:1), in whom is nothing good (Rom. 3:10–18; 7:18), who are utterly unable to please God (Rom. 8:8), and are spiritually poor, blind, oppressed captives of sin (Luke 4:18) shocks and outrages them, and they vehemently reject it (vv. 28–30). The gospel also teaches that salvation comes only to those who humble themselves, acknowledge their spiritual poverty, mourn over their sin, while hungering and thirsting (Matt. 5:3–6) for the divine righteousness that comes only through faith in the Lord Jesus Christ (Rom. 3:22; Gal. 2:16; Phil. 3:9), and those who reject that truth cannot be saved. The sobering reality is that those who rely on their self-righteousness, external morality, legalism, and religious rituals merely make comfortable homes for demons (see the exposition of Luke 11:24–28 in chapter 7 of this volume).

Throughout our Lord's ministry, it was the moral, self-righteous, religious people who resisted and hated Him. When, as noted above, He described the synagogue crowd in His hometown of Nazareth as spiritually impoverished, blind, and oppressed (Luke 4:18), they were so outraged that they tried to kill Him (vv. 28–30). After his call to salvation and apostleship, Levi (Matthew) gave a reception at his house in Jesus' honor (Luke 5:27–29). He invited his friends who, like the tax collector he had been, were the despised outcasts of Jewish society. Appalled that the Lord would associate with such riffraff, "the Pharisees and their scribes began grumbling at His disciples, saying, 'Why do you eat and drink with the tax collectors and sinners?'" (v. 30). Overhearing them, "Jesus answered and said to them, 'It is not those who are well who need a physician, but those who are sick. I have not come to call the righteous but sinners to repentance'" (vv. 31–32). Like all self-righteous people, the religious leaders did not see themselves as sinners and therefore cut themselves off from salvation; there was no point in calling them to repentance, since they did not believe they had anything for which to repent. Both the rich young ruler (Luke 18:18–27) and the prodigal son's older brother (Luke 15:25–30) illustrate the truth that religion, morality, and legalism deceive people into thinking that they are rightly related to God and worthy of His favor. But the truth is that God does not accept superficial self-righteousness, like that of the scribes and Pharisees (Matt. 5:20); only those to whom God imputes righteousness through faith (Gen. 15:6; Rom. 4:5) will enter His kingdom.

Amazingly, the reason Jesus gave for calling that generation wicked was not any of its thoughts and outward vile behaviors that He could have named, but because **it** looked **for a sign.** At first glance there does not seem to be anything wrong with that request, certainly not enough to qualify those making it as wicked and deserving of divine judgment. But as noted above, by demanding a sign they were claiming that Jesus was to blame for their rejection of Him because He supposedly had not given them enough evidence. That, in their minds, justified their conclusion that He was a servant of Satan, not of God.

There have been various suggestions as to what type of sign they were seeking in addition to the countless miracles Jesus had already performed over the course of His ministry. Some speculate that they expected Him to move stars, or rearrange the constellations; others that they wanted Him to move a tree, or reverse the flow of water in a stream, or fly up into the air and spin around. The truth is that they had no particular sign in mind; they were merely taunting Him (cf. 11:16). They were in essence daring the Lord to do something that would change their minds about Him.

The issue was not lack of evidence, but self-righteous moralism. That wicked generation hated Jesus' diagnosis of their sinful hearts, and no amount of evidence would convince them to accept Him if He did not change His diagnosis—not even His resurrection (cf. Matt. 28:11–15). But their knowledge of Jesus' miracles—the reality of which they never denied—rendered them profoundly guilty of rejecting inarguable evidence and hating both Him and God His Father (John 15:24), since no one can love the Father while hating His Son (v. 23). That firsthand knowledge, which other generations were not privileged to see, also marked that Jewish generation as singularly wicked for rejecting Jesus. The greater light they received brought with it greater potential for judgment (cf. 10:13–15; Heb. 10:26–31).

In spite of their protests, the people of Israel would justify Jesus' characterization of them as a wicked generation a few months after this incident. Just days after euphorically, enthusiastically hailing Him as the Messiah at the triumphal entry, they would turn on Jesus and scream for His execution.

THE FINAL SIGN

and yet no sign will be given to it but the sign of Jonah. For just as Jonah became a sign to the Ninevites, so will the Son of Man be to this generation. (11:29b–30)

No sign of the kind that wicked generation was demanding would **be given to it.** The Lord would, however, work a miracle sign that would point unmistakably to Him as God, Messiah, and Savior, which He identified as **the sign of Jonah.** Earlier in Galilee Jesus had described this sign in more detail:

> An evil and adulterous generation craves for a sign; and yet no sign will be given to it but the sign of Jonah the prophet; for just as Jonah was three days and three nights in the belly of the sea monster, so will the Son of Man be three days and three nights in the heart of the earth. (Matt. 12:39–40; cf. 16:4)

The story of Jonah, the reluctant prophet from a small village near Naza-reth (2 Kings 14:25) was well-known to Jesus' hearers. Commanded by God to go to Nineveh and proclaim its impending judgment (Jonah 1:1–2), he instead fled in the opposite direction. Boarding a ship bound for Tarshish (probably a city in what is now Spain), Jonah intended to get as far away from Nineveh as possible rather than bring the message of salvation to the hated Gentiles. But the Lord intervened and stirred up a powerful storm. Acknowledging that his disobedience was the cause of the storm, Jonah urged the sailors to throw him overboard. God provided a large sea creature (perhaps a whale or a whale shark) to swallow Jonah and save him from drowning. Jonah repented, went to Nineveh, and his preaching resulted in a massive revival.

   Jonah became a sign to the Ninevites because of his miracu-lous deliverance from certain death, which convinced them that he spoke for God. His experience is analogous to that of **the Son of Man, who would be** a similar sign **to** His **generation.** Both proclaimed judgment and called for repentance. Jonah was swallowed by a deadly sea creature; Jesus was swallowed into the grave. Jonah was miraculously delivered from certain death; Jesus was actually raised from the dead. Jonah's deliverance from the clutches of death ushered him into a great and powerful ministry, as the Lord's resurrection did for Him.

The final and greatest sign, then, was Christ's resurrection. But even this most powerful and convincing sign, like all the rest the Lord performed, failed to persuade those whose hearts were hardened against Him (John 12:37). The final sign highlighted the wretchedness of sinful unbelief. The leaders of Israel, who knew He was dead and came to life, bribed the soldiers to lie (Matt. 28:11–15).

THE FINAL SENTENCE

The Queen of the South will rise up with the men of this generation at the judgment and condemn them, because she came from the ends of the earth to hear the wisdom of Solomon; and behold, something greater than Solomon is here. The men of Nineveh will stand up with this generation at the judgment and condemn it, because they repented at the preaching of Jonah; and behold, something greater than Jonah is here. (11:31–32)

Two historic Old Testament figures symbolically stand in judgment on the wicked generation that rejected Jesus. The **Queen of the South,** known in the Old Testament as the Queen of Sheba (1 Kings 10:1–13), **will rise up with the men of this generation at the judgment and condemn them** for a number of reasons. She made an arduous journey of several weeks **from the ends of the earth** (Sheba was located in southwest Arabia, more than a thousand miles from Jeru - salem), her purpose being **to hear the wisdom of Solomon,** while the wisdom of Jesus was readily accessible to the people of His generation. She was a pagan idolater, with no knowledge of the true God, while they were steeped in the Old Testament. They were invited to come to Jesus

(Matt. 11:28–30), while there is no indication the she was invited to visit Solomon. Yet she was saved from her sin after believing what Solomon told her about the true God, while they rejected salvation truth from the King infinitely wiser and **greater than Solomon.** That is a damning indictment of that wicked generation.

The men of Nineveh will also **stand up with this generation at the judgment and condemn it.** Like the Queen of Sheba, the Ninevites had far fewer privileges and much less information than the generation that rejected Jesus. The messenger who came to them, Jonah, was a foolish, rebellious prophet, while Jesus, the messenger to Israel, is the sinless Son of God. Jonah went to Nineveh to proclaim the city's doom (Jonah 3:4); Jesus came "to seek and to save that which was lost" (Luke 19:10). Jonah performed no miracles in Nineveh, while Jesus performed countless miracles throughout Israel. Yet the pagan idolaters of Nineveh **repented at the preaching of Jonah** while the ultra-religious people of Israel rejected the one **greater than Jonah.** Their rejection proved that they deserve the sentence to eternal punishment that awaits them at the Great White Throne judgment.

THE REASON FOR JUDGMENT

No one, after lighting a lamp, puts it away in a cellar nor under a basket, but on the lampstand, so that those who enter may see the light. The eye is the lamp of your body; when your eye is clear, your whole body also is full of light; but when it is bad, your body also is full of darkness. Then watch out that the light in you is not darkness. If therefore your whole body is full of light, with no dark part in it, it will be wholly illumined, as when the lamp illumines you with its rays." (11:33–36)

The universal experience of light and darkness in the physical world provides a doorway into understanding the concept of light and darkness in the spiritual world. Here light is a metaphor for understanding divinely revealed truth, since light reveals (Eph. 5:13) but darkness conceals (1 Cor. 4:5). Failing to understand and apply the truth of the

gospel is the reason unrepentant sinners will face judgment. In this illustration Jesus gave three reasons why the generation that rejected Him
faces eternal judgment for rejecting His light: the possibility of sight, the
problem of sight, and the pretense of sight. He then concluded His illustration by pointing out the preciousness of sight.

THE POSSIBILITY OF SIGHT

**No one, after lighting a lamp, puts it away in a cellar nor under a
basket, but on the lampstand, so that those who enter may see the
light.** (11:33)

It would be pointless for someone, **after lighting a lamp,** to put
it away in a cellar or hide it **under a basket.** Since the purpose of light
is to reveal, the logical thing to do after lighting a lamp is to put it **on the
lampstand, so that those who enter** the room **may see the light.** As
noted above, the Lord's opponents had accused Him of not providing
enough proof for them to believe in Him. The point of this illustration is
that it would have been foolish for Him to have withheld evidence. In
reality, they had plenty of light, far more than what had been available to
either the Queen of Sheba, who believed, or the people of Nineveh, who
repented.

God's person provides light. He "is light, and in Him there is no
darkness at all" (1 John 1:5). He "dwells in unapproachable light" (1 Tim.
6:16; cf. Dan. 2:22), and in His light we see light (Ps. 36:9). God's Word also
provides light. In Psalm 119:105 the psalmist wrote, "Your word is a lamp
to my feet and a light to my path." But the most significant manifestation
of God's light is in the person of the Lord Jesus Christ. He is the "true Light
which, coming into the world, enlightens every man" (John 1:9; cf. 3:19);
the "Sunrise from on high" (Luke 1:78; cf. Isa. 42:1–7; and the "Light of the
world" (John 8:12; 9:5; 12:35–36, 46). Through Him the light of the glory of
God was revealed (2 Cor. 4:6).

THE PROBLEM OF SIGHT

The eye is the lamp of your body; when your eye is clear, your whole body also is full of light; but when it is bad, your body also is full of darkness. (11:34)

This statement reveals the heart of the issue. The problem was not lack of light, but lack of sight. The light of the truth was everywhere, but the spiritually blind refused to see it. The Lord Jesus Christ had for all intents and purposes flooded Israel with the truth concerning His deity and messiahship. His miracles further demonstrated His divine and absolute mastery over death, the forces of hell, and the physical world. But having seen all those miraculous works that pointed unmistakably to Jesus' deity (John 5:36; 10:25, 37–38; 14:11; 15:24) the religious leaders, along with the majority of the Jewish people, rejected Him. They could not accept His indictment of their external, ritualistic, legalistic religion. Stubbornly clinging to their self-righteousness, they sought to explain away Christ's miracles by attributing them to the power of Satan rather than God. Though they considered themselves guides to the blind (Rom. 2:17–19), they were themselves blind guides (Matt. 15:14; 23:16, 24) willfully blinded by their hatred of Jesus and His message (and by Satan's deception [2 Cor. 4:4]). In the words of Jesus, "This is the judgment, that the Light has come into the world, and men loved the darkness rather than the Light, for their deeds were evil. For everyone who does evil hates the Light, and does not come to the Light for fear that his deeds will be exposed" (John 3:19–20).

Since **the eye is the lamp of** the **body,** the ability to see depends on its condition. When it is **clear,** the **whole body also is full of light.** Light enters the brain through the eye, bringing comprehension of all that the light reveals. Therefore **when** the eye **is bad,** the **body also is full of darkness.** *Haplous* (**clear**) has the basic meaning of "single," "open," or "holding nothing back." A related word can be translated "generosity." When their eyes are wide open, people see everything. On the other hand *ponēros* (**bad**) describes eyes clouded by sin and evil. Those whose eyes are bad are spiritually blind and cannot see the light of the truth. The light of the glory of God shining in the face of Jesus Christ (2 Cor. 4:6) is completely obscured to those whose eyes are blinded by sin.

THE PRETENSE OF SIGHT

Then watch out that the light in you is not darkness. (11:35)

Knowing that they would indignantly deny that they were blind, the Lord issued this warning. *Skopeō* (**watch out**) could be translated, "keep a watchful eye on," "note carefully," "pay attention to," or "be concerned about." This strong warning was a call to careful self-examination. The danger that what they thought was **light** in them could actually be **darkness** was very real. Such self-deception marks every false system of belief apart from the gospel of Jesus Christ.

Tragically, those lost in the darkness of such systems imagine themselves to be enlightened. Sinners who think the darkness they are in is light are in a deadly dangerous situation. As the apostle Paul notes, they have become "futile in their speculations, and their foolish heart [is] darkened. ...Professing to be wise, they [have become] fools ...For they exchanged the truth of God for a lie, and worshiped and served the creature rather than the Creator, who is blessed forever. Amen" (Rom. 1:21, 22, 25).

The frightening reality for those who persistently refuse to repent is that God may judicially confirm them in their hardened condition. Those who persistently refuse to repent may eventually be unable to do so (Matt. 13:13–15; cf. Isa. 6:8–10; 29:10; 44:18; John 12:39–40; Acts 28:26–27; Rom. 11:7–8). Because he knew that "now is 'the acceptable time ... now is the day of salvation'" (2 Cor. 6:2), Paul pleaded with unbelievers, "We beg you on behalf of Christ, be reconciled to God" (2 Cor. 5:20).

THE PRECIOUSNESS OF SIGHT

If therefore your whole body is full of light, with no dark part in it, it will be wholly illumined, as when the lamp illumines you with its rays. (11:36)

For those willing to repent and turn from the sin that blinds them, the gift of sight opens up limitless vistas of blessing. The Lord's language is expansive: **Your whole body is full of light,** He declared, **with no dark part in it ... as when the lamp illumines you with its rays.**

Becoming a believer means having one's spiritual eyes opened to the truths revealed in God's Word (Ps. 119:18, 105, 130; 2 Peter 1:19). Having been "called . . . out of darkness into His marvelous light" (1 Peter 2:9) Christians walk in the light (1 John 1:5–7), are children of light (Eph. 5:8; 1 Thess. 5:5), and enjoy fellowship with the Light of the world (John 8:12). They are, and eternally will be, grateful for the light that floods their souls through God's grace.

Characteristics of False Religionists (Luke 11:37–54)

9

Now when He had spoken, a Pharisee asked Him to have lunch with him; and He went in, and reclined at the table. When the Pharisee saw it, he was surprised that He had not first ceremonially washed before the meal. But the Lord said to him, "Now you Pharisees clean the outside of the cup and of the platter; but inside of you, you are full of robbery and wickedness. You foolish ones, did not He who made the outside make the inside also? But give that which is within as charity, and then all things are clean for you. But woe to you Pharisees! For you pay tithe of mint and rue and every kind of garden herb, and yet disregard justice and the love of God; but these are the things you should have done without neglecting the others. Woe to you Pharisees! For you love the chief seats in the synagogues and the respectful greetings in the market places. Woe to you! For you are like concealed tombs, and the people who walk over them are unaware of it." One of the lawyers said to Him in reply, "Teacher, when You say this, You insult us too." But He said, "Woe to you lawyers as well! For

you weigh men down with burdens hard to bear, while you yourselves will not even touch the burdens with one of your fingers. Woe to you! For you build the tombs of the prophets, and it was your fathers who killed them. So you are witnesses and approve the deeds of your fathers; because it was they who killed them, and you build their tombs. For this reason also the wisdom of God said, 'I will send to them prophets and apostles, and some of them they will kill and some they will persecute, so that the blood of all the prophets, shed since the foundation of the world, may be charged against this generation, from the blood of Abel to the blood of Zechariah, who was killed between the altar and the house of God; yes, I tell you, it shall be charged against this generation.' Woe to you lawyers! For you have taken away the key of knowledge; you yourselves did not enter, and you hindered those who were entering." When He left there, the scribes and the Pharisees began to be very hostile and to question Him closely on many subjects, plotting against Him to catch Him in something He might say. (11:37–54)

By the final year of our Lord's life, His ministry consisted primarily of warning and judgment, and was marked by a constantly escalating conflict with the Jewish religious leaders. Seething with hatred because of His repeated denunciations of them and their theology, the spiritually blind, hypocritical leaders of apostate Judaism wanted Him dead (cf. John 11:53). Their hatred finally reached its climax when, against all reason and revelation, they manipulated the Romans into crucifying their own Messiah, bringing divine wrath down on their heads.

Many superficially picture the Lord's earthly ministry as one of performing kind deeds and miracles, while gently teaching on love and peace and being surrounded by women and children. But that is only part of the story. Jesus not only graciously proclaimed the truth, but also strongly condemned those who twisted and perverted it. It is true that He promised eternal heaven to those who received Him (Matt. 19:29; John 3:15–16), but it is also true that He promised everlasting hell to those who rejected Him (Matt. 7:21–23; 25:41–46; John 3:36). Jesus, the incarnate God of truth, the living personification of the holy law of

God, could not avoid conflict with sin and error.

Christ's life and ministry illustrate the crucial significance of truth. In a sense, all people affirm truth's importance. The routine day to day affairs of temporal life depend on people telling the truth, and without some degree of truthfulness life disintegrates and becomes chaotic. That is why liars are reviled, and sometimes held legally culpable. But truth is infinitely important in the spiritual realm, because nothing is as important as knowing the truth about salvation.

Satan, the father of lies (John 8:44), the ruler of the evil world system, opposes salvation truth (John 12:31; 14:30; 16:11; 1 John 5:19). His kingdom of darkness spawns an endless stream of religious liars and deceivers, who have led people astray ever since Adam and Eve. Deception today is greater than ever, due to its accumulation through human history and its exposure by the widespread reach of modern media. And in an age where the promoting of tolerance and diversity as the highest virtues has left people both unable and unwilling to distinguish truth from error, deception dominates. Even many who call themselves Christians advocate tolerating false teachers in the name of love, acceptance, peace, and unity. They ignore the reality that such people are savage, ravenous wolves (Matt. 7:15; Acts 20:29) disguised as messengers of truth, who keep people from true salvation (see the discussion of v. 52 below). But Jesus taught that false spiritual teaching comes from Satan's hell and sends people there. He aimed His most severe warnings and most stern judgments at those who outwardly seemed to be the most religious adherents to God and Scripture.

But being religious is not a virtue. False religion is not man ascending godward to the pinnacle of nobility, but descending to the lowest level of blasphemous depravity. As Paul wrote in Romans 1:18–23, religion is man foolishly abandoning the true God and creating false systems of his own making. False prophets and false teachers are in reality hypocrites, who create the illusion that they are something they are not. Instead of giving lost sinners the saving truth of the gospel, they reroute them from the narrow way of salvation onto the broad path that leads to eternal damnation (Matt. 7:13–14). Their outward display of piety is nothing but an insincere charade of godliness. Because they are devoid of true spiritual power they are to be avoided, not applauded (2 Tim. 3:5).

And, when they claim to represent the true God and Jesus Christ, they are the most dangerous.

Like that of all hypocritical false teachers, the religion of the scribes and Pharisees was an empty deception. They had no real love for God, since they rejected His Son (John 8:42; 15:23; 1 John 2:23), no experience of the Holy Spirit's power, no knowledge of the truth, no genuine righteousness, and no interest in real repentance. The Lord publicly denounced them as hypocrites (Matt. 15:7; 22:18; 23:13, 15, 23, 25, 27, 29), facing the severest judgment because of their willful rejection of Him (Matt. 23:33). His seemingly harsh rebuke of them was, at the same time, an act of mercy. Jesus' goal was not only to warn others about the false teachers, but also to warn them of their true spiritual condition. Unless they acknowledged and repented of their hypocrisy and embraced the truth in Him, they could not be saved.

In this passage there is a clear occasion among many where Jesus exposed the Jewish religious leaders as doomed deceivers. The phrase **now when He had spoken** connects this passage with His message in verses 29–36. After Jesus had finished speaking **a Pharisee asked Him to have lunch** (the earlier of the two main meals of the day) **with him.** A meal with someone was the sign of friendship in Israel. The invitation is thus surprising, and even more so since Jesus had just rebuked the nation and by implication its leaders. Pharisees refused to have meals with non-Pharisees, especially those associated with sinners (cf. 5:29–32). This man may have breached Pharisaic separation rules out of curiosity, since there is no indication that he had any evil motive for inviting the Lord (cf. 7:36–50). Jesus accepted his invitation **and He went in, and reclined at the table,** the common position for an extended meal and conversation (7:36–37, 49; 14:15; Matt. 9:10; 26:7, 20; John 12:2; 13:12, 23, 28).

The Pharisees were one of the four main Jewish sects along with the Sadducees (the wealthy, elite priests), the Zealots (political revolutionaries who sought independence from Rome), and the Essenes (ascetic monastics). Their name likely derives from a Hebrew verb meaning "to separate." The Pharisees viewed themselves as separated from and superior to everyone else (cf. John 7:49) because of their unmatched zeal for the Mosaic law and the rabbinic traditions.

The Pharisees originated during the intertestamental period, likely as an offshoot of the Hasidim (the "pious ones," who opposed the Hellenizing of Jewish culture under the wicked Seleucid king Antiochus Epiphanes). Unlike the Sadducees, who tended to be wealthy priests or Levites, the Pharisees were laymen, generally from the middle class. Although few in number (there were about 6000 at the time of Herod the Great), their popularity with the people throughout the land gave them significant influence in the Sanhedrin (cf. Acts 5:34–40).

The Lord's confrontation on this occasion reveals two defining characteristics of false religionists: what they love, and what they lack.

FALSE RELIGIONISTS ARE
CHARACTERIZED BY WHAT THEY LOVE

When the Pharisee saw it, he was surprised that He had not first ceremonially washed before the meal. But the Lord said to him, "Now you Pharisees clean the outside of the cup and of the platter; but inside of you, you are full of robbery and wickedness. You foolish ones, did not He who made the outside make the inside also? But give that which is within as charity, and then all things are clean for you. But woe to you Pharisees! For you pay tithe of mint and rue and every kind of garden herb, and yet disregard justice and the love of God; but these are the things you should have done without neglecting the others. Woe to you Pharisees! For you love the chief seats in the synagogues and the respectful greetings in the market places. Woe to you! For you are like concealed tombs, and the people who walk over them are unaware of it." (11:38–44)

The Pharisees' false religion was marked by five features that they loved: the symbolic, the sinful, the simplistic, the secondary, and the showy.

FALSE RELIGIONISTS LOVE THE SYMBOLIC

When the Pharisee saw it, he was surprised that He had not first ceremonially washed before the meal. (11:38)

When Jesus took His place at the table **the Pharisee . . . was surprised that He had not first ceremonially washed before the meal** (cf. Matt. 15:1–2; Mark 7:1–5). This had nothing to do with hygiene. His shock was not because the Lord's hands were physically dirty, but because He had not performed the elaborate ritual washing to make them **ceremonially** clean. Such washing was not commanded in the Old Testament, but had developed as part of the extrabiblical traditions of the elders (Matt. 15:2; Mark 7:3) that would later be collected in the Mishnah (third century A.D.). It symbolized holiness and a desire to be clean from all the defilements of the world. But this was merely another empty act of symbolism that could not address the corruption of the heart. The **Pharisee** was amazed that Jesus ignored the tradition, and since he was the host, he no doubt felt insulted. But the Lord refused to affirm man-made regulations that violated the commandments of God (Matt. 15:3–6). He was willing to insult this man to bring him face-to-face with his spiritual bankruptcy.

FALSE RELIGIONISTS LOVE THE SINFUL

But the Lord said to him, "Now you Pharisees clean the outside of the cup and of the platter; but inside of you, you are full of robbery and wickedness. (11:39)

Although the Pharisee said nothing, **the Lord** knew his mind and understood that he was troubled because his guest had ignored the ritual washing. Immediately, unapologetically and without deference, Jesus confronted the man's superficiality and **said to him, "Now you Pharisees clean the outside of the cup and of the platter; but inside of you, you are full of robbery and wickedness."** This was an appropriate illustration for Jesus to use at a meal. Any decent host would make certain that the parts of the dishes people ate from were clean. But spiritually speaking, the **Pharisees** did just the opposite, and took great care to **clean the outside of the cup and of the platter.** In the symbolism of the Lord's illustration, the Pharisees scrupulously cleaned the parts of the dishware that were inconsequential while leaving the eating surfaces filthy and unsanitary. The point is that despite their outward devotion to ritual, ceremony, and tradition, on the **inside** they were **full of robbery and wickedness** (cf. Matt. 23:25–28). They "loved the darkness rather than the Light, for their deeds were evil" (John 3:19). Their souls fed on pride, lust, and deception.

The two terms Jesus used graphically described their inner corruption. *Harpagēs* (**robbery;** "plunder," "pillage," "booty") refers to something seized by violent force. In classical Greek it was sometimes used of rape. False religion ravages and plunders people's temporal possessions and their eternal souls—and the Pharisees were guilty of doing both (20:47; Matt. 23:13, 15). *Ponēria* (**wickedness**) could also be translated "evil," "depravity," "malice," or "badness,"—all of which aptly describe these hypocrites whom Jesus called sons of hell (Matt. 23:15).

The external religion of the Pharisees was a sham. They exalted symbols on the outside and cherished sin on the inside; their preoccupation with external rituals caused them to overlook the significant issue of their wicked hearts. It is a sure mark of false religion that the more symbols there are the less spiritual reality there is.

FALSE RELIGIONISTS LOVE THE SIMPLISTIC

You foolish ones, did not He who made the outside make the inside also? But give that which is within as charity, and then all things are clean for you. (11:40–41)

Living in the compartmentalized world of their own religious system prevented the Pharisees from thinking deeply, honestly, or, in today's expression, outside the box. To address the host and his guests as **foolish ones** was certainly unconventional, but nonetheless accurate. Jesus was not doing what He prohibited in Matthew 5:22; this was an accurate assessment, not a coarse epithet. *Aphrones* (**foolish ones**) describes those who are ignorant, lack common sense, and think shallowly and superficially. In the New Testament it describes those who trust in their riches (Luke 12:20), are ignorant of religious truth (Rom. 2:20), question or deny the resurrection (1 Cor. 15:36), or reject the Christian faith (1 Peter 2:15). In contrast Paul exhorted believers, "Do not be foolish, but understand what the will of the Lord is" (Eph. 5:17).

Christ's rhetorical question, **"Did not He who made the outside make the inside also?"** was an unmistakable rebuke. To think that holy God would only be concerned about their observance of external rituals and not about their hearts was the height of folly. Such simplistic thinking reveals their shocking ignorance of the Old Testament (cf. Deut. 10:16; 1 Sam. 16:7; Ps. 51:6; Isa. 1:11–20; 19:13–14; Jer. 29:13; Joel 2:12–13; Amos 5:21–24; Mic. 6:7–8). The apostle Paul, himself once a Pharisee (Acts 23:6), summarized the Old Testament's teaching when he wrote, "He is a Jew who is one inwardly; and circumcision is that which is of the heart, by the Spirit, not by the letter; and his praise is not from men, but from God" (Rom. 2:29). God wants the heart.

It is best to understand the Lord's words, **But give that which is within as charity, and then all things are clean for you,** as an exhortation to His hearers to demonstrate their hearts for God by giving to the poor. In that sense it is reminiscent of His words to the rich young ruler: "If you wish to be complete, go and sell your possessions and give to the poor, and you will have treasure in heaven; and come, follow Me" (Matt. 19:21). All of their external religious trappings—almsgiving, prayers, fasting—were hypocritical as long as they kept plundering, pillaging, and ravaging people both physically and spiritually. Their unreasonably shallow, self-serving perspective kept them from focusing on what was in their hearts.

FALSE RELIGIONISTS LOVE THE SECONDARY

But woe to you Pharisees! For you pay tithe of mint and rue and every kind of garden herb, and yet disregard justice and the love of God; but these are the things you should have done without neglecting the others. (11:42)

This is the first of three woes that Jesus directed at the Pharisees as He pronounced judgment on their foolish, sinful, simplistic approach to spiritual truth. **Woe** is not primarily a sentimental expression of sorrow, but a declaration of judgment (cf. Isa. 3:9, 11; 5:8, 11, 18, 20, 21, 22; 10:1; 29:15; 30:1; 45:9; Matt. 23:13, 15, 16, 23, 25, 27, 29).

What elicited this first woe was the Pharisees' devotion to what was of secondary importance. They diligently paid their **tithe of mint and rue and every kind of garden herb,** even though the Old Testament commands regarding tithing (e.g., Lev. 27:30–33; Deut. 14:22–29; 26:12–15) did not extend to such trivial items. **Yet** their inward corruption and failure to obey the law's two great commands, to love God and their neighbors (Matt. 22:36–40), led them to **disregard justice and the love of God.** Instead, they focused on the minute details of their manmade regulations. Tithing and obeying God from the heart in minor matters prescribed in the Old Testament **are the things** the Pharisees **should have done,** but **without neglecting** justice or failing to love God. Void of spiritual life, they were left to pursue the secondary, outward forms of religious piety in a hopeless attempt to establish their self-righteousness.

FALSE RELIGIONISTS LOVE THE SHOWY

"Woe to you Pharisees! For you love the chief seats in the synagogues and the respectful greetings in the market places. Woe to you! For you are like concealed tombs, and the people who walk over them are unaware of it." (11:43–44)

The second woe Jesus pronounced on the **Pharisees** reveals the underlying motive behind everything they did. Their **love** of the showy displays of prominence—**the chief seats** (the ones for dignitaries in the front facing the congregation) **in the synagogues and the respectful greetings in the market places,** the places of honor at banquets (Matt. 23:6), wearing long robes (Mark 12:38) and being called Rabbi (Matt. 23:7)—demonstrated their insatiable desire for status. The Pharisees were hypocritical, self-righteous, proud, contemptuous of the common people (John 7:49), lacked justice and mercy, and pillaged and raped people's possessions and souls. Nevertheless they wanted to be loved, admired, revered, respected, and placed themselves in an elevated position above everyone else.

The attitude of the Pharisees was the antithesis of true spiritual leadership. Jesus instructed His followers that humble service, not demanding pride, is the hallmark of genuine spiritual leaders:

> Do not be called Rabbi; for One is your Teacher, and you are all brothers. Do not call anyone on earth your father; for One is your Father, He who is in heaven. Do not be called leaders; for One is your Leader, that is, Christ. But the greatest among you shall be your servant. Whoever exalts himself shall be humbled; and whoever humbles himself shall be exalted. (Matt. 23:8–12; cf. Luke 14:8–11)

The Pharisees, like their Old Testament counterparts, failed miserably to properly shepherd God's flock (Isa. 56:10–12; Jer. 10:21; 23:1–2; 50:6; Ezek. 34:2–10; Zech. 10:2–3). They were so bent on seeking their own glory that they refused to believe in their own Messiah revealed to them in person (John 5:44). Their self-promotion was a form of idolatry; Christ was a threat to their well-crafted satanic system.

The Lord pronounced one final **woe** on the Pharisees. It reveals that not only would they be judged for their own hypocrisy, but also for their evil influence on others. Despite their outward show of holiness, Jesus likened them to **concealed tombs,** whom **people . . . walk over . . .** and **are unaware of it.** The Old Testament prohibited touching a corpse (Num. 19:11–22) or a grave (v. 16), and those who did so became ceremonially unclean. Therefore graves in Israel were clearly marked so people would not inadvertently touch them and defile themselves. Having led the people astray, the Pharisees were like unmarked graves, defiling the souls of those who came into contact with them.

FALSE RELIGIONISTS ARE
CHARACTERIZED BY WHAT THEY LACK

One of the lawyers said to Him in reply, "Teacher, when You say this, You insult us too." But He said, "Woe to you lawyers as well! For

**you weigh men down with burdens hard to bear, while you your-
selves will not even touch the burdens with one of your fingers. Woe
to you! For you build the tombs of the prophets, and it was your
fathers who killed them. So you are witnesses and approve the
deeds of your fathers; because it was they who killed them, and you
build their tombs. For this reason also the wisdom of God said, 'I will
send to them prophets and apostles, and some of them they will kill
and some they will persecute, so that the blood of all the prophets,
shed since the foundation of the world, may be charged against this
generation, from the blood of Abel to the blood of Zechariah, who
was killed between the altar and the house of God; yes, I tell you, it
shall be charged against this generation.' Woe to you lawyers! For
you have taken away the key of knowledge; you yourselves did not
enter, and you hindered those who were entering." When He left
there, the scribes and the Pharisees began to be very hostile and to
question Him closely on many subjects, plotting against Him to
catch Him in something He might say.** (11:45–54)

After Jesus finished His condemnation of the Pharisees **one of
the lawyers said to Him in reply, "Teacher, when You say this,
You insult us too."** Also called teachers of the law (Luke 5:17) and
most frequently scribes (sixty-three times in the New Testament), **lawyers**
were experts in the interpretation and application of the Mosaic and rabbinic law. They were usually, but not always, Pharisees (they are distinguished from them by being mentioned separately; [5:21, 30; 6:7; 11:53;
15:2; Matt. 5:20; 12:38; 15:1; 23:2, 13, 14, 15, 23, 25, 27, 29; Mark 7:1, 5; John
8:3. Mark 2:16 refers to "the scribes of the Pharisees," and Acts 23:9 to "the
scribes of the Pharisaic party."]). They were given the respectful title of
rabbi ("great one"), though others who taught the word of God might
also receive that title (cf. John 1:38, 49; 3:2; 6:25, where it is given to Jesus).
Since the lawyers developed the religious system the Pharisees practiced, to insult the Pharisees was to **insult** them **too.**

In response to the lawyer's protest over the insults, Jesus pronounced three woes on them (though all six woes in this passage apply
to both the Pharisees and the lawyers). They reveal three things that false
religionists lack: spiritual power, spiritual life, and spiritual truth.

FALSE RELIGIONISTS LACK SPIRITUAL POWER

But He said, "Woe to you lawyers as well! For you weigh men down with burdens hard to bear, while you yourselves will not even touch the burdens with one of your fingers. (11:46)

The first **woe** directed **to** the **lawyers** exposes false religion's inherent lack of power to relieve the sin-burdened heart. Even the law of Moses can only reveal to people how sinful they are (Isa. 64:6; Rom. 3:20; 7:7; Gal. 3:10; James 2:10); it has no power to change the heart. As the apostle Paul wrote in Romans 8:3, "For what the Law could not do, weak as it was through the flesh, God did: sending His own Son in the likeness of sinful flesh and as an offering for sin, He condemned sin in the flesh" (cf. 3:21, 28; 10:4; Gal. 2:16, 21; 3:11; Phil. 3:9).

Thus for the lawyers to **weigh men down with burdens hard to bear** (the rabbinical interpretations of the law and the "traditions of the elders" [Mark 7:3]) in an impotent effort to give them the means to earn righteous standing with God was both cruel and hypocritical. *Phortia* (**burdens**) describes a massive burden, far beyond the capability of anyone to carry, such as a ship's cargo (Acts 27:10). Having usurped the authority to interpret the law (cf. Matt. 23:2), the lawyers required people to bear burdens that no one could carry (cf. Acts 15:10).

Nor were the lawyers interested in helping them in the slightest way, **not even** to **touch** (the Greek verb translated **touch** has the connotation of "to touch lightly," or "to brush") the **burdens with one of** their **fingers.** The truth was, the lawyers could not sustain the burdens they imposed on themselves, much less the people. But they were experts in finding ways of avoiding some of the more onerous burdens imposed by their legalistic system and deceiving themselves about achieving righteousness before God. Leon Morris writes,

> On the sabbath, they taught, a man may not carry a burden "in his right hand or in his left hand, in his bosom, or on his shoulder." But he may carry it "on the back of his hand, or with his foot or with his mouth or with his elbow, or in his ear or in his hair or in his wallet (carried) mouth downwards, or between his wallet and his shirt, or in the hem of his shirt, or in his shoe or in his sandal (*Shabbat* 10:3). Multiply this by all the regulations of the Law and ordinary people have a burden beyond bearing even to know what they might do and might not do.

> But there is also a multitude of loopholes for a lawyer who knew the
> traditions which enabled him to do pretty well what he wished. (*The
> Gospel According to St. Luke*, The Tyndale New Testament
> Commentaries [Grand Rapids: Eerdmans, 1975], 205–6)

The lawyers had no mercy, grace, or power to offer the common people, while hopelessly struggling under the crushing burden that they had imposed on themselves. Their inability and indifference were in stark contrast to Jesus' promise, "Come to Me, all who are weary and heavy-laden, and I will give you rest. Take My yoke upon you and learn from Me, for I am gentle and humble in heart, and you will find rest for your souls. For My yoke is easy and My burden is light" (Matt. 11:28–30).

False religion does not have the power to bring people into right relation to God. Nor do its leaders have the power to produce true spiritual life. They are blind guides of the blind (Luke 6:39), and both will end up in the eternal pit of hell. Yet it is the purpose of all false religion to carry out an elaborate deception as it gathers the damned into its influence.

FALSE RELIGIONISTS LACK SPIRITUAL LIFE

Woe to you! For you build the tombs of the prophets, and it was your fathers who killed them. So you are witnesses and approve the deeds of your fathers; because it was they who killed them, and you build their tombs. For this reason also the wisdom of God said, 'I will send to them prophets and apostles, and some of them they will kill and some they will persecute, so that the blood of all the prophets, shed since the foundation of the world, may be charged against this generation, from the blood of Abel to the blood of Zechariah, who was killed between the altar and the house of God; yes, I tell you, it shall be charged against this generation.' (11:47–51)

The obvious reason for false religionists' lack of spiritual power is their lack of spiritual life; they are "dead in [their] trespasses and sins" (Eph. 2:1), and being "in the flesh [they] cannot please God" (Rom. 8:8). They have not received a new heart (Ezek. 36:26) and the indwelling

Holy Spirit (v. 27), and hence have no capacity to honor, obey, or serve God. All who follow them are led into eternal condemnation and death.

This second **woe** directed specifically at the lawyers unmasks their spiritual deadness. They thought themselves superior to their ancestors because they built or embellished **the tombs of the prophets** while their apostate **fathers** had **killed** those very prophets (Neh. 9:26; Jer. 2:30). The scribes and Pharisees "buil[t] the tombs of the prophets and adorn[ed] the monuments of the righteous, and [said], 'If we had been living in the days of our fathers, we would not have been partners with them in shedding the blood of the prophets'" (Matt. 23:29–30).

But despite the superficial homage they paid to the martyred prophets, the scribes and Pharisees were no different than their ancestors. In both the Old and New Testaments, apostate Israel rejected the prophets and eventually refused to believe in the Messiah who they predicted would come. Jesus turned their veneration of the prophets on its head when He declared, **You are witnesses and approve the deeds of your fathers; because it was they who killed them, and you build their tombs.** In spite of their claim to be different than their ancestors, they had the same rejection of spiritual truth as did their fathers. The only way to truly honor the prophets was not to embellish their tombs, but to obey the word of God that they proclaimed, which the scribes and Pharisees clearly did not do. Even worse, they rejected the Messiah of whom the prophets so frequently wrote, and would eventually kill Him, just as their fathers had done to the prophets. Far from being better than their ancestors, the scribes and Pharisees were in fact far worse. The attention they paid to the prophets' tombs symbolically linked what their fathers did to what they were planning to do to the most glorious One ever promised by the prophets.

The Lord continued His rebuke, declaring in verse 49, **"For this reason also the wisdom of God said, 'I will send to them prophets and apostles, and some of them they will kill and some they will persecute.'"** The apostate religious leaders' future actions would prove the truth of Jesus' assertion that they were no better than their fathers. Since the quote attributed to **the wisdom of God** is not found in the Old Testament, it is best to translate it with the sense of "God in His wisdom said . . ." The **prophets and apostles** whom the apostate leaders of

Judaism would **kill** and **persecute** were the New Testament apostles and prophets. John the Baptist (Matt. 14:3–12), Stephen (Acts 7:58–60), the apostle James, the brother of John (Acts 12:1–2), James the Lord's brother (whose death was recorded by the first-century Jewish historian Josephus) and others (cf. Acts 26:10) were killed, while Peter and John (Acts 4:1–3), all the apostles (Acts 5:18–41), and others (Acts 8:1) were persecuted. Their mistreatment of the gospel preachers would conclusively demonstrate Christ's point that the scribes and Pharisees were as wicked and godless as their ancestors. In fact, they were much worse.

The Lord's shocking declaration that **the blood of all the prophets, shed since the foundation of the world,** would **be charged against this generation** reveals just how much worse the generation alive at that time was than those who killed the prophets. That God's accumulated wrath would fall on one generation is not unprecedented. The generation alive at the time of the flood experienced the judgment that resulted from generations of wickedness, as will the generation alive during the final eschatological time of the tribulation (Rev. 6–19). **This generation,** the one alive when Jesus lived, was culpable for **the blood of all the prophets, shed since the foundation of the world** because it had the most accumulated revelation, yet engaged in the same sins as previous generations. They had the teaching of the prophets in the Old Testament, they had heard John the Baptist, the twelve apostles, the seventy evangelists and, most significant, they had had the unprecedented privilege of hearing the profound truth of heaven from the lips of Jesus, God incarnate. And they had seen His divine power over demons, disease, death, and nature in a massive, unmistakable display of undenied miracles.

The judgment in view here is temporal, involving the death of tens of thousands of souls, as well as the destruction of the nation of Israel as an entity. Just a few decades later this generation would experience that temporal fury of God such as had not been felt since the Babylonian captivity. The revolt against Rome in A.D. 66–70 resulted in the destruction of nearly one thousand towns and villages throughout Israel. Jerusalem was taken after a siege, its buildings razed, and the temple destroyed. Tens of thousands of Jews throughout Israel were massacred, and thousands of others sold into slavery. This generation would indeed "fill up ... the measure of the guilt of [its] fathers" (Matt. 23:32). And that earthly judgment obviously led to final hell.

The phrase, **from the blood of Abel to the blood of Zechariah, who was killed between the altar and the house of God,** encompasses all the Old Testament martyrs. **Abel** was the first person in history to be murdered, killed by his brother Cain because of his jealousy over Abel's faithfulness in obeying God's commandments. Some think that the **Zechariah** in view here is the son of Jehoiada the priest, who was stoned to death in the temple court by order of King Joash (2 Chron. 24:20–22). But his death was not near the conclusion of the Old Testament, and there were many more martyrs after him.

No speculation is needed because Jesus made clear which of the more than two dozen Zechariahs mentioned in the Old Testament He was referring to. In Matthew 23:35 He called him "Zechariah, the son of Berechiah." This was the prophet Zechariah, the author of the book of Zechariah (Zech. 1:1) whose martyrdom, though not recorded in Scripture, took place near the close of the Old Testament. Evidently Zechariah the son of Berechiah was also killed **between the altar and the house of God** (cf. Joab, who was executed at the altar itself [1 Kings 2:28–34]). The collective guilt for the deaths of all those righteous martyrs would **be charged against** that wicked **generation** that had filled up God's wrath to the top.

FALSE RELIGIONISTS LACK SPIRITUAL TRUTH

"Woe to you lawyers! For you have taken away the key of knowledge; you yourselves did not enter, and you hindered those who were entering." When He left there, the scribes and the Pharisees began to be very hostile and to question Him closely on many subjects, plotting against Him to catch Him in something He might say. (11:52–54)

False religion is void of spiritual power because it is void of spiritual life, and that derives from the absence of spiritual truth. The third and final **woe** against the **lawyers,** and the last of the six aimed at both them and the Pharisees, makes that explicit. They were supposed to be inter-preters and teachers of the law, but in reality they had **taken away the key of knowledge**—accurate interpretation of Scripture under the illu-minating direction of the Holy Spirit. Since they are "devoid of the Spirit" (Jude 19) and blinded by Satan (2 Cor. 4:4), false teachers inevitably twist and distort the meaning of Scripture (2 Peter 3:15–16). In effect, Jesus declares that they lock up the truths of Scripture and throw away the key!

As their rejecting Christ reveals, the scribes and Pharisees could not correctly understand the Old Testament, which pointed to Him (John 5:39; cf. Luke 24:27; Rev. 19:10). Their traditions increasingly obscured the truth contained in the Old Testament, turning it into a maze of riddles, allegories, secret meanings, and obscure interpreta-tions, all designed to reinforce their cleverness and sell their false system of self-righteousness. Not only were they unable to **enter** the kingdom of God themselves, they also **hindered those who were entering.** That is the most severe condemnation given by our Lord, as is clear in the words of Hebrews 10:29–31:

> How much severer punishment do you think he will deserve who has trampled under foot the Son of God, and has regarded as unclean the blood of the covenant by which he was sanctified, and has insulted the Spirit of grace? For we know Him who said, "Vengeance is mine, I will repay." And again, "The Lord will judge His people." It is a terrifying thing to fall into the hands of the living God.

Sadly, but predictably, the Pharisees and scribes failed to heed Jesus' mercifully severe warnings. Instead of repenting of their sins, repu-diating their false system of religion, and calling for divine mercy, they became even more aggressively hostile to Him. **When He left there,** Luke noted, **the scribes and the Pharisees began to be very hostile.** *Enechō* (**hostile**) could be translated, "hold a grudge." It was not merely that they disagreed with Him theologically; their animosity toward Jesus was personal due to His publicly exposing them as false teachers. Their vicious hostility prompted them **to question Him closely on many subjects.** The Greek verbs translated **plotting** and **catch** are hunting terms. The former means "to lie in wait," or "to ambush"; the latter describes hunting and capturing a wild animal. The vivid language reveals their desperation to trap Jesus **in something He might say.**

Having utterly failed to do so, they eventually resorted to bringing in false, lying witnesses against Jesus at His trial (Matt. 26:59–61).

The church of Jesus Christ must in every time and place be ever vigilant against false teachers who pretend to be moral, love God, and teach truth, yet in reality are sinful, self-seeking fools, devoid of spiritual power, spiritual life, and spiritual truth. Because they are guilty of "speaking perverse things, to draw away the disciples after them" (Acts 20:30), they are not to be welcomed in the name of tolerance, but rejected as "those who cause dissensions and hindrances contrary to the teaching" of the gospel of Jesus Christ (Rom. 16:17; cf. 2 Tim. 3:5; Titus 3:10; 2 John 10–11). The strong words of 2 Peter and Jude stand as the warnings to the church.

A Certain Cure for Hypocrisy
(Luke 12:1–12)

10

Under these circumstances, after so many thousands of people had gathered together that they were stepping on one another, He began saying to His disciples first of all, "Beware of the leaven of the Pharisees, which is hypocrisy. But there is nothing covered up that will not be revealed, and hidden that will not be known. Accordingly, whatever you have said in the dark will be heard in the light, and what you have whispered in the inner rooms will be proclaimed upon the housetops. I say to you, My friends, do not be afraid of those who kill the body and after that have no more that they can do. But I will warn you whom to fear: fear the One who, after He has killed, has authority to cast into hell; yes, I tell you, fear Him! Are not five sparrows sold for two cents? Yet not one of them is forgotten before God. Indeed, the very hairs of your head are all numbered. Do not fear; you are more valuable than many sparrows. And I say to you, everyone who confesses Me before men, the Son of Man will confess him also before the angels of God; but he who denies Me before men will be denied

before the angels of God. And everyone who speaks a word against the Son of Man, it will be forgiven him; but he who blasphemes against the Holy Spirit, it will not be forgiven him. When they bring you before the synagogues and the rulers and the authorities, do not worry about how or what you are to speak in your defense, or what you are to say; for the Holy Spirit will teach you in that very hour what you ought to say." (12:1–12)

Since it cannot offer the true knowledge of God, man, sin, and salvation, false religion does not provide the truth that accesses the power for people to please God and receive His salvation. All false religious leaders claim to have the truth, but in reality none of them do. And since they do not know the truth themselves, empty hypocrites cannot lead others to it. Along with their devotees, they all perish.

The Greek word *hupokritēs* (hypocrite) was originally a secular term referring to an actor who played a role on stage. But in the New Testament it became a religious term, used exclusively in the negative sense of one who claims to speak for God but does not—a hypocrite. The original theatrical definition of *hupokritēs* figuratively expresses the nature of spiritual deceivers. An actor attempts to play a convincing role on the stage, pretending to be someone that he is not. So do religious deceivers. Even today most commonly the words "hypocrite," and "hypocrisy" have religious overtones. While all hypocritical spiritual leaders cheat people out of their earthly possessions, the eternal consequences of their unconscionable deception are far more damaging. Although they pretend to speak for God, they are fraudulent liars and deceivers (1 Tim. 4:2), who cause people to forfeit to judgment their eternal souls. These hypocrites the Pharisees, Jesus said, actually made people into fellow sons of hell (Matt. 23:15).

The Bible reveals specific characteristics of hypocrites. First, by pretending to be something they are not, they focus on outward appearance and hide the truth of who they really are. Jesus applied Isaiah's condemnation of the hypocrites of his day to the scribes and Pharisees when "He said to them, 'Rightly did Isaiah prophesy of you hypocrites, as it is written: "This people honors Me with their lips, but their heart is far away from Me:"'" (Mark 7:6). In a pompous, self-serving display of their supposed spirituality, the religious hypocrites of Jesus' day sounded trumpets to call attention to their giving (Matt. 6:2), prayed on the street corners for all to see (v. 5), made it obvious that they were fasting by having a mournful expression on their faces and neglecting their appearance (v. 16), enlarged their phylacteries and the tassels on their garments (Matt. 23:5), sought out the most important seats at banquets and in the synagogue (v. 6), and craved respectful public greetings and the honored title Rabbi (v. 7).

Viewing themselves as spiritually superior to the common people (cf. Isa. 65:5), hypocrites are condescendingly quick to find fault with them. In a pointed and humorous image Jesus said of such people,

> How can you say to your brother, "Let me take the speck out of your eye," and behold, the log is in your own eye? You hypocrite, first take the log out of your own eye, and then you will see clearly to take the speck out of your brother's eye. (Matt. 7:4–5)

For hypocrites to presume to criticize the faults of others is as absurd as someone with a gigantic log in his eye presuming to be able to remove a tiny splinter from someone else's eye.

Hypocrites respond with malice to those who expose them. Desperately trying to trap Jesus into making an incriminating statement, the Jewish religious leaders asked Him about the explosive issue of paying the poll tax required by the Romans. Perceiving both their malice (Matt. 22:18) and their hypocrisy (Mark 12:15), Jesus refuted their attempt to trap Him (Matt. 22:19–21).

Hypocrites also lack discernment. In Luke 12:54–57 Jesus rebuked those who were able to look at certain indicators and predict the weather (vv. 54–55), but were unable to recognize the obvious signs that the Messiah, God in human flesh, was among them (vv. 56–57).

Their disdain for those whom they regard as spiritually inferior causes hypocrites to lack compassion. Luke 13:11–13 describes Jesus' healing of a woman who had suffered from a crippling disease for eighteen years. Indignant at this blatant violation of the rabbinical Sabbath restrictions, a synagogue leader enjoined the people to seek healing on one of the other six days. Jesus' stern rebuke exposed the man's unfeeling hypocrisy:

But the Lord answered him and said,"You hypocrites, does not each of you on the Sabbath untie his ox or his donkey from the stall and lead him away to water him? And this woman, a daughter of Abraham as she is, whom Satan has bound for eighteen long years, should she not have been released from this bond on the Sabbath day?" (vv. 15–16)

This incident was but one of many when Jesus pronounced divine judgment on hypocrites. Seven times in Matthew 23 (vv. 13, 15, 16, 23, 25, 27, 29), the Lord addressed the scribes and Pharisees using the phrase,"Woe to you," which is an expression of divine condemnation and judgment. Jesus concluded His parable of the faithful and unfaithful slaves (Matt. 24:45–51) by declaring that the disloyal slave would be assigned to hell with the hypocrites. And in a shocking act of judgment, God took the lives of the two most notorious hypocrites in the early church, Ananias and Sapphira (Acts 5:1–11). Not only does God judge unbelievers for their hypocrisy, He also warns believers to avoid it (Rom. 12:9; cf. James 3:17; 1 Peter 2:1).

Hypocrisy plagued Israel throughout her history. God said to Ezekiel regarding the Jewish people of his day,

They come to you as people come, and sit before you as My people and hear your words, but they do not do them, for they do the lustful desires expressed by their mouth, and their heart goes after their gain. Behold, you are to them like a sensual song by one who has a beautiful voice and plays well on an instrument; for they hear your words but they do not practice them (Ezek. 33:31–32; cf. Isa. 58:1–11; Zech. 7:5–6).

Micah lamented that Israel's "leaders pronounce judgment for a bribe, her priests instruct for a price and her prophets divine for money. Yet they lean on the Lord saying, 'Is not the Lord in our midst? Calamity will not come upon us'" (Mic. 3:11). Admonishing the survivors of Babylon's destruction of Judah for their hypocrisy, Jeremiah said,

The Lord has spoken to you, O remnant of Judah, "Do not go into Egypt!" You should clearly understand that today I have testified against you. For you have only deceived yourselves; for it is you who sent me to the Lord your God, saying, "Pray for us to the Lord our God; and whatever the Lord our God says, tell us so, and we will do it." So I have told you today, but you have not obeyed the Lord your God, even in whatever He has sent me to tell you. Therefore you should now clearly understand that you will die by the sword, by famine and by pestilence, in the place where you wish to go to reside. (Jer. 42:19–22)

Psalm 78:36–37, Isaiah 29:13, and Romans 2:17–23 also describe Israel's hypocrisy.

The New Testament also records instances of hypocrisy. In addition to Ananias and Sapphira, Luke 20:20 describes "spies [sent from the religious leaders; v. 19] who pretended to be righteous, in order that they might catch [Jesus] in some statement, so that they could deliver Him to the rule and the authority of the governor." Paul encountered "false brethren secretly brought in, who had sneaked in to spy out our liberty which we have in Christ Jesus, in order to bring us into bondage" (Gal. 2:4; cf. 2 Cor. 11:13, 26). Even the apostle Peter temporarily fell into hypocrisy (Gal. 2:11–14).

But preeminent in the Bible's rogues' gallery of hypocrites were the scribes and Pharisees, the dominant force in the religious culture of first-century Israel. Over the course of His ministry, they became increasingly angry over Jesus' relentless exposure of their hypocrisy. Their opposition reached its peak when they tried to explain His miraculous powers as coming from Satan, not God (see the exposition of Luke 11:15 in chapter 6 of this volume). In response, the Lord pronounced six curses on the scribes and Pharisees (11:42, 43, 44, 46, 47, 52).

As chapter 12 opens, the majority of the people, having been swayed to that blasphemous view, were becoming fixed in their resentment, resistance, animosity, and rejection of Jesus. Gone was the sensibility, curiosity, enthusiasm, and excitement that marked the early years of His ministry; the people had indeed become "a wicked generation" (11:29). As a result, Jesus' ministry was largely one of warning and judgment. Those are the threatening themes of the discourse that begins in 12:1 and runs through 13:9.

The opening verse of chapter 12 sets the scene. The Greek phrase translated **under these circumstances** is better rendered "meanwhile," "at that time," or "during that period." Jesus gave this discourse during the same general period of time as the events recorded in chapter 11. The phrase **so many thousands** literally means tens of thousands. An immense crowd of **people had gathered together** to witness the ongoing conflict between the Lord and the scribes and Pharisees (11:53–54). There were so many there that the people **were stepping on one another** trying to get close enough to hear the dialogue between the Lord and His opponents. The result was a kind of mob scene.

Whatever dialogue may have been going on ended and Jesus turned to address the largely hostile crowd. Before He spoke to the people about hypocrisy, however, He directed His words to warn **His disciples first of all** to **beware of the leaven of the Pharisees, which is hypocrisy.** The word translated **disciples** is the plural form of the noun *mathētēs*, which refers to a learner or student. Not all of them had believed in Jesus, but unlike the majority of the crowd who had rejected Him, they were at least still interested in Him. Jesus warned them to **beware** ("give heed to," "pay attention to," "keep on the lookout for," "guard against") **the leaven** (permeating influence; cf. Matt. 16:6, 11–12; Mark 8:15) **of the Pharisees.** They needed to avoid all the corrupting influence of apostate false teachers since, as Paul said, "bad company corrupts good morals" (1 Cor. 15:33).

In verses 2–12, Jesus gave three essential, non-negotiable obligations that will keep people from the eternal disaster of being a hypocrite: honor the Father, honor the Son, and honor the Spirit. It is only by focusing on the triune God that one can avoid falling under the damning influence of false religion. Simply put, those who are not Trinitarians cannot avoid hell, since it is impossible to honor the Father without honoring the Son, and impossible to honor the Son without honoring the Spirit. There is an interlocking chain of testimony: the Spirit testifies to the Son (John 15:26), the Son reveals the Father (Luke 10:22; John 1:18), and the Father glorifies and honors the Son (John 8:54).

HONOR THE FATHER

But there is nothing covered up that will not be revealed, and hidden that will not be known. Accordingly, whatever you have said in the dark will be heard in the light, and what you have whispered in the inner rooms will be proclaimed upon the housetops. I

**say to you, My friends, do not be afraid of those who kill the body
and after that have no more that they can do. But I will warn you
whom to fear: fear the One who, after He has killed, has authority
to cast into hell; yes, I tell you, fear Him! Are not five sparrows
sold for two cents? Yet not one of them is forgotten before God.
Indeed, the very hairs of your head are all numbered. Do not fear;
you are more valuable than many sparrows.** (12:2–7)

Jesus gave three compelling reasons for honoring the Father.
First, He will uncover what is hidden. The statement **there is nothing
covered up that will not be revealed, and hidden that will not be
known** expresses a frequent theme of our Lord's teaching (cf. 8:17;
Matt.10:26; Mark 4:22). It echoes the closing verse of Ecclesiastes, where
Solomon warned that "God will bring every act to judgment, everything
which is hidden, whether it is good or evil" (Eccl. 12:14). The apostle Paul
wrote of the "day when, according to my gospel, God will judge the
secrets of men through Christ Jesus" (Rom. 2:16), and exhorted the
Corinthians, "Do not go on passing judgment before the time, but wait
until the Lord comes who will both bring to light the things hidden in the
darkness and disclose the motives of men's hearts; and then each man's
praise will come to him from God" (1 Cor. 4:5).

The point is that while hypocrites may succeed in their deception for a time, no one ultimately gets away with hypocrisy. What hypocrites successfully conceal from people will eventually be uncovered.
Some will be exposed in this life, as Paul told Timothy (1 Tim. 5:24–25); all
will be exposed in the future, when "the Son of Man is going to come in
the glory of His Father with His angels, and will then repay every man
according to his deeds" (Matt. 16:27; cf. Rom. 2:5–6).

The Lord's warning, **Accordingly, whatever you have said in
the dark will be heard in the light, and what you have whispered
in the inner rooms will be proclaimed upon the housetops,**
metaphorically reinforces the truth that sins will eventually be exposed.
What hypocrites try to hide in the darkness is clearly visible to God, as the
oldest book in the Bible reveals: "There is no darkness or deep shadow
where the workers of iniquity may hide themselves" (Job 34:22; cf. Ps.
139:12; Isa. 29:15; Jer. 23:24; Heb. 4:13). The **inner rooms** of which Jesus

spoke were storerooms (the same Greek word is so translated in v. 24), built in the middle of houses away from the exterior walls, which were more easily dug through by thieves. Such inner rooms were used to store valuables, but could also serve as a location for private conversations, or prayer (Matt. 6:6). The point is that hypocrisy cannot be permanently hidden, as Darrell L. Bock notes:

> This figure of speech describes our most private practices. This is a classic reversal theme: the most private of acts and utterances become the most public. It is this exposure that makes hypocrisy useless in the long run and the heroic deed done in private an object of admiration eventually. The contrasts are strong: darkness versus light and private whispering versus public preaching. (*Luke 9:51–24:53*, Baker Exegetical Commentary on the New Testament [Grand Rapids: Baker, 1996], 1135)

Hypocrites will one day be seen for what they really are.

A second reason to fear God is the reality that He will punish hypocrites in hell. Hypocrites are preoccupied with what people think. But it is foolish, Jesus said, to **be afraid of** humans, **who** in the worst case scenarios can only **kill the body and after that have no more that they can do.** On the other hand, Jesus went on to **warn** people **whom to fear:** rather, they are to **fear the One who, after He has killed, has authority to cast into hell.** *Gehenna* (**hell**) refers to the valley of Hinnom, located just outside of Jerusalem. Within that valley the apostate Jews had built a place of worship, where they sacrificed their children to the abominable pagan god Molech by burning them in fire (Jer. 7:31). That shrine was defiled by godly King Josiah as part of his reforms (2 Kings 23:10), and eventually the site became Jerusalem's city dump. Because it was a place where fires were constantly burning, *gehenna* came to be used figuratively to speak of eternal hell (cf. Matt. 5:22, 29, 30; 10:28; 18:9; 23:15, 33; Mark 9:43, 45, 47; James 3:6).

The one with the **authority to cast into hell** is not, as some imagine, Satan. Satan is neither the one who sends people to hell, nor is he the ruler of hell. On the contrary he himself will in a sure future day be cast into hell (Rev. 20:10), where he will be its most notorious prisoner for all eternity. Nowhere in Scripture is there a command to fear Satan. Believers have been completely delivered from him in the present, "because greater is He who is in [them] than he who is in the world"

(1 John 4:4), and in the future he will have no influence on us because "the God of peace will [quickly] crush Satan under [our] feet" (Rom. 16:20). So instead of fearing Satan, believers are to resist him (James 4:7; 1 Peter 5:9), be wary of his schemes (Eph. 6:11), and avoid giving him an opportunity to lure them into sin (Eph. 4:27; 1 Peter 5:8). God is the one to be feared (Prov. 23:17; 24:21; 2 Cor. 7:1; Eph. 5:21; 1 Peter 2:17; cf. Job 28:28; Pss. 19:9; 34:11; 111:10; Prov. 1:7; 9:10; Acts 9:31).

Here is another strong passage in our Lord's teaching that refutes the false idea that there is no hell. To insist that **hell** is a reference to the grave only destroys the contrast here and makes nonsense out of the Lord's statement. If there is no hell, then God would be unable to do anything to a person other than what men could do. Both could kill someone, who then would merely go out of existence. Jesus' whole point is that God is to be feared because He alone has the authority to both kill sinners and after death cast them into eternal torment.

A final reason to fear God is that nothing escapes His knowledge. Jesus used two illustrations to demonstrate God's omniscient knowledge of even the most insignificant details. **Are not five sparrows sold for two cents?** He asked. **Sparrows** are common small birds that were often eaten by the poor. They were so inexpensive that **five** could be bought for only **two cents** (a cent was one sixteenth of a day's pay for an average worker). **Yet** despite their insignificance **not one of them is forgotten before God.** He knows of every sparrow in the world. Not only that, He also knows the number of **hairs** on everyone's **head**—more than 100,000 on average. Such omniscience is the source of great comfort to His children (cf. Matt. 6:25–34), who have nothing to **fear,** since they **are more valuable than many sparrows.** But while this truth is comfort to believers, it should be a cause of terror to hypocrites, whose fraudulent self-righteousness will avail them nothing in light of God's complete and detailed knowledge of their true unregenerate condition.

HONOR THE SON

And I say to you, everyone who confesses Me before men, the Son of Man will confess him also before the angels of God; but he who

denies Me before men will be denied before the angels of God. (12:8–9)

The phrase **and I say to you** marks a transition in the Lord's flow of thought. The means to honor the Father is to honor the Son, because "he who does not honor the Son does not honor the Father who sent Him" (John 5:23; 8:41–42; 14:6; Acts 4:10–12; 1 John 4:14; 2 John 7). The term **everyone** is all-inclusive; only the one who **confesses** the Son **before men** honors God. **Confesses** translates a form of the verb *homologeō*, which literally means, "to agree," or "to say the same thing." To confess Christ is to affirm what is true about His person, works, and words. It is to accept the Father's testimony, "This is My beloved Son, in whom I am well-pleased" (Matt. 3:17) and "confess with [the] mouth Jesus as Lord, and believe in [the] heart that God raised Him from the dead" (Rom. 10:9).

The essence of confessing Jesus as Lord is self-denial, submitting all aspects of one's life to His sovereign control as a slave to his master (cf. Luke 7:8). In Luke 9:23–24 Jesus declared, "If anyone wishes to come after Me, he must deny himself, and take up his cross daily and follow Me. For whoever wishes to save his life will lose it, but whoever loses his life for My sake, he is the one who will save it" (cf. Gal. 2:20; Col. 3:3).

A true confession of Christ will result in the complete transformation wrought by regeneration and sanctification. "By this the children of God and the children of the devil are obvious," wrote the apostle John, "anyone who does not practice righteousness is not of God, nor the one who does not love his brother" (1 John 3:10). Those who make such a confession will inevitably manifest it openly **before men** both with their words and with their changed lives in willing and grateful submission to Christ.

Whether a person confesses or does not confess Christ will determine that person's eternal destiny. On the one hand, if a person **con - fesses** Him **before men, the Son of Man will confess him also before the angels of God.** But on the other hand, Jesus warned that the person **who denies** Him **before men will be denied before the angels of God.** Angels are frequently associated with judgment in the New Testament (9:26; Matt. 13:39–42, 49–50; 16:27; 25:31, 41; Mark 8:38; 2 Thess. 1:7;

Rev. 14:10, 14–15). Those who fail to genuinely confess Christ as Lord will one day hear Him say, "I never knew you; depart from Me, you who practice lawlessness" (Matt. 7:23). The sure way to miss out on heaven is to deny Christ, as the scribes and Pharisees had done. But just as sure a way to gain hell is to make an insincere, superficial confession of Christ (Matt. 7:21–22). Heaven belongs only to those who honor the Father by truly honoring the Son.

Honor the Spirit

And everyone who speaks a word against the Son of Man, it will be forgiven him; but he who blasphemes against the Holy Spirit, it will not be forgiven him. When they bring you before the synagogues and the rulers and the authorities, do not worry about how or what you are to speak in your defense, or what you are to say; for the Holy Spirit will teach you in that very hour what you ought to say. (12:10–12)

Having discussed the one to fear, the Father, and the one to confess, the Son, the Lord introduced the one to hear, the Holy Spirit. No one comes to the Father except through the Son, and no one comes to the Son except through the Spirit. Avoiding the damning judgment that comes to those caught up in hypocritical false religious systems requires belief in the person and work of each member of the Trinity. The Father must be acknowledged as sovereign judge and lawgiver, the Son as sovereign Savior and Lord, and the Spirit as sovereign revealer. The Father is the one whose holy law has been violated; the Son is the one whose death paid the penalty for that violation and satisfied God's wrath; the Spirit is the one whose revelation about the Father's law and the Son's death must be received. Just as Christ perfectly revealed the Father, so also does the Holy Spirit perfectly reveal Christ, both in Scripture and the work of regeneration.

The apostle John revealed how to know when a person's message is truly from the Spirit of God and not a human or demonic source when he wrote,

> By this you know the Spirit of God: every spirit that confesses that Jesus Christ has come in the flesh is from God; and every spirit that does not confess Jesus is not from God; this is the spirit of the anti-christ, of which you have heard that it is coming, and now it is already in the world (1 John 4:2–3).

Every one claiming to have a message from God either speaks the truth about Christ from the Spirit of God, or a lie from the spirit of antichrist. Those are the only two options, and there is no middle ground. Emphasizing the significance of a true confession of Jesus Christ, John Piper observes,

> Jesus is the litmus test of reality for all persons and all religions. He said it clearly: "The one who rejects me rejects him who sent me" (Luke 10:16). People and religions who reject Christ reject God. Do other religions know the true God? Here is the test: Do they reject Jesus as the only Savior for sinners who was crucified and raised by God from the dead? If they do, they do not know God in a saving way.
>
> That is what Jesus meant when he said, "I am the way, and the truth, and the life. No one comes to the Father except through me" (John 14:6). Or when he said, "Whoever does not honor the Son does not honor the Father who sent him" (John 5:23). Or when he said to the Pharisees, "If God were your Father, you would love me" (John 8:42).
>
> It's what the apostle John meant when he said, "No one who denies the Son has the Father. Whoever confesses the Son has the Father also" (1 John 2:23). Or when he said, "Everyone who ... does not abide in the teaching of Christ, does not have God." (2 John 9)
>
> There's no point in romanticizing other religions that reject the deity and saving work of Christ. They do not know God. And those who follow them tragically waste their lives. (*Don't Waste Your Life* [Wheaton, Ill.: Crossway, 2003], 39)

The Holy Spirit's testimony to Christ is the only way to know the truth about Him. No one will ever be able to confess Jesus as Lord except by the work of the Holy Spirit (1 Cor. 12:3). Saving faith comes from hearing the word concerning Christ (Rom. 10:17), and the Spirit is the author of Scripture (2 Peter 1:21). Those who confess Christ do so because they have heard and believed the truth about Him that is revealed in Scripture. The Holy Spirit produces in the elect and believing sinner the conviction of sin (John 16:8), and then does His life-giving (2 Cor. 3:6) work of regeneration (John 3:7–8) through the gospel contained in Scripture (1 Peter 1:23).

It is against that backdrop of honoring the Son that the Lord's warning is given. **Everyone who speaks a word against the Son of Man, it will be forgiven him; but he who blasphemes against the Holy Spirit, it will not be forgiven him** (cf. Matt. 12:31; Mark 3:28–29). If speaking **a word against the Son of Man** could not **be forgiven** then no one could be saved. Every Christian is a converted blasphemer who broke God's law, rebelled against His rule, and rejected the truth about His Son. By not being with Christ, they were against Him (Luke 11:23). It is only to blaspheming sinners that Jesus offered grace and salvation (Luke 5:32; 19:10).

But if a person **blasphemes against the Holy Spirit, it will not be forgiven him.** To blaspheme the Holy Spirit is to reject His testimony concerning the Lord Jesus Christ. The Spirit reveals the truth of salvation in Christ, and those who speak evil of that revelation, as the Pharisees had done (Luke 11:15), reject the testimony of the Holy Spirit to Christ (cf. John 15:26). Having cut themselves off from the only source of divine, saving truth, they cannot be saved.

Two passages in Hebrews illustrate the desperate plight of such people. In 6:4–6 the writer of Hebrews warned,

> For in the case of those who have once been enlightened and have tasted of the heavenly gift and have been made partakers of the Holy Spirit, and have tasted the good word of God and the powers of the age to come, and then have fallen away, it is impossible to renew them again to repentance, since they again crucify to themselves the Son of God and put Him to open shame.

Those who received that warning had seen all the evidence the Holy Spirit provided. They had heard the preaching of the gospel, with its offer of grace, mercy, and forgiveness, and witnessed the miraculous signs performed by the apostles (Heb. 2:2–4) that confirmed that their message was from God. Since they rejected all that the Holy Spirit had revealed concerning the Son and Savior, they could never be saved.

There is a similar warning against rejecting the Holy Spirit's testimony to Christ in chapter 10. Once again the writer addressed Jewish people who had been exposed to the truth of the gospel, but were in danger of rejecting it. For those who "go on sinning willfully after receiving the knowledge of the truth," the writer warned, "there no longer remains a sacrifice for sins" (v. 26). There is absolutely no provision for forgiveness of sins apart from the gospel of Christ. Those who reject it face "a terrifying expectation of judgment and the fury of a fire which will consume the adversaries" (v. 27). Eternal punishment in hell awaits those who turn their back on the truth about Jesus Christ. They face even more severe punishment than those who rejected the law of Moses (v. 28), since they have "trampled under foot the Son of God, and . . . regarded as unclean the blood of the covenant by which [they were] sanctified, and [have] insulted the Spirit of grace?" (v. 29). They will experience God's vengeance and punishment for rejecting the Spirit's testimony to the Son (vv. 30–31).

Jesus concluded this section with a promise for those who honor the Spirit by believing His testimony to the Son: **When they bring you before the synagogues and the rulers and the authorities, do not worry about how or what you are to speak in your defense, or what you are to say; for the Holy Spirit will teach you in that very hour what you ought to say.** Believers need not worry that severe trials will shatter their faith in Christ. The Spirit will permanently remain their comforting, strengthening teacher (cf. 1 John 2:20, 27), and will turn their trials into blessing (1 Peter 4:12–14). He is the protecting "power of God," who keeps the believer secure through "various trials" and causes those trials to be "the proof" of his faith—which gives him confidence he is really saved. That is a gift "more precious than gold" (1 Peter 1:5–7). His indwelling presence and empowerment will permanently keep their faith alive, and they will persevere no matter how severe their trials become (Luke 21:19). Even if they are brought **before the synagogues** (i.e., the synagogue courts) or **the rulers and the authorities** (whether Jewish or Gentile), they need **not worry about how or what** they **are to speak in** their **defense, or what** they **are to say. The Holy Spirit will teach** them **in that very hour what** they **ought to say.** He will make certain that to the end of their lives, no matter what the circumstances, what they say will confirm their profession of faith in Jesus Christ. Far from shattering their faith, those trials will provide an opportunity for their greater testimony (Luke 21:12–13).

Despite the plethora of religions, philosophies, worldviews, and beliefs, humanity may be divided into two categories: those who seek honor for themselves (Matt. 6:2), and those who live to honor the triune God. The former receive their reward—honor from men—in this life (Matt. 6:2, 5, 16), and after death will receive eternal punishment. The latter, having believed the Spirit's testimony to the Son, will receive eternal honor from the Father (John 12:26) in the glory of heaven.

The Rich Fool
(Luke 12:13–21)

11

Someone in the crowd said to Him, "Teacher, tell my brother to divide the family inheritance with me." But He said to him, "Man, who appointed Me a judge or arbitrator over you?" Then He said to them, "Beware, and be on your guard against every form of greed; for not even when one has an abundance does his life consist of his possessions." And He told them a parable, saying, "The land of a rich man was very productive. And he began reasoning to himself, saying, 'What shall I do, since I have no place to store my crops?' Then he said, 'This is what I will do: I will tear down my barns and build larger ones, and there I will store all my grain and my goods. And I will say to my soul, "Soul, you have many goods laid up for many years to come; take your ease, eat, drink and be merry."' But God said to him, 'You fool! This very night your soul is required of you; and now who will own what you have prepared?' So is the man who stores up treasure for himself, and is not rich toward God." (12:13–21)

This text provides an opportunity to introduce, in general, the biblical perspective on money, about which the Lord Jesus Christ had much to say. He taught that it is an index to a person's character, so much so that people's view of money is evidence of whether or not their salvation is genuine. After his conversion Zaccheus said, "Behold, Lord, half of my possessions I will give to the poor, and if I have defrauded anyone of anything, I will give back four times as much" (Luke 19:8). In response Jesus declared, "Today salvation has come to this house, because he, too, is a son of Abraham" (v. 9). The immediate change in his attitude toward money was evidence of his spiritual transformation. Jesus affirmed the reality of Zaccheus's salvation based on his willingness to part with his money for the glory of God and to help others.

On the other hand, the rich young synagogue ruler who sought eternal life also heard Jesus' call to repent and follow Him. But when the Lord tested his willingness to give all his possessions to the poor (Matt. 19:21), this man's reaction was the opposite of Zaccheus's. Instead of responding eagerly at any cost to receive the life he sought by obedient faith as Zaccheus had, "he went away grieving; for he was one who owned much property" (v. 22). Zaccheus's changed attitude toward money was evidence of spiritual transformation and true repentance; the rich young ruler's refusal to abandon his materialism manifested his lack of repentance and superficial interest in the spiritual realm.

How people view money is thus an effective barometer of their spirituality. Money is neither good nor bad in itself; corrupt people can put it to evil uses, while good people can put it to righteous uses. Though it is morally neutral, what people do with their money reflects their life priorities. In the words of Jesus, "Where your treasure is, there your heart will be also" (Luke 12:34).

The Bible does not forbid the possession of money; in fact, it teaches that "God [gives the] power to make wealth" (Deut. 8:18), and "richly supplies us with all things to enjoy" (1 Tim. 6:17). That blessing made many godly men in Scripture, such as Job (Job 1:3), Abraham (Gen. 13:2), Isaac (Gen. 26:13), Jacob (Gen. 30:43), Boaz (Ruth 2:1), Solomon (1 Kings 10:23), and Joseph of Arimathea (Matt. 27:57) extremely wealthy. God promised His people that their obedience to Him would result in necessary material, as well as abundant spiritual blessings (Deut. 15:4–6; 26:15; 28:11).

But while the Bible does not forbid possessing money, it does forbid loving it, warning that "the love of money is a root of all sorts of evil, and some by longing for it have wandered away from the faith and pierced themselves with many griefs" (1 Tim. 6:10). Later in that chapter, Paul exhorted Timothy to "instruct those who are rich in this present world not to be conceited or to fix their hope on the uncertainty of riches" (v. 17). To love money is idolatry.

As such, it is also futile and foolish. "Do not weary yourself to gain wealth," the book of Proverbs counsels, "cease from your consideration of it. When you set your eyes on it, it is gone. For wealth certainly makes itself wings like an eagle that flies toward the heavens" (Prov. 23:4–5). Solomon, one of the wealthiest men who ever lived, was wise enough to know that "he who loves money will not be satisfied with money, nor he who loves abundance with its income" (Eccl. 5:10).

Loving money leads to all kinds of problems. Achan's love of money brought disaster to himself, his family, and his people (Josh. 7:1–25). Balaam's love of money prompted his foolish attempt to curse God's people (Num. 22–24), which in turn cost him his life (Num. 31:8). Delilah's love of money led her to betray Samson (Judg. 16:4–6), which ultimately led to the death of thousands (Judg. 16:27–30). Judas's love of money caused him to betray the Lord Jesus Christ (Matt. 26:14–16) and suffer eternal torment in hell (Matt. 26:24; Acts 1:25). Ananias's and Saphira's love of money led them to lie to God (Acts 5:1–2), and brought about their executions through instant divine judgment (Acts 5:5, 10).

The love of money causes people to forget God. Aware of that dangerous reality Agur wisely prayed, "Give me neither poverty nor riches; feed me with the food that is my portion, that I not be full and deny You and say, 'Who is the Lord?'" (Prov. 30:8–9).

Idolizing money causes people to trust in their riches rather than God. Despite his great wealth Job proclaimed that he was innocent of such perverse trust:

> If I have put my confidence in gold,
> And called fine gold my trust,
> If I have gloated because my wealth was great,
> And because my hand had secured so much …

That too would have been an iniquity calling for judgment,
For I would have denied God above.
(Job 31:24–25, 28; cf. Ps. 52:7; Prov. 11:28)

Loving money causes people to be deceived. In Mark 4:19 Jesus warned of "the deceitfulness of riches, and the desires for other things," which "enter in and choke the word, and it becomes unfruitful." Money can produce a deadly spiritual deception. It can be a barrier to people believing the gospel. It can deceive unsaved people who possess it into thinking that all is well in their lives. Such people wrongly assume that their wealth is a sign of God's blessing and favor.

Loving money can cause people to lie, steal, and cheat, compromising their professed convictions rather than resting in God's gracious promises (Matt. 6:25–34; Phil. 4:19).

Loving money is linked to pride. As they were poised to enter the Promised Land Moses cautioned the children of Israel,

> Beware that you do not forget the Lord your God by not keeping His commandments and His ordinances and His statutes which I am commanding you today; otherwise, when you have eaten and are satisfied, and have built good houses and lived in them, and when your herds and your flocks multiply, and your silver and gold multiply, and all that you have multiplies, then your heart will become proud and you will forget the Lord your God who brought you out from the land of Egypt, out of the house of slavery. (Deut. 8:11–14)

In summation, loving money can cause people to be unfaithful to God (Mal. 3:8), and ignore the needs of others (1 John 3:17; cf. Prov. 3:27).

The Bible condemns obtaining money illegitimately, such as by stealing (whether directly [Ex. 20:15; Eph. 4:28], or by fraud [Ps. 37:21; Hos. 12:7; Amos 8:5; Mic. 6:11]), charging exorbitant interest (Ex. 22:25; Lev. 25:36–37; Neh. 5:7, 10; Ps. 15:5; Prov. 28:8) or gambling, which foolishly and wastefully trusts in chance rather than in the providence of God.

In contrast, the Bible lists several legitimate ways to obtain money, including gifts (Acts 20:35; Phil. 4:16), investments (Matt. 25:27), saving (Prov. 21:20; 30:25), wise planning (Prov. 27:23–24), and, primarily, work (Ex. 20:9; Prov. 6:6–8; 14:23; 24:30–34; 28:19; Eph. 4:28; 2 Thess. 3:10; 1 Tim. 5:8).

Those who love money may feel that they never have enough of it. Those who love material things usually abuse credit (cf. Prov. 6:1–5;

11:15; 17:18; 20:16; 22:7)—leading to an eventual lack of resources. People may also lack money because of stinginess (Prov. 11:24), impulsiveness (hastiness; Prov. 21:5), lack of discipline (Prov. 10:4; 13:18), laziness (Prov. 14:23; 19:15; 20:13; 24:30–34), indulgence (Prov. 21:17; 23:21), and craftiness or scheming (Prov. 28:19).

In the opening verses of this chapter Jesus had warned the largely hostile crowd against the deadly danger of hypocritical false religion (vv. 1–12). As He continued his message, the Lord issued a second warning, against materialistic greed. These were by no means randomly chosen sample sins. Rather, they reflect the two essential realms that exist: the material realm, and the spiritual realm. Hypocrisy relates to the spiritual realm; greed to the material world. Those two sins are closely linked. False religion is the love of error; materialism is the love of wealth. People can be deceived by the material world as well as by false religion. Further connecting the two sins, false teachers are inevitably after money (cf. Mic. 3:5; 2 Peter 2:1–3, 14). The Pharisees, for instance, were models of the union of both sins. Not only were they the leading purveyors of false religion in Israel, but they were also "lovers of money" (Luke 16:14). Both their teaching and motive were corrupt.

Christ's instruction on the danger of hypocritical false religion, His solemn warning against blaspheming the Holy Spirit, and His revelation of elevated truths regarding the Trinity was suddenly and surprisingly interrupted. While He was speaking on those topics **someone in the crowd** blurted out, **"Teacher, tell my brother to divide the family inheritance with me."** This man was indifferent to the profound spiritual truths which the Lord was communicating and eager only to fulfill his own selfish desires. Driven by his crass materialism and growing tired of waiting impatiently for Jesus to finish, he interrupted Him.

His request, although inappropriate under the circumstances, was not unusual. By calling Jesus **teacher** (*didaskale*) the man acknowledged Him to be a rabbi, and rabbis routinely arbitrated such civil and family disputes. His request that the Lord **tell** his **brother to divide the family inheritance with** him suggests that his brother was also present. No details are given about the man's motives or the legitimacy of his claim under the Old Testament laws of inheritance (cf. Num. 27:1–11; Deut. 21:15–17). In any case, he was not asking Jesus to weigh his claim on its merits, but rather to arbitrarily rule in his favor.

Refusing to intervene in the dispute Jesus **said to him, "Man** (an unsympathetic response; the term, like the English word "mister," was used to address strangers) **who appointed Me a judge or arbitrator over you?"** Though all spiritual judgment has been granted to Him by the Father (John 5:22, 27), Jesus did not come to judge mundane matters involving earthly possessions, but for a far more significant purpose: "He came to bring men to God, not to bring property to men" (Leon Morris, *The Gospel According to St. Luke,* Tyndale New Testament Commentaries [Grand Rapids: Eerdmans, 1975], 212).

Jesus seized the opportunity offered by the man's request to warn of the danger of greed. That warning unfolds in three sections: the admonition, the anecdote, and the application.

THE ADMONITION

Then He said to them, "Beware, and be on your guard against every form of greed; for not even when one has an abundance does his life consist of his possessions." (12:15)

The word **them** encompasses the entire crowd. The Lord directed this warning to all who were listening, not merely to the man who had interrupted His message. Refusing to sit in judgment on a dispute about money, Jesus instead rendered a far more important judgment on the sin of greed.

Orate (**beware**) is the present imperative form of the verb *oraō* (to see). It means here "to observe," "to recognize," or "to perceive." Jesus challenged His hearers to recognize and be on **guard** (this form of the verb *phulassō* means "take care," "look out for," "avoid," or "flee from") **against every form of greed.** *Pleonexia* (**greed**) can also be translated "covetousness," and refers to an inordinate desire for riches. *The Louw-Nida Greek-English Lexicon of the New Testament* appropriately defines *pleonexia* as "a strong desire to acquire more and more material possessions or to possess more things than other people have, all irrespective of need." As Solomon wisely observed, "He who loves money will not be satisfied with money, nor he who loves abundance with its income" (Eccl. 5:10).

Greed is as damning as false religion, since it is a form of idolatry (Eph. 5:5; Col. 3:5). To focus one's life on the acquisition of material possessions is to worship and serve the creature rather than the Creator (Rom. 1:25). And as Jesus went on to say, **not even when one has an abundance does his life consist of his possessions. Abundance** translates a form of the verb *perisseuō*, which means, "to exceed," "to surpass," "to have more than enough," or "to overflow" (cf. its use in Luke 9:17; 15:17; 21:4). But even such an abundance of material **possessions** does not provide real **life.** The word translated **life** is not *bios* (existence; biological life) but *zōē* (meaningful, purposeful, eternal life). Fulfilling, satisfying life that enjoys eternal peace, joy, hope, and blessing from salvation is not attainable from the material world, no matter how much one possesses.

THE ANECDOTE

And He told them a parable, saying, "The land of a rich man was very productive. And he began reasoning to himself, saying, 'What shall I do, since I have no place to store my crops?' Then he said, 'This is what I will do: I will tear down my barns and build larger ones, and there I will store all my grain and my goods. And I will say to my soul, "Soul, you have many goods laid up for many years to come; take your ease, eat, drink and be merry."' But God said to him, 'You fool! This very night your soul is required of you; and now who will own what you have prepared?' (12:16–20)

To illustrate to His hearers the folly of seeking fulfillment in riches, the Lord **told them a parable.** It was another of His simple, agrarian stories that all present on that occasion would have understood. Like the man who had interrupted His discourse, the imaginary man in the Lord's story was consumed with the pursuit of riches. **"The land of a rich man,"** Jesus began, **"was very productive."** There is no implication of any wrongdoing, dishonesty, or crime in his success; he just had a bumper crop.

Farmers are dependent for their success on circumstances and factors beyond their control. Hence, they should be most grateful to God for His providential control of those factors. But instead of thinking of what he could do to express his thankfulness, **he began reasoning to himself, saying, "What shall I do, since I have no place to store my crops?"** The huge harvest presented a dilemma, since he had insufficient room to store it. Selling the excess risked flooding the market and driving down the price that he could get. After musing on the problem, he decided to **tear down** his **barns and build larger ones, and there** to **store all** his **grain and** his **goods.** By rebuilding larger barns on the site of the existing ones, he would increase his storage capacity without having to build on productive crop land.

His selfish indulgence (illustrated by the repeated personal pronouns "I" and "my") gives insight into the heart of a materialist. Instead of considering giving some of his wealth to God or the poor, this man's only thought was how he could best use his resources for his own benefit. Pleased with his decision, he continued his soliloquy: **'And I will say to my soul, "Soul, you have many goods laid up for many years to come; take your ease, eat, drink and be merry."'** This miserly decision was nothing but blatant, unabashed hedonism.

But as was often the case in Jesus' stories, there was an unexpected twist in this one. Just when this man imagined himself to be set for life, God took his life. After he finished making his self-centered plans **God said to him, 'You fool! This very night your soul is required of you; and now who will own what you have prepared?'** *Aphrōn* (**fool**) refers to someone mindless, lacking sense, ignorant, destitute of knowledge and truth. He had foolishly forgotten God (cf. Pss. 14:1; 53:1), as well as his own mortality. To leave God out of one's plans is the height of folly. James wrote,

> Come now, you who say, "Today or tomorrow we will go to such and such a city, and spend a year there and engage in business and make a profit." Yet you do not know what your life will be like tomorrow. You are just a vapor that appears for a little while and then vanishes away. Instead, you ought to say, "If the Lord wills, we will live and also do this or that." But as it is, you boast in your arrogance; all such boasting is evil. (James 4:13–16)

Failing to consider his own mortality left him to contemplate bitterly the materialist's worst nightmare, aptly expressed by Solomon:

> Thus I hated all the fruit of my labor for which I had labored under the sun, for I must leave it to the man who will come after me. And who knows whether he will be a wise man or a fool? Yet he will have control over all the fruit of my labor for which I have labored by acting wisely under the sun. This too is vanity. (Eccl. 2:18–19; cf. Pss. 39:4–6; 90:10; 103:15–16)

There is no bigger fool than he who does not prepare for the life to come.

THE APPLICATION

So is the man who stores up treasure for himself, and is not rich toward God." (12:21)

The principle expressed in Jesus' parable applies to every **man who stores up treasure for himself, and is not rich toward God—** every person who pursues earthly riches instead of storing up treasure in heaven (Matt. 6:19–20). The location of a person's treasure reveals the true condition of his or her heart (v. 21). It reveals whether they have love for themselves and their possessions, or love for God; whether they worship material things, or worship God; whether they seek fulfillment in this life, or in the life to come; whether they store up treasure on earth only to lose it forever, or store up treasure in heaven and keep it forever.

The antidote to foolish, sinful, materialistic greed is to use what God has given us for His glory and the benefit of others.

Anxiety-Free Living
(Luke 12:22–34)

12

And He said to His disciples, "For this reason I say to you, do not worry about your life, as to what you will eat; nor for your body, as to what you will put on. For life is more than food, and the body more than clothing. Consider the ravens, for they neither sow nor reap; they have no storeroom nor barn, and yet God feeds them; how much more valuable you are than the birds! And which of you by worrying can add a single hour to his life's span? If then you cannot do even a very little thing, why do you worry about other matters? Consider the lilies, how they grow: they neither toil nor spin; but I tell you, not even Solomon in all his glory clothed himself like one of these. But if God so clothes the grass in the field, which is alive today and tomorrow is thrown into the furnace, how much more will He clothe you? You men of little faith! And do not seek what you will eat and what you will drink, and do not keep worrying. For all these things the nations of the world eagerly seek; but your Father knows that you need these things. But seek His kingdom, and these things will be added to

you. Do not be afraid, little flock, for your Father has chosen gladly to give you the kingdom. Sell your possessions and give to charity; make yourselves money belts which do not wear out, an unfailing treasure in heaven, where no thief comes near nor moth destroys. For where your treasure is, there your heart will be also." (12:22–34)

It is an amazing and ironic truth that while ours is perhaps the most affluent, indulged, and comfortable society ever, it is also the most stressed out, worried, and anxiety-ridden one. No worry goes unnamed, undefined, uncataloged, undiagnosed, or unmedicated; worries merely go unrelieved. It is frightening to believe one is trapped in an inexplicable universe; to be nothing more than the chance product of a blind, unguided, random, purposeless process of evolution that did not have man in mind. The thought that there is no one home in the universe results in a sense of cosmic alienation, loneliness, and angst. The anxiety that results takes many forms, to which humanistic psychology gives labels such as obsessive-compulsive disorder, panic disorder, post-traumatic stress syndrome, social anxiety disorder, general anxiety disorder, as well as specific phobias, such as fear of heights, enclosed places, mice, spiders, or snakes. Anxiety affects millions of people and treating it (usually by drugs) is a big business.

The best the world can hope for in superficially dealing with anxiety is to manage it and mask its impact. The Lord Jesus Christ, however, offers a radically different solution to anxiety—He promises to eliminate it. In this passage Jesus forbids worry concerning either the material world or the spiritual realm. In verse 22 He prohibited worry about the physical needs of life when **He said to His disciples, "For this reason I say to you, do not worry about your life, as to what you will eat; nor for your body, as to what you will put on."** In verse 32 He declared that those who believe in Him have nothing to fear in the spiritual realm either: **"Do not be afraid, little flock, for your Father has chosen gladly to give you the kingdom."** The Lord also dealt with worry and anxiety in the Sermon on the Mount (Matt. 6:25, 28, 31, 34; cf. 10:19), indicating that this was a frequent theme of His teaching.

Worry stems from two things: ignorance and, especially, unbelief.

Many Christians needlessly worry because they do not understand the depth of revelation on God's gracious love and care. But there are others who understand God's nature and promises, yet fall into worry anyway. To be needlessly ignorant is a sin, but to knowingly distrust God's self-revelation in Scripture is an even greater sin.

In this passage the Lord Jesus Christ revealed six truths about God that if misunderstood or mistrusted result in worry: divine priority, provision, privilege, preference, paternity, and pleasure.

WORRY FAILS TO UNDERSTAND DIVINE PRIORITY

And He said to His disciples, "For this reason I say to you, do not worry about your life, as to what you will eat; nor for your body, as to what you will put on. For life is more than food, and the body more than clothing. (12:22–23)

The **disciples,** or learners, included the Twelve, others who had believed in Jesus, and those who were still undecided about Him (cf. v. 41). In this discourse (12:1–13:9) the Lord was teaching them about life in the kingdom of God. As noted in the previous chapter of this volume, Jesus was interrupted by a man who demanded that He order his brother to divide the family inheritance with him. Jesus refused, and then told a parable that illustrates the folly of greed (12:13–21). The phrase **for this reason** connects what Jesus was about to say with what He had just said. He had confronted His hearers with a choice. They could, like the foolish man in the parable, store up treasure on earth. Or they could be rich toward God and store up treasure in heaven (12:21; cf. Matt. 6:19–21). Jesus also expressed that truth in the Sermon on the Mount when He declared, "No one can serve two masters; for either he will hate the one and love the other, or he will be devoted to one and despise the other. You cannot serve God and wealth" (Matt. 6:24).

The Lord's teaching might have caused those listening to wonder how their earthly needs would be met if they stored up their treasure in heaven. Jesus reassured them that there was no need for **worry about** their lives, **as to what** they would **eat; nor for** their bodies, **as to what** they would **put on.** The present imperative form of the verb translated **worry** indicates that absence of worry is to continually characterize believers. They need not worry because their trustworthy and loving heavenly Father, the one who clothes the flowers and feeds the birds (vv. 24–28), will provide everything they need. Instead of worrying, they are to cast all their anxiety on Him, knowing that He cares for them (1 Peter 5:7; cf. Phil. 4:19). He may ask them to give up everything, as Jesus did the rich young ruler (Luke 18:22; cf. 9:57–62; Matt. 13:44–46), since those who would follow Christ must deny themselves (Luke 9:23; cf. 5:11, 28; 19:8; Matt. 19:27). But God will continue to sustain those who give Him their highest worship until His purpose for their lives is fulfilled.

Though ancient people, even those in first-century Israel, faced a daily challenge in merely obtaining enough food and clothing to survive (cf. 1 Tim. 6:8) **life,** Jesus told them, **is more than food, and the body more than clothing.** The priority for those in His kingdom is to glorify God by fulfilling the purpose for which He has called them.

WORRY FAILS TO UNDERSTAND DIVINE PROVISION

Consider the ravens, for they neither sow nor reap; they have no storeroom nor barn, and yet God feeds them; how much more valuable you are than the birds! (12:24)

To illustrate His point that God will care for His people, Jesus urged His hearers to **consider the ravens.** As He did earlier in the Sermon on the Mount (Matt. 6:26), the Lord chose birds as an example of God's care for His creatures. Christ's hearers were very familiar with birds. In addition to its numerous native birds Israel, bounded on the east by barren desert and on the west by the Mediterranean Sea, is a major flyway for migratory birds. Hundreds of millions of birds seasonally pass through Israel each year.

Ravens were despised and unclean (Lev. 11:13–15), and are incapable of generating their own food supply, since **they neither sow nor reap.** Also, unlike humans and some animals (e.g., ants; cf. Prov. 6:6–8; 30:25), they do not store food for the long term, having neither **store-**

room nor barn. They survive solely because **God** has designed and made available the food they require to exist.

Scripture repeatedly speaks of God's providential care for His creatures. Job 38:41 asks rhetorically, "Who prepares for the raven its nourishment when its young cry to God and wander about without food?" The psalmist notes that all God's creatures "wait for [Him] to give them their food in due season" (Ps. 104:27; cf. 145:15). Arguing from the lesser to the greater, Jesus then drove home His point. Because God's children are **much more valuable . . . than the birds,** He will not fail to supply their needs until His purpose for their lives ends and He calls them to glory. "The young lions do lack and suffer hunger," wrote David, "but they who seek the Lord shall not be in want of any good thing" (Ps. 34:10). Late in his life he added, "I have been young and now I am old, yet I have not seen the righteous forsaken or his descendants begging bread" (Ps. 37:25; cf. Isa. 33:15–16). Those who disobey and forget God may temporarily be deprived of resources as a result of His chastening (cf. Hag. 1:1–11). Nor is God's providential provision an excuse for laziness (Prov. 20:4; 24:30–34; 2 Thess. 3:10–12). But until their allotted lifespan is over (see the next point), the Lord will sustain those who are His. Thus the sheep of the Great Shepherd can say triumphantly with David, "The Lord is my shepherd, I shall not want" (Ps. 23:1).

WORRY FAILS TO UNDERSTAND DIVINE PRIVILEGE

And which of you by worrying can add a single hour to his life's span? If then you cannot do even a very little thing, why do you worry about other matters? (12:25–26)

People have always been concerned about their health. That concern has in recent times mushroomed into a multibillion dollar industry of vitamins, food supplements, diet plans, health clubs, obsessive exercise, and medicines. It is certainly good to be disciplined and moderate in eating and to otherwise take care of one's physical body. Doing so can aid the health that may enable one to make the most of God's purpose for their life. But many—including some Christians—go beyond that reasonable concern and are obsessed with physical well-being. Paul, however, while acknowledging the benefits of bodily discipline (cf. 1 Cor. 9:25–27) emphasized the greater benefit of spiritual discipline, which leads to godliness (1 Tim. 4:7–8).

All of that worry is foolish and useless. Not only does it take believers' focus off God's priority in their lives, and deny His providential care, worry also ignores His privilege of sovereignly determining their lifespan. Jesus' rhetorical question, **Which of you by worrying can add a single hour** (lit., "cubit"; used here metaphorically as in Matt. 6:27 to refer to the length of one's life) **to his life's span?** emphasizes that no amount of anxiety can add to one's lifetime nor the lifespan that God has determined. Worry is destructive to health and well-being. Since people **cannot do even** the **very little thing** of adding even one hour to their lives, Jesus asked, **why** should they **worry about other** related **matters** such as food and clothing? Their heavenly Father will sustain the lives of those who obey His Word until the end of their God-determined time. On the other hand sin may shorten that time from what it might have been (cf. 1 Cor. 11:29–30; 1 John 5:16).

WORRY FAILS TO UNDERSTAND DIVINE PREFERENCE

Consider the lilies, how they grow: they neither toil nor spin; but I tell you, not even Solomon in all his glory clothed himself like one of these. But if God so clothes the grass in the field, which is alive today and tomorrow is thrown into the furnace, how much more will He clothe you? You men of little faith! And do not seek what you will eat and what you will drink, and do not keep worrying. (12:27–29)

According to evolutionary mythology, humans are nothing more than highly evolved animals. It is true that people share a common bond with plants and animals, since all were created by God. Only humans, however, were created in His image and have the capacity to love, serve, and worship Him. In this section of His discourse, our Lord turned from the issue of food to that of clothing. Having illustrated the former with God's care for birds, Jesus used plants to illustrate His provision of clothing. He revealed God's compassionate preference for those made in His image—especially His children—arguing in a typical Jewish way from the lesser to the greater.

Lilies is a generic term for flowering plants, not a reference to a specific species. **They neither toil nor spin** to make their own clothes, but freely and effortlessly grow within the order of earth's life. Their delicate beauty, however, is unsurpassed by any man-made garment. **Not even Solomon,** the most lavishly dressed man in Israel's history, **in all his glory clothed himself like one of these** ephemeral flowers. Yet they serve no spiritual purpose other than testifying that God is a God of beauty, goodness, order, design, and variety.

The point of the Lord's illustration is that God prefers His people over the birds and plants that He cares for (cf. v. 24). Jesus asked rhetorically, **If God so clothes the grass in the field, which is alive today and tomorrow is thrown into the furnace, how much more will He clothe you?** The question reflects the common use of dried **grass** to fuel the clay ovens used for cooking. If God **so** majestically **clothes** the perishable **grass** that is alive one day and thrown into the fire the next, He will certainly **clothe** His children. Therefore to be consumed with fear, doubt, and worry is to be guilty of having **little faith**—a common rebuke by our Lord (cf. 8:25; Matt. 6:30; 8:26; 14:31; 16:8; 17:20). Lack of faith expresses a lack of trust in God's knowledge of His children's needs, wisdom to know how to meet them, desire to meet them, or power to meet them. Such a weak view of the Creator and Provider dishonors God, produces worry, and restricts the flow of God's blessings (James 1:6–8). Therefore the Lord commanded His disciples, **Do not seek what you will eat and what you will drink, and do not keep worrying.** The pursuit of food and clothing can never be the preoccupation of their lives, so that they live as if diminishing the glory of God.

WORRY FAILS TO UNDERSTAND DIVINE PATERNITY

For all these things the nations of the world eagerly seek; but your Father knows that you need these things. But seek His kingdom, and these things will be added to you. (12:30–31)

Here for the first time in this discourse Jesus spoke of God as the Father of believers. The fatherhood of God is encouraging, for it guarantees that He will supply all their needs (Phil. 4:19)—the very **things** (e.g., what to eat, drink, and wear) **the nations of the world eagerly seek.** *Epizēteō* (**eagerly seek**) is a strengthened form of the verb *zēteō* and means "to search intensely for," "to seek diligently," or "to strongly desire." Those outside of God's kingdom have no claim on Him—no promises, pledges, or guarantees. The only good in their lives comes from common grace. Their father, Satan (John 8:44), makes no promises and provides no benefits. Being dead to spiritual things (Eph. 2:1), "having no hope and without God in the world" (v. 12), and being "darkened in their understanding, excluded from the life of God because of the ignorance that is in them" (4:18), the unregenerate focus on material things. They even create false gods in a vain attempt to help them in their quest, but those gods are only a reflection of evil men and demons—wicked, devious, selfish, violent, untrustworthy, indifferent, capricious, and merciless. Far from expecting help from such gods, the best people can hope for is to placate them.

In striking contrast to the lifeless gods of the pagans, our heavenly **Father knows that** we **need these** material **things** that the unregenerate so desperately seek. Not only does He know, He also sympathizes, and has unlimited resources and power to meet every need of His children. Understanding God's fatherhood removes any legitimate cause for worry, fear, or anxiety.

Paradoxically, believers do not receive the things they need by directly pursuing them. Instead they come indirectly; when they **seek** God's **kingdom . . . these things will be added to** them. Simply stated, our focus is not to be on food, clothes, money, houses, cars, or other material possessions, but rather on worshiping, serving, and proclaiming Christ, living obediently to the Word, and pursuing truth, holiness, and love. "Therefore if you have been raised up with Christ," Paul exhorted the Colossians, "keep seeking the things above, where Christ is, seated at the right hand of God. Set your mind on the things above, not on the things that are on earth" (Col. 3:1–2).

The consuming interest of the believer's life is the kingdom of God, the sphere of salvation where God rules as King and Lord. Everything is to be done for the honor and advance of the lordship of Christ. The Christian life begins with the repentance, self-denial, humility, mourning over sin, and hunger and thirst for righteousness that accompany saving faith, and results in a life of worship, service, and obedience. Those who set their souls to seek the kingdom glories, Jesus promised, will find that God will meet their earthly needs.

The truth that God takes care of His people was well-known to the Jewish people, having been clearly taught in the Old Testament. In Psalm 34 David exulted,

> O taste and see that the Lord is good;
> How blessed is the man who takes refuge in Him!
> O fear the Lord, you His saints;
> For to those who fear Him there is no want.
> The young lions do lack and suffer hunger;
> But they who seek the Lord shall not be in want of any good thing. . . .
> The eyes of the Lord are toward the righteous
> And His ears are open to their cry. . . .
> Many are the afflictions of the righteous,
> But the Lord delivers him out of them all. (vv. 8–10, 15, 19)

Evildoers "will wither quickly like the grass and fade like the green herb" (Ps. 37:2). But on the other hand, God promises to provide for all His peoples' needs:

> Trust in the Lord and do good;
> Dwell in the land and cultivate faithfulness.
> Delight yourself in the Lord;
> And He will give you the desires of your heart.
> Commit your way to the Lord,
> Trust also in Him, and He will do it. . . .
> Evildoers will be cut off,
> But those who wait for the Lord, they will inherit the land. . . .
> The humble will inherit the land
> And will delight themselves in abundant prosperity. . . .
> I have been young and now I am old,
> Yet I have not seen the righteous forsaken
> Or his descendants begging bread. (vv. 3–5, 9, 11, 25)

Isaiah also records God's promise to care for His people:

You who are far away, hear what I have done;
And you who are near, acknowledge My might.
Sinners in Zion are terrified;
Trembling has seized the godless.
"Who among us can live with the consuming fire?
Who among us can live with continual burning?"
He who walks righteously and speaks with sincerity,
He who rejects unjust gain
And shakes his hands so that they hold no bribe;
He who stops his ears from hearing about bloodshed
And shuts his eyes from looking upon evil;
He will dwell on the heights,
His refuge will be the impregnable rock;
His bread will be given him,
His water will be sure. (Isa. 33:13–16)

God will abundantly provide for those who belong to Him, are faithful to Him, and seek His kingdom above all else (Matt. 6:33).

WORRY FAILS TO UNDERSTAND DIVINE PLEASURE

Do not be afraid, little flock, for your Father has chosen gladly to give you the kingdom. Sell your possessions and give to charity; make yourselves money belts which do not wear out, an unfailing treasure in heaven, where no thief comes near nor moth destroys. For where your treasure is, there your heart will be also. (12:32–34)

This promise of giving His own the kingdom is the highpoint of our Lord's teaching on this occasion. The Bible reveals that God was pleased to offer His Son as a sacrifice for sin (Isa. 53:10) and Jesus, "for the joy set before Him endured the cross" (Heb. 12:2). For that reason, God also takes pleasure in His people, those whom Christ redeemed through His death and dwells within. Therefore there is no need for the redeemed, affectionately addressed here as the **little flock,** to be worried or fearful, **for** their **Father has chosen gladly,** not reluctantly, **to give** them **the kingdom.** *Eudokeō* (**gladly**) means "to delight in," or "to take pleasure in." It is God's good pleasure to grant the kingdom in all its fullness to His children. All of its riches of righteousness, peace, and joy

(Rom. 14:17) are theirs as "heirs of God and fellow heirs with Christ" (Rom. 8:17), with whom He will "freely give [them] all things" (v. 32; cf. Matt. 25:21, 23, 34; Luke 22:29; 2 Cor. 9:8; Eph. 1:3–14; James 2:5; 2 Peter 1:3–4). Here is yet another reason that worry is foolish and unnecessary for believers. Since God has freely given them all the glorious riches of His kingdom, how much more willingly will He give them what they need to serve Him in that kingdom?

Knowing that some in His audience were not yet in the salvation kingdom, however, the Lord closed His discourse with an invitation to enter it. But His command, **Sell your possessions and give to charity,** must have shocked and puzzled many in the crowd, as did the one that followed: **Make yourselves money belts which do not wear out, an unfailing treasure in heaven, where no thief comes near nor moth destroys.** Those radical statements seem contrary to the gospel, as if salvation is earned by good deeds. But they merely reiterate a principle Jesus repeatedly emphasized. In the Sermon on the Mount He had made a similar statement:

> Do not store up for yourselves treasures on earth, where moth and rust destroy, and where thieves break in and steal. But store up for yourselves treasures in heaven, where neither moth nor rust destroys, and where thieves do not break in or steal; for where your treasure is, there your heart will be also. (Matt. 6:19–21)

What He said here is exactly what He said to the rich young ruler when He challenged him, "Go and sell your possessions and give to the poor, and you will have treasure in heaven; and come, follow Me" (Matt. 19:21). Earlier in Luke's gospel Jesus said, "If anyone wishes to come after Me, he must deny himself, and take up his cross daily and follow Me" (Luke 9:23; cf. 14:27), while in Luke 14:33 He declared, "So then, none of you can be My disciple who does not give up all his own possessions."

Jesus' concluding statement, **For where your treasure is, there your heart will be also,** interprets and clarifies His meaning. Salvation comes only from embracing Jesus the Messiah by grace through faith (John 1:12; 3:16; 3:36; 5:24; cf. Eph. 2:8–9). Salvation is for the desperate, the humble, who mourn over their sin and hunger and thirst for righ-teousness. But how a person views money and possessions is a measure of the genuineness of repentance and faith. Anything that vies for a person's allegiance to Christ is a roadblock to salvation. As Jesus succinctly put it, "You cannot serve God and wealth" (Matt. 6:24; Luke 16:13). Those who would enter the kingdom of God must submit unreservedly to the rule of the King. They store up their treasure securely in heaven, rather than on earth, understanding that, as the missionary and martyr Jim Elliot wrote, "He is no fool who gives what he cannot keep to gain what he cannot lose" (Elisabeth Elliot, *Shadow of the Almighty* [New York: Harper & Row, 1979], 247).

Anticipating Christ's Return (Luke 12:35–48)

13

"Be dressed in readiness, and keep your lamps lit. Be like men who are waiting for their master when he returns from the wedding feast, so that they may immediately open the door to him when he comes and knocks. Blessed are those slaves whom the master will find on the alert when he comes; truly I say to you, that he will gird himself to serve, and have them recline at the table, and will come up and wait on them. Whether he comes in the second watch, or even in the third, and finds them so, blessed are those slaves. But be sure of this, that if the head of the house had known at what hour the thief was coming, he would not have allowed his house to be broken into. You too, be ready; for the Son of Man is coming at an hour that you do not expect." Peter said, "Lord, are You addressing this parable to us, or to everyone else as well?" And the Lord said, "Who then is the faithful and sensible steward, whom his master will put in charge of his servants, to give them their rations at the proper time? Blessed is that slave whom his master finds so doing when he comes. Truly I

say to you that he will put him in charge of all his possessions. But if that slave says in his heart, 'My master will be a long time in coming,' and begins to beat the slaves, both men and women, and to eat and drink and get drunk; the master of that slave will come on a day when he does not expect him and at an hour he does not know, and will cut him in pieces, and assign him a place with the unbelievers. And that slave who knew his master's will and did not get ready or act in accord with his will, will receive many lashes, but the one who did not know it, and committed deeds worthy of a flogging, will receive but few. From everyone who has been given much, much will be required; and to whom they entrusted much, of him they will ask all the more." (12:35–48)

The Bible teaches that human history will end when the Lord Jesus Christ returns to earth to take His people to be with Him, establish His kingdom, and punish the wicked. The second coming of the Son of God marks the end of the world as we know it. Scripture is as clear and trustworthy on Christ's second coming as it is historical on His first coming. The return of the Lord Jesus in full glory is an essential, central doctrine of the Christian faith, not a secondary, speculative sideshow. Acceptance of it is mandatory, not optional.

In fact, in some ways the doctrine of the second coming is the most important truth of all. It identifies and describes the culmination of redemptive history, encompassing the judgment of the wicked, the blessing of the righteous, and the final and permanent exaltation and glory of the King of kings and Lord of lords. It unambiguously marks the end of history, when God's purpose from before history's beginning will be completed after its conclusion. Every detail revealed in Scripture concerning the culmination of God's redemptive saga will be fulfilled with absolute precision. Therefore anyone who depreciates, obscures, misrepresents or abandons the truth concerning Christ's return comes perilously close to bringing divine judgment upon themselves:

> I testify to everyone who hears the words of the prophecy of this book: if anyone adds to them, God will add to him the plagues which are written in this book; and if anyone takes away from the words of the book

of this prophecy, God will take away his part from the tree of life and from the holy city, which are written in this book. (Rev. 22:18–19)

Yet despite the Bible's clear warning against tampering with the doctrine of the second coming, many well-intended Christians do just that. Although Scripture's description of the rest of redemptive history is precise and accurate, they somehow imagine that the end of the story is vague and uncertain. But tampering with the doctrine of the second coming corrupts biblical prophecy and tarnishes the glory of the Lord Jesus Christ.

Some deny the second coming altogether, such as the adherents of the eschatological view known as hyper-preterism or full preterism. Mainstream preterism holds that the tribulation prophecies in Revelation 6–19 were fulfilled in the past. The only event left on the prophetic calendar is the literal, bodily return of Jesus Christ to end history and bring judgment on the wicked. Hyper-preterists take that view one step further. Misinterpreting Jesus' words in Matthew 24:34, "Truly I say to you, this generation will not pass away until all these things take place," hyper-preterists insist that *all* of biblical prophecy—including the second coming of Christ—was fulfilled in the events surrounding the Roman destruction of Jerusalem in A.D. 70.

This radical view of prophecy relegates not only Christ's second coming, but also the resurrection of the dead and the great white throne judgment to the past. Adherents say that no prophecy of Scripture remains to be fulfilled, so that this present universe is the new heavens and the new earth promised in Isaiah 65:17, 66:22, 2 Peter 3:13, and described in Revelation 21 and 22. Sin will never be finally purged from God's creation. Satan has already been defeated as much as he is going to be. There is no physical, bodily existence beyond the grave; believers exist as eternally disembodied spirits in God's presence, while unbelievers are cast from His presence to live forever in the same form. Hyper-preterists treat such passages as 1 Thessalonians 4:16–17, 1 Corinthians 15:22–24, 53–54, and Philippians 3:21, which clearly promise a bodily resurrection from the dead, as allegories describing spiritual, not literal, realities.

Such radical views of prophecy have disastrous consequences, undermining virtually every fundamental doctrine of the Christian faith.

As noted above, they deny both the second coming of Christ and the bodily resurrection of the saints. But denying the literal, bodily return of Christ means denying His bodily ascension, since as the angels told the apostles, "This Jesus, who has been taken up from you into heaven, will come in just the same way as you have watched Him go into heaven" (Acts 1:11). Even more alarming, denying the bodily resurrection of believers entails denying the bodily resurrection of Christ, whose resurrection is the pattern for all who will rise from the dead (1 Cor. 15:20–23). Amazingly, some hyper-preterists have no qualms about taking their view to that extreme and, in a lame effort to be consistent, conclude that Christ, too, rose from the grave spiritually, not physically.

Of course, denying the bodily resurrection of Jesus Christ destroys the Christian faith. The apostle Paul bluntly warned the Corinthian believers, some of whom were, like contemporary hyper-preterists, denying the bodily resurrection (1 Cor. 15:12), "If Christ has not been raised, your faith is worthless; you are still in your sins" (v. 17). Like Hymenaeus and Philetus before them, hyper-preterists "have gone astray from the truth saying that the resurrection has already taken place, and … upset the faith of some" (2 Tim. 2:18). (I critique hyper-preterism in my book *The Second Coming* [Wheaton, Ill.: Crossway, 1999], 9–13.)

At the other end of the spectrum from those who deny the second coming are those who sensationalize Scripture's teaching on that future reality. They do so by interpreting the Bible's teaching regarding the future through the lens of current events. That approach to prophecy has generated endless speculation about how certain people or events supposedly have fulfilled various prophecies. For example, some were convinced that the catastrophic events of the First World War heralded the coming of the Apocalypse. Later, others suggested that Hitler, Mussolini, or Stalin were the Antichrist.

After the Second World War a spate of books appeared claiming that the rebirth of Israel as a nation in 1948 triggered the countdown to Armageddon. Like the hyper-preterists, their authors misinterpreted Jesus' words in Matthew 24:34. They claimed the "generation" of which the Lord spoke was the one alive in 1948, and hence Armageddon could not be more than forty years away. All were, of course, proved wrong when the rapture, tribulation, and Armageddon failed to materialize by the end of the 1980's.

Even worse, despite the Lord's explicit declaration, "But of that day or hour no one knows, not even the angels in heaven, nor the Son, but the Father alone" (Mark 13:32; cf. Acts 1:7), there has been no shortage of date setting regarding Christ's return. One popular writer on biblical prophecy convinced thousands of people that the rapture and the beginning of the tribulation would take place in 1988. He wrote a runaway best seller, *88 Reasons Why the Rapture Will Be in 1988,* wherein he boldly predicted that the rapture would take place in September of that year during Rosh Hashanah (the Jewish New Year). Undaunted when the rapture failed to take place as predicted, the book's author wrote another book the following year purporting to give *89 Reasons Why the Rapture Will Be in 1989*. Needless to say, that book also was wrong. Still another false prophet wrongly claimed that the Lord would return in 1994. Seventeen years later he predicted that Christ's return would take place in 2011. All predictions were bogus.

But while some deny the second coming outright and others sensationalize it, far more Christians simply appear to be indifferent to it. To them, the return of the Lord is a tertiary doctrine of limited importance, generating endless speculation and controversy while having little practical value in everyday lives. An earthbound Christianity, with its man-centered theology, "Christian" psychology, pragmatism, and pseudo-sanctified materialism (prosperity gospel), is too focused on the here and now to have any real interest in the second coming. The implication is that this life, which is but a fleeting vapor that soon vanishes (James 4:14), is more important than the life to come. What God has planned for the future is far more blessed than anything this present life can offer. To lose sight of the reality that no earthly benefit can compare to the joy and blessing Christ will deliver when He returns is disobedient and foolish.

Underscoring its profound significance, the Bible reveals at least ten reasons why the Lord Jesus Christ must return to earth bodily in the same manner that He left (Acts 1:11).

First, the promise of God demands it. The Old Testament contains more than three hundred prophecies of the coming Messiah, more than one hundred of which were fulfilled in the first coming of Jesus Christ.

That leaves at least two hundred prophecies remaining to be fulfilled at His second coming. For example, in Psalm 2:6–9 God promised that His Son would be King over all the earth and rule with a rod of iron. Isaiah 9:6–7 describes His reign as from David's throne. Micah 4:3 and Jeremiah 23:5 also speak of Christ's earthly rule. Zechariah 14:4–9 graphically describes His return to earth to reign as King. God cannot lie (Titus 1:2) and will not change His mind (Num. 23:19). The promises He has made demand that the Lord Jesus Christ return to fulfill them.

Second, the claims of Jesus demand it. During His earthly ministry He repeatedly referred to His second coming (e.g., Matt. 24:27, 30, 37, 39, 44; Mark 13:26; 14:62; John 14:2–3). He gave an extended and detailed discourse (Matt. 24–25) on the events surrounding His return, and alluded to it in numerous parables (e.g., Matt. 24:45–51; 25:1–13; 25:14–30; Luke 19:12–27). The concluding chapter of the Bible records Jesus' promise to come again in His own words (Rev. 22:7, 12, 20). Christ's veracity and credibility are thus inextricably tied to His second coming.

Third, the testimony of the Holy Spirit demands it. The "Spirit of truth" (John 14:17; 15:26; 16:13) inspired the human writers of Scripture (2 Peter 1:20–21), who repeatedly wrote of Christ's return (e.g., 1 Cor. 1:4–7; Phil. 3:20; Col. 3:4; 1 Thess. 4:16–17; Titus 2:13; Heb. 9:28; James 5:7–8; 1 Peter 1:13; 5:4; 1 John 3:2). The Spirit, along with the Father and the Son, testifies that Jesus Christ will return to earth in triumph and glory.

Fourth, God's program for the church demands it. Having gone to prepare a place in heaven for His people (John 14:2), Jesus will one day return to take them there (v. 3). The New Testament pictures the church as betrothed to Christ (2 Cor. 11:2), who will one day return for His bride (cf. 1 Cor. 1:7; Phil 3:20; 1 Thess. 1:10; Titus 2:13) and take her to the marriage feast (Rev. 19:6–9).

Fifth, the corruption of the world demands it. The return of Jesus Christ is the blessed hope of believers. But for the unbelieving world it is the terrifying prospect of immediate judgment, as the Lord Jesus Christ brings destruction, devastation, and death to the ungodly (cf. John 5:25–29; 2 Thess. 1:7–10; Jude 14–15; Rev. 19:11–16) and establishes His righteous kingdom. The final chapter of earth's history will be written by Jesus, the world's rightful heir (Heb. 1:2; cf. Rev. 5:1–5), when He returns.

Sixth, the future of Israel demands it. The elect remnant of Israel will one day repent and be saved. In Ezekiel's vivid imagery, the dry bones will come to life (Ezek. 37) when, as God promised

> I will pour out on the house of David and on the inhabitants of Jerusalem, the Spirit of grace and of supplication, so that they will look on Me whom they have pierced; and they will mourn for Him, as one mourns for an only son, and they will weep bitterly over Him like the bitter weeping over a firstborn" (Zech. 12:10).

Paul wrote that "all Israel will be saved" when "the deliverer [the Lord Jesus Christ] will come from Zion He will remove ungodliness from Jacob" (Rom. 11:26). That promised cleansing and salvation of Israel requires Jesus to return to earth.

Seventh, the vindication of Christ demands it. It is inconceivable that the last view of Jesus the world will have is one of Him hanging on a cross between two criminals. No unbelievers saw any of His post-resurrection appearances. His resurrection glory, seen only by believers, has not yet been manifested to the world, but that will change one day. At Christ's second coming, the whole world will see "the sign of the Son of Man ... appear in the sky, and then all the tribes of the earth will mourn, and they will see the Son of Man coming on the clouds of the sky with power and great glory" (Matt. 24:30; cf. Rev. 1:7). Jesus, who was publicly mocked, spit upon, scourged, and crucified, must return to reveal Himself to the world as its King and Lord.

Eighth, the judgment of Satan demands it. The usurper who is the present ruler of this world (John 12:31; 14:30; 16:11; cf. 2 Cor. 4:4; Eph. 2:2; 6:12; 1 John 5:19) will not be allowed to maintain his rule forever. Jesus must and will return to vanquish him, destroy his kingdom of darkness, and sentence him to eternal punishment in hell (Rev. 20:2, 10).

Ninth, the hope of believers demands it. Their longing "for the blessed hope and the appearing of the glory of our great God and Savior, Christ Jesus" (Titus 2:13) will not go unrequited. So central to the Christian faith is hope in Christ's return that 2 Timothy 4:8 defines Christians as those who "have loved His appearing." The Lord must return so that "the proof of [believers'] faith, being more precious than gold which is perishable, even though tested by fire, may be found to result in praise and glory and honor at the revelation of Jesus Christ" (1 Peter 1:7).

Finally, the groaning of creation demands it. Romans 8:18–22 personifies creation as groaning under the pain of the curse brought about by the fall (v. 22) and waiting "eagerly for the revealing of the sons of God" (v. 19) when "the creation itself also will be set free from its slavery to corruption into the freedom of the glory of the children of God" (v. 21). That will happen when Jesus Christ returns.

The return of Jesus Christ launches a sequence of events that will mark the end of the universe and this world in their present state. There will be a nuclear holocaust of unimaginable proportions as "the heavens will pass away with a roar and the elements will be destroyed with intense heat, and the earth and its works will be burned up" (2 Peter 3:10; cf. v. 12). Before that happens there will be a final judgment and sentencing to the eternal lake of fire of all the ungodly at the great white throne of God (Rev. 20:11–15). Preceding that judgment, Christ will reign for a thousand years on the earth in His millennial kingdom (Rev. 20:4). Before the advent of the millennial kingdom, Jesus will return in judgment (Matt. 25:31–46) in what is commonly known as the second coming, although the term is broader (Rev. 19:11–21). Before the second coming, the tribulation, the seventieth week of Daniel's prophecy of the seventy weeks (Dan. 9:24–27), will take place for seven years prior to the Lord's return (Rev. 6–19). It will be an unprecedented outpouring of divine judgment. Before the tribulation there will be the rapture of the church, the trigger that sets in motion all of those subsequent events.

Described in three key passages (John 14:1–3, 1 Cor. 15:51–53; 1 Thess. 4:16–17), the rapture is a signless event and could take place at any time. It is to be distinguished from Christ's return at the end of the tribulation. At the rapture, Christ comes for His saints (John 14:3; 1 Thess. 4:16–17), but not to earth. He meets them in the air (1 Thess. 4:17) to take them with Him to heaven (John 14:2–3) to receive their rewards (1 Cor. 3:10–15; 4:1–5; 2 Cor. 5:10) and participate in the marriage feast of the Lamb (Rev. 19:7). In contrast, seven years later, at Christ's return at the end of the tribulation He comes not for His saints, but with His saints (Rev. 19:14; cf. vv. 7–8), who descend with Him from heaven to earth (Zech. 14:4). In addition, the rapture passages mention no accompanying judgment. Nor is there any reference to the church in Revelation 6–19, which describes the tribulation. (For further evidence that the rapture will precede the tribulation, and hence is to be distinguished from the Lord's posttribulational return in judgment, see *Revelation 12–22*, The MacArthur New Testament Commentary [Chicago: Moody, 2000], 212–13.)

This section of Luke 12 reveals the second coming to be both certain and uncertain. The Lord Jesus Christ expressed both realities in verse 40 when He declared that "the Son of Man is coming [a certain event] at an hour that you do not expect [an uncertain time]." The Bible associates various signs with Christ's return at the conclusion of the tribulation, but none of them reveal the exact day and hour when it will occur (Matt. 24:36; 25:13). Because no events are specifically prophesied to precede it, the time of the rapture cannot be determined. Thus, the chronological sequence that it sets in motion (cf. Dan. 7:25; 12:7, 11–12; Rev. 13:5–6) is missing the key piece of information needed to determine when the Lord will return—when that sequence starts. That is one reason why date setting is so irresponsible. The New Testament is clear that these events are imminent, meaning they could start at any time with no warning sign (Heb. 10:25; James 5:7–9; 1 Peter 4:7; 1 John 2:18; Rev. 1:1; cf. Paul's use of "we" and "us" in 1 Thess. 4:15, 17; Titus 2:12–13).

The proper response to that reality in every generation is watchfulness (Matt. 24:42–44; Mark 13:33–37; Luke 21:34–36). In this passage Jesus both exhorted His followers to remain at all times ready for His return, and told them why such readiness is important.

THE EXHORTATION TO READINESS

"Be dressed in readiness, and keep your lamps lit. Be like men who are waiting for their master when he returns from the wedding feast, so that they may immediately open the door to him when he comes and knocks. Blessed are those slaves whom the master will find on the alert when he comes; truly I say to you, that he will gird himself to serve, and have them recline at the table, and will come up and wait on them. Whether he comes in the second watch, or even in the third, and finds them so, blessed are those slaves. But be sure of this, that if the head of the house had known at what hour the thief was coming, he would not have

allowed his house to be broken into. You too, be ready; for the Son of Man is coming at an hour that you do not expect." (12:35–40)

Jesus exhorted His hearers to be ready for His return by means of four simple analogies from everyday life: clothing, lamps, servants, and thieves.

CLOTHING

"Be dressed in readiness, (12:35*a*)

This phrase literally reads "let your loins be girded," and takes into account the long, flowing robes worn by both men and women in Jesus' day. Before they could work, fight, or run, people needed to gather up the loose material and tie it with a sash or belt. As they prepared for the Passover meal, God commanded the people of Israel, "Now you shall eat it in this manner: with your loins girded, your sandals on your feet, and your staff in your hand; and you shall eat it in haste—it is the Lord's Passover" (Ex. 12:11). After his dramatic victory over the prophets of Baal, Elijah "girded up his loins and outran Ahab to Jezreel" (1 Kings 18:46). When he sent his servant Gehazi to heal the Shunamite woman's son, Elisha instructed him, "Gird up your loins and take my staff in your hand, and go your way; if you meet any man, do not salute him, and if anyone salutes you, do not answer him; and lay my staff on the lad's face" (2 Kings 4:29). The Lord commanded Job, "Gird up your loins like a man, and I will ask you, and you instruct Me!" (Job 38:3; cf. 40:7). When He commissioned Jeremiah for his prophetic ministry God said to him, "Now, gird up your loins and arise, and speak to them all which I command you" (Jer. 1:17). Peter's exhortation in 1 Peter 1:13 literally reads, "Gird up the loins of your minds." Jesus' words are a call to **readiness** in light of His imminent return.

LAMPS

and keep your lamps lit. (12:35*b*)

Lamps have only one function: to provide light. In this case, as it often is, light is a figure for knowledge. This is not the time, Jesus warned, to be ignorant of these truths, stumbling around in the darkness; people need to be watchful and make certain that their lamp of knowledge is always **lit.** Later He would use lamps to illustrate the danger of spiritual unpreparedness in the parable of the bridesmaids. Unlike the wise virgins, the foolish ones (Matt. 25:1–12) allowed their lamps to go out. As a result, they were shut out of the wedding by the bridegroom, illustrating metaphorically the danger of spiritual unpreparedness.

The apostle Paul echoed this same warning when he wrote,

> Do this, knowing the time, that it is already the hour for you to awaken from sleep; for now salvation is nearer to us than when we believed. The night is almost gone, and the day is near. Therefore let us lay aside the deeds of darkness and put on the armor of light. Let us behave properly as in the day, not in carousing and drunkenness, not in sexual promiscuity and sensuality, not in strife and jealousy. But put on the Lord Jesus Christ, and make no provision for the flesh in regard to its lusts. (Rom. 13:11–14)

Because Jesus could return at any moment, people need to keep alert, have their lamps always lit, and not be lost in spiritual darkness.

SERVANTS

Be like men who are waiting for their master when he returns from the wedding feast, so that they may immediately open the door to him when he comes and knocks. Blessed are those slaves whom the master will find on the alert when he comes; truly I say to you, that he will gird himself to serve, and have them recline at the table, and will come up and wait on them. Whether he comes in the second watch, or even in the third, and finds them so, blessed are those slaves. (12:36–38)

Weddings in ancient Israel did not start or stop at a specific time. When the preparations were complete, the guests were summoned (cf. Matt. 22:2–4). The celebration could cover up to seven days, depending on how many people were there and how long the food lasted. The **men who** were **waiting for their master** to return **from the wedding feast** could not have known the exact time that he would return. Therefore, they needed to be constantly vigilant, **so that they** could **immediately open the door to him when he** arrived at home.

The master would not fail to reward **those slaves whom** he found **on the alert when he** returned. In an incredible reversal of roles to demonstrate the master's pleasure at such readiness, Jesus says he proceeded to **gird himself to serve** the ones who served him **and** had **them recline at the table** as his equals as he waited **on them.** That is what Jesus Himself did for His beloved disciples (John 13:1–5; cf. Matt. 20:28; Luke 22:27) and will again do at the marriage feast of the Lamb in heaven (Luke 13:28–30). No matter when he arrived—even if it was **in the second watch, or even in the third** (e.g., 9 p.m. to 3 a.m.)—His ready servants would be **blessed.**

THIEVES

But be sure of this, that if the head of the house had known at what hour the thief was coming, he would not have allowed his house to be broken into. You too, be ready; for the Son of Man is coming at an hour that you do not expect. (12:39–40)

In this final analogy the picture is not of a returning master, but of a robbed master. The opening phrase, **But be sure of this,** introduces a truth to be treated as both obvious and emphatic. Looking back on the incident, it is self-evident **that if the head of the house had known at what hour the thief was coming, he would not have allowed his house to be broken into.** Thieves often dug through the walls of houses, and had he known when the thief was going to strike, the master surely would have been ready to prevent or thwart his attempt.

The element of surprise associated with a thief's clandestine arrival fits the point of the unexpectedness of the Lord's return. In Revelation 3:3 Jesus warned the church at Sardis, "Remember what you have received and heard; and keep it, and repent. Therefore if you do not wake up, I will come like a thief, and you will not know at what hour I will come to you." Both 1 Thessalonians 5:2–4 and 2 Peter 3:10 liken the coming of the Day of the Lord to that of a thief.

Jesus summarizes the four analogies He had just given in a concluding exhortation: **You too, be ready; for the Son of Man is coming at an hour that you do not expect.** The only way to avoid spiritual loss is to be ready at all times for Christ's return.

Readiness starts with salvation. Earlier in Luke's gospel Jesus had called people to repent or face rejection when He returns:

> If anyone wishes to come after Me, he must deny himself, and take up his cross daily and follow Me. For whoever wishes to save his life will lose it, but whoever loses his life for My sake, he is the one who will save it. For what is a man profited if he gains the whole world, and loses or forfeits himself? For whoever is ashamed of Me and My words, the Son of Man will be ashamed of him when He comes in His glory, and the glory of the Father and of the holy angels. (9:23–26)

But readiness also involves sanctification. In 2 Peter 3:14 Peter exhorted his readers, "Therefore, beloved, since you look for these things [the cataclysmic destruction of the earth and the heavens described in verses 10–13], be diligent to be found by Him in peace, spotless and blameless" (cf. v. 11). The redeemed demonstrate their readiness for Christ's return by pursuing a godly life.

THE IMPORTANCE OF READINESS

Peter said, "Lord, are You addressing this parable to us, or to everyone else as well?" And the Lord said, "Who then is the faithful and sensible steward, whom his master will put in charge of his servants, to give them their rations at the proper time? Blessed is that slave whom his master finds so doing when he comes. Truly I say to you that he will put him in charge of all his possessions. But if that slave says in his heart, 'My master will be a long time in coming,' and begins to beat the slaves, both men and women, and to eat and drink and get drunk; the master of that slave will come on a day when he does not expect him and at

an hour he does not know, and will cut him in pieces, and assign him a place with the unbelievers. And that slave who knew his master's will and did not get ready or act in accord with his will, will receive many lashes, but the one who did not know it, and committed deeds worthy of a flogging, will receive but few. From everyone who has been given much, much will be required; and to whom they entrusted much, of him they will ask all the more." (12:41–48)

The Lord taught this same principle in Matthew 24:44–51 (cf. Mark 13:33–37 and the similar teaching in the parable of the talents [Matt. 25:14–30]), indicating that it was a recurring theme of His teaching. Uncertain of who the analogies in the previous point were addressed to **Peter,** acting as he often did as the spokesman for the rest, **said, "Lord, are You addressing this parable to us, or to everyone else as well?"** Jesus did not answer directly but indirectly with another parable, one involving two servants. The first is faithful and represents believers, who are ready for Christ's return and will be blessed. The other is unfaithful, and represents unbelievers, who are not ready for His return and will be punished. Since all people fall into one of those two categories, Jesus' parable encompasses everyone.

THE FAITHFUL SERVANT

And the Lord said, "Who then is the faithful and sensible steward, whom his master will put in charge of his servants, to give them their rations at the proper time? Blessed is that slave whom his master finds so doing when he comes. Truly I say to you that he will put him in charge of all his possessions. (12:42–44)

As noted above, **the faithful and sensible steward** represents genuine believers. They manage well the spiritual riches God has entrusted to their care, and are ready for Christ's return. *Pistos* (**faithful**), as always in the New Testament, has the meaning of "believing," indicating that this servant represents the redeemed. *Phronimos* (**sensible**) is the result of salvation and describes a thoughtful, prudent, discreet believer, who has the wisdom that is from above (cf. James 3:17). Believers understand the urgency and importance of living in the hope of their Lord's return. They have not only utilized the resources available to everyone; the revelation of God in creation (Rom. 1:18–32) and the law of God written in the hearts of all people (Rom. 2:15), but also when exposed to the gospel, they believed it, repented, and were saved. Like the faithful steward, they acted responsibly. **Put in charge of his** master's **servants** and instructed **to give them their rations at the proper time,** he did exactly that. His master would not fail to reward him for carrying out his will; **blessed is that slave,** Jesus said, **whom his master finds so doing when he comes.** When He returns Jesus too will reward those who have faithfully carried out His will. Just as the master **put** the faithful servant **in charge of all his possessions,** so also will the Lord give His faithful servants corresponding responsibility in the kingdom (cf. 12:32; 2 Tim. 2:12).

THE UNFAITHFUL SERVANT

But if that slave says in his heart, 'My master will be a long time in coming,' and begins to beat the slaves, both men and women, and to eat and drink and get drunk; the master of that slave will come on a day when he does not expect him and at an hour he does not know, and will cut him in pieces, and assign him a place with the unbelievers. And that slave who knew his master's will and did not get ready or act in accord with his will, will receive many lashes, but the one who did not know it, and committed deeds worthy of a flogging, will receive but few. From everyone who has been given much, much will be required; and to whom they entrusted much, of him they will ask all the more." (12:45–48)

In contrast to the faithful slave the unfaithful **slave,** ignoring the exhortation in verse 40, said **in his heart, "My master will be a long time in coming."** Lacking a sense of urgency, he continued to do whatever satisfied him. And that included brutality inflicted on **the slaves, both men and women,** as well as continuing **to eat and drink and**

get drunk. Instead of properly managing the resources placed in his charge, he used and abused them for his own gluttonous and drunken pleasure. He lived under the illusion that he had plenty of time to enjoy his sin before his master returned.

Many people live their lives under the same illusion, assuming they can do as they please and turn to God just before the end. Such reasoning is both foolish and dangerous, since no one knows when he or she will die, or when the Lord will return. Nor does that faulty reasoning take into account the deadly danger of apostasy (cf. Heb. 6:4–8). It fails to realize that God may harden the hearts of those who persist in hardening theirs so that they reach a point where they cannot repent and believe (John 12:37–40; Rom. 1:24, 26, 28; Heb. 10:26–27).

Illustrating the danger of such faulty reasoning, the unfaithful slave miscalculated the time of his master's return. He was caught unprepared when his **master** came back **on a day when he** did **not expect him and at an hour he** did **not know.** In a drastic and severe act of punishment symbolizing God's judgment on the wicked, his master **cut him in pieces and** assigned **him a place with the unbelievers.** With the word **unbelievers,** the metaphor becomes reality. The **place** where the unprepared will spend eternity is hell, where pleasure is replaced by everlasting pain as "there will be weeping and gnashing of teeth" (Matt. 24:51).

But while all unbelievers will be sentenced to hell, our Lord makes clear here that the degree of their punishment will differ. Jesus alluded to that fact by describing, in addition to the defiant slave mentioned above, two other types of unfaithful slaves. The first was a **slave who knew his master's will and did not get ready or act in accord with his will.** He was not wickedly defiant, but only distracted; he did not abuse his master's resources nor flagrantly defy his master's will, but neither did he obey him. As a result, he was unprepared for his return. Unlike the defiant slave, who received the severer punishment of being cut in pieces, this slave would **receive** the lesser punishment of **many lashes.** A third slave **did not know** his master's will. His ignorance did not exonerate him from judgment, since he **committed deeds worthy of a flogging.** However, he received the least severe punishment of the three, receiving **but few** lashes.

Jesus' concluding words provide the basis for the differing degrees of punishment in hell. **From everyone who has been given much,** He warned, **much will be required; and to whom they entrusted much, of him they will ask all the more.** The degree of punishment for unbelievers is directly related to their knowledge of the truth. The more truth people know, the more dangerous it is for them to reject it. In light of Christ's imminent return, to defiantly reject the gospel, be indifferent to it, or be ignorant of it risks eternal tragedy. The exhortation to all is, "Behold, now is 'the acceptable time,' behold, now is 'the day of salvation'" (2 Cor. 6:2). Everyone is called to "repent and believe in the gospel" (Mark 1:15; cf. Acts 17:30; 26:20), because those who refuse to do so will perish (Luke 13:1–5; John 3:18) and face God's eternal wrath (John 3:36).

The warning in Hebrews 10:26–31 is sobering:

> For if we go on sinning willfully after receiving the knowledge of the truth, there no longer remains a sacrifice for sins, but a terrifying expectation of judgment and the fury of a fire which will consume the adversaries. Anyone who has set aside the Law of Moses dies without mercy on the testimony of two or three witnesses. How much severer punishment do you think he will deserve who has trampled under foot the Son of God, and has regarded as unclean the blood of the covenant by which he was sanctified, and has insulted the Spirit of grace? For we know Him who said, "Vengeance is mine, I will repay." And again, "The Lord will judge His people." It is a terrifying thing to fall into the hands of the living God.

The Tragedy of
Wasted Opportunity
(Luke 12:49–59)

14

"I have come to cast fire upon the earth; and how I wish it were already kindled! But I have a baptism to undergo, and how distressed I am until it is accomplished! Do you suppose that I came to grant peace on earth? I tell you, no, but rather division; for from now on five members in one household will be divided, three against two and two against three. They will be divided, father against son and son against father, mother against daughter and daughter against mother, mother-in-law against daughter-in-law and daughter-in-law against mother-in-law." And He was also saying to the crowds, "When you see a cloud rising in the west, immediately you say, 'A shower is coming,' and so it turns out. And when you see a south wind blowing, you say, 'It will be a hot day,' and it turns out that way. You hypocrites! You know how to analyze the appearance of the earth and the sky, but why do you not analyze this present time? And why do you not even on your own initiative judge what is right? For while you are going with your opponent to appear before the magistrate, on your way

there make an effort to settle with him, so that he may not drag you before the judge, and the judge turn you over to the officer, and the officer throw you into prison. I say to you, you will not get out of there until you have paid the very last cent." (12:49–59)

Unarguably, history's most infamous example of missed opportunity is Judas Iscariot. He had the privilege, granted only to eleven other men, of living and traveling with, and experiencing for three years the presence of Jesus Christ, the Lord of glory incarnate. Yet inconceivably, after that intense personal companionship with the incomparably perfect Son of God, observing daily all the miracles He performed and hearing His unparalleled teaching, Judas betrayed Him and sold Him out for a paltry sum. Against the pure glory of Jesus, Judas appears as the most profoundly wretched man who ever walked on earth. Jesus pronounced his doom when He said of him, "Woe to that man by whom the Son of Man is betrayed! It would have been good for that man if he had not been born" (Matt. 26:24). Judas, who on earth knew intimately the Lord of heaven, will spend eternity away from His presence in hell, relentlessly tormented by his accusing conscience and the memory of his wasted opportunity. But it is the nature of hell that, though those who suffer without relief regret their pain, they do not change their attitude toward the One they rejected.

While in a personal sense Judas is unique, in a categorical sense he is not. There were many Judases in Jesus' day, if not in degree, then certainly in kind. There were many who rejected Him after being exposed to His teaching, seeing His miracles, and witnessing His perfectly holy life. That generation in Israel was the most privileged one in all of human history, being the only one to have God incarnate walk among them. But it was a Judas generation that rejected Jesus despite being eyewitnesses to massive, irrefutable evidence of who He was. The most privileged generation in human history became its most tragic example of wasted opportunity.

Every generation since, including our own, has had its share of Judases. There have always been many who, though exposed to the monumental evidence that clearly reveals Jesus' true identity, refuse to believe. Like Judas, they too will suffer the most severe eternal consequences for wasting their opportunity (cf. Heb. 10:26–31). In this passage Jesus addressed a warning to all such people.

The Jewish messianic expectation, based on their understanding of the Old Testament, was that the Messiah's arrival would usher in unparalleled peace. One of the most well-known messianic passages calls Messiah the "Prince of Peace" (Isa. 9:6). Isaiah 55:12 promised that the nation would be "led forth with peace" in Messiah's kingdom (cf. 66:12; Ps. 72:7; Ezek. 34:25), when God promised to make an everlasting covenant of peace with them (Ezek. 37:26).

In the New Testament Zacharias, the father of John the Baptist, expressed his confident hope that Messiah would "guide our feet into the way of peace" (Luke 1:79). In John 14:27 Jesus promised His followers, "Peace I leave with you; My peace I give to you; not as the world gives do I give to you. Do not let your heart be troubled, nor let it be fearful" (cf. 16:33). Quoting Isaiah 57:19 Paul wrote that Messiah "came and preached peace to [those] who were far away, and peace to those who were near" (Eph. 2:17), and added in Colossians 1:20 that He made that peace "through the blood of His cross" (cf. Luke 2:14; Acts 10:36; Rom. 5:1).

Tragically, Israel forfeited the peace that God had promised when they rejected the Messiah through whom it was to be realized. There could be no national or worldwide peace until Messiah set up His earthly kingdom that was a future reality. In the meantime as redemptive history unfolds, the gospel offers personal peace that comes from salvation only through faith in Jesus. Having rejected the Prince of Peace, Israel had no hope for His kingdom of peace. Neither was there any hope for personal peace.

As noted in chapter 10 of this volume, chapter 12 of Luke's gospel marks a turning point in our Lord's ministry. By now the majority of the Jewish people were hardened in their rejection of Him, and His ministry became largely one of warning. Beginning with the concluding verses of this chapter, those warnings became increasingly urgent and frequent (vv. 56, 59; cf. 13:3, 5, 9, 24–30, 35, 14:24; 19:41–44). In this passage Jesus gave three warnings concerning missed opportunity. He warned of the certainty of coming judgment, the reality of present strife, and the danger of lacking discernment.

THE CERTAINTY OF COMING JUDGMENT

"I have come to cast fire upon the earth; and how I wish it were already kindled! But I have a baptism to undergo, and how distressed I am until it is accomplished! (12:49–50)

The gospel divides all of humanity into two categories, both for time and eternity: the saved and the lost; the redeemed and the unredeemed; those who will spend eternity in heaven, and those who will spend it in hell.

The phrase **I have come** is a technical term used in several places by the Lord to speak of His mission, which He defined in Luke 19:10 when He said that "the Son of Man has come to seek and to save that which was lost" (cf. Matt. 9:13). "Do not think that I came to abolish the Law or the Prophets," He cautioned, "I did not come to abolish but to fulfill" (Matt. 5:17). In John 5:43 Jesus declared to the hostile Jewish leaders, "I have come in My Father's name, and you do not receive Me; if another comes in his own name, you will receive him." Jesus told those listening to His discourse on the bread of life, "I have come down from heaven, not to do My own will, but the will of Him who sent Me" (John 6:38). Jesus is the good shepherd, who "came that [His sheep might] have life, and have it abundantly" (John 10:10). He came "as Light into the world, so that everyone who believes in [Him] will not remain in darkness" (John 12:46); He "did not come to judge the world, but to save the world" (v. 47). On the night before His death Jesus said to the Twelve, "I came forth from the Father and have come into the world; I am leaving the world again and going to the Father" (John 16:28). He told Pilate, "For this I have come into the world, to testify to the truth" (John 18:37).

Although He came to save the lost, Jesus' mission was also one of judgment; He came to **cast fire upon the earth. Fire** is used frequently in Scripture as a picture of God's judgment (e.g., Deut. 32:22; 2 Sam. 22:9; Pss. 21:9; 78:21; 97:3; Isa. 26:11; 29:6; 30:33; 66:15–16; Jer. 4:4; 15:14; 21:12; Lam. 2:3–4; 4:11; Ezek. 21:31; 22:21, 31; Amos 1:4, 7, 10, 12, 14; 2:2, 5; 5:6; Nah. 1:6; Luke 3:9, 16–17; 2 Thess. 1:7–8; Heb. 10:27). The Jewish people were familiar with the Old Testament's predictions of God's fiery judgment, but they believed it would fall on the Gentiles. They never expected that, at Messiah's coming, judgment would fall on them. But Jesus came to save only the lost sinners who repent and believe, and to judge those who refuse to do so, Jew or Gentile. "For judgment I came into this world," He said, "so that those who do not see may see, and that those who see may become blind" (John 9:39; cf. 5:22–30).

Just as fire not only consumes what is combustible, but also purifies what is not, the gospel is a fire that either purges or punishes. Those who believe, it purges; those who reject, it consumes (John 3:18). It is "to the one an aroma from death to death, to the other an aroma from life to life" (2 Cor. 2:16).

The Lord's exclamation, **How I wish it were already kindled** indicates that the judgment to which He referred was yet to take place. The event that would kindle the fire of judgment was His death, which Jesus described as a **baptism** He had to **undergo. Baptism** refers to His immersion under divine judgment (cf. Mark 10:38); before He judged unbelievers for their sin, Christ Himself was judged by God for the sins of believers. That took place at the cross when He "redeemed us from the curse of the Law, having become a curse for us" (Gal. 3:13; cf. Isa. 53:5–6, 11–12; Rom. 4:25; 2 Cor. 5:21; 1 Peter 2:24). In that verse Paul expressed the essential, non-negotiable doctrine of penal substitution, which "states that God gave Himself in the person of his Son to suffer instead of us the death, punishment and curse due to fallen humanity as the penalty for sin. This understanding of the cross of Christ stands at the very heart of the gospel" (Jeffrey, Steve, Michael Ovey, and Andrew Sach, *Pierced for Our Transgressions* [Wheaton, Ill.: Crossway, 2007], 21).

So appalling for the sinless Son of God was the thought of bearing sin and being separated from the Father that He exclaimed, **How distressed I am until it is accomplished!** Although Gethsemane was the most agonizing time of anticipation, Jesus lived His life in a perpetual Gethsemane. There was never a time when He was not aware of the suffering that lay before Him. **Distressed** translates a form of the verb *sunechomai*, which has the basic meaning of being seized, gripped (as with fear), or under the control of something. It is used in Luke 8:37 to speak of the Gerasenes being "gripped with great fear" after Jesus cast out demons into a herd of pigs. In Luke 19:43 it refers to Jerusalem being hemmed in by the Romans during the siege of A.D. 70; in Luke 22:63 it is used of the men holding Jesus, and in 2 Corinthians 5:14 of Christ's love controlling

believers. In Philippians 1:23 Paul used it when he wrote to the Philippians that he was "hard-pressed from both directions, having the desire to
depart and be with Christ, for that is very much better," but realized that
"to remain on in the flesh [was] more necessary for their sake" (v. 24). The
distress of Christ as He agonized in the garden was not a sign of weakness, but of absolute, pure holiness being revealed by the thoughts of
bearing sin and divine judgment. It was the only possible response. How
could the sinless Son not be distressed in agony so that He sweated blood!

Accomplished translates a form of the same verb used of Jesus'
triumphant cry from the cross, "It is finished!" (John 19:30). In my commentary on that verse I noted,

> It was a shout of triumph; the proclamation of a victor. The work of
> redemption that the Father had given Him was accomplished: sin was
> atoned for (Heb. 9:12; 10:12), and Satan was defeated and rendered
> powerless (Heb. 2:14; cf. 1 Peter 1:18–20; 1 John 3:8). Every requirement
> of God's righteous law had been satisfied; God's holy wrath against sin
> had been appeased (Rom. 3:25; Heb. 2:17; 1 John 2:2; 4:10) every
> prophecy had been fulfilled. Christ's completion of the work of
> redemption means that nothing needs to be nor can be added to it.
> Salvation is not a joint effort of God and man, but is entirely a work of
> God's grace, appropriated solely by faith (Eph. 2:8–9). (*John 12–21*, The
> MacArthur New Testament Commentary [Chicago: Moody, 2008], 356)

The Lord was hard-pressed between the suffering and the purpose;
between the pain and the plan; between enduring the cross "for the joy
set before Him" (Heb. 12:2) and desiring to be restored to the glory that
He had had in the Father's presence before coming into the world (John
17:5); between His own will and the Father's. Yet He never wavered, and at
the end said in the garden, "Not My will, but Yours be done" (Luke 22:42).

THE REALITY OF PRESENT STRIFE

**Do you suppose that I came to grant peace on earth? I tell you, no,
but rather division; for from now on five members in one household will be divided, three against two and two against three.
They will be divided, father against son and son against father,
mother against daughter and daughter against mother, mother-**

in-law against daughter-in-law and daughter-in-law against mother-in-law."(12:51–53)

The dividing that the gospel of Christ brings is for both time and eternity. In this discourse Jesus gave a parable involving just and unjust servants that illustrated eternal separation (see the exposition of 12:41–48 in the previous chapter of this volume). The faithful steward represents those who are ready for Christ's return; who are obedient to the gospel, believe in Jesus, confess Him as Lord, and are saved (Rom. 10:9). They will be rewarded with blessedness forever in heaven. The unfaithful stewards (whether defiant, distracted, or ignorant) represent unbelievers, who do not believe in Jesus, accept the gospel, or repent. They will be sentenced to varying degrees of eternal, conscious punishment in hell.

But how they respond to Jesus will not only divide people in eternity, but also in time, as the Lord's rhetorical question, **Do you suppose that I came to grant peace on earth? I tell you, no, but rather division,** reveals (cf. Matt. 10:34). It was reasonable for the Jewish people, based on the Old Testament teaching noted earlier in this chapter, to **suppose** that Messiah would bring **peace.** But Jesus told them that He came not to bring peace, **but rather division.** When there is no peace between sinners and God, there will be no peace between people, but rather strife and conflict.

To illustrate His point Jesus chose society's most fundamental unit, the family (cf. a similar illustration in Micah 7:6). He often used the phrase **from now on** to describe something that was beginning, and would continue to be that way in the future (e.g., Matt. 23:39; 26:29; Luke 5:10; 22:69; John 8:11; 13:19; 14:7). Jesus, who came as the Prince of Peace to reconcile sinners to God (2 Cor. 5:18–20), was and would continue to be, at the same time, the great divider (cf. John 7:43; 9:16; 10:19).

In the Lord's hypothetical illustration **five members in one household will be divided, three against two and two against three. They will be divided, father against son and son against father, mother against daughter and daughter against mother, mother-in-law against daughter-in-law and daughter-in-law against mother-in-law.** (Six members of the household are named, but there are only five individuals, since the mother of the son and the mother-in-law of the daughter-in-law [her son's wife] are the same person.) This illustration has played out innumerable times in real families since Jesus' day. The offense of the gospel often causes those who reject and hate it to make outcasts of even family members who believe it. In Matthew 10:21 Jesus revealed how far family division over Him could go:"Brother will betray brother to death, and a father his child; and children will rise up against parents and cause them to be put to death." But He made the following comforting promise to those who lose their earthly families because of the gospel:"Everyone who has left houses or brothers or sisters or father or mother or children or farms for My name's sake, will receive many times as much, and will inherit eternal life" (Matt. 19:29).

THE DANGER OF LACKING DISCERNMENT

And He was also saying to the crowds, "When you see a cloud rising in the west, immediately you say, 'A shower is coming,' and so it turns out. And when you see a south wind blowing, you say, 'It will be a hot day,' and it turns out that way. You hypocrites! You know how to analyze the appearance of the earth and the sky, but why do you not analyze this present time? And why do you not even on your own initiative judge what is right? For while you are going with your opponent to appear before the magistrate, on your way there make an effort to settle with him, so that he may not drag you before the judge, and the judge turn you over to the officer, and the officer throw you into prison. I say to you, you will not get out of there until you have paid the very last cent." (12:54–59)

These two illustrations are a strong warning to those whose lack of discernment puts them in danger of missing out on salvation. The Jewish people, in particular their religious leaders, viewed themselves as being "a guide to the blind, a light to those who are in darkness, a corrector of the foolish, a teacher of the immature, having in the Law the embodiment of knowledge and of the truth" (Rom. 2:19–20). Yet they failed to discern the monumental and unparalleled reality that God's

Son the Messiah was among them and proved who He was by an incalculable array of supernatural miracles. That shocking lack of discernment in the face of such evidence rendered them permanently blind, darkened, foolish, and immature. They had failed to comprehend the true purpose of the law, which is to point people to Christ (Gal. 3:24), and they failed to confess Him as Lord (Rom. 10:9–10). In these analogies Jesus rebuked them for two things: failing to discern the time, and failing to discern the threat.

FAILING TO DISCERN THE TIME

And He was also saying to the crowds, "When you see a cloud rising in the west, immediately you say, 'A shower is coming,' and so it turns out. And when you see a south wind blowing, you say, 'It will be a hot day,' and it turns out that way. You hypocrites! You know how to analyze the appearance of the earth and the sky, but why do you not analyze this present time? (12:54–56)

The people of Jesus' day lacked the tools of modern meteorologists, such as satellite photos, Doppler radar, and sophisticated computer forecasting models. Yet through making simple observations on familiar patterns, they were able to make accurate short-term weather predictions. **"When you see a cloud rising in the west,** Jesus reminded them, **"immediately you say, 'A shower is coming,' and so it turns out."** Rain generally enters Israel from clouds that form over the Mediterranean Sea to the **west.** When the people noticed **a cloud rising in the west** they correctly surmised, as did Elijah (1 Kings 18:44–45), that **a shower** was **coming.** They also understood that **when** there was **a south wind blowing** from off the deserts in that direction it would **be a hot day.**

Then the Lord applied those two illustrations to His hearers. **You hypocrites!,** He said, **You know how to analyze the appearance of the earth and the sky, but why do you not analyze this present time?** Jesus often referred to the Jewish people, especially their religious leaders, as **hypocrites** (e.g., 13:15; Matt. 6:2, 5, 16; 7:5; 15:7; 22:18; 23:13, 15,

23, 25, 27, 28, 29). Their spirituality was false; their allegiance to God a sham; their virtue superficial; their religion external; their hearts evil.

At first glance, the connection between predicting the weather and hypocrisy may not be readily apparent. But Christ's point is that they were able to routinely reach weather conclusions based on far less evidence than His unparalleled words (Matt. 7:28–29; John 7:46), supernatural works (John 10:25), and sinless life (John 8:46) provided. That evidence conclusively proved Jesus was the Messiah, God incarnate. Their hypocrisy in this instance was in pretending not to have enough evidence to convince them that Jesus was who He claimed to be and demanding more signs from Him (see the discussion of that point in chapter 8 of this volume).

The Jewish people rejected Jesus not because they lacked evidence, but because He was not a military leader overthrowing their enemies and exalting Israel. They also deeply resented His diagnosis of their spiritual condition and saw His claim to be God as blasphemy. When He described them as spiritually impoverished, captive, blind, and oppressed (Luke 4:18), the spiritually proud Jews in the synagogue of His hometown of Nazareth

> were filled with rage as they heard these things; and they got up and drove Him out of the city, and led Him to the brow of the hill on which their city had been built, in order to throw Him down the cliff. But passing through their midst, He went His way. (vv. 28–30)

In John 8:37 He declared to the hostile Jewish religious leaders, "You seek to kill Me, because My word has no place in you." His claim to be God led them to attempt to stone Him (John 8:58–59; 10:31). John 1:11 notes that Christ "came to His own, and those who were His own did not receive Him," because "the Light has come into the world, and men loved the darkness rather than the Light, for their deeds were evil" (3:19).

The people and their leaders had all the light they needed (cf. John 12:35), but chose to reject it. Their spiritual blindness and the judgment it would bring moved the Savior to tears:

> When He approached Jerusalem, He saw the city and wept over it, saying, "If you had known in this day, even you, the things which make for

peace! But now they have been hidden from your eyes. For the days will come upon you when your enemies will throw up a barricade against you, and surround you and hem you in on every side, and they will level you to the ground and your children within you, and they will not leave in you one stone upon another, because you did not recognize the time of your visitation." (Luke 19:41–44)

Failing to properly recognize the **present time** caused them to miss their opportunity (cf. Gen. 6:3; Heb. 6:4–6). Although thousands of individuals would later believe in Jesus and be converted (cf. Acts 2:41; 4:4), the nation as a whole rejected Him then and continues to do so. Israel's failure to discern the times resulted in catastrophic judgment on the nation, which came in A.D. 70 at the hands of the Romans and continues until now. Zechariah prophesied that the judgment on the Jewish nation will not be lifted until they repent and embrace Jesus Christ as Lord (Zech. 12:10).

FAILING TO DISCERN THE THREAT

And why do you not even on your own initiative judge what is right? For while you are going with your opponent to appear before the magistrate, on your way there make an effort to settle with him, so that he may not drag you before the judge, and the judge turn you over to the officer, and the officer throw you into prison. I say to you, you will not get out of there until you have paid the very last cent." (12:57–59)

Jesus' question, **Why do you not even on your own initiative judge what is right?** was a challenge for each person there to examine his or her life. Specifically, He called them to **judge what is right,** by examining their lives with reference to sin. By way of illustration, Jesus chose a situation they would all have been familiar with. He asked them to picture themselves **going with** their **opponent to appear before the magistrate** on a legal matter, presumably involving a financial debt. The *archōn* (**magistrate**) was the official who conducted the preliminary hearing. If he found sufficient cause to proceed with the case, he would turn it over to the **judge** who, if he found the accused guilty, would **turn** him **over to the officer** in charge of the debtor's prison, **and the officer** would **throw** him **into prison.** If that happened, Jesus warned, they would **not get out of there until** they had **paid the very last cent.**

The Lord's point is that those who properly assess themselves will discern their issues of guilt before they stand before the judge and he settles them. In a spiritual sense, this pictures sinners on their way to the great white throne judgment, where they will be found guilty and sentenced to eternal punishment in hell (Rev. 20:11–15). Jesus urges them to carefully discern the horrendous threat of that judgment and embrace the gospel message before it is too late. As the writer of Hebrews warns, "It is appointed for men to die once and after this comes judgment" (Heb. 9:27).

In the face of this terrifying reality God offers the good news of salvation—free and complete pardon to all who believe in Jesus Christ (2 Cor. 5:18–20; Col. 2:13–14; 1 Peter 2:24). Those who accept that pardon and trust in Him will never face judgment (John 5:24; Rom. 5:1; 8:1), since He bore God's just wrath against all the sins of all who would ever believe and fully satisfied the demands of God's justice (Rom. 3:26; 2 Cor. 5:21). God showed His approval of that accomplishment by raising Him from the dead (1 Thess. 1:10). As John Calvin eloquently wrote, "By His obedience, He has wiped off our transgressions; by His sacrifice, appeased the divine anger; by His blood, washed away our sins; by His cross, borne our curse; and by His death, made satisfaction for us" ("Calvin's Reply to Sadoleto," in John C. Olin, ed., *A Reformation Debate* [Reprint; Grand Rapids: Baker, 1976], 66–67). Therefore sinners can confidently heed the call to "seek the Lord while He may be found; call upon Him while He is near" (Isa. 55:6; cf. 2 Cor. 6:2), trusting in Jesus' promise that "the one who comes to Me I will certainly not cast out" (John 6:37).

Living on Borrowed Time
(Luke 13:1–9)

15

Now on the same occasion there were some present who reported to Him about the Galileans whose blood Pilate had mixed with their sacrifices. And Jesus said to them, "Do you suppose that these Galileans were greater sinners than all other Galileans because they suffered this fate? I tell you, no, but unless you repent, you will all likewise perish. Or do you suppose that those eighteen on whom the tower in Siloam fell and killed them were worse culprits than all the men who live in Jerusalem? I tell you, no, but unless you repent, you will all likewise perish." And He began telling this parable: "A man had a fig tree which had been planted in his vineyard; and he came looking for fruit on it and did not find any. And he said to the vineyard-keeper, 'Behold, for three years I have come looking for fruit on this fig tree without finding any. Cut it down! Why does it even use up the ground?' And he answered and said to him, 'Let it alone, sir, for this year too, until I dig around it and put in fertilizer; and if it bears fruit next year, fine; but if not, cut it down.'" (13:1–9)

We live in an era unlike any other in history, an era in which the media provides instant mass communication that keeps people in touch with what is happening all over the world. But the relentless ocean of detailed information, pictures, and videos that floods our TV screens, computer monitors, and cell phones also ensures that we are not isolated from calamities, no matter where they happen. Deadly natural disasters such as earthquakes like those in Mexico, Chile, China, or Japan, tsunamis in the Indian Ocean, volcanic eruptions in Iceland or the Philippines, hurricanes along the eastern seaboard and Gulf coast of the United States, typhoons in Asia, wildfires in Australia or the American Southwest, avalanches in Europe, epidemics in third-world countries, famines in Africa, as well as man-made disasters, such as wars, terrorism, genocide, crimes, riots, and accidents, along with social and economic crises throughout the world, all flood our senses, causing people everywhere to experience vicariously all the pain, sorrow, suffering, and death those catastrophes bring.

That life on this fallen, sin-cursed planet is filled with trouble, sorrow, pain, and suffering is more evident than ever, but has always been the clear testimony of Scripture. One of Job's self-appointed counselors accurately declared, "Man is born for trouble, as sparks fly upward" (Job 5:7), an assessment with which Job agreed: "Man, who is born of woman, is short-lived and full of turmoil" (Job 14:1). "Why did I ever come forth from the womb to look on trouble and sorrow," Jeremiah lamented, "so that my days have been spent in shame?" (Jer. 20:18).

Even more disturbing is the perception that God sometimes seems distant and unconcerned about the world's troubles. Job cried out despondently, "Why do You hide Your face and consider me Your enemy?" (Job 13:24). The psalmist asked pensively, "Why do You stand afar off, O Lord? Why do You hide Yourself in times of trouble?" (Ps. 10:1). Speaking for Israel the sons of Korah asked, "Why do You hide Your face and forget our affliction and our oppression?" (Ps. 44:24). Isaiah wrote, "Truly, you are a God who hides Himself, O God of Israel, Savior!" (Isa. 45:15). David too had moments of doubt and discouragement. In Psalm 13:1 he asked despairingly "How long, O Lord? Will You forget me forever? How long will You hide Your face from me?" (cf. Pss. 77:7–9; 88:14), while in Psalm 22:1 he expressed his anguish in words later uttered by the Lord Jesus

Christ in application to His experience on the cross: "My God, my God, why have You forsaken me?" (cf. Matt. 27:46).

The universality of suffering and God's seeming indifference to it prompts many to ask why He allows bad things to happen to good people. But that question misses the point. No one is truly good, because "there is no man who does not sin" (1 Kings 8:46); "there is no one who does good" (Ps. 14:1); in God's "sight no man living is righteous" (Ps. 143:2); no one can say, "I have cleansed my heart, I am pure from my sin" (Prov. 20:9); "there is not a righteous man on earth who continually does good and who never sins" (Eccl. 7:20). Since "all have sinned" (Rom. 3:23) and "the wages of sin is death" (Rom. 6:23), everyone deserves death. The real question is not why bad things happen to good people, but why good things happen to bad people. That they do reflects God's compassion, grace, and mercy to undeserving sinners.

Because redeemed sinners still live in a fallen world, bad things also happen to believers. But unlike what happens to unbelievers, when believers experience the same calamities, they are not judgments, but remedial trials to benefit them spiritually and bring honor to God. Scripture says that God permits this for several important reasons.

First, God allows bad things to happen to His people to test the validity of their faith. Not for His benefit since He, of course, knows every person's heart (Ps. 44:21; Acts 15:8). But the tests and trials Christians undergo reveal to those being tested whether their faith is genuine. Peter wrote,

> In this [salvation] you greatly rejoice, even though now for a little while, if necessary, you have been distressed by various trials, so that the proof of your faith, being more precious than gold which is perishable, even though tested by fire, may be found to result in praise and glory and honor at the revelation of Jesus Christ. (1 Peter 1:6–7; cf. Deut. 8:2; 2 Chron. 32:31; Prov. 17:3)

Second, God allows bad things to happen to His people to teach them not to depend on themselves, but on His divine resources. "For we do not want you to be unaware, brethren," Paul wrote to the Corinthians, "of our affliction which came to us in Asia, that we were burdened excessively, beyond our strength, so that we despaired even of life; indeed, we had the sentence of death within ourselves so that we would not trust in ourselves, but in God who raises the dead" (2 Cor. 1:8–9; cf. 12:7–10).

Third, God allows bad things to happen to His people to remind them of their heavenly hope. Paul revealed the path of trials to hope when he told the Romans, "We also exult in our tribulations, knowing that tribulation brings about perseverance; and perseverance, proven character; and proven character, hope; and hope does not disappoint" (Rom. 5:3–5; cf. 2 Cor. 4:17–18). Trials take believers to the place where they hope for heaven, where none of the disappointments and suffering of this life will exist or be remembered.

Fourth, God allows bad things to happen to His people to reveal to them what they really love. Those who love the Lord will seek the proven character that suffering produces (Rom. 5:3–4), and willingly suffer in the process of being made more like the Lord Jesus Christ (cf. Acts 5:41; 1 Peter 4:13). On the other hand, those whose affections are set on worldly things will react with disappointment, despair, and even anger when trials take those things from them.

Fifth, God allows bad things to happen to His people to teach them obedience. The psalmist acknowledged, "Before I was afflicted I went astray, but now I keep Your word. . . . It is good for me that I was afflicted, that I may learn Your statutes" (Ps. 119:67, 71). Trouble is discipline from the Lord, which God uses to help believers increase in obedience and holiness (Heb. 12:5–11).

Sixth, God allows bad things to happen to His people so He can show them His compassion (Ps. 103:13). Believers never know God more intimately than when He comforts them in their affliction. It is then that the God of all comfort is near (cf. 2 Cor. 1:4–5).

Seventh, God allows bad things to happen to His people to prepare them for greater usefulness (James 1:2–4). The more they are tested and refined by trials, the more effective their service will be.

Finally, God allows bad things to happen to His people so they can be better equipped to comfort others in their trials, as was the case with Peter (Luke 22:31–32). Second Corinthians 1:4, 6 says,

> [God] comforts us in all our affliction so that we will be able to comfort those who are in any affliction with the comfort with which we ourselves are comforted by God. . . . But if we are afflicted, it is for your comfort and salvation; or if we are comforted, it is for your comfort, which

is effective in the patient enduring of the same sufferings which we also suffer.

And the overarching truth that covers all these purposes is that God, in these hard realities, "causes all things to work together for good to those who love God, to those who are called according to His purpose" (Rom. 8:28).

To the Jewish people of Jesus' day, the explanation of why bad things happened to people was singular and simple: calamities were always God's judgment on sin. In the Old Testament Job's friends reflected that mindset. They continually accused him of hidden sin and exhorted him to confess it. "Remember now," asked Eliphaz, "who ever perished being innocent? Or where were the upright destroyed?" (Job 4:7; cf. 8:20; 22:5–10). The disciples asked Jesus concerning a man born blind, "Rabbi, who sinned, this man or his parents, that he would be born blind?" (John 9:2).

But their theology was wrong; calamities are not God's way of singling out especially wicked people for punishment, as if those who die in a calamity are worse than those who survive. The truth is that all people are guilty sinners deserving of death, and everyone is living on borrowed time. God withholds judgment for a time because He is patient and merciful (Ex. 34:6; Num. 14:18; Pss. 86:15; 103:8)—even to pagan Gentiles (Jonah 3–4), while only those who fear Him savingly will experience God's forgiveness and blessing forever (Ps. 103:17–18). His patience toward those who reject Him will eventually come to an end (Gen. 6:3; Hos. 4:17; 5:6; 9:12).

God's patience provides an opportunity for salvation by giving people time to repent. Paul rebuked those who "think lightly of the riches of His kindness and tolerance and patience, not knowing that the kindness of God leads [them] to repentance" (Rom. 2:4), and offered himself as an example of Christ's perfect patience toward those who believe in Him and receive eternal life (1 Tim. 1:16). Peter wrote that "the Lord is ... patient toward you, not wishing for any to perish but for all to come to repentance" (2 Peter 3:9).

Jesus rejected the faulty theology that views calamity as God's judgment on particularly wicked people and taught that all sinners are living on borrowed time. He did so both through direct instruction, and by means of illustrations.

The Instruction

Now on the same occasion there were some present who reported to Him about the Galileans whose blood Pilate had mixed with their sacrifices. And Jesus said to them, "Do you suppose that these Galileans were greater sinners than all other Galileans because they suffered this fate? I tell you, no, but unless you repent, you will all likewise perish. Or do you suppose that those eighteen on whom the tower in Siloam fell and killed them were worse culprits than all the men who live in Jerusalem? I tell you, no, but unless you repent, you will all likewise perish." (13:1–5)

Christ's instruction called to mind two sensational disasters with which His hearers were familiar. After discussing those calamities, the Lord turned His attention to the true calamity that faces everyone.

THE TEMPLE CALAMITY

Now on the same occasion there were some present who reported to Him about the Galileans whose blood Pilate had mixed with their sacrifices. And Jesus said to them, "Do you suppose that these Galileans were greater sinners than all other Galileans because they suffered this fate? I tell you, no, (13:1–3*a*).

The phrase **on the same occasion** connects this section of the Lord's discourse with the preceding one, in which He had discussed judgment (12:49–59). This was the third time that this discourse, which began in 12:1, was interrupted (cf. 12:13, 41), as Christ's teaching on judgment prompted a serious and real ethical query so that **some** of those **present** asked **Him about the Galileans whose blood Pilate had mixed with their sacrifices.**

Pontius **Pilate** was the fifth Roman governor of Judea. He had been appointed by Tiberius in A.D. 26 and remained in office until he was removed in A.D. 36. Pilate was proud, arrogant, and cynical (cf. John 18:38), and at the same time weak and vacillating. The incident referred to on this occasion was typical of Pilate's rule as governor, which was marked by insensitivity and brutality. Reversing the policy of earlier Roman governors, Pilate had made a grand entrance by marching his troops into Jerusalem carrying standards bearing images that the Jews viewed as idolatrous. The populace protested vehemently against what they viewed as a sacrilege. Pilate ignored their protests and ordered them, on pain of death, to stop the protest. But they called his bluff, and dared him to carry out his threat of execution. Sane enough to be unwilling to massacre many people, Pilate was forced to remove the offending standards. The story is indicative of his poor judgment, stubbornness, arrogance, and vacillation. Pilate again enraged the Jews by taking money from their temple treasury to build an aqueduct to bring water to Jerusalem. In the ensuing protest riots, his soldiers beat and slaughtered many of the protesters.

The specific incident mentioned here involving **the Galileans whose blood Pilate had mixed with their sacrifices** is consistent with what is known of Pilate's character. Such incidents were all too common at that time in Israel (cf. Darrell L. Bock, *Luke 9:51–24:53,* Baker Exegetical Commentary on the New Testament [Grand Rapids: Baker, 1996], 1205). These Galileans may have been involved in some rebellious act against the Romans, who then tracked them to Jerusalem and slaughtered them there. The incident took place in the temple grounds, since the temple was the only place in Israel where sacrifices were offered. It probably happened at Passover, when large numbers of Galileans would have been offering sacrifices. The constant tension between Jews and Romans, coupled with Pilate's brutality, no doubt resulted in many similar unrecorded incidents. Whatever the particulars, Pilate sent his soldiers into the place of sacrifice and slaughtered the Galilean Jews. The ethical question was whether those poor Galileans were worse sinners than all the other people in the temple who were not killed. Their theology, as stated earlier, forced them to this dilemma. If suffering was always a judgment on sin, then these had to be the worst sinners. But they were in the very act of repentance and obedience to God's command to sacrifice.

The Lord understood the thoughts and replied, **"Do you suppose that these Galileans were greater sinners than all other Galileans because they suffered this fate?** That is exactly what they thought. But He said, **I tell you, no."** That answer had to have caught them off guard, since it emphatically rejected their conventional theological wisdom. (Both here and in verse 5 *ouchi* [**no**] is in the emphatic position at the beginning of the sentence.) According to that view, the Galileans in question were worse sinners than others in the temple, or for that matter in Galilee, therefore God allowed them to be slaughtered.

It is true that God sometimes immediately judges sinners for a specific sin, as He did Herod (Acts 12:21–23). There are also built-in judgments for sinful behavior, such as alcohol abuse leading to cirrhosis of the liver, immorality leading to sexually transmitted diseases, or criminal behavior leading to a violent death. Those judgments are not in view here. Jesus was not referring to the inevitable consequences of sin, but rather to catastrophic calamities that fall on people seemingly without discrimination.

For example, half a century after this incident the Roman town of Pompeii would be destroyed by a cataclysmic eruption of Mount Vesuvius. In modern times it was excavated, revealing pornographic images and brothels that testified to its immoral lifestyle. Some might therefore consider its destruction to be God's judgment. But the surrounding towns were no less immoral, and not all of Pompeii's residents engaged in that sordid lifestyle. There may even have been some Christians there who perished along with the rest. Throughout history accidents, natural disasters, crime, and war have killed unbelievers at all points of the moral spectrum, as well as believers. For the unbelievers this means eternal judgment in hell, but for believers it brings eternal blessing in heaven.

The Lord's point is that those who perish in such calamities are no worse sinners than those who survive. Those who live do so because though they deserve to die, God withholds what they deserve for a time in mercy. He allows sinners to live because He is compassionate, gracious, merciful, and "patient toward [them], not wishing for any to perish but for all to come to repentance" (2 Peter 3:9). But God uses calamities to remind all people that death is often an imminent surprise for which they need to be prepared. The exhortation of Jim Elliot, missionary and martyr, is fitting: "When it comes time to die, make sure that all you have to do is die" (cited in Elisabeth Elliot, *Through Gates of Splendor* [Wheaton, Ill.: Tyndale, 1981], 253).

THE TOWER CALAMITY

Or do you suppose that those eighteen on whom the tower in Siloam fell and killed them were worse culprits than all the men who live in Jerusalem? I tell you, no, (13:4–5*a*)

The people of Jerusalem and Judea looked down on the Galileans as inferior (cf. John 7:52). But Jesus' follow up question, **Or do you suppose that those eighteen on whom the tower in Siloam fell and killed them were worse culprits than all the men who live in Jerusalem?** referred to an incident involving Jerusalemites. Like the previous one involving Galileans, nothing further is known about this incident. Siloam is a section of Jerusalem near the southeast corner of the city wall. Water flowed into the pool of Siloam (John 9:7) from the Gihon spring in the Kidron Valley through a tunnel constructed by Hezekiah (2 Kings 20:20). (The pool of Siloam has recently been redis-covered. See "The Pool of Siloam Revealed" [www.bibleplaces.com/poolofsiloam.htm].) A **tower,** perhaps associated with the construction of the Roman aqueduct, **fell and killed** eighteen people. That tragic calamity did not happen to them because those folks were the dregs of Jerusalem's society, since Jesus specifically declared that they **were** not **worse culprits** (lit., "debtors"; i.e., to God for violating His law) **than all the** other **men who** lived **in Jerusalem.** This second illustration rein-forced the Lord's point that natural calamity is not simply God's way of singling out particularly evil people for judgment.

THE TRUE CALAMITY

but unless you repent, you will all likewise perish (13:3*b*, 5*b*)

This twice-repeated phrase introduces the inevitable calamity that everyone faces. That most severe judgment, from which no one escapes, is that **unless** people **repent,** when they die they **will all likewise** (not in the same manner, but with the same certainty) **perish** eternally (cf. Heb. 9:27). In the terms of the Lord's analogy, they need to settle their case before they face the divine judge and it is too late (see the exposition of 12:58–59 in the previous chapter of this volume).

Most of the Jewish people were caught up in a works-righteousness system that forced people to view themselves as good based on selective and superficial perception. Consequently, they refused to see themselves as sinners and therefore rejected (Matt. 11:20) Jesus' call for them to repent (Matt. 4:17), just as they had John the Baptist's before Him (Matt. 3:2). Ultimately, it was because Jesus rejected the Jewish people's hypocritical self-righteousness, categorized them as spiritually blind and impoverished, and boldly confronted their need for repentance that they plotted to murder Him.

Repentance involves two elements. First, sinners must change their mind about their sinfulness. They must acknowledge that God's law is absolutely holy and binding on them, that they have violated it, and deserve eternal punishment in hell. Repentant sinners must first agree that God's diagnosis of their wretched, sinful condition is just and accurate, and that they are powerless to deliver themselves from sin's death grip on them.

The second element of repentance is to affirm that Jesus Christ is the only Savior (cf. Luke 24:47). Repentance is not merely turning from sin, but also turning to God through Christ (cf. 1 Thess. 1:9–10). (I discuss repentance in my books *The Gospel According to Jesus* [Revised and expanded anniversary edition. Grand Rapids: Zondervan, 1988, 1993, 2008] and *The Gospel According to the Apostles* [Nashville: Word, 1993, 2000].)

THE ILLUSTRATION

And He began telling this parable: "A man had a fig tree which had been planted in his vineyard; and he came looking for fruit

on it and did not find any. And he said to the vineyard-keeper, 'Behold, for three years I have come looking for fruit on this fig tree without finding any. Cut it down! Why does it even use up the ground?' And he answered and said to him, 'Let it alone, sir, for this year too, until I dig around it and put in fertilizer; and if it bears fruit next year, fine; but if not, cut it down.'" (13:6–9)

This penetrating parable concludes Luke's record of the Lord's monumental evangelistic sermon that began in 12:1. It reinforces Jesus' point that everyone is living on borrowed time.

A **parable** is an extended analogy or illustration intended to elucidate one point, not an allegory where most or all of the elements carry a symbolic meaning. This is a simple and straightforward analogy that would have been readily understandable to those in an agrarian society. **Fig** trees were common in Israel (fig trees and figs are mentioned more than fifty times in Scripture). Under favorable conditions, they could reach a height of twenty-five feet. In addition to providing fruit, fig trees were an excellent source of shade (cf. John 1:48).

The Lord's story opens with Him inventing **a man** who **had a fig tree which had been planted in his vineyard.** Since it was protected, well-watered, and fertilized, a **vineyard** was an ideal place to plant **a fig tree.** Repeatedly, at the appropriate season, **he came looking for fruit on it,** but to his dismay he **did not find any.** This was an unexpected turn of events, since fig trees normally bore fruit every year, and this one was planted in an especially favorable location. In frustration, he expressed his disappointment and **said to the vineyard-keeper, "Behold, for three years I have come looking for fruit on this fig tree without finding any. Cut it down! Why does it even use up the ground?"** The last statement was not an expression of concern that the barren tree was wasting nutrients that other plants could use. It was rather an expression of disgust over the fruitless tree's uselessness.

But the keeper interceded **and said to him, "Let it alone, sir, for this year too, until I dig around it and put in fertilizer; and if it bears fruit next year, fine; but if not, cut it down."** He proposed giving the tree one more year to bear fruit in which he would work on it by cultivating and fertilizing the soil around it. Then **if it** bore **fruit** the **next**

year, fine; but if not, he agreed that it should be **cut down.** The Greek grammar of those two clauses provides a key to understanding the parable. The fig tree represents Israel (see below). The first conditional clause, **if it bears fruit,** is a third class condition, which expresses something that is unlikely to happen. The next conditional clause, **if not, cut it down,** is a first-class condition, which expresses something likely to happen. The parable illustrates the tragic reality that Israel would continue to fail to bear spiritual fruit even after the arrival of Jesus as Messiah, and would finally be destroyed. Like the tree in the parable, Israel was living on borrowed time and demonstrated little reason to hope for anything different in the future.

Five implications, which sum up the Lord's teaching in this section, may be drawn from this parable.

First, the solitary **fig tree** has an individual application, both national and personal. The national application is to Israel, which like this tree was planted in very fertile, well-tended ground (Isa. 5:1–2). The people of Israel had received continual blessings from God, including "the adoption as sons, and the glory and the covenants and the giving of the Law and the temple service and the promises ... the fathers, and from whom is the Christ according to the flesh" (Rom. 9:4–5). But despite those rich privileges Israel, like the fig tree, failed to produce spiritual life (Isa. 5:3–4; cf. Matt. 21:18–20). The nation was already apostate before Jesus began His ministry. His forerunner John the Baptist had denounced the people as hypocrites (Matt. 3:7), and warned of coming judgment (v. 10). And nothing changed during our Lord's time in the land.

In fact, in the last year of Jesus' ministry, the people remained fixed in unbelief and judgment was fast approaching. There was still time to repent and live before the crucifixion; time for them to hear and believe teaching from Jesus and to repent in the face of more displays of His miraculous power—including one of the most remarkable of all, the raising of Lazarus from the dead (John 11:1–45). But because of their hardened hearts, there was little hope that they would bear the fruit of repentance (cf. Luke 13:34–35; 19:41–44; 20:9–18; 21:20–24). The axe of divine judgment would fall and Israel would be destroyed in a holocaust by the Romans a mere four decades later.

The final four implications are personal. The second one is that those who fail to produce the spiritual fruit that accompanies salvation will be **cut down** in judgment.

Third, judgment is near; **next year** in the parable. At any moment the unsaved could perish, lose their last chance of salvation, and face eternal punishment.

Fourth, the delay in divine judgment is not due to any worthiness on the part of sinners, as the vineyard owner's disgusted statement, **Why does it even use up the ground?** illustrates.

Finally, God's patience with those living on borrowed time is not permanent. Therefore the Bible exhorts sinners to "seek the Lord while He may be found; call upon Him while He is near" (Isa. 55:6). Jesus warned that generation, "For a little while longer I am with you, then I go to Him who sent Me" (John 7:33); "I go away, and you will seek Me, and will die in your sin; where I am going, you cannot come" (John 8:21). For those living on borrowed time "now is the acceptable time, behold, now is the day of salvation" (2 Cor. 6:2), before their time is up and their eternal destiny sealed.

Christot Creates Conflict in the Synagogue
(Luke 13:10–17)

16

And He was teaching in one of the synagogues on the Sabbath. And there was a woman who for eighteen years had had a sickness caused by a spirit; and she was bent double, and could not straighten up at all. When Jesus saw her, He called her over and said to her, "Woman, you are freed from your sickness." And He laid His hands on her; and immediately she was made erect again and began glorifying God. But the synagogue official, indignant because Jesus had healed on the Sabbath, began saying to the crowd in response, "There are six days in which work should be done; so come during them and get healed, and not on the Sabbath day." But the Lord answered him and said, "You hypocrites, does not each of you on the Sabbath untie his ox or his donkey from the stall and lead him away to water him? And this woman, a daughter of Abraham as she is, whom Satan has bound for eighteen long years, should she not have been released from this bond on the Sabbath day? As He said this, all His opponents were being humiliated; and the entire crowd was rejoicing over all the

glorious things being done by Him. (13:10–17)

One of the great gospel paradoxes is that Jesus Christ, the Prince of Peace, who came to bring peace to the souls of men and to the world, has generated more conflict than anyone else who has ever lived. When He was an infant, Simeon told His parents, "Behold, this Child is appointed for the fall and rise of many in Israel, and for a sign to be opposed" (Luke 2:34). Then, in an unsuccessful attempt to eliminate Him, Herod brutally slaughtered all the male infants in the vicinity of Bethlehem (Matt. 2:16).

Throughout His ministry the Lord faced supernatural conflict. At the outset of His public ministry, He defeated Satan in a direct confrontation (Luke 4:1–13). Jesus further confronted the forces of hell by repeatedly casting out demons (Matt. 9:32–33; 12:22; 15:21–28; Mark 1:39; 3:11–12; Luke 4:31–37, 41; 6:18; 7:21; 8:26–33; 9:37–43; 11:14; 13:11–12, 31–32), demonstrating His absolute power and authority (Luke 4:36) over all of Satan's kingdom.

Jesus also was involved in continual conflict and controversy with the general Jewish populace (cf. John 1:11). His characterization of the self-righteous people of Nazareth as spiritually impoverished, captive, blind, and downtrodden so outraged them that they tried to kill Him on the spot by throwing Him off a cliff (Luke 4:16–30; cf. Mark 6:1–6). Even His own half-brothers rejected and mocked Him (John 7:2–9). The fickle crowd who hailed Him as Messiah at the triumphal entry would turn on Him a few days later during Passion Week and demand His execution in the most painful way.

But the Lord's most constant conflict was with the Jewish leaders, especially the architects of the popular form of apostate Judaism—the scribes and Pharisees. They were jealous (Matt. 27:18) of His enormous popularity and angry at His condemnation of their hypocrisy. In an attempt to discredit Him, they denounced Jesus as a blasphemer (Matt. 9:3; 26:65; John 10:33) and a liar (John 8:13), were appalled that He associated with "sinners" (Matt. 9:11; 11:19; Luke 7:39; 15:1; 19:7) and claimed that He was one (John 9:24), condemned Him for violating their non-biblical rabbinic traditions (Matt. 15:1–2), accused Him of being demon possessed (Mark 3:22; John 7:20; 8:48, 52; 10:20) and in league with Satan

(Matt. 9:34; 12:24; Luke 11:15), and otherwise blasphemed Him (Luke 22:65). They challenged His authority (Matt. 21:23; John 2:18), plotted to kill Him (Matt. 26:3–4), arrested Him, put Him through a series of mock trials, and persuaded the Romans to execute Him by crucifixion.

Jesus confronted that corrupt, hypocritical religious establishment by cleansing the temple at the outset of His ministry (John 2:13–22), and again shortly before His death (Luke 19:45–48). He unmasked the religious leaders' hypocrisy (Matt. 6:2, 5, 16; 15:7; 22:18; 23:13–30; Luke 12:1, 56; 13:15), hard-hearted unbelief (Matt. 11:20; John 12:37) that manifested itself by demanding further signs from Him (Matt. 12:38; 16:1; Luke 11:16; John 4:48; 6:30), and exposed their spiritual blindness (Matt. 15:14; 23:16, 17, 19, 24, 26; Luke 6:39; John 9:39–41).

On the night before His death, Jesus warned His followers that they would not escape the same hostility and opposition that He had faced:

> If the world hates you, you know that it has hated Me before it hated you. If you were of the world, the world would love its own; but because you are not of the world, but I chose you out of the world, because of this the world hates you. Remember the word that I said to you, "A slave is not greater than his master." If they persecuted Me, they will also persecute you; if they kept My word, they will keep yours also. (John 15:18–20; cf. Matt. 5:10–12, 44; 10:23; 13:21; Mark 10:30; Luke 21:12)

The Lord's warning proved true as the infant church also faced fierce hostility recorded in the book of Acts. On the very day the church was born the Jews began the persecution by mockingly accusing the apostles of being drunk (2:1–13). Soon after, when Peter and John healed a lame man and preached an evangelistic sermon, the Sanhedrin ordered them to stop speaking and teaching in the name of Jesus (4:1–22). Jealous of the apostles' popularity, the Sanhedrin imprisoned them, beat them and again ordered them not to speak in the name of Jesus (5:17–42). Later Stephen's fearless speech before the Sanhedrin so infuriated them that they stoned him to death (6:9–7:60). That incident sparked an outbreak of persecution, spearheaded by Saul of Tarsus, against the entire church at Jerusalem (8:1–4). Herod Agrippa, seeking to please the Jews, executed the apostle James and imprisoned Peter (12:1–19).

After his dramatic conversion on the way to Damascus Saul,

whose name was changed to Paul, faced intense, lifelong opposition everywhere he went—just as the Lord had promised him (9:16). That hostility began in Damascus (9:19–25) when, to the consternation and outrage of the Jewish community, the former persecutor of Christians began boldly proclaiming that Jesus was the Son of God. After a dramatic escape from Damascus (9:23–25; cf. 2 Cor. 11:32–33), the apostle went to Jerusalem, where he faced further hostility (9:28–29).

Fierce opposition dogged him no matter where he went on his missionary journeys. At Antioch "when the Jews saw the crowds, they were filled with jealousy and began contradicting the things spoken by Paul, and were blaspheming" (13:45). At Iconium "the Jews who disbelieved stirred up the minds of the Gentiles and embittered them against the brethren" (14:2). Paul was stoned and left for dead (14:19–20) at Lystra; beaten and imprisoned at Philippi (16:16–24); forced to flee from Thessalonica (17:1–10) and Berea (17:13–14); confronted by pagan idolatry and challenged by Greek philosophers at Athens (17:16–34); opposed by the Jews (18:5–6) and hauled before the Roman proconsul (vv. 12–17) at Corinth; opposed by both the Jews (19:8–10) and the Gentiles (vv. 23–41) at Ephesus; savagely beaten by rioting Jews and taken into custody by the Romans at Jerusalem (21:27–23:22) and put on trial before the Roman governors Felix (24:1–23) and Festus (25:1–22), and King Agrippa (25:23–26:32). Finally, after a harrowing voyage to Rome, Paul was rejected by many of the Jews there (28:17–29). In addition to the historical record in Acts, Paul referred numerous times in his epistles to the unceasing conflict that he experienced in his ministry (1 Cor. 4:12; 2 Cor. 1:8–10; 4:8–9, 17; 6:4; 7:4–5; 12:10; Gal. 5:11; 1 Thess. 3:1–7; 2 Tim. 1:12, 15–16; 2:8–10; 3:10–11; 4:6, 14–17; cf. Acts 20:19, 23 and Paul's summary in 2 Cor. 11:23–33). Speaking Spirit-inspired truth validated by his own experience, Paul taught that conflict is to be expected in the Christian life, since "all who desire to live godly in Christ Jesus will be persecuted" (2 Tim. 3:12; cf. Rom. 12:14; Phil. 1:28–30; 2 Thess. 1:4–7; Titus 2:8).

In the early years of the church, most of the conflict was generated by the Jews. Eventually, however, the Romans became the church's main antagonists, persecuting it for political, religious, social, and economic reasons (for a detailed explanation of those reasons, see *John 12–21*, The MacArthur New Testament Commentary [Chicago: Moody, 2008], 167–69).

The initial persecution of Christians by the Roman government was instigated by Nero after the devastating fire of A.D. 64 destroyed much of Rome. According to tradition, both Peter and Paul were in Rome and were martyred during that persecution. Toward the end of the first century, another Roman persecution broke out during the reign of Domitian. For the next century and a half, persecution was sporadic and, like those under Nero and Domitian, localized. The first empire-wide persecution came during the reign of Decius in A.D. 250. Decius ordered that everyone offer a sacrifice to the gods and the emperor. Those who refused were subject to arrest, imprisonment, torture, and execution. Decius's persecution, however, was cut short by his death in battle the following year. The last and most violent empire-wide persecution began in A.D. 303 during Diocletian's reign. This persecution was a determined effort to obliterate Christianity altogether. All copies of the Scripture were ordered to be destroyed, and Christians were commanded to offer sacrifices to the Roman gods or face execution. The persecution began to subside when Constantine and his co-emperor Licinius issued an edict granting freedom of worship (A.D. 313). But Licinius reneged on the agreement, allowing persecution to continue in parts of the empire until Constantine became the sole emperor in A.D. 324.

During the Middle Ages persecution against true believers was launched by the Roman Catholic Church, which had replaced secular Rome as the dominant power in Europe. The Inquisition and the St. Bartholomew's Day massacre, are only examples of the millennium of killing believers that marked the Roman Church's efforts to stamp out the preaching of the true gospel. In more recent times, countless thousands of believers continue to be imprisoned or killed by atheistic and Islamic regimes.

Returning to the conflict recorded in this passage, we see that it centered on the Sabbath, the observance of which was at the heart of Judaism. And this was not the first time the Lord had clashed with the religious leaders over the Sabbath (cf. Matt. 12:1–14; Luke 14:1–6; John 5:1–18; 9:1–41). As Lord of the Sabbath (Luke 6:5), Jesus had absolute authority to do as He pleased on that day. But the man-made Sabbath restrictions were so crucial to first-century Judaism that it was inconceivable to the Jewish leaders that anyone who violated them could be from

God (John 9:16). Their religious system was based on self-righteousness, good works, and the performance of various religious rituals and ceremonies. Jesus destroyed the illusion that such pleases God. He pointed out that instead of being spiritually rich, they were spiritually bankrupt; instead of being free, they were in bondage to sin, Satan, death, and judgment. Everyone is unable to keep God's law, not even its two most fundamental commandments, to love God and their neighbor with all their human faculties (Luke 10:25–37).

The Jews were trapped in their own system. They knew of their inability to keep God's law, but instead of repenting, they had developed a system in which they thought to obtain eternal life by keeping (at least externally) some selected and representative commandments (cf. the rich young ruler's question in Matt. 19:16). Chief among those were the extrabiblical regulations with which they had embellished the Sabbath (for a list of some of those regulations, see *Luke 6–10*, The MacArthur New Testament Commentary [Chicago: Moody, 2011], 3–4).

In our Lord's conflict with false religion on this particular Sabbath day, He exposed its error, its spiritual source (Satan), and its hypocrisy.

JESUS' CONFLICT WITH ERROR

And He was teaching in one of the synagogues on the Sabbath. (13:10)

On this Sabbath Jesus, as was His custom (Luke 4:16), **was teaching in one of the synagogues.** The numerous synagogues that existed in Israel provided a convenient venue for the Lord's teaching wherever He went. There were many synagogues in Galilee (since the minimum number of Jewish men required to form a synagogue was ten most, if not all of its 240 cities and villages would have had at least one, and many locations would have had multiple). In the more populous region of Judea, there would have been far more. For example, according to the Jeru - salem Talmud there were arguably 480 synagogues in Jerusalem alone.

Synagogues existed primarily for instruction in the Scriptures. In a synagogue Sabbath service, a passage from the Old Testament would be read, after which a teacher would explain its meaning to the congregation. The synagogues did not function like the Jerusalem temple, since only at the temple could offerings and sacrifices be offered and the feasts and ceremonies celebrated. But after the Babylonians destroyed the temple in 586 B.C., the Jewish exiles began gathering in small groups to hear the teaching of God's Word (cf. Ezek. 8:1; 14:1; 20:1; 33:31). Those informal gatherings eventually developed into the network of synagogues of Jesus' time.

A synagogue had no full-time pastors, teachers, or priests, and anyone approved by the ruler of the synagogue could teach the Old Testament. Oversight and leadership in the synagogues was in the hands of selected elders (cf. Mark 5:22) consisting of laymen, the chief of which was the *archisunagōgos*, or ruler of the synagogue (v. 14; cf. Acts 18:8). It was his responsibility to conduct the worship service and approve the teachers. Throughout His ministry Jesus had frequently taught in the synagogues (Matt. 4:23; 9:35; 13:54; Mark 1:21; Luke 4:15, 31–33; 6:6; John 6:59; 18:20). However as the reaction of this synagogue ruler indicates, synagogues were becoming less receptive to Him. In fact, this passage marks the last recorded appearance of Jesus in a synagogue.

Apparently, the source of the conflict, as on so many occasions previous, was the Lord's **teaching.** As Luke has clearly established, apostate Israel hated His message, because it indicted their religious system of legalism, merit, and self-righteousness. Though the Lord's message was a condemnation of damning apostate religion, it was not only that. The positive thrust of His preaching was salvation from sin and participation in the kingdom of God (Mark 1:14–15; Luke 4:43; 8:1; 9:11). Referred to thirty-one times in Luke's gospel, the kingdom of God is the realm in which God reigns over those who believe in Him. Jesus' message was that by confessing Him as Lord, repentant, believing sinners could be delivered from deception, false religion, Satan's kingdom, sin, and eternal judgment and enter God's kingdom. In His just-concluded sermon (12:1–13:9) Jesus challenged His hearers to enter the kingdom by turning from false religion, fearing God, yielding their lives to the Holy Spirit, rejecting materialism, and pursuing entrance into His kingdom, before it was too late and judgment fell on them. His message in the synagogue would have contained a similar exhortation to repent and believe the gospel message of forgiveness and salvation and the blessings of His kingdom (cf. 5:31–32; 6:20–23; 6:46–49; 9:23–26; 12:8–9; 14:25–33).

Truth, when it is taught where error prevails, inevitably produces conflict, and error prevailed in the synagogue (as it does in all false religious places). The Lord's message has provoked and always will provoke hostility from those who were content in their self-righteousness religion (cf. Luke 4:28–30; 6:11; 11:53). This occasion was no exception, as the synagogue ruler's reaction shows (see the discussion of v. 14 below).

JESUS' CONFLICT WITH SATAN

And there was a woman who for eighteen years had had a sickness caused by a spirit; and she was bent double, and could not straighten up at all. When Jesus saw her, He called her over and said to her, "Woman, you are freed from your sickness." And He laid His hands on her; and immediately she was made erect again and began glorifying God. (13:11–13)

The conflict intensified as the narrative shifted its focus from the Lord's teaching in the synagogue that day to one of those in attendance: **a woman who for eighteen years had had a sickness** caused by a spirit. The exact nature of her condition is not specified; *astheneia* (sickness) simply means "weakness." Whatever it was, it was so debilitating that **she was bent double, and could not straighten up at all.** The Greek text introduces her with the phrase *kai idou* ("and behold"), which "shuts out the idea that this woman was in the synagogue from the start and presents her as slowly and painfully making her way into it while Jesus was in the midst of his teaching" (R. C. H. Lenski, *The Interpretation of St. Luke's Gospel* [Minneapolis: Augsburg, 1946], 734).

But even worse than her terrible physical affliction was the social stigma that went with it. As noted in the previous chapter of this volume, the Jews believed that intense suffering was related to God's punishment for sin. So not only was she an outcast because of that presumed divine displeasure, but in the Jewish social perception of women, she was regarded as second-class. Worst of all, her **sickness** had been **caused by** an evil **spirit,** either by indwelling her or afflicting her (as Satan did Job; Job 2:7).

As she shuffled into the synagogue **Jesus saw her.** Taking note of her pitiable state, **He called her over and said to her, "Woman, you are freed from your sickness"** (cf. 4:33–35; 7:21; Mark 1:23–26; 5:2–13; 7:25–30; 9:17–27; Acts 10:38). **And He laid His hands on her; and immediately she was made erect again and began glorifying God** (5:25–26; 7:16; 17:14–15; 18:43). Without confronting or even referring to the demon, with merely a word and a touch, the Lord broke the evil spirit's hold over her. She was completely and permanently freed from her physical malady, as the perfect tense of the verb indicates. Nothing is said about her having faith—whether she believed Jesus could heal her and sought Him out, or was just coming to the synagogue as she always did. The text does not reveal her spiritual condition before or after her healing, or whether she became a true believer in Jesus Christ that day. What Jesus did was completely sovereign, and totally independent of any faith element from her.

JESUS' CONFLICT WITH HYPOCRITES

But the synagogue official, indignant because Jesus had healed on the Sabbath, began saying to the crowd in response, "There are six days in which work should be done; so come during them and get healed, and not on the Sabbath day." But the Lord answered him and said, "You hypocrites, does not each of you on the Sabbath untie his ox or his donkey from the stall and lead him away to water him? And this woman, a daughter of Abraham as she is, whom Satan has bound for eighteen long years, should she not have been released from this bond on the Sabbath day?" As He said this, all His opponents were being humiliated; and the entire crowd was rejoicing over all the glorious things being done by Him. (13:14–17)

The **synagogue official,** as noted above, was the one who oversaw all aspects of the synagogue's operation. Not surprisingly, this man was a prototypical legalist, far more concerned about the minutiae of rituals, ceremonies, and regulations than he was about the suffering of people.

Such an attitude is all too typical of false religion. Martin Luther's pastoral concern for the common people, who were subjected to crushing burdens by the Roman Catholic Church, helped trigger the Reformation. It was the sale of indulgences (essentially "get out of jail free" passes from purgatory) that was the final straw for Luther. In 1517 the Roman Catholic preacher Johan Tetzel arrived in the vicinity of Wittenberg selling indulgences, using as part of his sales pitch the catchy advertising jingle, "As soon as the coin in the coffer rings, the soul from purgatory springs." Appalled and horrified that his parishioners were flocking to purchase them, Luther posted his famous Ninety-Five Theses condemning indulgences. That event sparked the Reformation.

The Pharisees, too, cared little for the common people, whom they contemptuously dismissed as "this crowd which does not know the Law [and] is accursed" (John 7:49). Jesus denounced them as those who "tie up heavy burdens and lay them on men's shoulders, but they themselves are unwilling to move them with so much as a finger" (Matt. 23:4). The dozens of paralyzing restrictions and regulations associated with it had turned the Sabbath from a day of rest into the most burdensome day of the week.

The synagogue ruler should have glorified and praised God because Jesus' miracle had demonstrated God's heart of mercy and compassion to a desperately needy woman. Instead, he was **indignant because Jesus had healed on the Sabbath.** *Aganakteō* (**indignant**) describes intense displeasure. Though furious that Jesus had broken their man-made Sabbath regulations, he could not deny that the Lord had performed a miracle (cf. Matt. 28:11–14; John 3:2; 7:31; 9:16; 11:47). The synagogue ruler's continued unbelief despite the undeniable miracle he had seen confirms the reality that miracles do not produce faith (Matt. 11:20; Luke 16:31; John 12:37). Saving faith is produced by the Holy Spirit in the hearts of the penitent.

Lacking the courage to confront Jesus directly, the head of the synagogue instead **began saying to the crowd in response, "There are six days in which work should be done; so come during them and get healed, and not on the Sabbath day."** By indicting the woman for allegedly violating the Sabbath, he intended to condemn Jesus.

But the man's criticism was misguided. In what sense **work** was done is not clear. Jesus merely spoke to the woman and laid His hands on her, while all she did was straighten up. Further, there is nothing in the law of God, or even in the rabbinic regulations, that prohibited doing deeds of mercy on the Sabbath, as Jesus pointed out. **"You hypocrites,"** He declared, encompassing both the synagogue ruler and all who shared his narrow legalism, **"does not each of you on the Sabbath untie his ox or his donkey from the stall and lead him away to water him?"** (cf. 14:5; Matt. 12:11). The Mishnah, the codification of Jewish rabbinic law, permitted animals to be led to food and water on the Sabbath so long as they carried no burden. That being the case, Jesus demanded to know why **"this woman, a daughter of Abraham"** (i.e., a Jewish woman; cf. Luke 19:9) **whom Satan has bound for eighteen long years, should . . . not have been released from this bond on the Sabbath day?** What better day to free her from the burden she had borne for so long than the Sabbath, the day of rest?

The result of the confrontation was twofold. First, **all** Christ's **opponents,** both the ruler and those who agreed with him, **were being humiliated.** Their heartless legalism and hypocrisy were unmasked and they were publicly put to shame. They were not, however, personally humbled in the righteous sense of acknowledging and repenting of their hard-hearted hypocrisy. **The entire crowd** of onlookers, on the other hand, **was rejoicing over all the glorious things being done by Him.** But although stunned and amazed by Christ's power to heal (cf. 4:36; 9:43), that does not necessarily mean that they put their full trust in Him. Some did (cf. 16:16), but others continued to reject Him, likely along with those who hailed Him as Messiah at the triumphal entry, then cried for His blood a few days later.

The woman's healing is analogous to God's sovereign work in salvation, and serves as a metaphor for what God offered to do for Israel. He passes by the religious and self-righteous and chooses the humble, bent over by the burden of their sin, without hope of deliverance by their own power, and sovereignly delivers them from Satan's power and lifts them up to praise and glorify Him.

The Increasing Influence of the Kingdom (Luke 13:18–21)

17

So He was saying, "What is the kingdom of God like, and to what shall I compare it? It is like a mustard seed, which a man took and threw into his own garden; and it grew and became a tree, and the birds of the air nested in its branches." And again He said, "To what shall I compare the kingdom of God? It is like leaven, which a woman took and hid in three pecks of flour until it was all leavened." (13:18–21)

The kingdom of God was the constant theme of our Lord's preaching and teaching. At the outset of His Galilean ministry, "Jesus came into Galilee, preaching the gospel of God, and saying, 'The time is fulfilled, and the kingdom of God is at hand; repent and believe in the gospel'" (Mark 1:14–15). Later in His Galilean ministry Jesus "began going around from one city and village to another, proclaiming and preaching the kingdom of God" (Luke 8:1). As He started the Sermon on the Mount He said to His disciples, "Blessed are you who are poor, for yours is the kingdom of God" (Luke 6:20). Confronted by hostile Jewish leaders during His ministry in Judea, the Lord responded, "If I cast out demons by the finger of God, then the kingdom of God has come upon you" (Luke 11:20). After being "questioned by the Pharisees as to when the kingdom of God was coming, [Jesus] answered them and said, 'The kingdom of God is not coming with signs to be observed; nor will they say, "Look, here it is!" or, "There it is!" For behold, the kingdom of God is in your midst'" (Luke 17:20–21). The Lord's post-resurrection ministry to the apostles consisted of "appearing to them over a period of forty days and speaking of the things concerning the kingdom of God" (Acts 1:3). Clearly, Jesus' ministry emphasized preaching the kingdom, because that was what the Father had sent Him to do (Luke 4:43).

The coming of the King had been heralded with much promise and hope. The angel Gabriel appeared to Zacharias and announced that his son John would be the forerunner of the Messiah (Luke 1:5–20). A few months later came the momentous angelic announcements to Mary (Luke 1:26–38) and Joseph (Matt. 1:20–23). She was to bear a son, conceived by the Holy Spirit. He would be the Messiah, the Son of God, Immanuel ("God with us"), who would save His people from their sins. Angels made a startling appearance to some shepherds on the night of Jesus' birth, announcing to them that the Savior, Messiah, and Lord had been born (Luke 2:8–14). John the Baptist's ministry to prepare the people for Messiah's coming and kingdom drew large crowds (Matt. 3:1–6). John's ministry reached its zenith when he pointed to Jesus standing nearby and uttered the dramatic words, "Behold, the Lamb of God who takes away the sin of the world!" (John 1:29)

At the outset of Jesus' ministry, huge crowds followed Him, hoping that He would be the one to free them from the yoke of the hated Romans and set up His reign. But as time went on and Jesus showed no signs of being the political and military deliverer that they were expecting, the people became disillusioned. Adding to their disenchantment with Jesus was the aggressive Jewish leaders' opposition to Him. They viewed Him as an extreme threat to their entire religious structure, as well as to the people's trust and confidence in them. They were also enraged by His condemnation of their blatant hypocrisy. Seeking to discredit and destroy Him, they spread the lie that Jesus performed His miracles by Satan's power (Matt. 9:34; 10:25; 12:24; Luke 11:15; cf. John 7:20;

8:48, 52; 10:20). Desperate to get rid of Him, the Jewish authorities long plotted His death, rejected Him as their king, and had Him executed.

After His resurrection, Jesus met with only 500 believers in Galilee (1 Cor. 15:6; cf. Matt. 28:10, 16–17), and when the church was born on the Day of Pentecost there were only 120 people present (Acts 1:15). From a human perspective, there did not seem to be much to Christ's kingdom, even to His closest followers. Jesus' inner circle consisted of only twelve men, and one of them was a traitor. It looked like a failed effort in a small nation—far from the aspirations of the Jews.

As the Lord's ministry progressed, it became increasingly apparent for those who truly believed in Him as Lord and Messiah that His kingdom was not developing as they had anticipated. In their minds the kingdom was more than spiritual and internal; more than just the sphere of salvation where God rules as King over His people. Like their fellow countrymen, the disciples also expected it to be external; to manifest itself in a blazing, outward show of power and glory as Messiah vanquished all of God's enemies and established His reign on earth in Jerusalem. That expectation prompted James and John to ask Jesus brazenly, "Grant that we may sit, one on Your right and one on Your left, in Your glory" (Mark 10:37). Like Pilate, the disciples wondered in what sense He was a king (Luke 23:1–3), and failed to grasp the reality that His kingdom at that time was not of this world (John 18:36). The visible, earthly kingdom in which the Son of God reigns in glory and majesty with absolute, sovereign power was not for His first coming, but His second in the future (Rev. 20:4–6; cf. Ps. 2:6–9).

The disciples had given up everything to follow Jesus (Matt. 19:27), but so far had little to show for it. They were a ragtag band, with no money except for what they carried in a small box (and from which Judas pilfered [John 12:6]), who depended on the support of others to supply their needs (Luke 8:3). As the Lord's ministry wound down, so did their hopes that the promised messianic kingdom they longed for would appear. Their perception of the kingdom as extremely small, weak, obscure, and despised prompted Christ's teaching in this passage. These two parables, which also appear in Matthew 13, illustrate the truth that its small beginnings are no measure of its final ending. They emphasize that the kingdom's external power, and internal influence will grow beyond what could be comprehended or expected.

THE EXTERNAL POWER OF THE KINGDOM

So He was saying, "What is the kingdom of God like, and to what shall I compare it? It is like a mustard seed, which a man took and threw into his own garden; and it grew and became a tree, and the birds of the air nested in its branches." (13:18–19)

The conjunction *oun* (so, or "therefore") connects these parables with the incident in the previous section (13:10–17). The Lord had interrupted his teaching in a synagogue (v. 10) to heal a woman who had been crippled for eighteen years by a demon-caused illness (v. 11). That demonstration of His power over Satan's kingdom revealed the presence of God's kingdom (cf. Luke 11:20). The Lord then continued His teaching with these two parables, which illustrate the truth that the divine kingdom both externally and internally would expand exponentially from its small beginnings.

Jesus' rhetorical question, **What is the kingdom of God like, and to what shall I compare it?** introduces the first analogy. In an agrarian illustration with which His hearers would have been familiar, Jesus likened the kingdom to **a mustard seed, which a man took and threw into his own garden. A mustard seed** was the tiniest common seed, and was proverbial in Jewish culture for something extremely small (cf. Matt. 17:20; Luke 17:6). Some misinformed critics claim that Jesus' statement in Matthew's account of this parable that the mustard seed "is smaller than all other seeds" (Matt. 13:32) is factually incorrect, since there are other seeds that are smaller. "Seeds," however, translates the plural form of the noun *sperma*, which when used in the New Testament literally (and not figuratively to speak of children or descendants), always refers to familiar seeds sown to produce food crops (Matt. 13:24, 27, 37, 38; Mark 4:31; 1 Cor. 15:35–38), not to all seeds in the plant kingdom. And as botanist Dr. L. H. Shinners explains,

The mustard seed would indeed have been the smallest of those likely to have been noticed by the people at the time of Christ. The principal field crops (such as barley, wheat, lentils, beans) have much larger seeds, as do vetches and other plants which might have been present as weeds (the biblical tares) among grain....There are various weeds and wild flowers belonging to the mustard, amaranth, pigweed, and chickweed families with seeds as small or smaller than mustard itself, but they would not have been particularly known or noticed by the inhabitants....The only modern crop plant of importance with smaller seeds than mustard is tobacco, but this plant is of American origin and was not grown in the Old World until the 16th century and later (cited in John A. Sproule, "The Problem of the Mustard Seed," *Grace Theological Journal* 1 [Spring 1980]: 40)

The point of the story is that the smallest seed **grew** into the largest garden plant (Matt. 13:32). The mustard tree is actually a large shrub that can reach a height of fifteen feet. It was big enough that **the birds of the air nested in its branches. Nested** translates a form of the verb *kataskēnoō*, which literally means "to pitch one's tent" and hence to settle permanently. The reference here is not to birds resting temporarily on the mustard plant's **branches**, but building permanent nests because it is so large and sturdy.

The point of this parable is that viewed from an external, visible perspective, the eventually large size of the kingdom was not perceivable at the start. As noted above, at this point there were only a small number of people who followed Jesus. The kingdom was obscure; it was not distinguished by any majesty, power, or public display. Those things will mark its consummation, not its beginning. Most of the Jewish people were unaware of it (Luke 17:20–21), since its present form was not Messiah's earthly reign, but the sphere of salvation where God reigns in the hearts of His people.

The Lord's illustration is also a powerful prophecy. The kingdom will steadily grow until its consummation, which will be amazingly out of proportion to its beginning. That will happen when the Lord Jesus Christ returns in glory (Rev. 19:11–15) and "the kingdom of the world [becomes] the kingdom of our Lord and of His Christ; and He will reign forever and ever" (11:15).

Despite its humble beginning, the kingdom will enlarge to become the mighty force that the prophets envisioned. In the end, God will establish His Son as king, and He will shatter the nations and rule them with a rod of iron (Ps. 2). Under His reign the righteous will flourish, and there will be peace (Ps. 72: 7). Isaiah predicted that when the suffering servant (Isa. 53) returns to reign over the earth Israel "will spread abroad to the right and to the left. And [her] descendants will possess nations and will resettle the desolate cities" (Isa. 54:3). God will fulfill His promise to Israel given through the prophet Micah:

> I will surely assemble all of you, Jacob, I will surely gather the remnant of Israel. I will put them together like sheep in the fold; like a flock in the midst of its pasture they will be noisy with men. The breaker goes up before them; they break out, pass through the gate and go out by it. So their king goes on before them, and the Lord at their head. (Mic. 2:12–13)

Later in his prophecy Micah recorded a further description of Messiah's earthly kingdom:

> And it will come about in the last days that the mountain of the house of the Lord will be established as the chief of the mountains. It will be raised above the hills, and the peoples will stream to it. Many nations will come and say, "Come and let us go up to the mountain of the Lord and to the house of the God of Jacob, that He may teach us about His ways and that we may walk in His paths." For from Zion will go forth the law, even the word of the Lord from Jerusalem. And He will judge between many peoples and render decisions for mighty, distant nations. Then they will hammer their swords into plowshares and their spears into pruning hooks; nation will not lift up sword against nation, and never again will they train for war. Each of them will sit under his vine and under his fig tree, with no one to make them afraid, for the mouth of the Lord of hosts has spoken. Though all the peoples walk each in the name of his god, as for us, we will walk in the name of the Lord our God forever and ever. "In that day," declares the Lord, "I will assemble the lame and gather the outcasts, even those whom I have afflicted. I will make the lame a remnant and the outcasts a strong nation, and the Lord will reign over them in Mount Zion from now on and forever. As for you, tower of the flock, hill of the daughter of Zion, to you it will come—even the former dominion will come, the kingdom of the daughter of Jerusalem." (4:1–8)

The One whose "goings forth are from long ago, from the days of eternity" (Mic. 5:2) "will arise and shepherd His flock in the strength of the Lord, in the majesty of the name of the Lord His God. And they will remain, because at that time He will be great to the ends of the earth" (v. 4).

Zechariah also describes the coming earthly kingdom:

"Sing for joy and be glad, O daughter of Zion; for behold I am coming and I will dwell in your midst," declares the Lord. "Many nations will join themselves to the Lord in that day and will become My people. Then I will dwell in your midst, and you will know that the Lord of hosts has sent Me to you. The Lord will possess Judah as His portion in the holy land, and will again choose Jerusalem." (2:10–12)

Thus says the Lord of hosts, "It will yet be that peoples will come, even the inhabitants of many cities. The inhabitants of one will go to another, saying, 'Let us go at once to entreat the favor of the Lord, and to seek the Lord of hosts; I will also go.' So many peoples and mighty nations will come to seek the Lord of hosts in Jerusalem and to entreat the favor of the Lord." Thus says the Lord of hosts, "In those days ten men from all the nations will grasp the garment of a Jew, saying, 'Let us go with you, for we have heard that God is with you.'" (8:20–23; cf. 14:9–21)

That the **birds of the air nested** in the mustard plant's branches may also signify that even those who are not a part of the kingdom will benefit from it. Birds were not part of the mustard plant and did not share its life; they merely built their nests in it. Similarly, the unbelieving nations of the world find protection, security, and temporal blessing because of the influence and growth of the kingdom.

The imagery derives from several passages in the Old Testament. Daniel records Nebuchadnezzar's dream in which he saw

a tree in the midst of the earth and its height was great. The tree grew large and became strong and its height reached to the sky, and it was visible to the end of the whole earth. Its foliage was beautiful and its fruit abundant, and in it was food for all. The beasts of the field found shade under it, and the birds of the sky dwelt in its branches, and all living creatures fed themselves from it. (Dan. 4:10–12)

Daniel's tree symbolized the Babylonian Empire (vv. 20–22), which provided benefits to the nations that it conquered. The same imagery described the greatness of Babylon's predecessor, Assyria:

Behold, Assyria was a cedar in Lebanon with beautiful branches and forest shade, and very high, and its top was among the clouds. The waters made it grow, the deep made it high. With its rivers it continually extended all around its planting place, and sent out its channels to all the trees of the field. Therefore its height was loftier than all the trees of the field and its boughs became many and its branches long because of many waters as it spread them out. All the birds of the heavens nested in its boughs, and under its branches all the beasts of the field gave birth, and all great nations lived under its shade. (Ezek. 31:3–6)

Earlier in Ezekiel God described Messiah's kingdom in similar terms, indicating that in that kingdom all the nations of the earth will be blessed:

Thus says the Lord God, "I will also take a sprig from the lofty top of the cedar and set it out; I will pluck from the topmost of its young twigs a tender one and I will plant it on a high and lofty mountain. On the high mountain of Israel I will plant it, that it may bring forth boughs and bear fruit and become a stately cedar. And birds of every kind will nest under it; they will nest in the shade of its branches. All the trees of the field will know that I am the Lord; I bring down the high tree, exalt the low tree, dry up the green tree and make the dry tree flourish. I am the Lord; I have spoken, and I will perform it." (17:22–24)

As the visible kingdom developed it brought many benefits to grace this sin-darkened world. Christianity has opposed social evils, produced many of the world's greatest scientists, promoted education, and in general given rise to much that has comforted and benefited mankind. In society, as well as in the family (1 Cor. 7:14), the unregenerate are blessed by their association with the redeemed subjects of the kingdom.

THE INTERNAL INFLUENCE OF THE KINGDOM

And again He said, "To what shall I compare the kingdom of God? It is like leaven, which a woman took and hid in three pecks of flour until it was all leavened." (13:20–21)

The previous parable emphasized the external growth of the kingdom; this one focuses on its internal influence. As He did in the first parable, Jesus introduced this one with a rhetorical question, **To what**

shall I compare the kingdom of God? His answer likens the kingdom to leaven, which symbolizes influence, often for evil (e.g., Matt. 16:6, 11, 12; 1 Cor. 5:6–8; Gal. 5:9). Here, however, it illustrates the positive influence of the kingdom.

Leaven was a fermented substance mixed into bread dough that permeated it and caused it to swell up, bubble up, and expand. Making bread was generally done by women, so in the parable **a woman** took the leaven and hid it **in three pecks** (about fifty pounds) **of flour until it was all leavened.** Over time, the leaven would transform the dough into something far better than unleavened dough, which produces hard, dry, flat, less appetizing crackers.

In the Lord's illustration **flour** represents the world, and **leaven** represents the kingdom. Like leaven, which is mixed into the dough and thus hidden from sight, the kingdom is hidden in the world. The glorious manifestation of the children of God (Rom. 8:18–21) has not yet happened, so it is not obvious to the world who the subjects of the kingdom are. But like leaven transforms dough the kingdom, though hidden, influences the world through the testimony and righteous lives of its subjects, the message of the gospel, and the convicting work of the Spirit.

Are Just a Few Being Saved?
(Luke 13:22–30)

18

And He was passing through from one city and village to another, teaching, and proceeding on His way to Jerusalem. And someone said to Him, "Lord, are there just a few who are being saved?" And He said to them, "Strive to enter through the narrow door; for many, I tell you, will seek to enter and will not be able. Once the head of the house gets up and shuts the door, and you begin to stand outside and knock on the door, saying, 'Lord, open up to us!' then He will answer and say to you, 'I do not know where you are from.' Then you will begin to say, 'We ate and drank in Your presence, and You taught in our streets'; and He will say, 'I tell you, I do not know where you are from; depart from me, all you evildoers.' In that place there will be weeping and gnashing of teeth when you see Abraham and Isaac and Jacob and all the prophets in the kingdom of God, but yourselves being thrown out. And they will come from east and west and from north and south, and will recline at the table in the kingdom of God. And behold, some are last who will be first and some are first who will be last." (13:22–30)

Throughout His ministry, Jesus clarified and expanded His teaching by answering questions that people asked Him (e.g., Matt. 13:10–11; 17:10–11; 21:20–21; 24:3–4; Mark 12:28–29; Luke 7:19–23; 12:41–53; 17:20–21; John 3:1–5, 9–10; 6:28–33; 8:33–59; 9:1–3; 12:34–36; 13:6–10, 36–38; 14:5–9, 22–24). On this occasion, the Lord was asked the very provocative question of whether only a few will be saved.

His reply was shocking. Instead of discussing percentages, He declared that many will desire to enter the kingdom but will not be able to do so. Those who do enter will do so with difficulty; they will have to fight their way in through the narrow door. Christ's perspective goes against the grain of contemporary evangelistic methodology. Unlike His reply, which demonstrates that salvation is very difficult, modern evangelism frequently presents the gospel in ways that make it seem easy.

Much of modern evangelism's methodology stems from the revival ministry and writings of Charles Grandison Finney (1792–1875). Often called "the father of modern revivalism," Finney was an attorney who became an evangelist after his conversion. He denied that the new birth is a supernatural work of God, and taught that salvation depends solely on the power of man's will. His ministry utilized pragmatic "new measures," such as emotionally-charged urging of people to come forward to the "anxious bench" (a forerunner of the modern altar call) and other tactics designed to manipulate people's wills.

It certainly is not wrong to invite people to come to Christ and embrace the salvation that He offers. Jesus called sinners to repent and enter His kingdom (Matt. 4:17; Luke 5:32), as did John the Baptist (Matt. 3:2), and the apostles (Mark 6:12; Acts 2:38; 3:19). The reason the church exists is to carry out its mandate to "Go therefore and make disciples of all the nations, baptizing them in the name of the Father and the Son and the Holy Spirit" (Matt. 28:19; cf. Luke 24:47). The issue is not whether to invite and even command lost sinners to repent and believe the gospel, but rather how to frame that invitation. This passage is vitally important, because it reveals how the Lord Jesus Christ invited sinners to come to salvation. But before recording that invitation in verses 24–30, Luke described in verses 22–23 the setting in which it took place.

As the scene opens, Jesus **was passing through** Judea **from one city and village to another, teaching, and proceeding on His**

way to Jerusalem (a journey Luke records in 9:51–19:27). His death and resurrection were only a matter of months away. As He crisscrossed Judea Jesus was constantly **teaching,** as He had done throughout His ministry (cf. 4:43; 8:1; Matt. 4:23; 11:1; Mark 6:2), because disseminating the truth was foundational. The purpose of all the miracles, signs, and wonders Jesus performed to affirm His deity as the Son sent from the Father was to validate His teaching. The goal of ministry is always to provide the foundation of biblical truth that is essential to salvation, leading to love, service, and worship of God. The constant theme of the Lord's instruction related to life in His kingdom, the sphere of salvation where God reigns over His people who love, serve, and worship Him (cf. the exposition of 13:18–21 in the previous chapter of this volume).

At some unidentified point along the way during Christ's ministry in Judea **someone** posed **to Him** a provocative question: **"Lord, are there just a few who are being saved?"** The question reflects the recognition of His followers that the point of His teaching related to salvation. The divine work of salvation is not deliverance from unfulfillment, dissatisfaction with life, poverty, or poor self-esteem. Salvation is deliverance from God's wrath and judgment into safety and eternal blessing through the sacrificial death of His Son. "Having now been justified by His blood," Paul wrote, "we shall be saved from the wrath of God through Him" (Rom. 5:9; cf. 1 Thess. 1:10; 5:9). The question was whether only a few were to be saved from divine judgment and eternal damnation in hell. It appeared to the questioner to be the case.

The question was an honest one, asked by a true follower of Christ. Those in the crowds who heard Him ran the gamut from outright enemies to curiosity seekers to the very interested to the genuinely saved believers. What level of interest this individual had in Christ is not known. His question, though, voiced what His followers had to be thinking. The Jewish people expected that when Messiah came, he would be welcomed by the entire nation, which would receive salvation (Isa. 45:17; 60:21–22). Messiah would establish his kingdom, in which Israel would play a leading role. In that kingdom the curse will be removed and righteousness and peace will prevail. Gentiles will also be saved (Isa. 56:6–7) and come to see Messiah reigning in glory on Mount Zion (Isa. 24:23; Zech. 8:22–23).

But after nearly three years of ministry, countless miracles, unmatched teaching, and crowds of thousands following Him, there were only a disappointingly small number of true believers who believed in Him savingly. So few in number were they that even He referred to them as a "little flock" (Luke 12:32; cf. the exposition of 13:18–19 in the previous chapter of this volume). The religious leaders of the nation had rejected Jesus, denouncing Him as being empowered by Satan. Many of the people had bought into that lie and also viewed Jesus' supernatural power as satanic. Many rejected Him because He did not meet their messianic profile and expectation. In fact, when a large crowd attempted to force Him into their preconceived role of political-military messiah, Jesus refused (John 6:14–15). But it was the puzzling conundrum that even among the large numbers who did follow Him very few were genuine believers.

The question, however, overlooks Old Testament history, which reveals that salvation had never been widespread in the past. When God destroyed the sinful pre-flood world, only eight people escaped that divine judgment (Gen. 7:13; 1 Peter 3:20). From the destruction of the wicked cities of Sodom and Gomorrah only Lot and his wife and daughters escaped (Gen. 19:16). The genuine, believing remnant of Israel was always small (Isa. 6:13; 10:20–22; Jer. 23:3; 31:7; 50:20), and salvation was always individual (Isa. 55:1), never national.

The fact that Jesus' answer did not address the question directly shows that it is not important how many people are being saved; what matters to each person is that he or she be one of them. Instead of responding to the question of quantity, Jesus focused on the quality of true believers' faith and gave a personal invitation to those present to receive the salvation that He offers. Four aspects of that invitation may be discerned: He called for spiritual exertion, temporal desperation, lack of relation, and eternal perception.

SPIRITUAL EXERTION

And He said to them, "Strive to enter through the narrow door; for many, I tell you, will seek to enter and will not be able." (13:23b–24)

Christ's invitation was radically different from those commonly used today. His message was not that God loves everyone unconditionally and desires to connect with sinners and fulfill all their personal dreams and ambitions. Nor was His goal to manipulate people into making a shallow commitment to Him. Jesus' words are sobering, threatening, and frightening enough to produce panic in the heart of a penitent, thoughtful soul. They also serve to banish halfhearted seekers who are unwilling to surrender unconditionally to His lordship (cf. Luke 14:33).

Compared to the rampant easy believism that underlies much of modern evangelism Jesus' invitation, which calls for strenuous exertion from the penitent sinner, seems almost heretical. It is true that salvation is solely by God's sovereign grace. No one can come to Christ unless the Father draws him (John 6:44, 65), nor can anyone know the Father except those to whom the Son chooses to reveal Him (Matt. 11:27). Those who are dead in their sins can be saved only by God's grace, not their own efforts (Eph. 2:1–10; Titus 3:3–5). Yet salvation is not apart from the will of the sinner. As noted above, John the Baptist, Jesus, and the apostles called for sinners to repent, and that is the church's message as well. Paul told the Greek philosophers on Mars Hill in Athens that "having overlooked the times of ignorance, God is now declaring to men that all people everywhere should repent" (Acts 17:30; cf. 26:20). Those commands make it clear that sinners are responsible for the choices that they make, and will be held accountable for not repenting and believing in the Savior.

Strive translates a form of the verb *agōnizomai*, from which the English word "agonize" derives. It is used only here in the Synoptic Gospels. The word means "to fight" (John 18:36; 1 Tim. 6:12; 2 Tim. 4:7), "to compete" in an athletic contest (1 Cor. 9:25), or "to struggle" (Col. 1:29; 4:12; 1 Tim. 4:10). The fight or struggle in view here is one of self-denial that produces real repentance. "If anyone wishes to come after Me," Jesus said, "he must deny himself, and take up his cross daily and follow Me" (Luke 9:23). Then He added the paradoxical statement that "whoever wishes to save his life will lose it, but whoever loses his life for My sake, he is the one who will save it" (v. 24). The message of the gospel is not self-fulfillment, but self-denial. Faith in Christ costs the sinner his selfish goals and desires, and may separate him from his family (Luke 14:26), possessions (Mark 10:17–22), even his life (John 12:25). But those who lose those ephemeral earthly things will gain in this life blessings, and in their eternal reward infinitely more.

The requirement that sinners **enter through the narrow door** further indicates the intensity of the struggle (cf. Matt. 7:13–14). The door is a tight fit, requiring those who enter through it to strip themselves of their personal baggage. It is also made hard to find by the many deceptive voices luring the unwary and undiscerning to the broad gate that leads to hell. Therefore many **will seek to enter and will not be able.**

The Lord brings salvation only to a heart marked by the repentance that always accompanies true saving faith. Quoting from Isaiah 40:3–4, John the Baptist described true repentance: "The voice of one crying in the wilderness, 'Make ready the way of the Lord, make His paths straight. Every ravine will be filled, and every mountain and hill will be brought low; the crooked will become straight, and the rough roads smooth'" (Luke 3:4–5). In my commentary on that passage in an earlier volume of this series I wrote,

> The words of Isaiah's prophecy quoted here also serve as an analogy of the repentance John preached. The wilderness pictures the sinful heart, and repentance involves bringing to light the deep, dark things of the heart, pictured by filling in the ravines, and humbling human pride, depicted in the imagery of bringing low the mountains and hills. The crooked, deceitful, devious perverse things must be made straight, and any other rough places in the heart, whether self-love, love of money, love of the world, the lust of the flesh, indifference, or unbelief, must be smoothed out. Only then will the truly repentant see the salvation of God. (*Luke 1–5*, The MacArthur New Testament Commentary [Chicago: Moody, 2009], 211. See also the discussion of true repentance in chapter 18 of that volume.)

TEMPORAL DESPERATION

Once the head of the house gets up and shuts the door, and you begin to stand outside and knock on the door, saying, 'Lord, open up to us!' (13:25a)

Not only is the door to the kingdom narrow, but it also can be shut. **Once** Christ, **the head of the house, gets up and shuts the door** there will be no admission; the opportunity to enter the kingdom will be permanently gone for those who are shut out. There is a sense of desperation and urgency in this picture; sinners, with only a limited time to respond to the gospel invitation, let that opportunity pass to be permanently shut out.

Scripture makes it clear that all the unredeemed are living on borrowed time (cf. the exposition of 13:1–9 in chapter 15 of this volume). God declared of the sinful, pre-flood world, "My Spirit shall not strive with man forever, because he also is flesh; nevertheless his days shall be one hundred and twenty years" (Gen. 6:3). Jesus told a parable about a rich, selfish fool who was greedily storing up earthly treasure for himself, only to have God say to him, "You fool! This very night your soul is required of you; and now who will own what you have prepared?" (Luke 12:20). "Be ready," Jesus exhorted His hearers, "for the Son of Man is coming at an hour that you do not expect" (Luke 12:40). Like a guilty person settling with their opponent before reaching the magistrate, sinners must settle with God before it is too late (Luke 12:58). Jesus warned those who told him of Pilate's slaughter of some Galileans, "Unless you repent, you will all likewise perish" (Luke 13:3; cf. 5). The story of a man giving a fig tree one more year to produce fruit symbolizes the reality that all who lack the genuine fruit of salvation are living on borrowed time (Luke 13:6–9). Eventually, God's patience toward those who reject the truth will end and He will judicially abandon them (Rom. 1:24,26,28). Therefore "now is 'the acceptable time,' behold, now is 'the day of salvation'" (2 Cor. 6:2).

Using the same imagery as that in the shocking parable of the wise and foolish virgins (Matt. 25:1–13), Jesus warned that those who miss their opportunity for salvation will **stand outside and knock on the door, saying, 'Lord, open up to us!'** That reaction expresses their surprise and horror at being permanently shut out of the kingdom of God. After all, they were religious people, many of whom claimed to have ministered in Jesus' name (Matt. 7:22). Clearly, hell will be populated not only by irreligious rejecters of God, but also by those who were outwardly religious and reverently spoke of Him.

LACK OF RELATION

then He will answer and say to you, 'I do not know where you are from.' Then you will begin to say, 'We ate and drank in Your presence, and You taught in our streets'; and He will say, 'I tell you, I do not know where you are from; depart from me, all you evildoers.' (13:25b–27)

The Lord's **answer, "I do not know where you are from"** (cf. Matt. 7:23), reveals the reason that those who squander their opportunity will be shut out of the kingdom. Despite their external religious façade, they had no relation to or life union with Christ.

Salvation results in a shared life with Jesus Christ. "I have been crucified with Christ," Paul wrote, "and it is no longer I who live, but Christ lives in me; and the life which I now live in the flesh I live by faith in the Son of God, who loved me and gave Himself up for me" (Gal. 2:20). Christians are in Christ (cf. Rom. 6:11, 23; 8:1; 1 Cor. 1:30; 2 Cor. 1:21; 5:17; Gal. 3:28; Phil. 1:1; 4:21; Col. 1:2, 28; 2 Tim. 3:12; 1 Peter 5:10, 14), and He is in them (John 6:56; 14:20; 15:4–5; 17:26; Rom. 8:10; Col. 1:27; 3:11; Eph. 3:17).

Shocked by His denial of any relationship with them, they **will begin to say, "We ate and drank in Your presence, and You taught in our streets."** Their protest that they **ate and drank in** His **presence** symbolizes their claim to have had a relationship with Him. They also claimed to have listened to Christ when He **taught in** their **streets.** How then could He shut them out of the kingdom?

But mere familiarity with Jesus does not bring salvation, as the Lord's reply drove home with crushing finality: **I tell you, I do not know where you are from; depart from me, all you evildoers** (cf. Ps. 6:8). They had no relationship with Him. They had never repented and been justified by God because they were covered with the righteousness of Christ through faith in Him. Rather, though religious and moral, they were still unrighteous **evildoers.** The sentence was final; their departure eternal.

ETERNAL PERCEPTION

In that place there will be weeping and gnashing of teeth when you see Abraham and Isaac and Jacob and all the prophets in the kingdom of God, but yourselves being thrown out. And they will come from east and west and from north and south, and will recline at the table in the kingdom of God. And behold, some are last who will be first and some are first who will be last." (13:28–30)

Jesus did not focus on His hearers' purposes, ambitions, desires, health, wealth, or anything else in this life. Instead He called them to have an eternal perspective and turn their attention to the threat of hell. **In that place,** Jesus warned, **there will be weeping and gnashing of teeth** (cf. Matt. 8:12; 13:42, 50; 22:13; 24:51; 25:30). The torment of hell will not be limited to the pain of punishment, but will include the remorse, shock, and surprise of those who ended up there despite thinking they were going to heaven. The more people in hell knew about the gospel, the more profound their remorse will be; their pain will be proportional to their level of rejection. And since their rejection will be eternal and incurable, so will their sin be and the judgment of that sin.

Intensifying the warning of torment for those denied entrance to the heavenly realm will be the bliss of those who enter it. Specifically, it should be contemplated by all Jewish people to consider that they will be left out of the kingdom if they reject Christ. **Abraham and Isaac and Jacob and all the prophets in the kingdom of God** will be there while they are **thrown out** of God's presence forever. The Jewish people prided themselves on being the children of Abraham, who had an inalienable right as heirs to the covenant promises God made with him and reiterated to the prophets. They expected to be saved because they were Abraham's descendants. Realizing that they who reject Christ will never with their three illustrious forefathers enjoy the rich blessings of the kingdom should make the reality of hell extremely bitter for them.

Even more painful than being left out of eternal life with their hero forefathers is the knowledge that their hated enemies, the Gentiles, **will come from east and west and from north and south, and will recline at the table in the kingdom of God** (cf. Matt. 8:11–12) from which they are excluded. That Gentiles will be in God's kingdom should come as no surprise, since that truth is clearly taught in the Old Testament (e.g., Isa. 2:2–4; 25:6; 56:6–7; 60:3; 66:19–24). But the Jews largely rejected that idea and even resented the thought that God would save Gentiles (see Jonah 1–3). Here Gentiles are depicted enjoying a lavish banquet—symbolic in the ancient Near East of life's most important events—in the kingdom. The banquet pictures the blessedness of fellowship with God (cf. Luke 22:29–30; Rev. 19:9).

Jesus' concluding statement, **And behold, some are last who will be first and some are first who will be last,** further intensifies the shock these lost Jews will feel. Not only will Gentiles be in the kingdom, but they will also be equal with the Jews who are there. In the realm of salvation "there is neither Jew nor Greek, there is neither slave nor free man, there is neither male nor female; for [the redeemed] are all one in Christ Jesus" (Gal. 3:28; cf. Eph. 2:11–16).

The lesson to be learned from Christ's model invitation to salvation is twofold. First, the true church of Jesus Christ must get the message right; a perverted, corrupted, altered, false, and easy invitation is powerless to save lost sinners. Further, false evangelism leaves people unconverted and subsequently skeptical of true gospel evangelism and therefore more open to further deception. The Lord Jesus Christ never watered down His message to avoid offending people; He made them either feel bad enough to repent, or furious enough to reject.

The message to the unredeemed is that God saves no one apart from genuine repentance. The battle to deny self and follow Christ is intense, the time is short, eternal destiny is at stake.

Who Really Killed Jesus?
(Luke 13:31–33)

19

Just at that time some Pharisees approached, saying to Him, "Go away, leave here, for Herod wants to kill You." And He said to them, "Go and tell that fox, 'Behold, I cast out demons and perform cures today and tomorrow, and the third day I reach My goal.' Nevertheless I must journey on today and tomorrow and the next day; for it cannot be that a prophet would perish outside of Jerusalem." (13:31–33)

From His birth the Prince of Peace was the target of murderers. It is, shockingly, a most remarkable reality about Christ's life that so many wanted to kill Him. After all, Jesus was without sin or evil, perfect, absolutely righteous, holy, compassionate, generous, and benevolent. He offered what everyone desperately needs: mercy and grace in the forgiveness of sin, eternal life, freedom from judgment, deliverance from eternal punishment in hell, and everlasting joy in heaven. Further, He offered those not as things to be earned, achieved, or merited, but as a free gift to be received. Ironically, the one who called for the very best in people brought out the very worst in them.

The attempts on Jesus' life began long before the outset of His public ministry. When He was still an infant Herod the Great, patriarch of the Herodian dynasty, ruled Judea. As an Idumean (Edomite) in league with Caesar, Herod was viewed with suspicion by the Jews. That heightened the fear that made him constantly anxious that someone would usurp his power. Herod was a sociopath whose paranoia reached a horrific climax when late in his reign magi arrived from the east declaring that the king of the Jews had been born and they were seeking him. Fearing a rival to his throne, Herod determined from the Jewish religious leaders that the Messiah was to be born in Bethlehem (Mic. 5:2) so he could kill him. Not sure exactly which child was the threat, he irrationally and brutally ordered the slaughter of all the boys two and under in that area in a vain attempt to kill Jesus in the mass murder (Matt. 2:13–18).

At the outset of His ministry the Lord cleansed the temple of the merchants and moneychangers who were corrupting His Father's house (John 2:13–17). Outraged, the Jewish authorities demanded to know by what authority He had so boldly acted. Knowing that already they desired to kill Him, "Jesus answered them, 'Destroy this temple, and in three days I will raise it up.'" As verse 21 notes, "He was speaking of the temple of His body."

Even the people of His hometown of Nazareth tried to kill Jesus the first time He spoke in their synagogue. They were outraged when He offended their spiritual pride by describing them as spiritually poor, blind, captive, and oppressed (Luke 4:18). And when He further reinforced that point by reminding them that they were like their ancestors who rejected the word of God, so that Elijah and Elisha went to minister to two humble, penitent Gentile outcasts, it was too much for their nationalistic pride and self-righteousness to bear. Infuriated, they exploded in an emotional effort to murder Him by throwing Him off a cliff (vv. 28–29).

The Jewish religious leaders—Pharisees, Sadducees, Herodians, scribes, chief priests, and high priests—collectively also sought to murder Jesus, because He violated and condemned their corrupt, apostate, self-righteous religion. Their hatred of Him for cleansing the temple intensified when Jesus affirmed His deity after healing a man on the Sabbath. "For this reason therefore," the apostle John notes, "the Jews [the religious leaders] were seeking all the more to kill Him, because He not only was breaking the Sabbath, but also was calling God His own Father, making Himself equal with God" (John 5:18). Throughout Christ's ministry they sought an opportunity to take His life (Matt. 26:3–4; Mark 3:6; Luke 19:47; John 7:1, 25; 11:53). Eventually, they succeeded in pressuring the Romans into crucifying Him (as He Himself had predicted [Matt. 16:21; 17:23; 21:33–46; Mark 10:32–34]). Following the lead of their rulers, the Jewish crowds too sought Jesus' death (Matt. 27:20–25).

Pilate, although he pronounced Jesus innocent (Luke 23:13–14, 22), in the end also wanted Him dead. Fearing a riot (Matt. 27:24), and even more that the Jewish leaders would report him to Caesar (John 19:12), Pilate ordered Jesus to be executed (Matt. 27:26). His soldiers gleefully carried out those orders (Matt. 27:27–31).

This passage introduces yet another villainous, would-be killer of Jesus, Herod Antipas. It may be divided into three sections: the Pharisees' warning, Herod's threat, and Jesus' response.

THE PHARISEES' WARNING

Just at that time some Pharisees approached, saying to Him, "Go away, leave here, (13:31*a*)

At first glance this seems puzzling. Why would the **Pharisees,** who hated Jesus and wanted to murder Him themselves, warn Him about Herod's similar intent? Though they hated Herod and resented that this Roman puppet king, who was half Idumean and half Samaritan, reigned over them, would it not accomplish their intent if he killed Jesus? Since they obviously were not motivated by concern for Jesus' safety, this warning suggests that their ultimate intent was to kill Jesus, but their immediate objective was to intimidate Him into silence—shut down His teaching.

At the time, Jesus was ministering in Perea (cf. Matt. 19:1; Mark 10:1; John 10:40–42), a region located east of the Jordan River opposite Samaria and Judea that, like Galilee, was also ruled by Herod Antipas. The Pharisees may have been trying to force Jesus to **leave** Perea and go to Judea, where the Sanhedrin had jurisdiction. After His strong words of warning that unbelieving Jews will be shut out of the kingdom (see the discussion of 13:23–30 in the previous chapter of this volume), they were even more determined to silence Him temporarily, and eventually permanently.

HEROD'S THREAT

for Herod wants to kill You. (13:31*b*)

Herod, as noted above, was Herod Antipas, a son of the long-tenured Herod the Great. After his death, Herod's kingdom was divided among three of his sons. Archelaus received Judea, Samaria, and Idumea; Philip, Ituraea and Trachonitis (Luke 3:1), northeast of Galilee; and Antipas, Galilee and Perea. Antipas is the Herod referred to in the Gospels' accounts of Jesus' ministry. He ruled from his father's death in 4 B.C. until A.D. 39. In addition to his not being Jewish, the Jews hated Antipas because he built his capital city, Tiberius (located on the west shore of the Sea of Galilee) on the site of a Jewish cemetery, thus defiling it. They were further outraged when he put idols in public places in Tiberius. While Jesus ministered extensively for one year throughout the small, compact area of Galilee, there is no record in the Gospels of Him ever visiting Tiberius.

Antipas, openly immoral, was publicly rebuked by John the Baptist for his illicit affair and marriage to his brother Philip's wife Herodias (Mark 6:17–18). In a desperate move to silence the bold preacher, the shamed Herod imprisoned John (Luke 3:20). Herodias, not surprisingly, held a bitter grudge against John and wanted him dead (Mark 6:19). Fearing both John (v. 20) and the people, who viewed him as a prophet (Matt. 14:5), Herod refused. Eventually, however, Herodias found a way to manipulate her husband into killing John. At Antipas's birthday celebration, her daughter (from her marriage to Herod's brother Philip) performed a lewd dance before Herod and his guests. Captivated sensually by her performance, Herod unwisely "promised with an oath to give her whatever she asked" (Matt. 14:7). Seizing the opportunity, Herodias prompted her daughter to reply, "Give me here on a platter the head of

John the Baptist" (v. 8). Too proud to break his foolish promise in front of his distinguished guests, Herod reluctantly ordered and executed John's beheading (Matt. 14:9–10).

Although the text does not say why Herod wanted to kill Jesus, there are several possible reasons. Since he had killed His forerunner and fellow preacher John the Baptist, Herod may have feared that Jesus might take vengeance on him. His guilt stemming from his beheading of John (cf. 9:7–9; Mark 6:14–16) also might have driven Herod to dread for his own life. He was well aware of Jesus' supernatural power (23:8; Matt. 14:1–2), and may have felt he needed to eliminate Jesus to protect himself. Further, knowing that Rome expected him to keep the peace, Herod may have been uneasy about the huge crowds that followed Jesus. If Jesus instigated a rebellion, Herod's career and power may have been in jeopardy with Rome, so he may have decided to head off a revolt by a preemptive strike against Him. It is also possible that, like his father, Antipas may have viewed Jesus as a potential rival for his throne. The Lord's refusal to see him (Luke 9:9; 23:8) could also have added to his uneasiness. Even when Herod eventually did meet Jesus during His mock trials He, unlike His interrogations by Annas, Caiaphas, and Pilate, refused to answer him (v. 9).

JESUS' RESPONSE

And He said to them, "Go and tell that fox, 'Behold, I cast out demons and perform cures today and tomorrow, and the third day I reach My goal.' Nevertheless I must journey on today and tomorrow and the next day; for it cannot be that a prophet would perish outside of Jerusalem." (13:32–33)

The Son of God was not in the least intimidated by Herod's threat to take His life. Disdainfully dismissing him and his threat, Jesus said to the Pharisees, **"Go and tell that fox, 'Behold, I cast out demons and perform cures today and tomorrow, and the third day I reach My goal.'"** For Jesus to make such a derogatory statement was highly unusual; Herod is the only individual in the New Testament for whom the Lord expressed such contempt. Foxes are wily, cunning, sneaky pests, known for their destructiveness; for example, the Song of Solomon refers to "the little foxes that are ruining the vineyards" (2:15). Thus, to call someone a **fox** was a demeaning, contemptuous insult, the equivalent in today's vernacular of calling someone a "varmint." Herod was not at all a noble, powerful lion but a mere fox; far more a nuisance than a threat. Just as a fox could not kill a man, so also Herod could not kill Jesus. He was powerless to alter the divine timetable.

Some may wonder whether Jesus' comment was a violation of the Mosaic law, which forbids speaking evil of a ruler (Ex. 22:28; Eccl. 10:20; cf. Acts 23:5). While that was normally the case, there were exceptions. God often directly rebuked Israel's rulers through the prophets. Speaking through Isaiah God said to Israel, "Your rulers are rebels and companions of thieves; everyone loves a bribe and chases after rewards. They do not defend the orphan, nor does the widow's plea come before them" (Isa. 1:23). In Ezekiel 22:27 God lamented that Israel's "princes within her are like wolves tearing the prey, by shedding blood and destroying lives in order to get dishonest gain." Hosea 7:3–7 records God's strong rebuke of Israel's wicked leaders:

> With their wickedness they make the king glad, and the princes with their lies. They are all adulterers, like an oven heated by the baker who ceases to stir up the fire from the kneading of the dough until it is leavened. On the day of our king, the princes became sick with the heat of wine; he stretched out his hand with scoffers, for their hearts are like an oven as they approach their plotting; their anger smolders all night, in the morning it burns like a flaming fire. All of them are hot like an oven, and they consume their rulers; all their kings have fallen. None of them calls on Me.

The prophets themselves also censured Israel's rulers. Samuel re-buked King Saul for failing to completely destroy the Amalekites (1 Sam. 15:16–19); Nathan rebuked King David for committing adultery with Bathsheba and then murdering her husband (2 Sam. 12:7–12); Elijah rebuked King Ahab for forsaking God's commandments and worshiping idols (1 Kings 18:18) and for murdering Naboth and stealing his vineyard (1 Kings 21:17–22). Jesus, not only a prophet, but also God incarnate, had every right to rebuke a "varmint" for thinking he could come into God's field and kill the Son of God. Jesus would die at God's appointed time, but not at the hands of Herod.

The message the Lord sent back to Herod through the Pharisees was one of defiance: **Behold, I cast out demons and perform cures today and tomorrow, and the third day I reach My goal.** He would continue His ministry of freeing people from oppression by the forces of hell, and curing their sicknesses. The phrase **today and tomorrow, and the third day** is a colloquial saying expressing completion (cf. Ex. 19:10–11). Jesus would continue to do what He had been doing day in and day out for the brief time remaining until His earthly ministry was completed. His goal was to do the Father's will (John 4:34; 5:30; 6:38) and lay down His life to complete the work of redemption (Matt. 20:28; John 6:51; 10:15, 17–18; Gal. 1:3–4; Eph. 5:2, 25; Titus 2:13–14; 1 John 3:16). Herod's threat could not and did not change Jesus' plans in the slightest.

Jesus then declared, **Nevertheless I must journey on today and tomorrow and the next day.** Disregarding Herod's impotent threat, He would continue moving day by day toward the goal God determined for Him and the completion of His work. Jesus would not die in Perea, **for it cannot be that a prophet would perish outside of Jerusalem.** It was necessary that Jesus, the final sacrifice, die in Jerusalem, the location of the temple where all the other sacrifices were made. This proverbial saying reflects the bitterly ironical truth that Jerusalem, the center of Jewish worship, was the scene of the deaths of many of the prophets. The innocent blood spilled by Manasseh (2 Kings 21:16) and Jehoiakim (24:4) included that of the prophets sent to rebuke them (Jer. 26:20–23). According to tradition, one of the prophets martyred under Manasseh's reign was Isaiah, sawn in two inside a hollow log (cf. Heb. 11:37). Second Chronicles 24:20–22 records the murder of Zechariah, the son of Jehoiada the priest:

> Then the Spirit of God came on Zechariah the son of Jehoiada the priest; and he stood above the people and said to them, "Thus God has said, 'Why do you transgress the commandments of the Lord and do not prosper? Because you have forsaken the Lord, He has also forsaken you.'" So they conspired against him and at the command of the king they stoned him to death in the court of the house of the Lord. Thus Joash the king did not remember the kindness which his father Jehoiada had shown him, but he murdered his son. And as he died he said, "May the Lord see and avenge!"

Jesus told a parable that summarized Israel's long history of killing God's prophets, which would culminate in His own death:

> And He began to tell the people this parable:"A man planted a vineyard and rented it out to vine-growers, and went on a journey for a long time. At the harvest time he sent a slave to the vine-growers, so that they would give him some of the produce of the vineyard; but the vine-growers beat him and sent him away empty-handed. And he proceeded to send another slave; and they beat him also and treated him shamefully and sent him away empty-handed. And he proceeded to send a third; and this one also they wounded and cast out. The owner of the vineyard said, 'What shall I do? I will send my beloved son; perhaps they will respect him.' But when the vine-growers saw him, they reasoned with one another, saying, 'This is the heir; let us kill him so that the inheritance will be ours.' So they threw him out of the vineyard and killed him. What, then, will the owner of the vineyard do to them? He will come and destroy these vine-growers and will give the vineyard to others." (Luke 20:9–16)

Herod did not kill Jesus, so who was responsible for His death? Over the centuries, the Jewish people have borne the brunt of the blame. Misguided zealots have denounced them as "Christ-killers," and used that charge to justify all sorts of evil, from persecution to hate crimes to pogroms, to mass murder. Sadly, some of that anti-Semitic activity has been carried out in the name of Jesus. But such abhorrent behavior flows from satanic motives, not from true love for Jesus Christ.

There is, however, a sense in which the Jews alive at the time of Christ were responsible for His death, as both the Old Testament and the New Testament attest. Isaiah 49:7 describes Messiah as "the despised One ... the One abhorred by the nation." Isaiah 53 predicted that the Jews at the end of history when they are saved will confess that they despised, forsook, oppressed, afflicted, and led Messiah to His death. This confession will take place when they finally look back on the one they "pierced" and mourn and are saved (Zech. 12:10; 13:1). Psalm 22:6–8 prophetically described His treatment at their hands:

> But I am a worm and not a man, a reproach of men and despised by the people. All who see me sneer at me; they separate with the lip, they wag the head, saying, "Commit yourself to the Lord; let Him deliver him; let Him rescue him, because He delights in him."

As noted earlier in this chapter, the Jewish leaders sought to kill Jesus from the outset of His ministry. But the final decision to murder Him was made in a council headed by the high priest, Caiaphas:

> Therefore the chief priests and the Pharisees convened a council, and were saying, "What are we doing? For this man is performing many signs. If we let Him go on like this, all men will believe in Him, and the Romans will come and take away both our place and our nation." But one of them, Caiaphas, who was high priest that year, said to them, "You know nothing at all, nor do you take into account that it is expedient for you that one man die for the people, and that the whole nation not perish."...So from that day on they planned together to kill Him. (John 11:47–50, 53)

The people shared the responsibility with their leaders for Jesus' death. At His trial before Pilate they joined them (Luke 23:13) in screaming, "Crucify, crucify Him!" (vv. 21, 23). They further assumed their share of the blame for Christ's death when they shouted, "His blood shall be on us and on our children!" (Matt. 27:25). Peter affirmed their guilt in his sermon on the Day of Pentecost when he addressed the "men of Israel," and reminded them that they had "nailed [Jesus] to a cross by the hands of godless men and put Him to death" (Acts 2:22–23). Peter concluded his sermon by declaring, "Therefore let all the house of Israel know for certain that God has made Him both Lord and Christ—this Jesus whom you crucified" (v. 36; cf. 3:12–15; 4:10).

But the Jewish people by no means bore the sole responsibility for Christ's death. It was Pilate, a Gentile, in collusion with Herod, also a non-Jew, who sentenced Him to death. And the actual execution was carried out by Roman soldiers. Thus, no one group alone bears the guilt for Jesus' death. As I wrote in *The Murder of Jesus,*

> In fact, the murder of Jesus was a vast conspiracy involving Rome, Herod, the Gentiles, the Jewish Sanhedrin, and the people of Israel— diverse groups who apart from this event were seldom fully in accord with one another. In fact, it is significant that the crucifixion of Christ is the *only* historical event where all those factions worked together to achieve a common goal. All were culpable. All bear the guilt together. The Jews as a race were no more or less blameworthy than the Gentiles. ([Nashville: Word, 2000], 5. Emphasis in original.)

A collective prayer offered in one of the earliest assemblies of believers ties together all the guilty parties: "For truly in this city there were gathered together against Your holy servant Jesus, whom You anointed, both Herod and Pontius Pilate, along with the Gentiles and the peoples of Israel" (Acts 4:27).

But their involvement was merely the instrumental means of Christ's death; the efficient cause was God Himself. The prayer just cited goes on to say, "to do whatever Your hand and Your purpose predestined to occur" (v. 28). Both the Old and New Testaments teach that Christ's death was ordained by God. Isaiah 53:10 says that "the Lord was pleased to crush Him, putting Him to grief." Peter said of Jesus that "this Man, delivered over by the predetermined plan and foreknowledge of God, you nailed to a cross by the hands of godless men and put Him to death" (Acts 2:23).

It is a great, providential irony that had the men involved in Christ's death understood the wisdom of God, "they would not have crucified the Lord of glory" (1 Cor. 2:8). They bear eternal guilt for their part in Christ's death. But God demonstrated His absolute sovereignty by overruling their evil deed for His own purpose:

> The Cross is therefore the ultimate proof of the utter sovereignty of God. His purposes are always fulfilled in spite of the evil intentions of sinners. God even works His righteousness *through* the evil acts of unrighteous agents. Far from making Him culpable for their evil, this demonstrates how all He does is good, and how He is able to work all things together for good (Romans 8:28)—even the most wicked deed the powers of evil have ever conspired to carry out. (*The Murder of Jesus*, 7. Emphasis in original.)

Divine Compassion for Those Deserving Condemnation (Luke 13:34–35)

20

"O Jerusalem, Jerusalem, the city that kills the prophets and stones those sent to her! How often I wanted to gather your children together, just as a hen gathers her brood under her wings, and you would not have it! Behold, your house is left to you desolate; and I say to you, you will not see Me until the time comes when you say, 'Blessed is He who comes in the name of the Lord!'" (13:34–35)

A proper view of God understands that He is not only sovereign and holy, but also gracious and compassionate. John Calvin, known for his emphasis on the biblical truth of God's absolute holiness and sovereignty, nonetheless cautioned, "Your idea of [God's] nature is not clear unless you acknowledge him to be the origin and fountain of all goodness" (*Institutes*, I.II.3).

Compassion is part of God's essential goodness. He proclaimed Himself to Moses on Mt. Sinai to be "compassionate and gracious, slow to anger, and abounding in lovingkindness and truth" (Ex. 34:6; cf. Ps. 103:8,

13). In Psalm 116:5 the psalmist declared, "Gracious is the Lord, and right-eous; yes, our God is compassionate." Isaiah reminded Israel, "The Lord longs to be gracious to you, and therefore He waits on high to have com-passion on you" (Isa. 30:18), while the prophet Joel encouraged his coun-trymen, "Now return to the Lord your God, for He is gracious and compassionate" (Joel 2:13). James reminded his suffering readers that "the Lord is full of compassion and is merciful" (James 5:11; cf. Pss. 40:11; 69:16; 111:4; Dan. 9:9; Jon. 4:2).

God dispenses His compassion according to His sovereign will. He declared to Moses, "I will be gracious to whom I will be gracious, and will show compassion on whom I will show compassion" (Ex. 33:19; cf. Rom. 9:15). His compassion is unfailing. In spite of God's devastating judgment on Israel, Jeremiah could still affirm, "The Lord's lovingkind-nesses indeed never cease, for His compassions never fail. They are new every morning; great is Your faithfulness" (Lam. 3:22–23; cf. v. 32). God's compassion inclines Him to forgive sin. After David sinned with Bath-sheba, he cried out to God, "Be gracious to me, O God, according to Your lovingkindness; according to the greatness of Your compassion blot out my transgressions" (Ps. 51:1). It was His compassion that prompted the Lord to forgive Israel's sins (Ps. 78:38). Isaiah 55:7 promises repentant sin-ners that God will show compassion on them and pardon their sins (cf. Mic. 7:19). The parable of the two sons (Luke 15:11–32) illustrates God's compassion for lost sinners.

God especially has demonstrated compassion for Israel. "The Lord was gracious to them and had compassion on them and turned to them because of His covenant with Abraham, Isaac, and Jacob, and would not destroy them or cast them from His presence until now" (2 Kings 13:23). In a lengthy prayer of national confession, the exiles who had returned to Jerusalem chronicled God's repeated compassion for Israel despite the people's relentless sin and rejection of Him (Neh. 9:17–38). Second Chronicles 36:15–16 notes that

> the Lord, the God of their fathers, sent word to them again and again by His messengers, because He had compassion on His people and on His dwelling place; but they continually mocked the messengers of God, despised His words and scoffed at His prophets, until the wrath of the Lord arose against His people, until there was no remedy.

Deuteronomy 32:9–11 likens God's tender, compassionate care for Israel to an eagle's care for its young:

> For the Lord's portion is His people; Jacob is the allotment of His inheritance. He found him in a desert land, and in the howling waste of a wilderness; He encircled him, He cared for him, He guarded him as the pupil of His eye. Like an eagle that stirs up its nest, that hovers over its young, He spread His wings and caught them, He carried them on His pinions.

Even when God's judgment sent His people into exile, He still showed them compassion (cf. 2 Chron. 30:9; Ps. 102:13). That foreshadows an even greater outpouring of divine compassion on Israel in the end times (cf. Deut. 30:3; Isa. 14:1; 49:10–16; 54:7–8; Jer. 30:18).

As God incarnate, the Lord Jesus Christ manifested divine compassion. He felt compassion for the crowds "because they were distressed and dispirited like sheep without a shepherd" (Matt. 9:36; cf. 14:14). Before feeding the four thousand "Jesus called His disciples to Him, and said, 'I feel compassion for the people, because they have remained with Me now three days and have nothing to eat; and I do not want to send them away hungry, for they might faint on the way'" (Matt. 15:32). Seeing two blind men, Jesus was "moved with compassion ... and touched their eyes; and immediately they regained their sight and followed Him" (Matt. 20:34). When a "leper came to Jesus, beseeching Him and falling on his knees before Him, and saying, 'If You are willing, You can make me clean'" (Mark 1:40) the Lord, "moved with compassion ... stretched out His hand and touched him, and said to him, 'I am willing; be cleansed'" (v. 41). He halted a funeral procession and raised a widow's son from the dead because "He felt compassion for her" (Luke 7:13).

In this section Jesus expressed His care for Israel in the form of a lament, which features compassion, condemnation, and conversion.

COMPASSION

"O Jerusalem, Jerusalem, the city that kills the prophets and stones those sent to her! How often I wanted to gather your children

together, just as a hen gathers her brood under her wings, and you would not have it! (13:34)

During His earthly ministry, Jesus manifested divine wrath and indignation toward sinners who rejected Him. He scathingly denounced the scribes and Pharisees as hypocrites, who fastidiously kept the minutiae of the law, but inwardly were corrupt and would not escape being sentenced to hell (Matt. 23:3–33). He also denounced the people of Israel as evil, adulterous, sinful, and unbelieving (Matt. 12:39; Mark 8:38; 9:19).

But the Lord also grieved for those who rejected Him, as exemplified in this passage. The agrarian imagery conveyed by His words, **How often I wanted to gather your children together, just as a hen gathers her brood under her wings,** pictures His desire to deliver rejecting Israel from divine judgment. He longed to protect them the way a mother hen shelters her chicks from a predator.

Christ's grief for lost sinners reflects God's grief. "I take no pleasure in the death of the wicked," God declared, "but rather that the wicked turn from his way and live. Turn back, turn back from your evil ways! Why then will you die, O house of Israel?" (Ezek. 33:11; cf. 18:23). In Jeremiah 13:16 God warned Israel through Jeremiah, "Give glory to the Lord your God, before He brings darkness and before your feet stumble on the dusky mountains, and while you are hoping for light He makes it into deep darkness, and turns it into gloom." Verse 17 records what God's reaction would be should that happen: "But if you will not listen to it, my soul will sob in secret for such pride; and my eyes will bitterly weep and flow down with tears, because the flock of the Lord has been taken captive." God would weep tears of grief through the eyes of Jeremiah over the judgment of His people.

Luke 19:41–44 records another display of Christ's divine grief for unbelieving Israel. Several months after the incident recorded in this passage, Jesus approached Jerusalem on His triumphal entry. Overcome with emotion, the Lord

> saw the city and wept over it, saying, "If you had known in this day, even you, the things which make for peace! But now they have been hidden

from your eyes. For the days will come upon you when your enemies will throw up a barricade against you, and surround you and hem you in on every side, and they will level you to the ground and your children within you, and they will not leave in you one stone upon another, because you did not recognize the time of your visitation."

The interjection **O** expresses the strong emotion (cf. Mark 9:19) that the Lord felt for Jerusalem (representing the entire nation, as in Ezek. 16:2–3; Mic. 1:5). The phrase **Jerusalem, Jerusalem** further indicates the intensity of Jesus' emotion. Repetition is a familiar way in Scripture of expressing emphasis and pathos. In Luke 10:41 Jesus replied to Martha's frustrated demand that He order her sister to help her, "Martha, Martha, you are worried and bothered about so many things." He solemnly warned Peter, "Simon, Simon, behold, Satan has demanded permission to sift you like wheat" (Luke 22:31). Jesus said to Paul when He appeared to him on the road to Damascus, "Saul, Saul, why are you persecuting Me?" (Acts 9:4). Overcome with grief at the news of Absalom's death, David "was deeply moved and went up to the chamber over the gate and wept. And thus he said as he walked, 'O my son Absalom, my son, my son Absalom! Would I had died instead of you, O Absalom, my son, my son!'" (2 Sam. 18:33).

Jesus described Jerusalem as **the city that kills the prophets and stones those sent to her.** Stoning was the prescribed form of execution for blasphemy (Lev. 24:14–16; cf. 20:1–3; Acts 6:11; 7:58–60). The parallel statements **kills the prophets** and **stones those sent to her** each contain present participles, indicating ongoing action. Israel had rejected and killed the prophets in the past (see the expositions of 13:33 in chapter 19 of this volume and 11:47–51 in chapter 9), was still doing it, and would continue to do so in the future. In the Beatitudes Jesus told His disciples, "Blessed are you when people insult you and persecute you, and falsely say all kinds of evil against you because of Me. Rejoice and be glad, for your reward in heaven is great; for in the same way they persecuted the prophets who were before you" (Matt. 5:11–12). In Matthew 23 Jesus denounced the Jewish religious leaders as "sons of those who murdered the prophets" (v. 31), and told them, "Therefore, behold, I am sending you prophets and wise men and scribes; some of them you will kill and crucify, and some of them you will scourge in your synagogues, and persecute from city to city" (v. 34).

Tragically, the people of Israel **would not** accept the protection, love, and salvation the Lord longed to give them. They would even kill the purest prophet, their own Messiah, instigate the imprisonment and execution of His brother James (Acts 12:1–3), stone Stephen (Acts 7:58–60), and go on persecuting and killing Christians (Acts 8:1; 26:10; 1 Cor. 15:9; 1 Tim. 1:13).

By doing so they continued their long history of distrust, disobedience, and rebellion against God that began when they were delivered from slavery in Egypt. They rebelled against Him at least ten times during their years of wandering in the wilderness (Ex. 14:10–12; 15:22–24; 16:1–3; 16:19–20; 16:27–30; 17:1–4; 32:1–35; Num. 11:1–3, 4–34; 14:3). As they, at last, stood on the brink of entering the Promised Land, Moses reiterated the law of God to the new generation of Israelites, those whose fathers had rebelled and died in the wilderness (Num. 14:1–38). He reminded them that obedience would bring blessing and disobedience cursing, and they promised to obey (Deut. 26:17). As an object lesson to reinforce that principle, the people were commanded to hold a dramatic ceremony after they entered Canaan. Half of the tribes were to stand on Mt. Ebal (near Shechem) and recite the blessings of obedience (Deut. 27:12), while the other six stood across the valley on Mt. Gerizim and recited the curses for disobedience (vv. 13–26).

Sadly, throughout subsequent history, Israel chose the path of disobedience, and has experienced the curses. From the repeated cycles of disobedience during the period of the judges, through the time of the divided kingdom, until the destruction and exile first of the northern kingdom of Israel and then the southern kingdom of Judah, Israel's history was largely one of rebellion, as 2 Kings 17:7–17 chronicles:

> Now this came about because the sons of Israel had sinned against the Lord their God, who had brought them up from the land of Egypt from under the hand of Pharaoh, king of Egypt, and they had feared other gods and walked in the customs of the nations whom the Lord had driven out before the sons of Israel, and in the customs of the kings of Israel which they had introduced. The sons of Israel did things secretly which were not right against the Lord their God. Moreover, they built for themselves high places in all their towns, from watchtower to fortified city. They set for themselves sacred pillars and Asherim on every high

hill and under every green tree, and there they burned incense on all the high places as the nations did which the Lord had carried away to exile before them; and they did evil things provoking the Lord. They served idols, concerning which the Lord had said to them, "You shall not do this thing." Yet the Lord warned Israel and Judah through all His prophets and every seer, saying, "Turn from your evil ways and keep My commandments, My statutes according to all the law which I commanded your fathers, and which I sent to you through My servants the prophets." However, they did not listen, but stiffened their neck like their fathers, who did not believe in the Lord their God. They rejected His statutes and His covenant which He made with their fathers and His warnings with which He warned them. And they followed vanity and became vain, and went after the nations which surrounded them, concerning which the Lord had commanded them not to do like them. They forsook all the commandments of the Lord their God and made for themselves molten images, even two calves, and made an Asherah and worshiped all the host of heaven and served Baal. Then they made their sons and their daughters pass through the fire, and practiced divination and enchantments, and sold themselves to do evil in the sight of the Lord, provoking Him.

As a result,

the Lord was very angry with Israel and removed them from His sight; none was left except the tribe of Judah. Also Judah did not keep the commandments of the Lord their God, but walked in the customs which Israel had introduced. The Lord rejected all the descendants of Israel and afflicted them and gave them into the hand of plunderers, until He had cast them out of His sight. (vv. 18–20)

The apostle Paul, quoting Isaiah, summarizes God's exasperation and sorrow for His disobedient people: "But as for Israel He says, 'All the day long I have stretched out my hands to a disobedient and obstinate people'" (Rom. 10:21; cf. Isa. 65:2).

CONDEMNATION

Behold, your house is left to you desolate; (13:35a)

Rejecting God's compassion results in His condemnation. The particle *idou* (**behold**) indicates that what follows is surprising and shocking. **House** symbolizes not only the temple, but also Jerusalem and the nation as a whole. Significantly, Jesus referred to **your** house, not God's. The nation had set its course; the day of opportunity was over; God had judicially abandoned them (cf. Rom. 1:24, 26, 28). Jesus "came to His own, and those who were His own did not receive Him" (John 1:11), because they "loved the darkness rather than the Light, for their deeds were evil" (3:19). They would soon disown "the Holy and Righteous One" and ask "for a murderer to be granted to [them]" (Acts 3:14). It was no longer God's house; the glory had departed and Ichabod was written on it (cf. 1 Sam. 4:21).

Isaiah 5:1–7 describes Israel's rejection of God's compassionate care and His subsequent judgment in the form of a parable or dirge. Verses 1–4 chronicle God's care for Israel and the nation's disobedience:

> Let me sing now for my well-beloved a song of my beloved concerning His vineyard. My well-beloved had a vineyard on a fertile hill. He dug it all around, removed its stones, and planted it with the choicest vine. And He built a tower in the middle of it and also hewed out a wine vat in it; then He expected it to produce good grapes, but it produced only worthless ones. "And now, O inhabitants of Jerusalem and men of Judah, judge between Me and My vineyard. What more was there to do for My vineyard that I have not done in it? Why, when I expected it to produce good grapes did it produce worthless ones?"

As a result, God would judge His people for their rejection of Him:

> "So now let Me tell you what I am going to do to My vineyard: I will remove its hedge and it will be consumed; I will break down its wall and it will become trampled ground. I will lay it waste; it will not be pruned or hoed, but briars and thorns will come up. I will also charge the clouds to rain no rain on it." For the vineyard of the Lord of hosts is the house of Israel and the men of Judah His delightful plant. Thus He looked for justice, but behold, bloodshed; for righteousness, but behold, a cry of distress. (vv. 5–7)

Centuries earlier, God had issued a similar warning to Solomon,

> If you or your sons shall indeed turn away from following Me, and do not keep My commandments and My statutes which I have set before you, and shall go and serve other gods and worship them, then I will cut off Israel from the land which I have given them, and the house which

I have consecrated for My name, I will cast out of My sight. So Israel will become a proverb and a byword among all peoples. (1 Kings 9:6–7)

The apex of Israel's turning away from God was their rejection and killing of the Lord Jesus Christ. Since that crime, the Jewish people have been under unrelenting judgment.

The first outbreak of divine cursing struck Israel with devastating force in A.D. 70. In the climactic event of the Jewish revolt against Rome that began in a.d. 66 the Romans, after a long siege, sacked Jerusalem and destroyed the temple. The first-century Jewish historian Josephus described the grim results:

> Caesar gave orders that they should now demolish the entire city and temple, but should leave as many of the towers standing as were of the greatest eminency ... and so much of the wall as enclosed the city on the west side. This wall was spared, in order to afford a camp for such as were to lie in garrison, as were the towers also spared, in order to demonstrate to posterity what kind of city it was, and how well fortified, which the Roman valor had subdued; but for all the rest of the wall, it was so thoroughly laid even with the ground by those that dug it up to the foundation, that there was left nothing to make those that came thither believe it had ever been inhabited. (*Wars of the Jews*, VII.1.1)

According to Josephus more than a million people died during the revolt, and almost one hundred thousand more were taken captive (*Wars*, VI.9.3).

In A.D. 439 Theodosius, ruler of the Eastern Roman Empire, issued a law denying Jews the same legal rights as others. Two centuries later the Byzantine Emperor Heraclius banished Jews from Jerusalem (A.D. 630).

Throughout the Middle Ages and the early modern period anti-Semitism was widespread in Europe. In the eleventh century Pope Urban II's passionate call for a crusade to free the Holy Land from the Muslims sparked an outbreak of violence against European Jews, who were also regarded as enemies of Christ. On their way to the Holy Land (which most of them did not reach), an undisciplined army composed largely of untrained peasants slaughtered thousands of Jews. Other Jews committed suicide rather than submit to forced conversion. The principle army of the crusaders massacred many of Jerusalem's Jewish inhabitants after they captured the city. England expelled its entire Jewish population in

1290, and there is no record of Jews in England until they were permitted to return in 1655. Other countries, such as France and Austria, also expelled some of their Jewish population. The Jews were often blamed for the devastating plague known as the Black Death (1348–50), and as a result were cruelly persecuted and killed. They were falsely accused of horrendous crimes, including ritual murder, faced forced conversion and baptism, and were often required to wear distinctive clothing that marked them as Jewish, such as armbands, badges, or special hats.

In recent times anti-Semitism has continued to pollute Western civilization. The nineteenth century witnessed pogroms and persecution in Russia, particularly after the assassination of Tsar Alexander II in 1881, which some blamed on the Jewish people. In a scandal that rocked France, Alfred Dreyfus, a young Jewish officer in the French army, was falsely accused of treason, imprisoned in the notorious Devil's Island prison, and after a public outcry, eventually exonerated. The twentieth century witnessed the unspeakable evil of the Holocaust, in which millions of Jews were systematically murdered under Hitler and Stalin. The modern state of Israel, founded in 1948, has faced relentless threats and assaults by her enemies. The threat of slaughter hangs over Israel's head today as the power and hatred of Islam increases exponentially.

For two thousand years the Jewish people have been a desolate house, a people punished by God. But that will end. In the most glorious hour of Israel's history, the nation returns to God. Through all of this history of being under God's curse, a remnant of Jews in every period has been saved (Rom. 1:16) and in Christ, they are one with all Gentile believers in the church (Rom. 10:12; 1 Cor. 12:13; Gal. 3:28; Col. 3:11).

CONVERSION

and I say to you, you will not see Me until the time comes when you say, 'Blessed is He who comes in the name of the Lord'" (13:35*b*)

Jesus' words in verses 34 and 35 may be viewed not only topically, but also chronologically. Considered in that sense, they reveal three aspects of God's dealing with Israel: past, present, and future.

God's past dealings with Israel are marked by two things: His special, gracious, covenantal love for Israel, and her special hatred for and rejection of His messengers.

The Lord's love for His people permeates the Old Testament. Moses reminded Israel, "Because [God] loved your fathers, therefore He chose their descendants after them. And He personally brought you from Egypt by His great power" (Deut. 4:37; cf. 10:15). Later in Deuteronomy he added,

> For you are a holy people to the Lord your God; the Lord your God has chosen you to be a people for His own possession out of all the peoples who are on the face of the earth. The Lord did not set His love on you nor choose you because you were more in number than any of the peoples, for you were the fewest of all peoples, but because the Lord loved you and kept the oath which He swore to your forefathers, the Lord brought you out by a mighty hand and redeemed you from the house of slavery, from the hand of Pharaoh king of Egypt. (Deut. 7:6–8)

In chapter 9 Moses reiterated to the Israelites that God was not giving them the land of Canaan because of their own righteousness (vv. 4–6), then recounted their history of sinning against Him to prove it (vv. 7–28). He concluded by reminding them that they were God's own people and inheritance (v. 29; cf. Isa. 43:1), and for that reason alone He was giving them the land.

But Israel repaid God's love with hatred and persecution of the messengers He sent to them, as noted in the exposition of verse 34 above. Because of that God has for the present time abandoned Israel. Centuries of disobedience have culminated in the nation's rejection (John 1:11; Acts 3:14–15) of their Messiah Jesus, who is the key to the fulfillment of all the promises (2 Cor. 1:20; cf. Acts 13:32–33). The Jewish people missed their opportunities and wasted their privileges (Rom. 3:1–2; 9:1–5) because "they stumbled over the stumbling stone" (Rom. 9:32). For the last two millennia Israel has been a desolate house, preserved as a people, but judicially punished by God.

But that is not the end of the story. There is a future for Israel in the plan of God beyond the remnant who are being saved during the church age. The **time** will come **when** Israel will **say** to Christ, **Blessed is**

He who comes in the name of the Lord (cf. Ps. 118:26). The term **until** encompasses all of God's covenant promises; **see** refers to spiritual recognition (cf. Luke 2:30; 2 Cor. 5:16). In that future day when they confess Jesus as their Messiah, Israel will recognize who He truly is. When the "Spirit of grace and of supplication" comes to them, they will "look on [Him] whom they have pierced; and they will mourn for Him" (Zech. 12:10). Then the fountain of cleansing will come to them from heaven. The rebels will be purged out and Israel saved (Zech. 13:1ff.). Their confession will be the words of Isaiah 53:

> Who has believed our message? And to whom has the arm of the Lord been revealed? For He grew up before Him like a tender shoot, and like a root out of parched ground; He has no stately form or majesty that we should look upon Him, nor appearance that we should be attracted to Him. He was despised and forsaken of men, a man of sorrows and acquainted with grief; and like one from whom men hide their face He was despised, and we did not esteem Him. Surely our griefs He Himself bore, and our sorrows He carried; Yet we ourselves esteemed Him stricken, smitten of God, and afflicted. But He was pierced through for our transgressions, He was crushed for our iniquities; the chastening for our well-being fell upon Him, and by His scourging we are healed. All of us like sheep have gone astray, each of us has turned to his own way; But the Lord has caused the iniquity of us all to fall on Him. He was oppressed and He was afflicted, yet He did not open His mouth; like a lamb that is led to slaughter, and like a sheep that is silent before its shearers, so He did not open His mouth. By oppression and judgment He was taken away; and as for His generation, who considered that He was cut off out of the land of the living for the transgression of my people, to whom the stroke was due? His grave was assigned with wicked men, Yet He was with a rich man in His death, because He had done no violence, nor was there any deceit in His mouth. But the Lord was pleased to crush Him, putting Him to grief; if He would render Himself as a guilt offering, He will see His offspring, He will prolong His days, and the good pleasure of the Lord will prosper in His hand. As a result of the anguish of His soul, He will see it and be satisfied; By His knowledge the Righteous One, My Servant, will justify the many, as He will bear their iniquities. Therefore, I will allot Him a portion with the great, and He will divide the booty with the strong; because He poured out Himself to death, and was numbered with the transgressors; Yet He Himself bore the sin of many, and interceded for the transgressors. (Isa. 53:1–12)

Despite the Lord's promise, however, many argue that God is permanently finished with Israel. They believe that there is no future for the nation, though individual Jews will continue to come to faith in Christ and be incorporated into the church. That is an essential tenet of covenant theology. Covenant theologians hold that the curses promised for Israel's disobedience were literally fulfilled. On the other hand, they argue that because Israel rejected Jesus Christ, it is no longer part of God's plan. Therefore the blessings promised for obedience are fulfilled spiritually in the church.

That view raises a number of difficulties. First, once the literal meaning of a passage is rejected, how can the spiritual sense be determined? If the normal rules of biblical interpretation do not apply to prophecy, who is to say what the spiritual meaning of the passages regarding Israel's future is? If the Bible does not mean what it says, to what authority can we turn to determine what it does mean? Further, if those prophecies are not to be taken literally, what meaning did they have for those to whom they were addressed? If the prophecies of Israel's future blessing really apply to the church, why were they addressed to Israel? And why was Israel literally cursed? Finally, spiritualizing those prophecies results in some glaring inconsistencies. As I noted in an earlier volume in this series:

> It is inconsistent to argue that the cursings [the prophecies regarding Israel] they pronounce apply literally to Israel, while the blessings they promise apply symbolically and spiritually to the church. An example of inconsistency in the spiritualizing method of interpreting prophecy comes from the angel Gabriel's words to Mary in Luke 1:31-33: "And behold, you will conceive in your womb and bear a son, and you shall name Him Jesus. He will be great and will be called the Son of the Most High; and the Lord God will give Him the throne of His father David; and He will reign over the house of Jacob forever, and His kingdom will have no end." If, as all conservative scholars agree, Jesus was literally conceived in Mary's womb, literally named "Jesus," literally became great, was literally "the Son of the Most High," will He not also literally reign on David's throne over Israel? Can the same passage be interpreted both literally and non-literally? (*Revelation 12–22*, The MacArthur New Testament Commentary [Chicago: Moody, 2000], 232)

Those who spiritualize the prophecies of Israel's future blessing admit that applying the literal, historical, grammatical and contextual method of hermeneutics—which they themselves apply to the non-prophetic portions of Scripture—to prophecy leads inevitably to the conclusion that there will be a future for Israel. Floyd Hamilton, an advocate of interpreting the prophecies regarding Israel non-literally acknowledges, "Now we must frankly admit that a literal interpretation of the Old Testament prophecies gives us just such a picture of an earthly reign of the Messiah as the premillennialist pictures" (*The Basis of Millennial Faith* [Grand Rapids: Eerdmans, 1942], 38). Loraine Boettner, who also advocated the non-literal view, agrees with Hamilton's assessment: "It is generally agreed that if the prophecies are taken literally, they do foretell a restoration of the nation of Israel in the land of Palestine with the Jews having a prominent place in that kingdom and ruling over the other nations" ("A Postmillennial Response [to Dispensational Premillennialism]," in Robert G. Clouse, ed., *The Meaning of the Millennium: Four Views* [Downers Grove, Ill.: InterVarsity, 1977], 95). To adopt a hermeneutical method for interpreting prophecy different from that used to interpret the rest of Scripture is entirely arbitrary. Those who advocate such a method do so because the literal interpretation of the prophecies regarding Israel's future is inconsistent with their theological preferences. Theology, however, should be based on exegesis, not determine it.

But what is really at stake here is God's faithfulness. To put it simply, can He be counted on to keep His promises? In both the Abrahamic and Davidic covenants God promised unconditionally that there would be a future for the chosen nation. The Davidic covenant, first given in 2 Samuel 7:12–17 and referred to throughout the Old Testament, promised that God will establish the Messiah as King, defeat all of Israel's enemies, and grant Israel prosperity and prominence. When Messiah comes to establish His kingdom, Israel will be saved (Rom. 11:25–26).

The Abrahamic covenant, first given in Genesis 12, and reaffirmed in chapters 13, 15, 17, 26, 28, and 35, is an irrevocable, unilateral, eternal promise from God. In it God vowed to make of Abraham's descendants a great nation and grant them a land even greater in extent than that of modern-day Israel. The Abrahamic covenant also promised personal salvation through Abraham's seed, the Lord Jesus Christ (Gal. 3:16).

God is faithful (1 Cor. 10:13; 1 Peter 4:19) and keeps His promises (Deut. 4:31; Josh. 21:43–45; 23:14). His faithfulness demands that He honor the covenants He made with Israel (cf. Neh. 9:26–32). For Him to fail to do so would call into question all of His promises, make His Word void, and undermine His integrity. But the Bible repeatedly emphasizes that God will keep His promises concerning Israel's future:

> "For the mountains may be removed and the hills may shake, but My lovingkindness will not be removed from you, and My covenant of peace will not be shaken," says the Lord who has compassion on you. (Isa. 54:10)

> "Behold, the days are coming," declares the Lord, "When I will raise up for David a righteous Branch; and He will reign as king and act wisely and do justice and righteousness in the land. In His days Judah will be saved, and Israel will dwell securely; and this is His name by which He will be called, 'The Lord our righteousness.'" (Jer. 23:5–6)

> Thus says the Lord, who gives the sun for light by day and the fixed order of the moon and the stars for light by night, who stirs up the sea so that its waves roar; the Lord of hosts is His name: "If this fixed order departs from before Me," declares the Lord, "then the offspring of Israel also will cease from being a nation before Me forever." Thus says the Lord, "If the heavens above can be measured and the foundations of the earth searched out below, then I will also cast off all the offspring of Israel for all that they have done," declares the Lord. (Jer. 31:35–37)

> "As I live," declares the Lord God, "surely with a mighty hand and with an outstretched arm and with wrath poured out, I shall be king over you. I will bring you out from the peoples and gather you from the lands where you are scattered, with a mighty hand and with an outstretched arm and with wrath poured out; and I will bring you into the wilderness of the peoples, and there I will enter into judgment with you face to face. As I entered into judgment with your fathers in the wilderness of the land of Egypt, so I will enter into judgment with you," declares the Lord God. "I will make you pass under the rod, and I shall bring you into the bond of the covenant; and I will purge from you the rebels and those who transgress against Me; I will bring them out of the land where they sojourn, but they will not enter the land of Israel. Thus you will know that I am the Lord." (Ezek. 20:33–38)

> For the sons of Israel will remain for many days without king or prince, without sacrifice or sacred pillar and without ephod or household idols. Afterward the sons of Israel will return and seek the Lord their God and David their king; and they will come trembling to the Lord and to His goodness in the last days. (Hos. 3:4–5)

> In that day I will set about to destroy all the nations that come against Jerusalem. I will pour out on the house of David and on the inhanbitants

of Jerusalem, the Spirit of grace and of supplication, so that they will look on Me whom they have pierced; and they will mourn for Him, as one mourns for an only son, and they will weep bitterly over Him like the bitter weeping over a firstborn. (Zech. 12:9–10)

In that day a fountain will be opened for the house of David and for the inhabitants of Jerusalem, for sin and for impurity.…"It will come about in all the land," declares the Lord,"that two parts in it will be cut off and perish; but the third will be left in it. And I will bring the third part through the fire, refine them as silver is refined, and test them as gold is tested. They will call on My name, and I will answer them; I will say, 'They are My people,' and they will say, 'The Lord is my God.'" (Zech. 13:1, 8–9)

And the Lord will be king over all the earth; in that day the Lord will be the only one, and His name the only one. All the land will be changed into a plain from Geba to Rimmon south of Jerusalem; but Jerusalem will rise and remain on its site from Benjamin's Gate as far as the place of the First Gate to the Corner Gate, and from the Tower of Hananel to the king's wine presses. People will live in it, and there will no longer be a curse, for Jerusalem will dwell in security. (Zech. 14:9–11)

For I do not want you, brethren, to be uninformed of this mystery—so that you will not be wise in your own estimation—that a partial hardening has happened to Israel until the fullness of the Gentiles has come in; and so all Israel will be saved; just as it is written, "the deliverer will come from Zion, He will remove ungodliness from Jacob." (Rom. 11:25–26. See also Jer. 30:10–11; 31:10; 33:17–21; Ezek. 16:60; Hos. 2:19; Zech. 8:20–23)

Scripture speaks clearly on this matter. It is not ambiguous. Nor does God's compassion for sinners obviate their responsibility. Those who accept His offer of salvation will receive His compassion and be converted. But the rebellious and disobedient who reject His invitation to salvation (see among many others Isa. 45:22; 55:1; Matt. 3:2; 4:17; 11:28–30; Mark 6:12; Acts 2:38; 3:19; 17:30; 26:20; Rev. 22:17) will face condemnation (John 3:18, 36; 5:29; 12:47–48; Acts 17:31; Rom. 2:5–9, 12; 2 Thess. 1:6–9; Heb. 9:27; 10:26–27; 2 Peter 3:7; Rev. 20:11–15). Of such people Jesus said, "You are unwilling to come to Me so that you may have life" (John 5:40; cf. 1:11; 12:37–41; Matt. 22:1–14; 23:37; Luke 14:15–24; Acts 7:51). The Bible teaches that sinners are responsible for their refusal to accept God's offer of salvation:

When they set their will to reject him, he respected their will, and accepted their rejection. Jerusalem was Messiah's own capital city; and in Jerusalem was the very house of God. Christ did not raise an army, nor use his miraculous powers to drive out his enemies from Jerusalem and throw Israel's rebellious priesthood out of his Father's house. Instead he let them throw him out of both the temple and the city; and what had been his Father's and his, he left in their hands. . . . It is an awesome thing to contemplate: if men use the free-will God has given them to reject the Saviour, neither God nor Christ will overrule that free-will or remove it. That does not mean, of course, that puny man has the power to defeat the will of the Almighty: it was always God's will that man's will should be free, and man be able to say no to God, if he chose. (David Gooding, *According to Luke* [Grand Rapids: Eerdmans, 1987], 263)

Confronting Hypocritical False Teachers (Luke 14:1–14)

21

It happened that when He went into the house of one of the leaders of the Pharisees on the Sabbath to eat bread, they were watching Him closely. And there in front of Him was a man suffering from dropsy. And Jesus answered and spoke to the lawyers and Pharisees, saying, "Is it lawful to heal on the Sabbath, or not?" But they kept silent. And He took hold of him and healed him, and sent him away. And He said to them, "Which one of you will have a son or an ox fall into a well, and will not immediately pull him out on a Sabbath day?" And they could make no reply to this. And He began speaking a parable to the invited guests when He noticed how they had been picking out the places of honor at the table, saying to them, "When you are invited by someone to a wedding feast, do not take the place of honor, for someone more distinguished than you may have been invited by him, and he who invited you both will come and say to you, 'Give your place to this man,' and then in disgrace you proceed to occupy the last place. But when you are invited, go and recline at the last place, so that when the one who has invited you comes, he may say to you, 'Friend, move up higher'; then you will have honor in the sight of all who are at the table with you. For everyone who exalts himself will be humbled, and he who humbles himself will be exalted." And He also went on to say to the one who had invited Him, "When you give a luncheon or a dinner, do not invite your friends or your brothers or your relatives or rich neighbors, otherwise they may also invite you in return and that will be your repayment. But when you give a reception, invite the poor, the crippled, the lame, the blind, and you will be blessed, since they do not have the means to repay you; for you will be repaid at the resurrection of the righteous." (14:1–14)

The Bible harshly condemns false teachers as greedy (Isa. 56:11; Jer. 6:13; 8:10; Mic. 3:5; Phil. 3:18–19; 2 Peter 2:1–3, 14) emissaries of Satan, whom Jesus said turn people away from the narrow path to heaven and instead lure them onto the broad path to hell (Matt. 7:13–15).

Scripture does not support the inclusiveness, tolerance of error, and willingness to embrace false teachers in the name of love and unity that marks the professing church today. On the contrary the Bible, using vivid and powerful language, denounces false teachers. In a litany of graphic expressions, they are called blind men who know nothing, "mute dogs unable to bark, dreamers lying down who love to slumber" (Isa. 56:10), demented fools (Hos. 9:7), reckless, treacherous men (Zeph. 3:4), ravenous wolves (Matt. 7:15), blind guides of the blind (Matt. 15:14; cf. 23:16), hypocrites (Matt. 23:13), fools (v. 17), whitewashed tombs full of bones (v. 27), serpents, a brood of vipers (v. 33), thieves and robbers (John 10:8), savage wolves (Acts 20:29), slaves of their own appetites (Rom. 16:18), hucksters peddling the Word of God (2 Cor. 2:17), false apostles, deceitful workers (2 Cor. 11:13), servants of Satan (v. 15), purveyors of a different gospel (Gal. 1:6–8), dogs, evil workers (Phil. 3:2), enemies of the cross of Christ (Phil. 3:18), those who are conceited and understand nothing (1 Tim. 6:4), men of depraved minds deprived of the truth (v. 5), men who have gone astray from the truth (2 Tim. 2:18), captives of the devil (v. 26), deceivers (2 John 7), ungodly persons (Jude 4), and unreasoning animals (v. 10). The Bible also pronounces severe judgment on them (Deut. 13:5; 18:20; Jer. 14:15; Gal. 1:8–9; Rev. 2:20–23).

Scripture harshly condemns false teachers because of the deadly danger they pose to people's eternal souls. They lead many astray from the truth of God's Word (Isa. 3:12; 9:16; Jer. 14:13; 23:26–27, 32; 50:6; Matt. 23:13, 15; 24:4–5, 24; Luke 11:46, 52; Rom. 16:17–18; Col. 2:4, 8, 18; 1 Thess. 2:14–16; 2 Tim. 3:13; Titus 1:10; 2 John 7)—especially concerning the need for repentance from sin (Jer. 6:14; 8:11; 23:21–22; Lam. 2:14; Ezek. 13:10, 16, 22).

One of the most sinister and deadly false teachers of recent decades was Jim Jones, founder of the People's Temple. Jones was a Communist and atheist (as well as a drug abuser and sexual predator), who deified himself and claimed to be the reincarnation of such religious and political figures as Jesus, Gandhi, Buddha, and Lenin. Jones ridiculed biblical Christianity, mocked the God of Scripture, and derided the Bible as a "paper idol." He cynically sought to further his Marxist socialist agenda by infiltrating the church (cf. Acts 20:29–30). Jones eventually led his followers to Guyana, where they founded the now infamous Jonestown settlement. There, on November 18, 1978, more than 900 people (tragically, at least 200 of them children), died in a mass murder-suicide ordered by Jones.

The Jonestown incident shocked the world. Yet the real tragedy was not that so many people died physically in a South American jungle, but that they died eternally. While few false teachers lead their followers to physical death as Jim Jones did, all lead them to eternal death.

The leaders of the Jewish people in Jesus' day were described by Him as making people "twice as much [sons] of hell as [themselves]" (Matt. 23:15). The people trusted them and believed that they would lead them to salvation. But the truth is that instead, as they had throughout much of the Old Testament history, the leaders of Israel led the people into God's eternal judgment (cf. Luke 13:24–29, 34–35).

Chief among Israel's false teachers were the Pharisees, one of four main Jewish sects, along with the Sadducees (the wealthy, elite priests), the Zealots (political revolutionaries who sought independence from Rome), and the Essenes (ascetic monastics). The Pharisees were devout religionists, extremely zealous for the Mosaic law (and their own extrabiblical traditions [cf. Mark 7:8–13]).

The sect originated during the intertestamental period, born out of a spiritual revolt against the influence of Greek and Roman thought and culture on the Jewish people. They called for a separation ("Pharisee" likely derives from a Hebrew verb meaning "to separate") from paganism and a return to a strict adherence to the Old Testament law. The Pharisees had no interest in politics (unlike the Sadducees and the Zealots), nor were they mystics (unlike the Essenes). In contrast to the Sadducees, who were mostly wealthy priests or Levites, the Pharisees were laymen, and generally came from the middle class. Although few in number (according to the first-century Jewish historian Josephus there were about 6,000 at the time of Herod the Great), they had widespread influence with the common people, to whom they taught the law in the local synagogues. (Ironically, the Pharisees viewed those common people in a condescending fashion as ignorant of the law and beneath them [cf. John 7:49].) Eventually, the rabbinic traditions that the Pharisees increasingly superimposed on the Old Testament became a crushing burden (Matt. 23:4), impossible for the people to bear (Acts 15:10).

The Sadducees ceased to be a force in Jewish life after the destruction of the temple in A.D. 70 and the Zealots' influence faded after the Bar Kochba revolt (A.D. 132–35) was crushed, leaving the Pharisees as the dominant force in Judaism. The Pharisees' theology was in many ways biblically correct. They believed in the resurrection (Acts 23:6–8), angels (Acts 23:8), demons, predestination, human responsibility, and Messiah's earthly kingdom.

While pretending to be devout, the Pharisees were actually hypocrites who failed to live up to even their own strict teaching regarding the law (Matt. 23:3). They abandoned the true religion of the heart for an external one, which they hoped would elicit the admiration and respect of the people, as well as God's approval (Matt. 6:1–5; 9:14; 12:2; 23:5–7, 23; Luke 11:38–39). The Pharisees' superficial, external righteousness, however, fell far short of what heaven demands (Matt. 5:20; 23:28; Luke 11:39–40). So despite their zeal for the law, they amounted only to "blind guides of the blind" (Matt. 15:14), who made their proselytes doubly worthy of the hell to which they themselves were headed.

Closely associated with the Pharisees were their scribes (5:21, 30; 6:7; 11:53; 15:2; Matt. 5:20; 12:38; 15:1; 23:2, 13, 15, 23, 25, 27, 29; Mark 7:1, 5;

John 8:3; Mark 2:16 refers to "the scribes of the Pharisees," and Acts 23:9 to "the scribes of the Pharisaic party"), the professional scholars who specialized in the interpretation and application of the Old Testament law. The scribes provided the theological foundation for the Pharisees' teaching.

There were Pharisees who were sympathetic to Jesus (John 9:15–16) and Paul (Acts 23:9) and a few even became believers (Acts 15:5). But all the rest hated and opposed Jesus, viewing the gospel of Christ as an attack on their religious system and them. That Jesus frequently denounced them in front of the people as hypocrites further enraged them.

This dramatic confrontation in which our Lord, as He frequently did, exposed the Pharisees' hypocrisy and pride can be broken into four features: the setting, the setup, the silencing, and the story.

THE SETTING

It happened that when He went into the house of one of the leaders of the Pharisees on the Sabbath to eat bread, (14:1*a*)

The phrase **it happened** indicates an unspecified time during the Lord's final journey to Jerusalem (recorded by Luke in 9:51–19:27). The exact location where this incident took place is not certain, although it most likely was in Perea. On this occasion Jesus, as He had done in the past (cf. Luke 7:36–50; 11:37–54), **went into the house of** a Pharisee **to eat bread** (i.e., have a meal, which would have been prepared in advance due to the Sabbath restrictions on food preparation). This was the home of **one of the leaders of the Pharisees,** possibly the ruler of the local synagogue or even a member of the Sanhedrin. The meal was the midday **Sabbath** meal, which took place after the morning meeting in the synagogue. This was a gathering of many of the elite Pharisees and scribes. Constantly seeking honor and prestige, the Pharisees associated only with those they considered equals or who would elevate their status. They would never invite to a meal those whom they considered beneath them. Thus, they were shocked and appalled when Jesus regularly associated with the outcasts of Jewish society (Matt. 9:10–11; Luke 15:1–2). Yet for reasons that will soon become apparent, they invited both Jesus, whom they hated, and a man who was himself a despised outcast.

THE SETUP

they were watching Him closely. And there in front of Him was a man suffering from dropsy. (14:1*b*–2)

Because of the Pharisees' animosity toward Him, the question naturally arises as to why Jesus was invited to the meal. Why He accepted the invitation is clear—it was to present once again the gospel to those religious sinners who desperately needed salvation. That the Pharisees had their own agenda is clear from the phrase **they were watching Him closely. Watching . . . closely** translates a form of the Greek verb *paratereō*, which means, "to observe carefully," "to be on the lookout," or "to pay heed to." But in the gospels the word takes on a sinister tone, and could be translated, "to lurk," "to spy," "to watch for an opportunity with malicious intent" (cf. 14:1; 20:20; Mark 3:2). Jesus was invited because they were setting Him up, hoping to entrap Him into breaking the rabbinic laws, which were particularly strict regarding the Sabbath.

The bait for their trap was **a man suffering from dropsy. Dropsy,** or edema, is a medical condition in which the body abnormally retains fluids, causing swelling. It is not a disease, but rather the symptom of a disease or condition related to the heart, lungs, kidneys, or liver. The rabbis viewed such a condition, however, as God's judgment for immorality, or as uncleanness due to the body's failure to eliminate (Lev. 15:1–3). Thus in their view this man was both immoral and ritually unclean. Since no Pharisee would have tolerated such a defiled person at the meal, they obviously planned to use him for a sinister purpose. And they were fairly sure that based on His pattern Jesus, seeing his dropsy, would do what they wanted.

And what they desired was to get Jesus to violate their Sabbath restrictions by healing the man (cf. Luke 6:6–11; 13:10–17). In their twisted minds, this would confirm their belief that He was not from God. That amazingly counterintuitive thinking graphically reveals the depths of their spiritual blindness and the hardness of their sin-darkened hearts. In effect, they were challenging Jesus to perform a miracle so they could justify rejecting Him. They would view the healing, in reality the very proof that He was God (cf. John 10:25, 37–38; 14:10–11), as evidence that He was neither God nor from God (John 9:16). They believed He was empowered by the devil (Matt. 12:24). In an astonishing display of duplicity and hypocrisy, these self-appointed guardians of the rabbinic law actually were encouraging Jesus to break it.

THE SILENCING

And Jesus answered and spoke to the lawyers and Pharisees, saying, "Is it lawful to heal on the Sabbath, or not?" But they kept silent. And He took hold of him and healed him, and sent him away. And He said to them, "Which one of you will have a son or an ox fall into a well, and will not immediately pull him out on a Sabbath day?" And they could make no reply to this. (14:3–6)

Jesus masterfully turned the tables on those who sought to trap Him and instead trapped them. Before He performed the healing as they knew He would, He responded to their challenge to His divine authority as Lord of the Sabbath (Luke 6:5) by asking the **lawyers and Pharisees, "Is it lawful to heal on the Sabbath, or not?"** Needless to say, ministering to a sick person was by no means a violation of any Old Testament regulation concerning the Sabbath (cf. Matt. 12:7). Rabbinic attachments, however, prohibited anyone from treating a sick person on the Sabbath unless that person was in imminent danger of death if left untreated until the next day. To do so, the rabbis taught, would constitute work and hence be a violation of the required Sabbath rest. Even matters of life and death were subject to their cruel, inflexible, and ridiculous man-made restrictions.

Jesus' question put the scribes and Pharisees on the horns of a dilemma. On the one hand, answering that it was lawful to do good on the Sabbath would officially authorize Him to heal the man and put them in agreement with that. They could not then indict Him for breaking the Sabbath. On the other hand, answering that it was not lawful might keep Jesus from performing the healing, once again preventing them from indicting Him. Faced with those two equally unpleasant alternatives, **they kept silent,** confounded in the face of a simple question with complex implications.

Leaving His opponents silently stuck on the horns of the dilemma, Jesus acted forcefully and decisively in defiance of their Sabbath regulations, and no doubt angry and grieved at their hardened hearts (cf. Mark 3:5). **He took hold of** the sick man and **healed him.** *Epilambanomai* (**took hold of**) is a forceful term, which has the idea of "seizing," or "grabbing" (cf. 23:26; Matt. 14:31; Acts 16:19; 18:17; 21:30, 33). The Lord's hands on him not only showed compassion to the sick man by letting him know that he was not an unclean outcast, but also left no doubt that He Himself was the healer. Instantly and completely the man's condition was cured and the excess fluids disappeared. Since the purpose of Christ for him was accomplished, Jesus **sent him away.** The Lord compassionately understood that he would have been eager to share the good news of his healing with his family and friends.

At that moment, the Pharisees must have thought that their plan had succeeded. Jesus had clearly violated their Sabbath restrictions by healing a man who by their standards was unclean, sinful, and under divine judgment. But before they could level their accusations Jesus, knowing what they were thinking, posed a new question. **"Which one of you will have a son or an ox fall into a well,"** He asked them, **"and will not immediately pull him out on a Sabbath day?"** Of course, if any of them had **a son** (for obvious reasons) **or an ox** (because of the financial cost of replacing it) that fell **into a well** they would **immediately pull him out,** even **on a Sabbath day.** They would not even allow their animals to go without water on the Sabbath (13:15). Why, then, should they object to Jesus reaching out on the Sabbath to save a man drowning in his own fluids?

This was not what the Pharisees had envisioned. Their plan to discredit Jesus had backfired. Humiliated by the Lord's exposure of their hypocrisy, **they could make no reply to** His challenge (cf. 13:17; 20:26). Things were about to get worse for them, however, as the Lord took the offensive, inventing a story as He often did, to condemn their pride and call for humility.

THE STORY

And He began speaking a parable to the invited guests when He noticed how they had been picking out the places of honor at the table, saying to them, "When you are invited by someone to a wedding feast, do not take the place of honor, for someone more distinguished than you may have been invited by him, and he who invited you both will come and say to you, 'Give your place to this man,' and then in disgrace you proceed to occupy the last place. "But when you are invited, go and recline at the last place, so that when the one who has invited you comes, he may say to you, 'Friend, move up higher'; then you will have honor in the sight of all who are at the table with you. . . . And He also went on to say to the one who had invited Him, "When you give a luncheon or a dinner, do not invite your friends or your brothers or your relatives or rich neighbors, otherwise they may also invite you in return and that will be your repayment. But when you give a reception, invite the poor, the crippled, the lame, the blind, and you will be blessed, since they do not have the means to repay you; for you will be repaid at the resurrection of the righteous." (14:7–10, 12–14)

Having turned the Pharisees' attempt to trap Him against them and shamed them into silence, Jesus used a parable to confront their pride and hypocrisy. There was also mercy in His words, which challenged them to repent and enter the kingdom.

The Pharisees may have been silenced, but Jesus still had much to say to them. A **parable** is not an allegory in which everything has a hidden, mystical, spiritual meaning, but an illustration, analogy, or metaphor used to make or clarify a point. In the sense that Jesus used them, parables are earthly stories that illustrate heavenly realities.

The **invited guests** were, as noted above, the scribes and Pharisees, who did not mingle with those whom they considered their inferiors. While they had been watching Him (v. 1), Jesus had been watching them. As they were filing in for the meal, **He noticed how they had been picking out the places of honor at the table.** A typical **table** would be U-shaped or an arrangement of separate tables in the middle of the room. At the head was the host, on either side of him the two most honored guests, and down the sides the remaining guests, all reclining on three-person couches. When the guests entered for this meal, there had been a less than subtle scramble as they began **picking out the places of honor at the table,** the ones nearest to the host.

Such behavior was consistent with the Pharisees' insatiable desire to be elevated in the sight of men. They "love[d] the place of honor at banquets and the chief seats in the synagogues" (Matt. 23:6; cf. Luke 20:46), and "the respectful greetings in the market places" (Luke 11:43). The honored guests were those who had honored the host (or were capable of doing so); the system of seeking honor from each other (John 5:44) was based on reciprocation. The whole scene was an exercise in self-promotion.

Jesus set His criticism of the guests' behavior at the luncheon in an illustration of a **wedding feast**—the most important of all community events. **"When you are invited by someone to a wedding feast,"** Jesus told them, **"do not take the place of honor, for someone more distinguished than you may have been invited by him, and he who invited you both will come and say to you, 'Give your place to this man,' and then in disgrace you proceed to occupy the last place."** Eagerly grabbing a place of **honor** could backfire if **someone more distinguished** (and therefore better able to reciprocate to the host) had **been invited.** In that case the host would make the less important man **give** his **place to** the more important one, and then in humiliation and **disgrace** the first man would **proceed to occupy the last place,** the least honorable of all. A far wiser course of action would be to **go and recline at the last place,** and then have the host **say, "Friend, move up higher."** That would result in even more **honor in the sight of all who** were attending the banquet. The principle here is reminiscent of Solomon's counsel in Proverbs 25:6–7: "Do not claim honor in the presence of the king, and do not stand in the place of great men; for it is better that it be said to you, 'Come up here,' than for you to be placed lower in the presence of the prince, whom your eyes have seen."

But Jesus was not merely advising the Pharisees on the proper etiquette for being a successful hypocrite. In reality, His words were designed to picture those who, in a display of spiritual pride and self-righteous arrogance, clamor for the chief places in the kingdom of God (cf. Mark 10:35–40), only to be sent by God, the host of heaven's banquet, to the remotest place in His domain.

One such status seeker was the Pharisee in a "parable [Jesus told] to some people who trusted in themselves that they were righteous, and viewed others with contempt" (Luke 18:9). He considered himself superior to the despised tax collector, haughtily declaring, "God, I thank You that I am not like other people: swindlers, unjust, adulterers, or even like this tax collector. I fast twice a week; I pay tithes of all that I get" (vv. 11–12). But in just such a reversal of positions as Jesus spoke of, the humble, repentant tax collector, not the proud Pharisee, entered the kingdom of salvation (v. 14).

As the host, **the one who had invited** Jesus was not, of course, involved in the battle for the important seat. He owned it. But the Lord rebuked his pride as well. **"When you give a luncheon or a dinner, do not** exclusively **invite your friends or your brothers or your relatives or rich neighbors,** He told him, **otherwise they may also invite you in return and that will be your repayment."** Reciprocity controlled the ethics and actions of the Pharisees' social structure. But it was a zero sum game with no winners, in which the participants' gains and losses of prestige evened out in the end. And even had there been clear winners in the earthly prestige game, there would not have been any places of honor for them in the kingdom.

In Jewish society an invitation to a meal with a Pharisee was a kind of currency; they exploited hospitality for the sake of self-glory and elevation. Disinterested kindness was foreign to them; everything they did was self-serving. Jesus' challenge to the host revealed the true path to eternal blessing: **"But when you give a reception, invite the poor, the crippled, the lame, the blind, and you will be blessed, since they do not have the means to repay you; for you will be repaid at the resurrection of the righteous."** Such outcasts would not be invited to a **reception** given by a Pharisee, since they had no way of reciprocating. Further, it was just such riffraff that the Pharisees sought to distance themselves from. But those true saints who demonstrated humility by inviting people who could not repay them will be **repaid** by

God **at the resurrection of the righteous** (cf. John 5:28–29; Acts 24:15), when they receive their eternal reward.

THE ASSUMPTION

For everyone who exalts himself will be humbled, and he who humbles himself will be exalted. (14:11)

This is the spiritual axiom or principle underlying Christ's exhortations to both the guests and the host. God is the unnamed person and power who both humbles the proud (Prov. 16:5; Isa. 2:11, 17; Dan. 4:37) and exalts the humble (Luke 1:51–52; James 4:10; 1 Peter 5:6). In Psalm 75:6–7 the psalmist wrote, "For not from the east, nor from the west, nor from the desert comes exaltation; but God is the Judge; He puts down one and exalts another" (cf. Matt. 23:12; Luke 18:14). Honor and blessing in God's kingdom eludes those who think they can earn it; salvation comes only to the humble (Matt. 5:3–5). Those bloated with the edema of pride will not pass through the narrow gate leading to salvation.

Whether Jesus explained the meaning of His parable to the guests is not revealed, though He probably did. His reference to the resurrection of the righteous would have made it clear to them that He was speaking of the kingdom (cf. the statement by one of the guests in v. 15). Yet, the Lord was under no obligation to explain anything to those who hard-heartedly rejected Him (cf. Matt. 13:10–13; 11:25).

In any case His message is clear. No one will enter the kingdom by merit, good works, righteous deeds, self-promotion, spiritual pride, or making and keeping extrabiblical laws. Salvation comes only to the humble, the broken and contrite who plead only for mercy and grace, and nothing more. Jesus described them as the poor in spirit, who mourn over their sin and are humble (Matt. 5:3–5). They are those who have obeyed James's exhortation to

> Submit therefore to God. Resist the devil and he will flee from you. Draw near to God and He will draw near to you. Cleanse your hands, you sinners; and purify your hearts, you double-minded. Be miserable and mourn and weep; let your laughter be turned into mourning and

your joy to gloom. Humble yourselves in the presence of the Lord, and He will exalt you. (James 4:7–10)

Such a one was Paul, a proud, zealous Pharisee, who eventually came to regard his self-righteous religious achievements as manure (Phil. 3:8) and cast himself wholly on the mercy of God for salvation:

> I thank Christ Jesus our Lord, who has strengthened me, because He considered me faithful, putting me into service, even though I was formerly a blasphemer and a persecutor and a violent aggressor. Yet I was shown mercy because I acted ignorantly in unbelief; and the grace of our Lord was more than abundant, with the faith and love which are found in Christ Jesus. It is a trustworthy statement, deserving full acceptance, that Christ Jesus came into the world to save sinners, among whom I am foremost of all. Yet for this reason I found mercy, so that in me as the foremost, Jesus Christ might demonstrate His perfect patience as an example for those who would believe in Him for eternal life. (1 Tim. 1:12–16)

Paul understood what these Pharisees did not. The way into the kingdom is not through self-promoting pride, but through self-effacing humility and acknowledging oneself to be a wretched sinner in need of God's gracious salvation provided through Jesus Christ.

An Invitation to God's Great Banquet
(Luke 14:15–24)

22

When one of those who were reclining at the table with Him heard this, he said to Him, "Blessed is everyone who will eat bread in the kingdom of God!" But He said to him, "A man was giving a big dinner, and he invited many; and at the dinner hour he sent his slave to say to those who had been invited, 'Come; for everything is ready now.' But they all alike began to make excuses. The first one said to him, 'I have bought a piece of land and I need to go out and look at it; please consider me excused.' Another one said, 'I have bought five yoke of oxen, and I am going to try them out; please consider me excused.' Another one said, 'I have married a wife, and for that reason I cannot come.' And the slave came back and reported this to his master. Then the head of the household became angry and said to his slave, 'Go out at once into the streets and lanes of the city and bring in here the poor and crippled and blind and lame.' And the slave said, 'Master, what you commanded has been done, and still there is room.' And the master said to the slave, 'Go out into the highways and

267

along the hedges, and compel them to come in, so that my house may be filled. For I tell you, none of those men who were invited shall taste of my dinner.'" (14:15–24)

The fifty-third chapter of Isaiah describes Jesus Christ, the Servant of the Lord and Messiah, as "a man of sorrows and acquainted with grief" (v. 3). The New Testament account of His life bears that out. While Jesus wept (Luke 19:41; John 11:35) and was grieved (Matt. 26:37–38; Mark 3:5), there is no indication in Scripture that He ever laughed. He told many somber, sobering stories, and even used sarcasm, but there is no record that He said anything to elicit laughter.

And yet the story He told in this text would surely have seemed like a joke to those who heard it. They would have seen it as laughable, ludicrous, ridiculous, impossible, inconceivable; a joke without a punch line; an impossible scenario. A great feast like the one of which the Lord spoke, given by a wealthy, prominent man, would have been the social event of the year. For some, it might have been the highlight of their lives. No one invited to such a banquet would have dreamed of refusing the invitation. Nor would such an important person invite the dregs of society to fill his banquet hall.

Jesus was still at the Sabbath-day meal at the home of a Pharisee described in the previous chapter of this volume. He had been invited in an attempt by the hostile Pharisees to trap Him into violating their man-made Sabbath restrictions by performing a healing (vv. 1–2). But He turned the tables on them and exposed their hypocrisy, shaming them into silence (vv. 3–6). Having silenced them, He then took the offensive and told a parable illustrating their duplicity, conceit, and hypocrisy (vv. 7–14).

The Lord had concluded His illustration with a reference to the resurrection and reward of the righteous. The scribes and Pharisees understood that He was referring to eternal life, and challenging them to humble themselves to receive it. Earning that resurrection was their supreme hope. They believed that by enduring the minute prescriptions, deprivation, self-sacrifice, and rituals of their religious system they would gain eternal life in God's kingdom. In all false religions the promise of a good life in the future after death motivates people to put up with the restrictions and burdens imposed on them in this life.

Jesus was speaking in familiar terms because the Old Testament pictured the resurrection of the righteous as a magnificent banquet in the presence of God:

> The Lord of hosts will prepare a lavish banquet for all peoples on this mountain; a banquet of aged wine, choice pieces with marrow, and refined, aged wine. And on this mountain He will swallow up the covering which is over all peoples, even the veil which is stretched over all nations. He will swallow up death for all time, and the Lord God will wipe tears away from all faces, and He will remove the reproach of His people from all the earth; for the Lord has spoken. And it will be said in that day, "Behold, this is our God for whom we have waited that He might save us. This is the Lord for whom we have waited; let us rejoice and be glad in His salvation." (Isa. 25:6–9; cf. Matt. 8:11–12; 22:2–14; Rev. 19:9)

The Lord's reference to the resurrection of the righteous as a banquet was not lost on the guests, who thought of that great future heavenly gathering. That connection prompted **one of those who were reclining at the table with Him** to say in response, **"Blessed is everyone who will eat bread in the kingdom of God!"** This was a beatitude; a toast directed at himself and his fellow Pharisees, affirming that they will be among the blessed at the heavenly banquet **in the kingdom of God.** It was not only a pronouncement of blessing on themselves, but also a scornful rebuke of the Lord's declaration that they were too proud to enter God's kingdom (cf. 14:11). His words bounced off their confidence that their Abrahamic ancestry (cf. John 8:33–59) and adherence to the traditions, regulations, and rituals would secure a place for them at God's banquet. Not only did they fully expect to be at that heavenly feast, but also to be in the seats of honor.

Jesus always sought to shatter unwarranted religious hope, and never encouraged anyone's false sense of security, so that arrogant, misguided assumption called for immediate and unmistakable correction. Following His example is essential to all true evangelism. Those with an unfounded assumption that they are headed for heaven need to know that they are fatally deceived. To expect heaven while rejecting Jesus Christ and His gospel is the most deadly and serious of all false hopes (cf. Heb. 10:26–31).

Jesus' illustration and its application was a direct assault on the delusional self-confidence of the Jewish people, in particular the scribes and Pharisees. It may be divided into four points: the invitation, the excuses, the inclusion, and the exclusion.

THE INVITATION

But He said to him, "A man was giving a big dinner, and he in -vited many; and at the dinner hour he sent his slave to say to those who had been invited, 'Come; for everything is ready now.' (14:16–17)

In His reply to the guest's smug and erroneous assumption that he and his fellow Pharisees would be in the kingdom, the Lord addressed the issue of who really will enter the kingdom. His reply was in the form of another parable, relating the responses of guests invited to a banquet. The words that describe that banquet are **big** and **many,** indicating a huge, grand, gala event, like the wedding feast in another of the Lord's parables given by a king to honor his son (Matt. 22:1–14). The host of this imaginary feast would be extremely wealthy, to afford an event of this magnitude.

The personal, formal invitations to the **dinner** would have come in two stages to the **invited** guests. The first, like invitations today, would have informed the recipient that they were invited to the event. Unlike modern invitations, however, the exact date and time would not have been specified due to the complexities of preparing the feast. When all was ready, a second invitation would notify the pre-invited guests that the banquet was about to begin. Thus in this story, when **the dinner hour** arrived, the host **sent his slave to say to those who had been invited, 'Come; for everything is ready now.'** The eagerly anticipated and long awaited dinner was about to begin.

THE EXCUSES

But they all alike began to make excuses. The first one said to him, 'I have bought a piece of land and I need to go out and look at it; please consider me excused.' Another one said, 'I have bought five yoke of oxen, and I am going to try them out; please consider me excused.' Another one said, 'I have married a wife, and for that reason I cannot come.' (14:18–20)

The food was ready, the invited guests had been notified, and the banquet was ready to start. But then the unthinkable happened. Shockingly, unbelievably the guests—not merely a few, but **all** of them—**began to make excuses** for not attending. This was completely contrary to expected behavior. No one invited to an extravagant dinner by a wealthy host would have refused to come, let alone everyone. It was so absurd as to be incomprehensible to the status-seeking scribes and Pharisees, who must have stared at the Lord in disbelief.

Jesus gave three sample excuses that heightened the absurdity of the situation by making it obvious that the guests had no rational reasons for refusing to attend. **The first one** protested, **'I have bought a piece of land and I need to go out and look at it; please consider me excused.'** This excuse makes no sense. After all, the **piece of land** would still be there after the banquet. And no one would buy property sight unseen, so he obviously had already gone **out** to **look at it.** Surely seeing a field was not more compelling than the honor and joy that would come from attending the banquet.

The second excuse was nonsense: **'I have bought five yoke of oxen,** another man said, **and I am going to try them out; please consider me excused.'** Once again, trying out the newly-purchased oxen was not urgent, and could have waited until after the banquet. And would he not have already tried out the oxen before he bought them? Further, that this man was able to afford **five yoke of oxen** suggests that he was a reasonably wealthy man himself; surely one of his servants could have tested the oxen for him. Why not attend the banquet and have both the oxen and the host's favor?

Another one offered a third absurdity: **'I have married a wife, and for that reason I cannot come.'** Given their low view of women, the Pharisees would have found this excuse the most laughable of all. In first-century Jewish society, women did not dictate to their husbands what they could do. Nor could the Old Testament exemption from military service and other duties for newly married men (Deut. 24:5; cf. 20:7) be construed as a valid excuse for not attending a banquet. This excuse, like the first two our Lord created, was transparently ridiculous.

THE INCLUSION

And the slave came back and reported this to his master. Then the head of the household became angry and said to his slave, 'Go out at once into the streets and lanes of the city and bring in here the poor and crippled and blind and lame.' And the slave said, 'Master, what you commanded has been done, and still there is room.' And the master said to the slave, 'Go out into the highways and along the hedges, and compel them to come in, so that my house may be filled. (14:21–23)

When **the slave came back and reported** these and many other similar excuses **to his master . . . the head of the household** understandably **became angry.** For the invited guests to meet his generosity and kindness with frivolous indifference and disdain was an outrageous act that insulted him personally and embarrassed him publicly. It was an egregious breach of social etiquette; unforgivable conduct made even worse by the lame and illegitimate excuses offered by the guests.

The head of the household decided that too much time, effort, and expense had gone into preparing the banquet to cancel it. The celebration would go on, but with a different and utterly unlikely set of guests. He **said to his slave, 'Go out at once into the streets and lanes of the city and bring in here the poor and crippled and blind and lame.'** In reality such people would have to be strongly persuaded, if not brought in, because they would be reluctant to come on their own, since they understood that social protocol would have obligated them to reciprocate. That they did not have the means to do. The notion that a wealthy, prominent man would invite poor, despised out-casts to such a banquet was as preposterous as imagining that the origi-nal guests would turn down his invitation en masse. There was not the slightest chance that either would have happened, much less both.

In the story the slave did as his master **commanded,** but after bringing people in off the city streets **there** was still **room** in the ban-quet hall. **'Go out into the highways and along the hedges, and compel them to come in,** the head of the household commanded, **so that my house may be filled.'** This latter group consisted of people even further down the social ladder than those brought in off the city streets. They were people with no home of their own; shady characters who lived outside of town in the brothels, seedy inns, and roadhouses along the **highways, and** even in the trees and bushes **along the hedges.** Because they were widely scattered, it would be more difficult and time consuming to round them up. And it would be even harder to **compel them to come in,** since they would be even more reluctant than the poor in town.

THE EXCLUSION

For I tell you, none of those men who were invited shall taste of my dinner.'" (14:24)

The despised outcasts would come and enjoy his banquet, but the head of the household vowed that **none of those men who were** originally **invited** would **taste of** his **dinner.** If not approving of bring-ing in the poor, the Pharisees would have understood and approved of that action; those foolish enough to turn down his invitation deservedly forfeited their privilege for good.

But at this point the parable ceased to be a hypothetical story, as the Lord drove the point directly at the scribes and Pharisees. Jesus used the phrase **I tell you** frequently in Luke's gospel to signal the application of truth to His audience (e.g., 11:8, 51; 12:5, 51; 13:3, 5, 24, 27; 15:7, 10; 17:34; 18:8, 14; 19:26). The head of the household represents God, who issued the invitation; the banquet represents salvation in His eternal kingdom;

the pre-invited guests are Israel (and Gentile proselytes); the first invitation was delivered by the Old Testament prophets (cf. Rom. 9:4–5). The
guests initially said yes to God's invitation; they accepted the Old Testament revelation that they were God's chosen people, and would therefore enter the kingdom (even though they rejected and murdered the
prophets; cf. Luke 13:34).

At the dinner hour, which Jesus called the "favorable year of the
Lord" (Luke 4:19), the second invitation was delivered by John (Matt. 3:2)
and Jesus (Matt. 4:17). Everything was ready. But like the fictional guests
in Jesus' illustration, those invited refused to attend. They had no interest
in the banquet of God if Jesus Christ was the door to the banquet hall.
They were not interested in Him, or His message. When He presented the
true gospel of salvation, they sought to kill Him (Matt. 26:59; Mark 14:1;
John 11:53). And like the guests in the illustration, they offered foolish
excuses. Two of those excuses had involved material possessions, the
third a relationship. Both of those types of excuses have been offered
throughout history by those who are more interested in the things of the
world than God's invitation to salvation. For that reason Jesus warned, "If
anyone comes to Me, and does not hate his own father and mother and
wife and children and brothers and sisters, yes, and even his own life, he
cannot be My disciple ... So then, none of you can be My disciple who
does not give up all his own possessions" (Luke 14:26, 33; cf. the discussion of those verses in chapter 23 of this volume).

Like the guests in the illustration, Israel said yes to God's original
invitation, and no to the second invitation; they said yes to God's promises,
but no to His Son. Uninterested, indifferent, and self-satisfied, they clung
tightly to the deceitfulness of riches and the cares of this world (8:14; cf.
Matt. 13:22; Mark 4:18–19) and missed God's heavenly banquet. As a
result, God was angry with them and abandoned them to judgment, leaving their house to them desolate (Luke 13:35). Spiritual judgment comes
on all unbelievers at death. Physical judgment fell on that generation in
A.D. 70 when the Romans massacred tens of thousands of Jews and
destroyed the temple. Judgment continues to fall on all who reject God's
invitation to salvation in Jesus and thus dishonor His Son. In John 3:36
John the Baptist warned, "He who believes in the Son has eternal life; but
he who does not obey the Son will not see life, but the wrath of God

abides on him." Paul described God's eternal wrath on unredeemed sinners when he wrote to the Thessalonians,

> For after all it is only just for God to repay with affliction those who afflict you, and to give relief to you who are afflicted and to us as well when the Lord Jesus will be revealed from heaven with His mighty angels in flaming fire, dealing out retribution to those who do not know God and to those who do not obey the gospel of our Lord Jesus. These will pay the penalty of eternal destruction, away from the presence of the Lord and from the glory of His power. (2 Thess. 1:6–9)

Instead of experiencing God as gracious host, those who reject His invitation to the heavenly banquet will one day face Him as sovereign judge and forever be shut out of His heaven (Rev. 20:10–15).

But the spiritually bankrupt, destitute, and humble, symbolized by the town (the believing Jewish remnant) and highway (believing Gentiles) dwellers, will be included in the banquet. These are repentant sinners, who acknowledge that they are unworthy to enter God's kingdom. They picture those who have the attitude of the publican, who "was even unwilling to lift up his eyes to heaven, but was beating his breast, saying, 'God, be merciful to me, the sinner!'" (Luke 18:13). They are so acutely aware of their unworthiness that the gospel messengers will have to compel them to come; that is, to persuade strongly, urge, and constrain them to respond to God's invitation to salvation. The verb translated "compel" in verse 23 is the same one used in Matthew 14:22 where Jesus made His disciples get into a boat, in Acts 26:11 of Paul's attempts before his conversion to force Christians to blaspheme, in Acts 28:19 of his being forced to appeal to Caesar, and in Galatians 2:3 of Titus not being compelled to be circumcised.

The gospel invitation came "to the Jew first" (Rom. 1:16), and those who responded with repentant faith entered God's eternal kingdom of salvation. With rare exceptions, however, the Pharisees, scribes, rabbis, priests, and most of the people of Israel through the years rejected God's invitation to salvation. The tragic result of unbelief and rejection of Jesus the Messiah is the forfeiture of eternal life in the kingdom.

Not only the Jewish people, but also everyone else who refuses God's invitation to salvation will be excluded from the kingdom. Like the foolish virgins, they will be left outside in the dark when night falls on the day of opportunity and the door to the kingdom is shut (Matt. 25:1–12). All those who reject the Lord Jesus Christ will be shut out of the blessings God has prepared in heaven for those who love His Son:"Things which eye has not seen and ear has not heard, and which have not entered the heart of man, all that God has prepared for those who love Him" (1 Cor. 2:9).

custom-tailored to your preferences. But that lightness will never fill you up with the true, saving gospel of Jesus Christ, because it is designed by man and not God, and it is hollow and worthless. In fact, it's worse than worthless, because people who hear the message of Christianity Lite think they're hearing the gospel—think they're being rescued from eternal judgment—when, in fact, they're being tragically misled.

The true gospel is a call to self-denial. It is not a call to self-fulfillment. And that puts it in opposition to the contemporary evangelical gospel, where ministers view Jesus as a utilitarian genie. You rub the lamp, and He jumps out and says you have whatever you want; you give Him your list and He delivers. (Nashville: Thomas Nelson, 2003, 1–2)

In contrast to "Christianity Lite," the true Christian gospel does not offer heaven on earth, but heaven in heaven. It produces genuine disciples of the Lord Jesus Christ, not superficial hangers on. This section, as the threefold repetition of the term "disciple" (vv. 26, 27, 33) indicates, is about what it means to be a genuine follower of Christ. It is an evangelistic call by Jesus to come to Him (v. 26), which is to come after Him (v. 27); to be a real disciple, not a would-be, potential, or peripheral one.

The Greek word translated "disciple" (*mathētēs*) is a broad term that identifies a learner or a student. In ancient Jewish culture, rabbis were itinerant, traveling about accompanied by their disciples. Though He was never recognized as one by the religious establishment, Jesus was often called a rabbi (e.g., Matt. 26:25; Mark 9:5; 11:21; John 1:38, 49; 3:2; 4:31; 6:25; 9:2; 11:8), in part because like the rabbis, He was a traveling teacher who had disciples. Those early disciples were at varying levels of commitment, ranging from the fully committed, to the nominally committed, to the uncommitted curiosity seekers. Over the course of His ministry, Jesus made the requirements for being a genuine disciple clearer and expressed them in more absolute terms. As a result, the superficial disciples began to abandon Him (John 6:60, 66; cf. Luke 8:13–14), especially as Israel's attitude toward Him hardened into unbelief and rejection. By the time His ministry drew to a close, Jesus had become even more definitive about discipleship. The term "disciple" underwent a metamorphosis, and took on a purer, more restricted meaning, so that by the book of Acts it became a synonym for "Christian" (11:26; cf. 26:28) and described those who were true redeemed believers in Jesus Christ (6:1–7; 9:1, 10, 19; 9:26,

36, 38; 11:29; 13:52; 14:20–22, 28; 15:10; 16:1; 18:23, 27; 19:9, 30; 20:1, 30; 21:4, 16).

The previous chapter of Luke's gospel closed with the Lord's pronouncement of judgment on the nation of Israel and its leaders for rejecting Him (see the exposition of 13:34–35 in chapter 20 of this volume). But Jesus still invited individuals to become His disciples, as He did in this passage (cf. 12:8; 18:18–24). This section comes at a strategic point in Luke's gospel. It is obvious from the preceding passages that the Jewish religious leaders, confident in their law-keeping, traditions, and rituals, did not know how to be saved, and therefore could not lead the people to salvation (cf. 6:39; Matt. 23:15). They trusted in their religious ceremonies and moral achievements, refusing to humble themselves, which resulted in their being shut out of the kingdom (14:24) along with all who followed them. They could lead no one to salvation. They only produced "sons of hell" (Matt. 23:15).

In contrast to the religious leaders' damning ignorance, Luke records Jesus' authoritative teaching on the true way of salvation. The Lord used several metaphors to describe salvation, such as entering God's kingdom (18:24), having eternal life (18:18), and being confessed by Him before God and the holy angels (12:8–9). Here He equated salvation with becoming His disciple.

Some, however, in serious error, misconstrue the Lord's teaching here and deny that it is an invitation to salvation. They suggest that Jesus is addressing here those who were already saved but not disciples following Him; those who had acknowledged Him as Savior, but not as Lord. Jesus was, they maintain, calling such people to move up from salvation to a higher level of commitment and become disciples; confusing Paul's terminology, we could say that He was urging them to stop being carnal Christians and become spiritual Christians (1 Cor. 3:1 KJV). But that turns our Lord from an evangelist into a deeper or higher life teacher— even though He explicitly said that He came "to seek and to save that which was lost" (Luke 19:10), and that He did "not come to call the righteous but sinners to repentance" (Luke 5:32). As noted above, in the book of Acts "disciple" is used synonymously with "Christian." Therefore to become a disciple of Christ is not to move to a higher plane in the Christian life, it is to be saved; to pass from death to life (John 5:24); from darkness to light (Acts 26:18); from Satan's kingdom to Christ's (Col. 1:13). (For a discussion of the so-called lordship debate, see my books *The Gospel According to Jesus* [Revised and expanded anniversary edition. Grand Rapids: Zondervan, 1988, 1993, 2008], and *The Gospel According to the Apostles* [Nashville: Word, 1993, 2000].)

What Jesus asked for in this passage is amazingly extreme. He did not call for a makeover, but demanded a takeover. He challenged sinners to acknowledge Him as sovereign Lord, divine dictator, ruler, controller, king, and master. Jesus never called for anyone to pray a short, easy prayer to receive eternal life. Nor did He manipulate anyone to make an emotional decision, or give a false assurance of salvation to shallow interest. He never taught that the way to heaven is broad and easy, but warned that "the gate is small and the way is narrow that leads to life, and there are few who find it" (Matt. 7:14), and said that people would have to force their way into it (Luke 16:16). "Not everyone who says to Me, 'Lord, Lord,' will enter the kingdom of heaven," He cautioned, "but he who does the will of My Father who is in heaven will enter" (Matt. 7:21). Only those who continue in His word (John 8:31) and whose lives manifest the fruit of salvation (John 15:8; cf. Matt. 3:8) are truly His disciples, and only disciples are saved from hell's judgment.

The Lord's evangelistic methodology is in striking contrast to that of today's pop church approach. Pastors and evangelists, pursuing mass responses, seek to eliminate barriers and make it as easy as possible for people to respond to the message. Jesus, however, did the opposite. He made extreme, exclusive, and absolute statements to discourage superficial responders. "Do not think that I came to bring peace on the earth" He declared, "I did not come to bring peace, but a sword" (Matt. 10:34). In two brief parables, Jesus likened salvation in God's kingdom to a hidden treasure and a valuable pearl, which people sold all that they possessed to obtain (Matt. 13:44–46). It may be necessary to give up families and possessions for His sake and the gospel's (Mark 10:29–30), and face the world's hatred (John 15:18–19; 16:1–3). The Lord solemnly warned would-be followers, "If anyone wishes to come after Me, he must deny himself, and take up his cross daily and follow Me" (Luke 9:23; cf. Matt. 10:38; 16:24–25), because "He who loves his life loses it, and he who hates his life in this world will keep it to life eternal" (John 12:25).

This passage does not reveal every aspect of salvation truth. It does not mention God's holiness, human sin, divine judgment, Christ's saving work on the cross, or salvation by grace through faith. Its focus is not on the objective facts of the gospel, but rather the subjective attitude of the radical, extreme faith commitment that must exist in the hearts of those who trust Christ savingly. Those who fall short of such commitment to Him will perish eternally (Matt. 7:21–23; 8:19–22; Luke 13:24–28). Heaven awaits those who give up everything; who repent, raise the empty hands of faith, and confess Jesus as Lord and themselves as His slaves as they receive the free gift of salvation.

This text reveals three things that mark true disciples of Jesus Christ: abandonment of past priorities, appraisal of present powers, and allegiance to future privileges.

ABANDONMENT OF PAST PRIORITIES

Now large crowds were going along with Him; and He turned and said to them, "If anyone comes to Me, and does not hate his own father and mother and wife and children and brothers and sisters, yes, and even his own life, he cannot be My disciple. Whoever does not carry his own cross and come after Me cannot be My disciple. . . . So then, none of you can be My disciple who does not give up all his own possessions. (14:25–27, 33)

Jesus summarized the priorities of the unregenerate under three general headings: self, relationships, and possessions. Even at this late stage, with rejection set and the cross only months away, Jesus still attracted **large crowds,** who **were going along with Him** as He made His final journey to Jerusalem. The exact location of this incident is not known (though some suggest that it was east of the Jordan in Perea). This was not the first teaching Jesus had done on this journey. Many who heard His teaching on this occasion also heard His extended discourse that Luke records in 12:1–13:9. That instruction includes several more components of His evangelistic preaching, such as His calling on His hearers to avoid the influence of false religion (12:1), understand that they are under God's scrutiny (12:2–3), fear God as the judge of sin (12:4–5), confess Jesus as Lord and Savior (12:8–9), listen to the Holy Spirit (12:10–12), abandon materialism (12:13–21), seek God's kingdom (12:22–34), be ready for the second coming (12:35–48), settle their accounts with God before it is too late (12:54–59), and realize that they are living on borrowed time (13:1–9). In this section on radically changed priorities the Lord calls for extreme devotion.

First, **anyone** who **comes to** Jesus for salvation must prefer God over his family. Coming to Christ is terminology for the initial expression of saving faith. A person who does so, Jesus declared, must **hate his own father and mother and wife and children and brothers and sisters.** The phrase **his own** stresses the natural priority of and normal affection for one's family. Salvation brings turmoil into the home as the new believer attempts to co-exist with non-believers. Family members who reject the gospel may even ostracize those who believe it. In Matthew 10:34–36 Jesus warned that families would be divided over Him:

> Do not think that I came to bring peace on the earth; I did not come to bring peace, but a sword. For I came to set a man against his father, and a daughter against her mother, and a daughter-in-law against her mother-in-law; and a man's enemies will be the members of his household. (cf. the exposition of Luke 12:51–53 in chapter 14 of this volume)

The Lord's teaching that it is necessary to **hate** one's family is not inconsistent with the Bible's commands that children are to honor their parents (Ex. 20:12), husbands love their wives (Eph. 5:25), wives love their husbands (Titus 2:4), and parents love their children (Titus 2:4; cf. Eph. 6:4). Hate in this context is a Semitic way of expressing preference. For example, God said in Malachi 1:2–3, "I have loved Jacob; but I have hated Esau" (cf. Rom. 9:13). The point is not that God had animosity toward Esau, but rather that He preferred Jacob by giving His promise through him. Similarly, when Genesis 29:31 records that Leah was unloved (the Hebrew word literally means "hated") by Jacob, it does not mean that he despised and detested her, but that he loved Rachel more (cf. Deut. 21:15–17). To hate one's family is to prefer God over them by disregarding what they desire if that conflicts with what God requires; it is to love God more and them less."He who loves father or mother more than Me is not worthy of Me," Jesus said, "and he who loves son or daughter more than Me is not worthy of Me" (Matt. 10:37). All other loves must be subordinate to loving God with all one's heart, soul, mind, and strength (Luke 10:27).

Jesus' words would have been clearly understood in the context of the first century. When Jewish people made a commitment to Jesus Christ, they would often alienate their families, as Darrell L. Bock notes:

> At that time a Jewish person who made a choice for Jesus would alien-ate his or her family. If someone desired acceptance by family more than a relationship with God, one might never come to Jesus, given the rejection that would inevitably follow. In other words, there could be no casual devotion to Jesus in the first century. A decision for Christ marked a person and automatically came with a cost. (Contemporary comparisons may be seen in certain formerly Communist Eastern European settings, in Moslem countries, or in tight-knit Asian families.) The modern Western phenomenon where a decision for Christ is pop-ular in the larger social community was not true of Jesus' setting, which complicates our understanding of the significance of a decision to associate with Christ. Today one might associate with Christ simply because it is culturally appropriate, rather than for true spiritual rea-sons. Such a "decision" was impossible in the first century. If one chose to be associated with Jesus, one received a negative reaction, often from within the home. (*Luke 9:51–24:53*, Baker Exegetical Com-mentary on the New Testament [Grand Rapids: Baker, 1996], 1285)

Second, a person who would come to Jesus must hate **even his own life** (cf. John 12:25), or **he cannot be** His **disciple.** The call to sal-vation is a call to self-denial (cf. Luke 17:33); it marks the end of sinners being the reigning authorities in their lives and calls for them instead to submit as slaves to Jesus' authority as Lord, King, and Master. That selfless-ness extends to the point of death, as Jesus' next statement, **Whoever does not carry his own cross and come after Me cannot be My dis-ciple** (cf. 9:23–25; Matt. 16:24) makes clear. The heavenly treasure is so valuable (Matt. 13:44), the pearl of salvation so precious (v. 46), that true disciples are willing to give up their lives, if God so wills, to gain eternal life. Jesus calls for complete self-abandonment.

It must be noted that this is not a meritorious pre-salvation work that somehow earns justification. Salvation, Paul insisted, is "by grace … through faith; and that not of yourselves, it is the gift of God" (Eph. 2:8).

Jesus declared that "no one can come to [Him] unless it has been granted him from the Father" (John 6:65). But salvation is not apart from the sinner's will. Jesus called people to "Repent and believe in the gospel" (Mark 1:15), and warned unbelievers, "Unless you repent, you will all likewise perish" (Luke 13:3, 5). Peter challenged his hearers to "Repent and return, so that your sins may be wiped away" (Acts 3:19), and Paul preached that "God is now declaring to men that all people everywhere should repent" (Acts 17:30; cf. 26:20). Those commands presuppose the sinner's responsibility to obey them, for which he is enabled by the Spirit of God.

Finally, a person who would **be** Christ's **disciple** must **give up all his own possessions.** The phrase **none of you** includes everyone and the word **all** encompasses not just money, but material goods as well. There are no exceptions or exemptions to these absolute, unqualified requirements. *Apotassō* (**give up**) literally means, "to take leave of" (Acts 18:18, 21; 2 Cor. 2:13), or "to say good-bye to" (Mark 6:46; Luke 9:61). It was his unwillingness to surrender his possessions that caused the rich young ruler to turn away from Christ (Luke 18:18–23) and be eternally lost. Jesus is not advocating socialism, or getting rid of everything and living a life of poverty. His point is that those who would be His disciples must recognize that they are stewards of everything and owners of nothing. And if the Lord asked them to give up all they would be willing, because loving obedience is their highest duty and joy. Leon Morris notes the implications of the Lord's teaching:

> The lesson is plain. Jesus does not want followers who rush into discipleship without thinking of what is involved. And He is clear about the price. The man who comes to Him must renounce all that he has. . . . These words condemn all half-heartedness. Jesus is not, of course, discouraging discipleship. He is warning against an ill-considered, faint-hearted attachment in order that men may know the real thing. He wants men to count the cost and reckon all lost for His sake so that they can enter the exhilaration of full-blooded discipleship. (*The Gospel According to St. Luke,* The Tyndale New Testament Commentaries [Grand Rapids: Eerdmans, 1975], 236–37)

APPRAISAL OF PRESENT POWERS

For which one of you, when he wants to build a tower, does not first sit down and calculate the cost to see if he has enough to complete it? Otherwise, when he has laid a foundation and is not able to finish, all who observe it begin to ridicule him, saying, 'This man began to build and was not able to finish.' Or what king, when he sets out to meet another king in battle, will not first sit down and consider whether he is strong enough with ten thousand men to encounter the one coming against him with twenty thousand? Or else, while the other is still far away, he sends a delegation and asks for terms of peace. (14:28–32)

These two illustrations demonstrate the importance of understanding the sacrifice required when making a commitment to Christ. As was true of all of Jesus' illustrations and parables, both describe situations familiar to His listeners. The point is that people count the cost before undertaking any important task in life. How much more important is it to count the cost before committing oneself to Him?

The first illustration pictures a man contemplating building a **tower.** This could have been a watchtower for protection from his enemies, or a storage tower for his goods. Either one would have been a visible construction project, and everyone in the community would have known about it. Preserving one's honor and avoiding bringing shame on oneself and one's family were elevated matters in the ancient Near East. Thus, for this man to have **laid a foundation and** then **not** been **able to finish** would have brought shame. It would have made him the laughingstock of the community, as **all who** saw the unfinished tower began **to ridicule him, saying, "This man** (a derogatory, contemptuous expression; cf. 5:21; 7:39) **began to build and was not able to finish** (*ekteleō;* to completely or totally finish a task)." To avoid such a devastating blow to his honor and prestige, a man considering building a tower would **first sit down and calculate the cost to see if he** had **enough to complete it.**

While the first illustration pictures a voluntary act, the second depicts a man thrust involuntarily into a dilemma beyond his control. Jesus asked His hearers to consider a **king** preparing **to meet another**

king commanding a stronger force to engage him **in battle.** Before confronting the attacking king in combat, would he **not first sit down and consider whether he is strong enough with ten thousand men to encounter the one coming against him with twenty thousand?** Would he not assess what logistics, terrain, weaponry, and what strategic or tactical advantages might outweigh his opponent's numerical superiority? If not, to proceed with the battle would be suicidal folly, both for the king and his men. If he had no possibility of victory, his only sensible recourse would be, **while the other** king **is still far away,** to send **a delegation and** negotiate **for terms of peace.**

In both stories Jesus showed the wisdom of carefully assessing the commitment involved in following Him. He did not want emotion-driven, superficial, self-seeking, temporary, transient followers, like those represented by the rocky and thorny soils in the parable of the sower (Matt. 13:20–22). Real faith endures to the end (Mark 13:13; cf. 1 John 2:19). John Stott writes concerning the importance of counting the cost of commitment,

> The Christian landscape is strewn with the wreckage of derelict, half-built towers—the ruins of those who began to build and were unable to finish. For thousands of people still ignore Christ's warning and undertake to follow him without first pausing to reflect on the cost of doing so. The result is the great scandal of Christendom today, so-called 'nominal Christianity.' In countries to which Christian civilization has spread, large numbers of people have covered themselves with a decent, but thin, veneer of Christianity. They have allowed themselves to become somewhat involved; enough to be respectable but not enough to be uncomfortable. Their religion is a great, soft cushion. It protects them from the hard unpleasantness of life, while changing its place and shape to suit their convenience. No wonder the cynics speak of hypocrites in the church and dismiss religion as escapism. (*Basic Christianity* [Downer's Grove, Ill.: Inter-Varsity, 1978], 108).

Avoiding temporary, false faith demands that sinners honestly assess their motives, examine the genuineness of their repentance, and determine whether they are ready to keep the commitment that Christ demands from His followers. None of those things, as noted above, are human works that can earn salvation, which is by faith alone. Rather, they are distinguishing marks of true faith, apart from which it is a non-saving delusion (James 2:14–26).

ALLEGIANCE TO FUTURE PRIVILEGES

Therefore, salt is good; but if even salt has become tasteless, with what will it be seasoned? It is useless either for the soil or for the manure pile; it is thrown out. He who has ears to hear, let him hear. (14:34–35)

At first glance, there seems to be a disconnect between these closing statements and the previous verses. But the Lord's use of **therefore** to introduce them indicates that He was in fact making a connection. The connection is that being His disciple concerns not only past relationships and present commitment, but also future continued allegiance.

Salt was widely used before the advent of refrigeration as a preservative. It was also associated in the Old Testament with the covenants (Lev. 2:13; Num. 18:19; 2 Chron. 13:5) and the sacrifices (Lev. 2:13; Ezra 6:9–10; Ezek. 43:23–24). Salt normally does not degrade, or else it would be of little value as a preservative. Sometimes, however, salt from the vicinity of the Dead Sea was contaminated with gypsum and, if not processed correctly, could lose its effectiveness **and become tasteless.** As the Lord's rhetorical question, **If even salt has become tasteless, with what will it be seasoned?** indicates, such salt is **useless either for the soil** (as fertilizer) **or for the manure pile** (since it would not decompose). It could only be used to keep footpaths free of vegetation, or be **thrown out.**

This illustration shows that Jesus does not want temporary disciples, but rather those who will commit to lifelong loyalty to Him. Only those disciples can be used by Him for good in this world. It is true that no one perfectly keeps his commitment to the Lord. There are times when it falters due to family pressures, selfishness, the allure of material possessions, or when believers wonder if they have the resolve to love and obey the Lord to the end. Moments of failure, however, do not invalidate the direction of the heart.

On the other hand, temporary disciples are ultimately useless to the Lord. Like contaminated salt, those contaminated by worldliness will be **thrown out** into eternal judgment (13:28; Matt. 8:12; 13:41–42, 50; 22:12–13; 25:30; John 15:6).

Jesus closed with the colloquial expression, **He who has ears to**

hear, let him hear. This familiar saying is a challenge to listen to, understand, and embrace His message (cf. Matt. 11:15; 13:9, 43; Mark 4:23). It is
an urgent call for people to respond before it is too late, and the judgment Jesus warned of in Luke 8:10 falls and "seeing they may not see, and
hearing they may not understand."

Heaven's Joy: Recovering the Lost (Luke 15:1–10)

24

Now all the tax collectors and the sinners were coming near Him to listen to Him. Both the Pharisees and the scribes began to grumble, saying, "This man receives sinners and eats with them." So He told them this parable, saying, "What man among you, if he has a hundred sheep and has lost one of them, does not leave the ninety-nine in the open pasture and go after the one which is lost until he finds it? When he has found it, he lays it on his shoulders, rejoicing. And when he comes home, he calls together his friends and his neighbors, saying to them, 'Rejoice with me, for I have found my sheep which was lost!' I tell you that in the same way, there will be more joy in heaven over one sinner who repents than over ninety-nine righteous persons who need no repentance. Or what woman, if she has ten silver coins and loses one coin, does not light a lamp and sweep the house and search carefully until she finds it? When she has found it, she calls together her friends and neighbors, saying, 'Rejoice with me, for I have found the coin which I had lost!' In the same way, I tell you, there

is joy in the presence of the angels of God over one sinner who repents." (15:1–10)

The Bible reveals the many attributes of God, both His incommunicable attributes (those true of Him alone, such as omnipotence, omnipresence, omniscience, immutability, and eternality) and communicable attributes (those also true to a far lesser degree of humans, such as righteousness, holiness, wisdom, love, compassion, grace, and mercy). Believers are very familiar with these. But one of God's attributes that is often overlooked is His joy. Though an eternally joyful God seems hard to accept, texts like First Chronicles 16:27 and Nehemiah 8:10 refer to that reality. Luke 10:21 even records that Jesus "rejoiced greatly in the Holy Spirit," while in John 15:11 and 17:13 Christ spoke of His own joy. Even enduring the cross as a "man of sorrows" (Isa. 53:3) He knew would bring Him joy, the joy of recovering lost sinners (Heb. 12:2).

God, who is by nature a savior (Matt. 1:21; John 3:16–18; 1 Tim. 2:3–4; Titus 1:3, 2:10, 13; 3:4, 6), brings Himself everlasting joy in recovering the lost. It is that joy which is expressed as the point of the three parables the Lord devised in this chapter (vv. 7, 10, 32). And God's joy in recovering the lost is not an obscure theme in Scripture. In Deuteronomy 30:9 God promised Israel that when He punished them for their disobedience and they repented (vv. 1–8) He would "again rejoice over [them] for good, just as He rejoiced over [their] fathers." In Psalm 105:43 the psalmist declared that God "brought forth His people with joy, His chosen ones with a joyful shout." Looking ahead to the future salvation of Israel, God said through Isaiah, "For as a young man marries a virgin, so your sons will marry you; and as the bridegroom rejoices over the bride, so your God will rejoice over you" (Isa. 62:5; cf. 65:19). Similarly, God declared through Jeremiah,

> Behold, I will gather them out of all the lands to which I have driven them in My anger, in My wrath and in great indignation; and I will bring them back to this place and make them dwell in safety. ... I will rejoice over them to do them good and will faithfully plant them in this land with all My heart and with all My soul. (Jer. 32:37, 41)

The prophet Zephaniah wrote,

> Shout for joy, O daughter of Zion! Shout in triumph, O Israel! Rejoice
> and exult with all your heart, O daughter of Jerusalem! The Lord has
> taken away His judgments against you, He has cleared away your ene-
> mies. The King of Israel, the Lord, is in your midst; You will fear disaster
> no more. In that day it will be said to Jerusalem: "Do not be afraid, O
> Zion; do not let your hands fall limp. The Lord your God is in your midst,
> a victorious warrior. He will exult over you with joy, He will be quiet in
> His love, He will rejoice over you with shouts of joy." (Zeph. 3:14–17)

God's joy is the source of believers' joy; it is a component of the kingdom
of God dispensed by the Holy Spirit to the redeemed (Rom. 14:17; cf.
15:13; Ps. 51:12; 1 Thess. 1:6). While Christians are blessed with a rich
measure of joy in this life (John 15:11; 16:20, 24; 17:13; Acts13:52; Rom.
15:13; Gal. 5:22; Phil. 4:4; 1 Peter 1:8; 1 John 1:4; 2 John 12), the full joy of
eternal perfection awaits them in heaven when as faithful slaves they
"enter into the joy of [their] master" (Matt. 25:21, 23). Believers' highest
joy in this life does not come from the trivial, insignificant, temporal
things of this world, but in the spiritual life and fellowship of lost sinners
found, restored, and united in Christ's true church. Believers' joy, as God's
joy, is the result of the greatness and glory of God's saving work.

Three points provide necessary background information for the
parables in this chapter. The first is clarity. These stories cannot be understood in a vacuum, but only in light of the cultural setting in which they
were given. What they meant to the people of Jesus' day is what He
intended them to mean to each and every succeeding generation. A
parable in a sense can be like a political cartoon, the point of which is
lost on those from a different society. The message of our Lord's parables
was clear to perceptive listeners living together in the common culture
of the time. Thus, the essential prerequisite for understanding the message of the parables is established by reconstructing the cultural setting
in which they were told.

The second is location. This chapter is centrally placed in Luke's
gospel. The introductory section (1:1–9:50) covers Luke's prologue, the
events surrounding Christ's birth, and His Galilean ministry. The middle
section (9:51–19:27), chronicles the Lord's ministry in Judea. The final
section (19:28–24:53), focuses on the passion of Christ; the events surrounding the cross, His death, resurrection, and post-resurrection appearances. The middle ten chapters, containing more than twenty parables,

are the heart and soul of our Lord's kingdom teaching. Chapter 15 is in the middle of those ten chapters, and the three parables it contains form the high point of Jesus' teaching in this section of Luke.

The final point is complexity. While illustrations and analogies and never allegories with mystical, hidden, secret meanings, parables can contain various features and layers. In each of these parables, the story itself is first and follows the same form or outline in all three. Something valuable (a sheep, coin, or son) is lost, sought, found or restored, and celebrated. The second layer consists of an ethical implication that everyone would have understood. Did the shepherd do the right thing in leaving the ninety-nine sheep to look for the one that was lost? Should the woman have dropped everything to search for her lost coin? Was the father right to take back the son who had wasted his inheritance? Third, there are theological implications in the lessons each parable teaches about the kingdom of God. The final layer involves what the parables teach about Christ. All three parables also illustrate an aspect of the lost sinner, who like a sheep is stupid and helpless; like a coin is senseless and inanimate, and like a rebel son is wicked and destitute. In each case the seeker (the shepherd, woman, and father) represents God, who after restoring the lost sinner rejoices along with all those in heaven.

With that as a background, the chapter opens on the foundational reality that sets the stage—**all the tax collectors** (despised traitors who extorted money from their fellow Jews to fill Rome's coffers) **and the sinners** (the irreligious and unrighteous riff-raff, whom the scribes and Pharisees considered beneath them and refused to associate with) **were coming near** Jesus **to listen to Him.** As a result, **both the Pharisees and the scribes began to grumble, saying, "This man receives sinners and eats with them."** William Barclay details the Pharisees' disdain for such people:

> The Pharisees gave to people who did not keep the law a general classification. They called them *the People of the Land*; and there was a complete barrier between the Pharisees and the People of the Land. The Pharisaic regulations laid it down, "When a man is one of the People of the Land, entrust no money to him, take no testimony from him, trust him with no secret, do not appoint him guardian of an orphan, do not make him the custodian of charitable funds, do not accompany him on a journey." A Pharisee was forbidden to be the guest

of any such man or to have him as his guest. He was even forbidden, so far as it was possible, to have any business dealings with him. It was the deliberate Pharisaic aim to avoid every contact with the people who did not observe the petty details of the law.... the strict Jews said, not "There will be joy in heaven over one sinner who repents," but, "There will be joy in heaven over one sinner who is obliterated before God." (*The New Daily Study Bible*, The Gospel of Luke [Louisville: Westminster John Knox, 2001], 236–37. Italics in original.)

That the Lord associated with the despised outcasts of Jewish society shocked and appalled the religious authorities, and drew their sharp criticism (cf. 5:29–32; 7:34–39; 19:7). But Christ associated with sinners because His mission was to "seek and to save that which was lost" (Luke 19:10) and consequently bring joy to God.

It is in the context of His conflict with the scribes and Pharisees that Jesus created the three parables that make up the chapter. They not only reveal that God and all heaven rejoice when the lost are found, but at the same time indict the scribes and Pharisees because they did not find joy in Jesus' mission of saving sinners. They claimed to know God, but in truth were abysmally ignorant of the heart of God toward the lost. They were just another generation like those whom Isaiah described as hypocrites who "draw near with their words and honor Me with their lip service, but they remove their hearts far from Me" (Isa. 29:13). These stories are the means by which the Lord exposes their complete alienation from God, His joy, and mission of salvation.

THE LOST SHEEP

So He told them this parable, saying, "What man among you, if he has a hundred sheep and has lost one of them, does not leave the ninety-nine in the open pasture and go after the one which is lost until he finds it? When he has found it, he lays it on his shoulders, rejoicing. And when he comes home, he calls together his friends and his neighbors, saying to them, 'Rejoice with me, for I have found my sheep which was lost!' I tell you that in the same way, there will be more joy in heaven over one sinner who repents

than over ninety-nine righteous persons who need no repentance.
(15:3–7)

By introducing the first two parables with a hypothetical question, the Lord drew the scribes and Pharisees deep into both the experience and thinking of the main characters. Having assumed that role in
their minds and affirmed that what the character in the story did was
right ethically they were trapped. There was no way to avoid the Lord's
clear and unmistakable application of the truth that it was right to recover
a valuable coin and sheep—was it less important to rescue a soul from
judgment?

This first story involves poor peasants in a village setting. The
man caring for a **hundred sheep** probably did not own all of them,
since it would have been unusual for one villager to have a flock that
large. Villagers would often consolidate their sheep into large flocks and
hire shepherds from the lower end of the village's social structure to take
care of them. They were reluctant to hire outsiders since such hired
hands, having no personal stake in the flock, were not concerned about
the sheep (John 10:12–13).

Even though such prominent Old Testament figures as Rachel
(Gen. 29:9), Jacob (Gen. 30:31; 31:4), the patriarchs of the twelve tribes of
Israel (Gen. 37:12–13; 47:3), Joseph (Gen. 37:2), Moses (Ex. 3:1), and David
(1 Sam. 16:19; 17:15, 20, 34) had been shepherds, and even God is
described as a shepherd (Gen. 48:15; Pss. 23:1; 80:1; Isa. 40:11; John 10:11,
14; Heb. 13:20; 1 Peter 2:25; 5:4; Rev. 7:17), shepherds were near the bottom
of the social ladder. Caring for sheep was the lowest of the legitimate
occupations, ranking just above the outcast line, below which were tax
collectors and other irreligious sinners. Shepherds were uneducated and
unskilled, and were increasingly viewed in the post-New Testament era
as dishonest, unreliable, and unsavory—so much so that they were not
permitted to testify in court. Sheep had to be watched and cared for
seven days a week, leaving shepherds unable to fully comply with the
Pharisees' man-made Sabbath regulations. Because they were in continual violation of those regulations, shepherds were perpetually ceremonially unclean. For Jesus to ask the scribes and Pharisees to imagine
themselves in the role of a shepherd was insulting. No Pharisee would

demean himself by becoming a shepherd, not even hypothetically. By challenging them to put themselves in the imaginary shepherd's place, the Lord once again attacked their overweening pride.

As the story opens, the shepherds (there would likely have been two or three for a flock of this size) had **lost one of** the sheep. This was a dangerous and potentially life-threatening situation, since sheep are defenseless against predators and unable to take care of themselves. For example, if they roll over onto their backs they are often unable to right themselves, which places them in grave danger, as Phillip Keller explains:

> The way it happens is this. A heavy, fat, or long fleeced sheep will lie down comfortably in some little hollow or depression in the ground. It may roll on its side slightly to stretch out or relax. Suddenly the center of gravity in the body shifts so that it turns on its back far enough that the feet no longer touch the ground. It may feel a sense of panic and start to paw frantically. Frequently this only makes things worse. It rolls over even further. Now it is quite impossible for it to regain its feet.
>
> As it lies there struggling, gases begin to build up in the rumen. As these expand they tend to retard and cut off blood circulation to the extremities of the body, especially the legs. If the weather is very hot and sunny a cast sheep can die in a few hours. If it is cool and cloudy and rainy it may survive in this position for several days. (*A Shepherd Looks At Psalm 23* [Grand Rapids: Zondervan, 1970], 61–62)

Losing one of the sheep was therefore a serious situation, which called for immediate action. Shepherds were accountable for their flock, and if a sheep wandered off, they were responsible to rescue it (cf. 1 Sam. 17:34–35), or produce evidence that it had been killed by a predator or stolen (cf. Gen. 31:39). It was this shepherd's duty to **leave the ninety-nine in the open pasture** under the care of others **and go after the one** that was **lost** and search for it **until he** found **it.**

In the Lord's story the shepherd found the lost sheep, so his search was successful. Having **found** it, the shepherd laid **it on his shoulders,** its stomach against his neck and its feet tied together in front of him, and started on the long, arduous journey home carrying the heavy animal (an adult sheep can weigh more than 100 pounds). Further, that he brought the sheep **home** to the village, not back to the open pasture from where he had set out on his search, implies that it was after nightfall and that he made the return trip in the dark.Yet, he did not do so unwillingly, but rejoicing.

After being lost, sought, and found, the sheep's safe return was celebrated. In his joy over finding the missing sheep, the shepherd called **together his friends and his neighbors, saying to them, "Rejoice with me, for I have found my sheep which was lost!"** The scribes and Pharisees, though loath to be shepherds, even in their minds for the sake of illustration, would have understood fully the monetary value of sheep, since they were "lovers of money" (Luke 16:14). They would have grasped the joyous celebration that would have ensued when the shepherd returned with the lost sheep. They would have agreed that, ethically, the shepherd's relentless pursuit of the lost sheep was his obligation.

Having drawn the scribes and Pharisees into the story, the Lord delivered a devastating application to them. **I tell you,** He solemnly declared, **that in the same way, there will be more joy in heaven over one sinner who repents than over ninety-nine righteous persons who need no repentance.** The contrast between the scribes and Pharisees, who were indifferent to the plight of the lost, and God, who seeks them and rejoices when they are found, is striking. That those who claimed to officially represent God did not understand His mission or share His joy at the recovery of lost sinners reveals that their thinking was alien to His. The scribes and Pharisees lived within the narrow confines of superficiality and triviality while all around them souls were perishing. They were hypocrites, false shepherds who knew nothing of the compassionate, caring, loving heart of God; they were depicted by the **ninety-nine** self-**righteous persons who** saw no **need** for personal **repentance** and brought no joy to heaven.

The story also contains Christological overtones. God incarnate in Jesus Christ is the good shepherd (John 10:11, 14), who came "to seek and to save that which was lost" (Luke 19:10). He has compassion on lost sinners, whom He likened to sheep without a shepherd (Matt. 9:36; Mark 6:34), and bore the full burden of their restoration to God by laying down His life for them (John 10:11; cf. Isa. 53:4–6; 1 Peter 2:24–25).

THE LOST COIN

Or what woman, if she has ten silver coins and loses one coin, does not light a lamp and sweep the house and search carefully until she finds it? When she has found it, she calls together her friends and neighbors, saying, "Rejoice with me, for I have found the coin which I had lost!" In the same way, I tell you, there is joy in the presence of the angels of God over one sinner who repents. (15:8–10)

Like the first story, this one also takes place in a village setting. As does the previous parable, this one presents a poor person of low social standing facing a major crisis—a woman who lost a coin of great value.

If the scribes and Pharisees were insulted that Jesus asked them to think like a shepherd, calling on them to imagine themselves in the place of a woman was an even greater insult. Shepherds were considered unclean, and in that male-dominated culture women were deemed insignificant and not worthy of respect. It should be noted that while the scribes and Pharisees resented being compared to a shepherd and a woman, God Himself did not. In Psalm 23 He not only pictured Himself as a shepherd (v. 1), but also as a woman (v. 5; preparing a table was women's work), while in His lament over Jerusalem, Jesus pictured Himself as a mother hen (Luke 13:34). It was mercy that prompted Jesus to assault their foolish pride, since only the humble can be saved (Matt. 5:5; James 4:6, 10).

The parable describes a **woman** who had lost one of her **ten silver coins.** The coin was a drachma (a Roman denarius), which represented a day's wage for a common laborer. While that may not seem like a large sum, in a bartering society, where money was not used as frequently as in most modern societies, it was a significant loss. The money may have been an emergency fund, to be used when needed to make critical purchases. A more likely possibility is that the coins represented the woman's dowry, given to her as a wedding gift by her father and providing security for the future.

How she lost it is not relevant to the story. It may be that she had strung the coins together and worn them around her neck and the cord broke, or she may have bound them up together in a rag as a sort of purse and the knot came undone. To carry out her desperate search, it was necessary for her to **light a lamp** even in the daytime, since houses usually had either no windows, or at best very small ones. When a quick look around failed to reveal the coin, she proceeded to **sweep the** dusty, hard-packed dirt floor of the **house and search carefully** and intensely for it.

At last, to her great joy, she found the missing coin. To celebrate, she called **together her** female **friends and neighbors** (both nouns are feminine) **saying, "Rejoice with me, for I have found the coin which I had lost!"** People in a small, tight-knit village would share each other's sufferings and joys, so a party celebrating the woman's joy at recovering what she had lost would have been appropriate. Are eternal souls worth less?

In terms of ethics, the Pharisees would once again have agreed that she had done what was necessary under the circumstances. All would agree that having lost a significant sum of money, there was nothing else for her to do but diligently search for it until she found it. This parable too was aimed squarely at them, as Christ's emphatic statement **I tell you** indicates. Yet they again failed to make the connection between their contemptuous disdain for lost souls and God's passionate concern for them. They failed to share in the **joy** that exists **in the presence of the angels of God,** who have a keen interest in the redemption that produces God's joy (cf. Matt. 18:10; 25:31; Luke 2:10–14; 1 Peter 1:12; Rev. 3:5), **over one sinner who repents.** The joy here is God's joy, the joy that fills heaven, and in which the angels and the redeemed share (cf. Rev. 4:8–11; 5:8–14).

The Lord's indictment of the scribes and Pharisees was clear and inescapable. How could they affirm the ethical responsibility of a shepherd to search for a lost sheep and a woman to search for a lost coin, while condemning Him for seeking to recover lost souls? How could they understand the joys of the humble men and women in a village over temporal recovery, and utterly fail to comprehend the joy of God in heaven over eternal salvation?

The theological and Christological elements of this brief parable are clear. The woman represents God in Christ seeking lost sinners in the cracks, dust, and debris of a dirty world of sin. He initiated the search for those sinners who belong to Him through His sovereign choice of them, since like the lifeless, inanimate coin, they can do nothing on their own (Eph. 2:1–3). Jesus came all the way from heaven to earth to search for His lost ones, pursuing sinners into every dark corner, and then shining the light of the glorious gospel (2 Cor. 4:5–6; 1 Tim. 1:11) on them. Having found the lost sinner, God in Christ restores him or her to His heavenly treasury, and then expresses joy in which the holy inhabitants of heaven share.

Recovering the lost requires costly grace. The sinless Son of God became a man, lived with sinners, bore God's wrath for sin on the cross, and rose in triumph from the grave. None of the false gods of the world's religions are like the true and living God, who seeks and saves unworthy sinners because He values them as His own; who makes His enemies His friends for the sheer joy that He receives in saving them.

Yet God's seeking and saving lost sinners does not happen apart from their repentance. That reality is not part of the sheep and coin stories, since they are not persons. It is, however, a theme of the last and longest of the three parables in this chapter, the tale of two sons and a loving father (vv. 11–32), which is the subject of the next chapter of this volume.

The Tale of Two Sons (Luke 15:11–32)

25

And He said, "A man had two sons. The younger of them said to his father, 'Father, give me the share of the estate that falls to me.' So he divided his wealth between them. And not many days later, the younger son gathered everything together and went on a journey into a distant country, and there he squandered his estate with loose living. Now when he had spent everything, a severe famine occurred in that country, and he began to be impoverished. So he went and hired himself out to one of the citizens of that country, and he sent him into his fields to feed swine. And he would have gladly filled his stomach with the pods that the swine were eating, and no one was giving anything to him. But when he came to his senses, he said, 'How many of my father's hired men have more than enough bread, but I am dying here with hunger! I will get up and go to my father, and will say to him, "Father, I have sinned against heaven, and in your sight; I am no longer worthy to be called your son; make me as one of your hired men."' So he got up and came to his father. But while he was still a long way off, his father saw him and felt compassion for him, and ran and embraced him and kissed him. And the son said to him, 'Father, I have sinned against heaven and in your sight; I am no longer worthy to be called your son.' But the father said to his slaves, 'Quickly bring out the best robe and put it on him, and put a ring on his hand and sandals on his feet; and bring the fattened calf, kill it, and let us eat and celebrate; for this son of mine was dead and has come to life again; he was lost and has been found.' And they began to celebrate. Now his older son was in the field, and when he came and approached the house, he heard music and dancing. And he summoned one of the servants and began inquiring what these things could be. And he said to him, 'Your brother has come, and your father has killed the fattened calf because he has received him back safe and sound.' But he became angry and was not willing to go in; and his father came out and began pleading with him. But he answered and said to his father, 'Look! For so many years I have been serving you and I have never neglected a command of yours; and yet you have never given me a young goat, so that I might celebrate with my friends; but when this son of yours came, who has devoured your wealth with prostitutes, you killed the fattened calf for him.' And he said to him, 'Son, you have always been with me, and all that is mine is yours. But we had to celebrate and rejoice, for this brother of yours was dead and has begun to live, and was lost and has been found.'" (15:11–32)

The Lord Jesus Christ was the master story teller. His stories were unequalled analogies clarifying spiritual truth. Although they had, above the surface, profound spiritual significance relating to the kingdom of God and salvation, they were, in themselves, stories drawn from everyday life experience that His hearers could relate to. Even Christ's fictional stories, like the rest of the Bible, stand in contrast to false religions, almost all of which draw their features out of myth and fantasy. The Bible is a real world book, true to fact and to common human experience. Even when the meanings of the Lord's stories were designed to conceal the truth from those who had rejected Him (Matt. 13:13–15; John 12:39–40), they were still clear and comprehensible stories. Even those who rejected the truth understood the analogies, though in the dark as to their spiritual significance and application.

This story is a clear illustration of that fact. The religious leaders understood the story exactly, but as to its spiritual meaning they were blind. Of all the Lord's parables, this one is the best known and most memorable. Commonly known as the parable of the prodigal son, it is in reality the story of two rebellious sons and their loving, gracious father. Though a child can grasp the tale, its meaning is probably the most rich and complex of Jesus' parables.

This story deserves more than just a barebones treatment; a mere superficial understanding that fails to grasp the depth and richness of its message. Since the Bible is an ancient Near Eastern book, its truths are presented in a cultural setting that is alien to our own. It has been all too easy for interpreters to rip this story out of its context, transport it into today's world, and treat it superficially and errantly. To do so is not only to miss the nuances, subtleties, and features that give this story its full divine message, but also to misrepresent the message of Jesus. And that is no small crime, especially in dealing with this most crucial salvation illustration.

To draw out of this magnificent story all that God put in it is to hear it in the context that Jesus' audience would have heard it. There were in their minds deeply ingrained social and religious ideas, cultural attitudes, generating predictable feelings and sensibilities typical of life and perception in the ancient Middle East. Even the most educated people of that time would have had their roots in simple, agrarian village life. Understanding some of the features of that life will illuminate the story for modern readers, and prevent superficial misrepresentation.

As noted in the previous chapter of this volume, the three parables in Luke 15 are Jesus' response to accusations made by His relentless adversaries, the scribes and Pharisees. They hated Him for confronting and exposing their self-righteous hypocrisy, and in return blasphemously accused Him of being empowered by Satan. One way they tried to discredit Jesus was by attacking Him for associating with the "unsynagogued" riffraff of Jewish society, the tax-collectors and sinners (15:1–2). That Jesus associated with Satan's people (as they viewed them) instead of God's people (as they viewed themselves) proved, they argued, that He could not be from God.

Like the parables of the lost sheep and the lost coin, this parable depicts God's joy over the salvation of the lost. But while the first two parables emphasize God's part in seeking sinners this third one, while touching on God as the seeker, focuses more on the human aspect of salvation—man's sin, rejection, repentance, and return to God. It is a dramatic, moving story of the sinner's desperate penitence and of God's love and eager forgiveness for such sorrow.

The story revolves around three characters: the younger son, the father, and the older son and how they acted within a culture whose ethical priority was to seek honor and avoid shame. Told to the protectors of honor and rejecters of shame, this story turns that ethical construct on its head. The younger son appears to be the extreme example of shame by his rebellion against all that is right. Then, in the eyes of the scribes and Pharisees, the father appears more shameful in accepting the son back. To all who understand the story, the older brother is the ultimate exhibition of shame, and he represents the scribes and Pharisees, who believed they were the most honorable and without shame. Those aspects of shame and honor will become clear as the story progresses.

THE YOUNGER SON

And He said, "A man had two sons. The younger of them said to his father, 'Father, give me the share of the estate that falls to me.' So he divided his wealth between them. And not many days later, the younger son gathered everything together and went on a journey into a distant country, and there he squandered his estate with loose living. Now when he had spent everything, a severe famine occurred in that country, and he began to be impoverished. So he went and hired himself out to one of the citizens of that country, and he sent him into his fields to feed swine. And he would have gladly filled his stomach with the pods that the swine were eating, and no one was giving anything to him. But when he came to his senses, he said, 'How many of my father's hired men

have more than enough bread, but I am dying here with hunger! I will get up and go to my father, and will say to him, "Father, I have sinned against heaven, and in your sight; I am no longer worthy to be called your son; make me as one of your hired men."' (15:11–19)

The story of the familiar younger of the two sons unfolds in three stages of shame: he made a shameless request, committed a shameless act of rebellion, and then shamefully repented.

A SHAMELESS REQUEST

And He said, "A man had two sons. The younger of them said to his father, 'Father, give me the share of the estate that falls to me.' So he divided his wealth between them. (15:11–12)

The story opens by introducing a **man** who **had two sons.** The common title of this story, the parable of the prodigal son, implies that it is primarily about the **younger** son. Such is not the case, however. Though he does not appear until the end, it is actually the older brother who is the main focus of the parable. The younger son's actions at the beginning set in motion the chain of events that led to his brother's sinful reaction and the indictment of Jesus' listeners. "Prodigal" is an archaic term that describes a spendthrift; an extravagantly self-indulgent or recklessly wasteful person. It accurately describes the younger son, as his actions reveal.

This young man made a startling request **to his father** and said to him, **"Father, give me the share of the estate that falls to me."** The scribes and Pharisees listening to this story would have been surprised and shocked by his brazen demand. This was an outrageous, unheard of request for a son to make to his father. It was disrespectful, and expressed an extreme lack of love and gratitude to the one who had provided everything for him. The scribes and Pharisees would have considered it shameful, reprehensible, unacceptable behavior, a flagrant violation of the fifth commandment, "Honor your father and your mother"

(Ex. 20:12; cf. Lev. 19:3; Mal. 1:6; Matt. 15:4).

For a son to say such a thing to his father in that culture was tantamount to saying that he wished that his father was dead, since he was not entitled to his share of the inheritance (one-third of the estate, since his brother was the firstborn [Gen. 25:31–34; Deut. 21:17]) while his father was still alive. Since his father retained control and oversight of the estate as long as he lived (cf. v. 31), he stood in the way of his son's plans. He wanted his freedom to leave the family and gratify his own selfish desires. Normally a son who shamed himself by making such a request would have been publically shamed by his father, perhaps disinherited, or possibly even dismissed from the family and considered dead (cf. vv. 24, 32).

Further evidence of the son's irresponsibility comes from the use of the term *ousias* (**estate**), used only here in the New Testament, instead of the usual term for inheritance, *klēronomia* (12:13; 20:14; Matt. 21:38; Mark 12:7). *Ousias* refers to property or material possessions, and its use suggests that he was unwilling to take the responsibility that came with his share of the estate. He evidently was not interested in managing his share for the family's future good, as those before him had done, but selfishly wanted to liquidate it to use it only for his own pleasure.

Word of the son's irresponsible and selfish request would have circulated throughout the village. The people would have expected the father to be furious with the son who had shamed and dishonored him and to take appropriate disciplinary action. Instead, in a surprising and unexpected turn of events, the father granted his son's request and **divided his wealth between** his sons. **Wealth** translates the Greek work *bios*, which literally refers to physical life. It encompasses here all that the previous generations of the family had produced and handed down to the current generation. Had the father done so of his own free will it might have been understandable. But to do so in response to his wicked son's impudent request was shocking. Instead of slapping him across the face for his insolence, the father gave him what he wanted. In the eyes of the religious leaders listening the father had, by this concession, acted shamefully himself! The Lord is making the spiritual point that God gives sinners the freedom to choose their course of iniquity.

A SHAMELESS REBELLION

And not many days later, the younger son gathered everything together and went on a journey into a distant country, and there he squandered his estate with loose living. Now when he had spent everything, a severe famine occurred in that country, and he began to be impoverished. So he went and hired himself out to one of the citizens of that country, and he sent him into his fields to feed swine. And he would have gladly filled his stomach with the pods that the swine were eating, and no one was giving anything to him. (15:13–16)

It did not take long for **the younger son** to take the next step in his downward plunge. Wasting no time, **not many days later** he **gathered everything** he had received **together.** *Sunagō* (**gathered together**) has the connotation here of turning **everything** into cash (the word was so used in extrabiblical Greek; cf. Walter Bauer, William F. Arndt, and F. Wilbur Gingrich, *A Greek-English Lexicon of the New Testament and Other Early Christian Literature* [Chicago: Univ. of Chicago, 1979], 782), since that was the only practical way he could have taken his share of the estate with him **on a journey into a distant country** for his sinful pleasure. Although he could not take possession of his inheritance until his father died, he was permitted to sell his share (necessarily at a discounted price) to a buyer willing to wait to take possession until the father died (much like investors today buy futures, hedging against the future by paying the purchase price now).

As if it were not bad enough that he dishonored his father, ignored his responsibility to the family, and set off on a wasteful course of sinful pleasure, he then travelled to a **distant country,** meaning a Gentile region (as was all territory outside of Israel). He wanted to sin beyond the range of all accountability, far away from his father and the villagers, who scorned him for his disgraceful behavior. His action symbolizes the foolishness of the sinner trying to flee from God, to whom he does not want to be answerable.

The people listening to the story would have wondered why the Lord did not bring in the older brother at this point to act as a mediator. That would have been expected. If he truly loved his father, he would have defended his honor from the irresponsible actions of his younger brother; if he loved his brother, he would have intervened to prevent him from ruining his life and heaping shame on everyone. He bears shame for his absence. The picture is of a loving, generous father who gave his all to two ungrateful, unloving sons, both of whom had absolutely no relationship to him, or to each other.

As he had planned, after arriving at his destination, the younger son **squandered his estate with loose living.** *Diaskorpizō* (**squandered**) literally means "to scatter" (Matt. 25:24, 26; 26:31; Luke 1:51; John 11:52; Acts 5:37). Through his reckless, wasteful, debauched lifestyle—including consorting with prostitutes (v. 30)—he squandered his fortune.

Sin's pleasures are fleeting (Heb. 11:25), however, and when the last of his money was gone, the party was over. His erstwhile friends, who had gladly binged with him, had no more use for him once **he had spent everything.** Hard on the heels of his bankrupting himself came another disaster, this one not of his own making: **a severe famine occurred in that country.** Famine was a dreaded and deadly scourge that was all too common in the ancient world. Famine drove both Abraham (Gen. 12:10) and Jacob and his family (Gen. 47:4) to seek refuge in Egypt, Isaac to seek refuge in the land of the Philistines (Gen. 26:1), and Ruth and her family to take refuge in Moab (Ruth 1:1). There were famines throughout Israel's history (2 Sam. 21:1; 1 Kings 18:1–2; 2 Kings 4:38; 8:1; Neh. 5:3; Lam. 5:10; Acts 11:28), often with appalling consequences—including cannibalism (2 Kings 6:25–29).

For the first time in his life **he began to be impoverished** (lit., "come up short," or, "be in need"). His own bad decisions, coupled with the severe external crisis brought about by the famine, brought him to an inconceivable level of desperation. He had forsaken his family, and his so-called friends had forsaken him. He was a stranger in a foreign land, with nowhere to go and no one to turn to for help. He was penniless, destitute, without resources. Seeking unrestrained pleasure, unabated lusts, and unrestricted behavior, he wound up instead with pain, emptiness on the brink of death. Yet despite his dire circumstances, he was not yet ready to humble himself, return home, seek restoration, and face the consequences of his shameful behavior.

Instead, he came up with a desperate plan. **He went and hired**

himself out to one of the citizens of that country, who **sent him into his fields to feed swine.** For a Jewish man to herd **swine** in a Gentile country was one of the most degrading occupations imaginable. The rabbinic writings pronounced a curse on those involved with swine (Leon Morris, *The Gospel According to St. Luke,* The Tyndale New Testament Commentaries [Grand Rapids: Eerdmans, 1975], 241). The word **hired** is a stretch for what Jesus meant, since it translates a form of the verb *kollaō,* which literally means "glued." This was not a job contract. He was a beggar and like persistent beggars the world over, he probably latched on to this man and would not let go. To get rid of him, the man would send him to feed the pigs, perhaps with no intention to pay him anything. He was reduced to fighting the pigs for the **pods that** they **were eating.** These were probably carob pods, which are virtually inedible for humans (although when crushed to powder, they can be used as a substitute for chocolate). Even his attempts at begging failed, for **no one was giving anything to him.**

The younger son's behavior exemplifies the sinner's wretched desires and his predicament graphically illustrates the sinner's desperate plight. To sin against God is to rebel against His fatherhood, disdain His honor and respect, spurn His love, and reject His will. Unrepentant sinners shun all responsibility and accountability to God. They deny Him his place, hate Him, wish He did not exist, refuse to love Him, and dishonor Him. They take the gifts He has given them and squander them in a life of self-indulgence, dissipation, and unrestrained lust. As a result they find themselves spiritually bankrupt, empty, destitute, with no one to help, nowhere to turn, and facing eternal death. And when all the self-help strategies fail, the sinner hits rock bottom. There is only one solution for those who, like this young man, find themselves in such a situation, which the next scene in the parable reveals.

A SHAMEFUL REPENTANCE

But when he came to his senses, he said, 'How many of my father's hired men have more than enough bread, but I am dying here with hunger! I will get up and go to my father, and will say to

him, "Father, I have sinned against heaven, and in your sight; I
am no longer worthy to be called your son; make me as one of
your hired men."' (15:17–19)

In the depths of his hopelessness and despair, the younger son,
facing starvation, **came to his senses** and remembered his rich and
generous father. **"How many of my father's hired men have more
than enough bread, but I am dying here with hunger!"** he reminded
himself. This statement further reveals his knowledge of his father's gracious, compassionate nature. **Hired men** were day laborers who were
generally unskilled and poor, living day to day on the temporary jobs
they could find at whatever wages they were offered (cf. Matt. 20:13–14).
Recognizing the reality that such people would be part of society, the Old
Testament law protected them and required their wages to be paid in a
timely manner (cf. Lev. 19:13; Deut. 24:14–15). But as the son knew well
and recalled, his father generously exceeded the requirements of the law
by making sure that the men he hired had **more than enough bread.**
That recollection gave him hope and, with no other option, with what the
scribes and Pharisees would see as brash audacity, he decided to **get up
and go to** his **father.** The worst that could happen would be no more
severe than what he faced, but he hoped at least to be treated with the
same mercy and compassion with which his father had always treated
his day laborers.

With that in mind, he rehearsed a brief confession to offer when
he arrived home: **"Father, I have sinned against heaven, and in
your sight; I am no longer worthy to be called your son; make me
as one of your hired men.'"** The best he could have expected, after
humbly confessing his shameful sin, was to be allowed to work toward
restitution (cf. Matt. 18:26) of all he had wasted and after that hope to be
reconciled with his father. The scribes and Pharisees would have agreed
that he needed to confess, repent, be humiliated, shamed, and perhaps
receive forgiveness and mercy, but only after making full restitution. In
their thinking, people earn their way back from shame.

The younger son's actions picture the kind of repentance that can
lead to salvation. He came to his senses and realized that his situation was
desperate. He remembered his father's goodness, compassion, generosity,

and mercy and trusted in them. In the same way, the repentant sinner takes stock of his situation and acknowledges his need to turn from his sin. He realizes that there is no one to turn to except the Father whom he has shamed and dishonored and by faith, with nothing to offer, turns to Him for forgiveness and reconciliation on the basis of His grace. The son acknowledged to his father that he had **sinned against heaven** (the Greek phrase could also suggest that he viewed his sins as piling up as high as heaven; cf. Ezra 9:6) **and in** his **sight.** In the same way the penitent sinner takes full responsibility for his sin and affirms its heinousness.

Repentance is the sinner's part in the process of being restored to God, and there is no true gospel apart from it. The call for sinners to repent is at the heart of all biblical evangelism, beginning in the Old Testament (cf. Pss. 32:5; 51:1–4, 14, 17; Isa. 1:16–18; 55:6–7; Ezek. 18:30, 32; 33:19; Jonah 3:5–10). In the New Testament repentance was central to the gospel preaching of John the Baptist (Luke 3:3–9), Jesus (Matt. 4:17; Luke 5:32; 13:3, 5; 24:46–47), the apostles (Mark 6:12), and the early church (Acts 2:38; 3:19; 5:31; 8:22; 17:30; 20:21; 26:20; 2 Cor. 7:9–11). Repentance must not be misconstrued as a meritorious, pre-salvation work since, though required of the sinner, it must be granted by God (Acts 11:18; Rom. 2:4; 2 Tim. 2:25).

Assuming that he would have to work to make restitution, the younger son did not expect to be welcomed back immediately into the family as a son, or even as one of the household servants. He only hoped that his father would be willing to accept him as **one of** his **hired men.** His empty lifestyle had filled him with remorse for the past, pain in the present, and the bleak prospect of even more suffering in the future as he worked the rest of his life to earn acceptance. But as it turned out, he drastically underestimated his father.

THE FATHER

So he got up and came to his father. But while he was still a long way off, his father saw him and felt compassion for him, and ran and embraced him and kissed him. And the son said to him, 'Father, I have sinned against heaven and in your sight; I am no

longer worthy to be called your son.' But the father said to his slaves, 'Quickly bring out the best robe and put it on him, and put a ring on his hand and sandals on his feet; and bring the fattened calf, kill it, and let us eat and celebrate; for this son of mine was dead and has come to life again; he was lost and has been found.' And they began to celebrate. (15:20–24)

Like the shameful story of his lost son, in the eyes of the religious leaders, the story of the father unfolds in three shameful stages: a shameful reception, a shameless reconciliation, and a shameless rejoicing.

A SHAMEFUL RECEPTION

So he got up and came to his father. But while he was still a long way off, his father saw him and felt compassion for him, and ran and embraced him and kissed him. And the son said to him, "Father, I have sinned against heaven and in your sight; I am no longer worthy to be called your son." (15:20–21)

Forced to his only option, the hopeful younger son **got up and came to his father.** The reception he was to receive was beyond his imagination, and shocked and stunned those legalists to whom the story was directed. The unexpected reception began to unfold **while he was still a long way off.** Before he entered the village Jesus said **his father saw him,** indicating that he had been watching, waiting, suffering silently, hoping himself that one day his shameful son would return. The scribes and Pharisees would have expected that if the son did return, the father, to maintain his own honor, would initially refuse to see him. Instead, he would make him sit in the village outside the gate of the family home for days in shame and disgrace. When he did finally grant his son an audience, it would be a cool reception as the son humbled himself before his father. He would be expected to tell his son what works he would need to perform to make full restitution for his prodigality, and for how long, before he could be reconciled as a son to his father. All of that was consistent with the rabbis' teaching that repentance was a good work performed by sinners that could eventually earn God's favor and forgiveness.

But that cultural expectation was shattered by Jesus when He said the father, on seeing his son, **felt compassion for him, and ran and embraced him and kissed him.** It was obviously represented as daylight, since he would not have been able to see his son at any great distance at night. The village would have been bustling with activity, and the father was determined to reach his son before he entered the village, with the intent to protect him from the shame of the taunts, scorn, and abuse that would be heaped upon him by the villagers as soon as they recognized him. The father's **compassion** for his son spurred him into action before the abuse could start.

To the utter amazement of the Lord's hearers, the details of the story convey that the father took the son's shame upon himself and then immediately reconciled him to the full honor of sonship. Incredibly, this shameful humbling is seen in his eagerness to reach him, because he **ran** to meet his son. Middle Eastern noblemen do not run. And **ran** translates a form of the Greek verb *trechō*, which was used of running a race in 1 Corinthians 9:24 and 26. Determined to reach his son before he entered the village received the taunts of the town, the father literally sprinted to him. For a man of his status and importance to run in public was, and still is, unheard of. Running necessitated gathering up the long robes worn by men and women alike and thus exposing the legs, which was considered shameful. He became at that time the object of shame— taking shame on himself to prevent shame on his son. Even more shocking was what he did when he reached the prodigal; he **embraced him** despite his impoverished filthiness and the vile rags he wore **and** repeatedly **kissed him.** That gesture of acceptance, love, forgiveness, and reconciliation would have further shocked the scribes and Pharisees. Here in this father the Lord Jesus Christ presents Himself, the one who left the glory of heaven, came to earth and bore the shame and humility to embrace repentant sinners, who come to Him in faith, and give them complete forgiveness and reconciliation.

The son's stunning reception by the horribly offended father took place solely by the grace of that father, apart from any works on the boy's part. When he finally could speak and make his rehearsed speech,

"Father, I have sinned against heaven and in your sight; I am no longer worthy to be called your son," he left out the last crucial phrase, **"make me as one of your hired men."** Why? Because there was no need to work to earn restoration and reconciliation. His father had received him back as a son. He did not have to crawl back one day at a time into his father's good graces, but was instantly forgiven, given mercy, and already reconciled. The son's reception is a true illustration of believers, who come in by repentance and faith directed toward God, pleading for His grace and forgiveness apart from works—and receiving full sonship.

A SHAMELESS RECONCILIATION

But the father said to his slaves, 'Quickly bring out the best robe and put it on him, and put a ring on his hand and sandals on his feet; (15:22)

The father then gave visible evidence of his reconciliation with his son. His actions would have further shocked those listening to this story. They would have found it incomprehensible that he would lavish honors on the son who had shamed and dishonored him. Turning to the household **slaves** who had followed him as he ran to meet his son, he said first of all, **"Quickly,** without delay, **bring out the best robe and put it on him."** The **best** or most important **robe** belonged to the patriarch, and was worn only on the most significant occasions. He was about to call for a grand, gala celebration, yet he gave his son the garment that he would normally have worn to such an event. The **ring** was the father's signet ring, which bore the family crest and was used to stamp the wax seal on documents to authenticate them. It signified the father's bestowing of privileges, rights, and authority on his son. **Sandals,** not usually worn by slaves, signified his full restoration to sonship. Just as the son returned to his father with nothing, so repentant, empty-handed sinners approach their heavenly Father, who justifies not the self-righteous, but the ungodly (Rom. 4:5).

The father's giving the robe and ring to his younger son would have shocked Christ's hearers. They knew that the robe and the ring by rights should have gone to the older brother. He would have first worn the father's formal robe at his own wedding—the single greatest event that could happen in a family. He should have received the ring as a symbol of his right as the firstborn to act on behalf of his father. But now, incredibly, his father had given them to his younger brother. Such lavish love and grace bestowed on a penitent, trusting sinner is incomprehensible to the legalistic mind. Legalism hates grace.

A SHAMELESS REJOICING

and bring the fattened calf, kill it, and let us eat and celebrate; for this son of mine was dead and has come to life again; he was lost and has been found.' And they began to celebrate. (15:23–24)

Overjoyed at his son's return, the father ordered his servants to prepare an extravagant celebration, dwarfing those of the shepherd who found his lost sheep (v. 6) and the woman who found her lost coin (v. 9). The **fattened,** grain-fed **calf** was reserved for events of utmost significance, such as the wedding of the firstborn son (cf. Matt. 22:2–4), or the visit of an important person (cf. 1 Sam. 28:24). By ordering his servants to prepare it so that the guests could **eat and celebrate,** the father re-vealed how important his son had become. Since a fattened calf could feed up to two hundred people, the entire village would have been invited. The shepherd had found an animal, the woman an inanimate object, and they celebrated with a few of their friends. But the father had found his **son,** who was **dead** and had **come to life again;** who **was lost,** but now had **been found,** and the entire village **began to celebrate** with him. All three celebrations reflect heaven's joy at the divine recovery of lost sinners (see the discussion of that truth in the previous chapter of this volume). And this party, like the first two, in reality honored not the one found, but the finder, who sought his son and gave him full reconciliation through his merciful forgiveness and gracious love.

THE OLDER SON

Now his older son was in the field, and when he came and approached the house, he heard music and dancing. And he summoned one of the servants and began inquiring what these things could be. And he said to him, 'Your brother has come, and your father has killed the fattened calf because he has received him back safe and sound.' But he became angry and was not willing to go in; and his father came out and began pleading with him. But he answered and said to his father, 'Look! For so many years I have been serving you and I have never neglected a command of yours; and yet you have never given me a young goat, so that I might celebrate with my friends; but when this son of yours came, who has devoured your wealth with prostitutes, you killed the fattened calf for him.' And he said to him, 'Son, you have always been with me, and all that is mine is yours. But we had to celebrate and rejoice, for this brother of yours was dead and has begun to live, and was lost and has been found.'" (15:25–32)

Some, simplistically, have argued that the older son represents Christians, since he remained at home and was outwardly obedient to his father. In reality, however, he represents the apostate legalists, in the form of the scribes and Pharisees. The older son's shameful role may be viewed under two headings: his truly shameful reaction, and his father's perceived shameful response.

A SHAMEFUL REACTION

Now his older son was in the field, and when he came and approached the house, he heard music and dancing. And he summoned one of the servants and began inquiring what these things could be. And he said to him, 'Your brother has come, and your father has killed the fattened calf because he has received him back safe and sound.' But he became angry and was not willing to go in; and his father came out and began pleading with him. But he answered and said to his father, 'Look! For so many years I

have been serving you and I have never neglected a command of yours; and yet you have never given me a young goat, so that I might celebrate with my friends; but when this son of yours came, who has devoured your wealth with prostitutes, you killed the fattened calf for him.' (15:25–30)

The **older son** had been out **in the field** all day overseeing the workers and was unaware of his brother's return and the subsequent party. When **he came** in from the field **and approached the house, he heard music and dancing.** That he knew nothing of the reconciliation and had not heard the sounds of the party earlier indicates the huge size of the family estate designed into the story. Surprised at finding a village-wide celebration in progress that he knew nothing about, **he summoned one of the servants** (perhaps one of the young boys hanging around the fringes of the party) **and began inquiring what these things could be.** He was not in the loop regarding the party, even though as the firstborn the responsibility for planning it should have fallen to him. Further, it was his resources, from his share of the estate, that were being used for the party, yet he had not been consulted. Legally, his father did not have to get his permission to use the resources, even though he had already dispersed to him the remaining two thirds of the estate. As noted above, the father retained control (according to the legal principle known as usufruct) of the estate as long as he lived. But his father's failure to consult him indicates once again that the older brother had no relationship with him or his younger brother. In terms of his relationship to his family he was metaphorically, as well as literally, far away in a field.

The servant's reply, **"Your brother has come, and your father has killed the fattened calf because he has received him back safe and sound,"** should have filled him with joy that his brother had returned and his father was being properly honored for his generosity. Instead it outraged and infuriated him that his father had **received** the prodigal back at all. Even worse from his perspective was the realization that his father had already reconciled with his brother (the Greek word translated **safe and sound** is used in the Septuagint, the Greek translation of the Old Testament, to refer to peace, not merely physical health), instead of making him work to make restitution for his waste and sin.

For years that older rebel had managed to conceal his true feelings of resentment toward his father and brother. All along, though, he had been wicked like his brother, only inwardly, not outwardly. But this event exposed his real attitude. In a burst of public display from long-cultivated private hatred, **he became angry and was not willing to go in** to celebrate with the others. He could not rejoice over the recovery of his lost brother because he had no love for his father. He failed to understand unmerited favor, free forgiveness, and deliverance from shame by the actions of the offended one endowed with the authority to forgive.

The scribes and Pharisees would have applauded his reaction. Finally, they must have thought, someone is upholding honor and acting righteously in anger over the son's shameful sin and the father's shameful forgiveness. They would have considered his father's actions outrageous and shameful, in the same way they considered Christ's associating with tax collectors and sinners wicked. And picturing them, the older son was a hypocritical legalist, doing what was expected of him on the outside, but inwardly filled with secret sins, such as bitterness, hatred, jealousy, anger, and lust (Matt. 23:28). The truth is, he was more profoundly and truly lost than his profligate younger brother, because he had spent his life convincing himself and others that he was good and morally upright. That made it impossible for him to acknowledge that he was in reality a wretched sinner. So it was with the scribes and Pharisees, they were "the righteous" that unlike "sinners" would not come to repentance (Matt. 9:13).

In contrast to their hard legalism and showing the same compassionate patience that he had toward his younger son, his **father came out and began pleading with him** to come to the celebration. The father's action symbolized God in Jesus Christ pleading with sinners (cf. Ezek. 18:31; 33:11; Luke 19:10) to come to salvation. This yet again would have surprised the self-righteous Jews, who would have expected the older son to be honored for his unwillingness to mingle in a celebration for a sinner led by a host whose love overpowered his devotion to the law.

All of the older son's pent up anger, bitterness, and resentment spilled out in a tirade that disregarded both his father's honor and his brother's blessing. Disrespectfully refusing to address him with the title

"Father," he bluntly **said to his father, "Look! For so many years I have been serving** (*douleuō*; to serve as a slave) **you."** To him, his **many years** of working under his father had been nothing but slavery. There was no love or respect for his father, merely toil and drudgery, waiting for him to die so he could inherit. It becomes clear that he wanted exactly what his younger brother wanted, all he could get of the estate for his own use, but chose a different path to obtaining it. Then, in a classic expression of self-righteous hypocrisy he declared, **"I have never neglected a command of yours"** (cf. Luke 18:21). Reflecting the amazing capacity for self-deception exhibited by hypocrites who think they are good, he lived under the illusion that he had never neglected any of his father's commands. The implied contrast is between his supposedly perfect behavior and his father's shameful behavior in his lenient treatment of his younger son. The older son saw himself as one of the "ninety-nine righteous persons who need no repentance" (Luke 15:7).

His outburst continued with allegations that his father had acted unfairly and unjustly. **"You have never given me a young goat,"** he complained, **"so that I might celebrate with my friends."** First, he declared that he had not been celebrated for his legalism. Heaven never holds a party for a self-righteous man. The second implication is that the people who really mattered to him, those that he would like to party with, were his friends, not his family. That was reminiscent of the Pharisees, who associated only with other Pharisees. In addition to allegedly ignoring his faithful service, he accused his father of showing favoritism to his younger brother. Refusing to acknowledge him as his brother or even name him, he disdainfully, contemptuously referred to him as **"this son of yours."** Then, painting the scene as black as he could, he reminded his father that his brother had **devoured** his **wealth with prostitutes,** and in spite of that, he had thrown a party to end all parties and **killed the fattened calf for him.**

The picture is striking. The legalistic older brother stood alone in the dark reviling his gracious father, who at the same time was being honored at the joyous celebration of his lost son's recovery. His actions graphically picture the scribes and Pharisees. They were unrepentant, self-righteous, hypocritical externalists, choosing to revile and scorn Jesus Christ, God incarnate, for reconciling sinners whom all Jewish religious society had rejected, instead of joining the heavenly banquet with those praising God for their salvation.

A SHAMEFUL RESPONSE

And he said to him, "Son, you have always been with me, and all that is mine is yours. But we had to celebrate and rejoice, for this brother of yours was dead and has begun to live, and was lost and has been found." (15:31–32)

The father's gracious, gentle response would have been considered the last shameful act in the story by the villagers had they known of it (as it was by the scribes and Pharisees listening to the story). They would have expected him to slap his son across the face for his insolent outburst. Instead, he addressed him in tender, endearing terms, reasoning with him and reaching out to him with the same compassionate love and mercy he had shown to his younger son. The word translated **son** is not *huios*, the term used in verses 11, 13, 19, 21, 24, 25 and 30, but the more affectionate term *teknon* ("child"). **"You have always been with me,"** he reminded him, **"and all that is mine is yours."** Although the father retained control over the estate, he had already given it to his son. Here is a picture of God's magnanimity, especially to the Jews, who were given the Scripture, the most generous common grace, and years of gospel opportunity (cf. Rom. 9:4–5). God's riches were given in greatest abundance and clarity to the Jews, and especially those very leaders who prided themselves on their knowledge of Scripture.

The father's concluding statement, **"But we had to celebrate and rejoice, for this brother of yours was dead and has begun to live, and was lost and has been found,"** returns to the theme of all three parables in this chapter—God's joy at recovering lost sinners. The younger son symbolizes those who seek God's salvation by grace, the older son those who seek salvation by works.

I give a more complete account of this wonderful parable in my book *A Tale of Two Sons* (Nashville: Thomas Nelson, 2008). In that book I wrote the following regarding the shocking, real-life ending to Jesus' parable:

With those words [v. 32], the parable of the prodigal son ended—but like a musical arrangement without a final, satisfying chord resolution. No more words, and Jesus simply walked away from the public venue where He was teaching. He moved into a more private context with His own disciples, where He began to tell them a whole new parable. The narrative reflects the shift in verse 33. "He also said to His disciples: 'There was a certain rich man ...'"

This is stunning. The ending is the thing in every story. We wait with anticipation for the finale. It's so vital that some readers can't resist turning to the end to see how the plot resolves before they read the actual story. But this story leaves us hanging. In fact, the Prodigal Son's story ends so abruptly that a textual critic with a low view of Scripture might very well suggest that what we have here is just a story fragment, unaccountably unfinished by the author. Or is it more likely that the ending was written down but somehow separated from the original manuscript and lost forever? There surely must be an end to this story somewhere, right?

But the abruptness of the ending doesn't leave us without the point; it *is* the point. This is the final blow in a long series of shocks that were built into Jesus' telling of the story. Of all the surprising plot twists and startling details, this is the culminating surprise: Jesus marvelously shaped the point and then simply walked away without resolving the tension between the father and his firstborn. But there is no missing fragment. He intentionally left the story unfinished and the dilemma unsettled. It is *supposed* to make us feel like we're waiting for a punch line or final sentence.

Surely the people in Jesus' original audience were left standing with their mouths hanging open as He walked away. They must have asked one another the same question that is on the tip of our tongues when we read it today: *What happened? How did the elder son respond? What is the end of the story?* The Pharisees, of all people would want to know, because the elder son clearly represented them.

It's easy to imagine that the guests in the story would be eager to hear how everything turned out. They were all still inside at the celebration, waiting for the father to come back inside. When he left the party so abruptly, people would conclude that something serious was going on. In a real-life situation such as this, it would begin to be whispered around among the guests that the elder brother was out there, very angry that people were celebrating something as reprehensible as the immediate, unconditional, wholesale forgiveness of a son who had behaved as badly as the prodigal. Everyone would want to study the father's expression when he came back inside to try to detect some clue about what happened. That's exactly *our* response, as listeners to Jesus' story.

But with all that pent-up expectation, Jesus simply walked away, leaving the tale hanging, unfinished, unresolved.

Incidentally, Kenneth E. Bailey, a Presbyterian commentator who was fluent in Arabic and a specialist in Middle-Eastern literature (he spent forty years living and teaching the New Testament in Egypt, Lebanon, Jerusalem and Cyprus) provides a fascinating analysis of the literary style of the Prodigal Son's story. The structure of the parable explains why Jesus left it unfinished. Bailey demonstrates that the parable divides naturally into two nearly equal parts, and each part is systematically structured in a kind of mirrored pattern (ABCD-DCBA) called a *chiasm*. It's a kind of parallelism that seems practically poetic, but it is a typical device in Middle Eastern prose to facilitate storytelling.

The first half—where the focus is completely on the younger brother—has eight stanzas or strophes, and in this case the parallels describe the prodigal's progress from departure to return:

Then He said: "A certain man had two sons.

A. Death—*And the younger of them said to his father, 'Father, give me the portion of goods that falls to me.' So he divided to them his livelihood.*

B. All Is Lost—*And not many days after, the younger son gathered all together, journeyed to a far country, and there wasted his possessions with prodigal living. But when he had spent all, there arose a severe famine in that land, and he began to be in want.*

C. Rejection—*Then he went and joined himself to a citizen of that country, and he sent him into his fields to feed swine. And he would gladly have filled his stomach with the pods that the swine ate, and no one gave him anything.*

D. The Problem—*But when he came to himself, he said, 'How many of my father's hired servants have bread enough and to spare, and I perish with hunger!*

D. The Solution—*I will arise and go to my father, and will say to him, "Father, I have sinned against heaven and before you, and I am no longer worthy to be called your son. Make me like one of your hired servants." And he arose and came to his father.*

C. Acceptance—*But when he was still a great way off, his father saw him and had compassion, and ran and fell on his neck and kissed him.*

B. All Is Restored—*And the son said to him, 'Father, I have sinned against heaven and in your sight, and am no longer worthy to be called your son.' But the father said to his servants, 'Bring out the best robe and put it on him, and put a ring on his hand and sandals on his feet.*

A. Resurrection—*And bring the fatted calf here and kill it, and let us eat and be merry; for this my son was dead and is alive again; he was lost and is found.' And they began to be merry."*

The second half shifts focus to the elder brother and progresses through a similar chiastic pattern. But it ends abruptly after the seventh strophe:

A. He Stands Aloof—*"Now his older son was in the field. And as he came and drew near to the house, he heard music and dancing. So he called one of the servants and asked what these things meant.*

    B. Your Brother; Peace (a feast); Anger—*And he said to him, 'Your brother has come, and because he has received him safe and sound, your father has killed the fatted calf.' But he was angry and would not go in.*

        C. Costly Love—*Therefore his father came out and pleaded with him.*

        D. My Actions, My Pay—*So he answered and said to his father, 'Lo, these many years I have been serving you; I never transgressed your commandment at any time; and yet you never gave me a young goat, that I might make merry with my friends.*

        D. His Actions, His Pay—*'But as soon as this son of yours came, who has devoured your livelihood with harlots, you killed the fatted calf for him.'*

        C. Costly Love—*And he said to him, 'Son, you are always with me, and all that I have is yours.*

    B. Your Brother; Safe (a feast); Joy!—*It was right that we should make merry and be glad, for your brother was dead and is alive again, and was lost and is found.'"*

A. The Missing Ending

The end of the parable is deliberately asymmetrical, as if to put extra stress on the lack of resolution. The ending simply isn't there.

We're *supposed* to notice that. Since the story stops abruptly with such a tender appeal, every hearer ought to take that plea to heart, meditate on it, personalize it, and see the gentle reasonableness of embracing the father's joy in the salvation of sinners. And, frankly, no one needed that sort of honest self-examination more than the legalistic scribes and Pharisees to whom Jesus told the story. The parable was an invitation first of all for them to forsake their pride and self-righteousness and reconcile with God's way of salvation. But furthermore, the same principle applies to everyone else, too—from wanton sinners like the Prodigal Son to sanctimonious hypocrites like the elder brother, and all kinds of people in between. Thus everyone who hears the story writes his or her own ending by how we respond to the kindness of God toward sinners.

It is an ingenious way to end the story. It leaves us wanting to pen the ending we would like to see. Anyone whose heart is not already hardened by self-righteous resentment ought to apprehend in the parable something about the glory of God's grace in Christ—especially His loving forgiveness and glad-hearted acceptance of penitent sinners. The person who catches even a glimpse of that truth would surely want to write something good—like this:

> Then the elder son fell on his knees before his father, saying, "I repent for my bitter, loveless heart, for my hypocritical service, and for my pride and self-righteousness. Forgive me, Father. Make me a true son, and take me inside to the feast." The father then embraced his firstborn son, smothered him with tearful, grateful kisses, took him inside, and seated him alongside his brother in dual seats of honor. They all rejoiced together and the level of joy [at] that already amazing celebration suddenly doubled. No one there would ever forget that night.

That would be the perfect ending. But I can't write the ending for anyone else—including the scribes and Pharisees. They wrote their own ending, and it was nothing at all like that one.

THE TRAGIC ENDING

Don't forget that Jesus told this parable—including the abrupt ending—chiefly for the benefit of the scribes and Pharisees. It was really a story about them. The elder brother represented them. The hanging resolution underscored the truth that the next move was theirs. The father's final tender plea was Jesus' own gentle appeal to them. If they had demanded to know the end of the parable on the spot, Jesus might well have said to them, "That is up to you." The Pharisees' ultimate response to Jesus would write the end of the story in real-life.

We therefore know how the tale really ended, then, don't we? It is not a happy ending. Instead, it's another shocking plot turn. In fact, it is the greatest shock and outrage of all time.

They killed Him.

Since the father figure in the parable represents Christ and the elder brother is a symbol of Israel's religious elite, in effect, the true ending to the story, as written by the scribes and Pharisees themselves, ought to read something like this: "The elder son was outraged at his father. He picked up a piece of lumber and beat him to death in front of everyone."

I told you it was a shocking ending.

You may be thinking to yourself, *No! That's not how the story ends. I grew up hearing that parable in Sunday school, and it's not supposed to have a tragic ending.*

Indeed, it seems like any rational person whose mind and heart is not utterly twisted by his own sanctimonious hypocrisy would listen to such a parable with deep joy and holy thankfulness for the generous grace that lifts a fallen sinner up, restores him to wholeness, and receives him again into his father's favor. Any humble-hearted individual who sees himself reflected in the Prodigal would naturally enter into the father's joy and celebration, rejoicing that Jesus would paint such a vivid portrait of divine grace. As we've seen from the very start, the clear message of the parable is about how eagerly Jesus receives sinners. It should end with joy, not tragedy. Everyone should join the celebration.

But the elder brother's heart was clearly (albeit secretly until now) hardened against his father. He had stored up years worth of resentment, anger, greed, and self-will—while wearing his father's favor as a badge of legitimacy. He never really understood or appreciated his father's goodness to him; but he was happy to receive it and milk it for whatever he could get out of it. He completely misinterpreted his father's kindness, thinking it was proof of his own worthiness; when in reality it was an expression of *the father's* goodness. And as soon as the father showed such lavish favor to the utterly unworthy prodigal brother, the elder brother's resentment quickly boiled over and his true character could not be concealed any longer.

Remember, the elder brother is a picture of the Pharisees. His attitude mirrored theirs exactly. If the elder son's behavior seems appalling and hard to understand for you and me, it was not at all hard to understand for the Pharisees. They were steeped in a religious system that cultivated precisely that kind of self-righteous, self-congratulatory, self-willed perspective with respect to the goodness and grace of God. They believed they had God's favor because they had earned it, pure and simple. So when Jesus showed favor to repentant tax collectors, prostitutes, and other lowlifes who clearly did not deserve any favor, the Pharisees resented it. They believed Jesus' kindness toward lowly sinners took the sheen off the emblem of their superiority, and they became angry in precisely the same way the elder son became angry.

Does it not seem remarkable that when Jesus brought his telling of the parable to such an abrupt halt—leaving off the ending completely—Luke's account is utterly silent regarding any kind of response from the Pharisees? They knew full well that the message of the parable was aimed at them and ought to have shamed them. But they asked no questions, made no protest, offered no commentary, asked for no further elaboration. The reason is that they understood the elder brother's attitude already. It made perfect sense to them. Perhaps they didn't even feel the lack of resolution to the same degree most listeners do, because to them the elder brother's complaint seemed perfectly reasonable. The way they would have *liked* to see the story resolved required *the father's* repentance. In their ideal scenario, the father would see the elder son's point, make a public apology to the elder son, publicly shame the Prodigal for his foolish behavior, and then perhaps even cast the Prodigal out forever. But the Pharisees surely saw the point Jesus was making clearly enough that they knew the story would never take a turn like *that*.

So they said nothing—at least nothing Luke (guided by the Holy Spirit) deemed important enough to record for us. Perhaps they simply turned and walked away. More likely, Jesus turned away from them.

In fact, let's assume there's no ellipsis at this point in the chronology of Luke's narrative. Luke 15 ends where the parable of the Prodigal Son ends. But Luke 16 continues with Jesus still speaking. This seems to be the record of one lengthy discourse. And in Luke 16:1, Jesus does indeed turn away from the scribes and Pharisees "to the disciples," and He begins to instruct them with another parable. This one is about the shrewdness of unbelievers and the impossibility of serving both God *and* money. Luke 16:14 says, "Now the Pharisees, who were lovers of money, also heard all these things, and they derided Him"—meaning they ridiculed Him.

So apparently they hung around, perhaps just on the periphery, after the parable of the Prodigal Son abruptly ended, undeterred in their opposition to Jesus. In fact, they were more determined than ever to silence Him, no matter what it took. And that attitude is what led them to write for themselves the tragic ending to the greatest parable of all time.

The Pharisees' hatred for Jesus grew from the day he told them the parable until they hatched a conspiracy to kill Him. "And the chief priests and the scribes sought how they might take Him by trickery and put Him to death" (Mark 14:1). In the end, they secured the grudging cooperation of the Roman authorities, and even the collusion of Herod—and they had Him crucified.

Christ's death on the cross occurred at their urging just a few months after this encounter in Luke 15. Then they congratulated themselves on a righteous act that they were certain would preserve the honor of Israel and the true religion they believed was embodied in their beloved traditions.

The Glorious Sequel

Here is the divine irony: when they did their worst, they accomplished God's best (Acts 2:22; 2 Corinthians 5:21; Isaiah 53). But even Jesus' death was not the end of the story. No grave could hold Jesus in its grip. He rose from the dead, signifying that He had conquered sin, guilt, and death once and for all. His dying on the cross finally produced the effectual blood atonement that had been shrouded in mystery for all the ages, and His resurrection was the proof that God accepted it.

Jesus' death therefore provided for us what the blood of bulls and goats could never accomplish: a full and acceptable atonement for sin. And His perfect righteousness gives us precisely what we need for our redemption: a complete covering of perfect righteousness equal to God's own divine perfection.

So there *is* true and blessed resolution to the story after all.

The Open Invitation

The invitation to be part of the great celebratory banquet is still open to all. It extends even to you, dear reader. And it doesn't matter whether you are an open sinner like the Prodigal Son, a secret one like his elder brother, or someone with characteristics from each type. If you are someone who is still estranged from God, Christ urges you to acknowledge your guilt, admit your own spiritual poverty, embrace your heavenly Father, and be reconciled to Him (2 Corinthians 5:20).

> And the Spirit and the bride say, "Come!" And let him who hears say, "Come!" And let him who thirsts come. Whoever desires, let him take the water of life freely. (Revelation 22:17)

Now, enjoy the celebration. (pp. 189–98. Emphasis in original.)

Investing Earthly Finances with an Eternal Focus (Luke 16:1–13)

26

Now He was also saying to the disciples, "There was a rich man who had a manager, and this manager was reported to him as squandering his possessions. And he called him and said to him, 'What is this I hear about you? Give an accounting of your management, for you can no longer be manager.' The manager said to himself, 'What shall I do, since my master is taking the management away from me? I am not strong enough to dig; I am ashamed to beg. I know what I shall do, so that when I am removed from the management people will welcome me into their homes.' And he summoned each one of his master's debtors, and he began saying to the first, 'How much do you owe my master?' And he said, 'A hundred measures of oil.' And he said to him, 'Take your bill, and sit down quickly and write fifty.' Then he said to another, 'And how much do you owe?' And he said, 'A hundred measures of wheat.' He said to him, 'Take your bill, and write eighty.' And his master praised the unrighteous manager because he had acted shrewdly; for the sons of this age are more shrewd in relation to their own kind than the sons of light. And I say to you, make friends for yourselves by means of the wealth of unrighteousness, so that when it fails, they will receive you into the eternal dwellings. He who is faithful in a very little thing is faithful also in much; and he who is unrighteous in a very little thing is unrighteous also in much. Therefore if you have not been faithful in the use of unrighteous wealth, who will entrust the true riches to you? And if you have not been faithful in the use of that which is another's, who will give you that which is your own? No servant can serve two masters; for either he will hate the one and love the other, or else he will be devoted to one and despise the other. You cannot serve God and wealth.** (16:1–13)

Of the nearly forty parables told by the Lord Jesus Christ in the Gospels, about one third of them deal in some way with money. That money played such a prominent role in the teaching of Jesus is not surprising, since it has a dominant role in society and the lives of individuals. People spend much of their time thinking about money; how to acquire it, spend it, save it, invest it, borrow it, keep track of it, and sometimes give it away. The widespread preoccupation with money that dominates today's society results in anxiety, covetousness, selfishness, greediness, discontent, idolatry, and pride.

Scripture has much to say about money, including how to obtain it, how to regard it, and how to use it.

The Bible reveals both right and wrong ways to obtain money. The most important way to make money is through work. Proverbs 14:23 says, "In all labor there is profit, but mere talk leads only to poverty" (cf. 6:6–11; 20:4; 28:19), and Paul wrote that those who refuse to work should not eat (2 Thess. 3:10).

Second, money can be obtained by saving for the future. "There is precious treasure and oil in the dwelling of the wise," wrote Solomon, "but a foolish man swallows it up" (Prov. 21:20; cf. 30:24–25).

Third, money can be obtained through proper assessment of one's resources and wise planning. Solomon advised, "Know well the condition of your flocks, and pay attention to your herds; for riches are not forever, nor does a crown endure to all generations" (Prov. 27:23–24).

Finally, money can be obtained through gifts (Phil. 4:16).

On the other hand, there are wrong ways to get money, including stealing (whether directly [Ex. 20:15; Eph. 4:28], or by fraud [Ps. 37:21; Hos. 12:7; Amos 8:5; Mic. 6:11]), charging exorbitant interest on loans (Ex. 22:25; Lev. 25:36–37; Neh. 5:7, 10; Ps. 15:5; Prov. 28:8), withholding from others what is due them (James 5:4), or gambling, which foolishly trusts in chance rather than in the providence of God.

Scripture reveals both the right way and the wrong way to regard money. The right attitude is to acknowledge that God owns everything (Ps. 50:10; Hag. 2:8), and is the source of people's ability to earn money (Deut. 8:17–18; cf. 1 Tim. 6:17).

The wrong way to regard money is to love it, which leads to disastrous consequences (1 Tim. 6:10). Loving money is destructive (1 Tim. 6:9), numbering among its victims Achan (Josh. 7:1–25), Balaam (Num. 22–24), Judas (Matt. 26:24; Acts 1:25), and Ananias and Saphira (Acts 5:1–10). Loving money leads to a lack of trust in God (Job 31:24–28; Prov. 11:28; 1 Tim. 6:17), results in ungratefulness and pride (Deut. 8:12–17), and causes people to behave foolishly (Luke 12:16–21), rob God (Mal. 3:8), and be indifferent to the needs of others (1 John 3:17).

The Bible also establishes the proper use of money. People are to earn it to support themselves (2 Thess. 3:10–12), their families (1 Tim. 5:8), and their nation (Rom. 13:6–7), as well as to help people in need (Matt. 6:2–3; James 2:15–16).

Above and beyond those things, there are some necessary biblical prerequisites to giving to kingdom purposes. First, those who would truly honor God in giving must transfer ownership of their money, possessions, time, and talents to Him. Second, they must make exalting Christ and proclaiming the gospel the supreme purpose of their lives. Finally, they must put themselves in a position to use their money to honor God by taking steps to get out of debt (paying bills, prioritizing spending, eliminating nonessential spending, selling items that perpetuate debt, refusing to borrow money for luxuries, pursuing contentment, etc.).

Several principles mark New Testament giving. First, Christian giving is entirely voluntary (cf. 2 Cor. 9:7). The argument that Christians are biblically mandated to tithe ten percent of their income is based on a flawed understanding of the Old Testament. (For a discussion of tithing, see *2 Corinthians*, The MacArthur New Testament Commentary [Chicago: Moody, 2003], 281–83; *Whose Money Is It, Anyway?* [Nashville: Word, 2000].) Far from being legalistic, giving is to be willing, joyful, eager, enthusiastic, and from the heart. It is also to be secret, unlike the showy public giving of legalists and hypocrites (Matt. 6:2–4), regular and systematic (1 Cor. 16:1–2), and motivated by love, not legalistic compulsion (2 Cor. 8:8).

In this parable and His application of it, the Lord redirects our attitudes and establishes His will for believers concerning wealth.

THE PARABLE

Now He was also saying to the disciples, "There was a rich man who had a manager, and this manager was reported to him as squandering his possessions. And he called him and said to him, 'What is this I hear about you? Give an accounting of your management, for you can no longer be manager.' The manager said to himself, 'What shall I do, since my master is taking the management away from me? I am not strong enough to dig; I am ashamed to beg. I know what I shall do, so that when I am removed from the management people will welcome me into their homes.' And he summoned each one of his master's debtors, and he began saying to the first, 'How much do you owe my master?' And he said, 'A hundred measures of oil.' And he said to him, 'Take your bill, and sit down quickly and write fifty.' Then he said to another, 'And how much do you owe?' And he said, 'A hundred measures of wheat.' He said to him, 'Take your bill, and write eighty.' And his master praised the unrighteous manager because he had acted shrewdly; for the sons of this age are more shrewd in relation to their own kind than the sons of light. (16:1–8)

Jesus, the unequalled storyteller, was very adept at teaching both from the expected, and the unexpected experiences of life. The main character in his fictional story is an unrighteous manager, guilty not only of incompetence, but also of embezzlement. However the Lord created him to teach a positive spiritual principle. Recognizing that incongruity, some have attempted to read between the lines to find a way to recast this man in a positive light. But there are no hidden details in this straightforward narrative, nor is there anything more to it than the details He gave. And it is precisely the surprise ending, in which the master praises the unrighteous manager instead of punishing him, that provides the point of the story. The unexpected response is a pattern that Jesus often used, following the rabbinic pattern of reasoning from the lesser to the greater. His point was that if an unrighteous man was shrewd in using money for his own selfish interests, how much more should righteous believers use all they possess for God's kingdom?

This parable was not addressed to the scribes and Pharisees, as the previous three had been (15:1–3), although they were still present and heard it (16:14). The primary audience was the **disciples.** The Lord turned from three evangelistic parables, in which He called those who rejected Him to repentance and salvation, to one aimed primarily at believers. He moved in a sense from giving a salvation message to one on discipleship.

The **rich man** was wealthy enough to have hired a **manager,** a steward or administrator who oversaw at least one aspect of his business. He would have been a free man, not a slave, of high social status, and bearing great responsibility. The debts that were owed to the rich man were too large to have been incurred by tenant farmers, which gives further testimony to the size of his operation.

That he had a manager overseeing his farming operation suggests that the rich man was probably an absentee landowner. That would help explain why he was unaware of what was happening until the **manager was reported to him.** *Diaballō* (**reported**) is related to the noun *diabolos*, which means "slanderer," or "accuser," and is the word translated "devil." *Diaballō* means "to accuse" or "bring charges" with a hostile intent. The accusation eventually reached the rich man that his manager was **squandering** (the same word used in 15:13 to describe the younger son's wasting his share of the estate) **his possessions.** Having found out about the situation the rich man took immediate action to protect his interests. **He called** the manager **and said to him, 'What is this I hear about you? Give an accounting of your management, for you can**

no longer be manager.' But having fired him, he allowed him to remain until he compiled a final **accounting of** his **management.** That gave him opportunity to do more harm.

The embezzling manager was now in a quandary, as expressed by his question, **"What shall I do?"** (cf. 3:10–14; 12:17; Acts 2:37). After his **master** took **the management away from** him he faced two unpleasant alternatives. On the one hand, he was **not strong enough to dig.** He was, in contemporary terms, a white-collar worker, and not capable of hard manual labor. Further, he no doubt saw such labor as beneath his dignity. The other alternative was equally unacceptable. If manual labor was beneath him, how much more would he have been **ashamed to beg?** The future looked bleak, and he saw no way out of his dilemma.

Then he had a sudden flash of inspiration; a "eureka moment," or epiphany. **"I know what I shall do,"** he exclaimed, **"so that when I am removed from the management people will welcome me into their homes."** The **people** to whom he referred were his master's debtors, with whom he had done business on behalf of his master. The solution he came up with would provide all the things he would need: a place to live, income, and status.

In addition to his mismanagement, the manager launched a new scheme to rob his master. **He summoned each one of his master's debtors** in turn and renegotiated their deals to lower the amount they owed. Since his master had not terminated him immediately, he still had access to their contracts. Apparently his absent master had not yet rescinded the manager's authority to act on his behalf, or word of that had not yet reached his debtors. The debts involved commodities, and were due to be paid at harvest time. By reducing what they were obligated to pay his master, he put them under obligation to him. Reciprocation was an integral part of Jewish society; if someone did a person a favor, that person was obligated to do one for him.

Jesus then gave two examples of the manager's deceitful dealings. **To the first** he said, **"How much do you owe my master?" And he said, "A hundred measures of oil." And he said to him, "Take your bill, and sit down quickly and write fifty."** One **hundred measures of** olive **oil** was 875 gallons, or the yield of about 150 olive trees, and was worth about one thousand denarii—more than three years' wages for a common laborer. The new deal, which cut the debt in half, created a significant loss for his master. The second debtor owed **a hundred measures of wheat.** The manager reduced his bill by twenty percent to **eighty** measures of wheat, once again defrauding his former master of a considerable amount of money (a hundred measures of wheat would have been equivalent to eight to ten years' wages for a common laborer). These were not cases where a debt was restructured due to extenuating circumstances, such as crop damage from weather or locusts, or price fluctuations. This was done solely to benefit the manager, by making the debtors to the master debtors to him.

Then came the shocking, unexpected conclusion to the story: **his master praised the unrighteous manager.** To those listening to the Lord relate this story, it would have seemed that he had taken leave of his senses. But the master did not praise the manager because he was wasteful, irresponsible, or a thief. He praised him **because he had acted shrewdly.** *Phronimōs* (**shrewdly**) means to act wisely and with insight. The manager took advantage of his opportunity, carefully working the situation to his own advantage. Since the debtors were now obligated to him, his future was secure.

The point of the parable is simple. **"The sons of this age"** (sinners; those outside of the kingdom of God), Jesus said, **"are more shrewd in relation to their own kind than the sons of light"** (believers; cf. John 12:36; Eph. 5:8; 1 Thess. 5:5). Sinners are more skilled and diligent in securing their temporal future in **this** present **age** than those whose citizenship is in heaven (Phil. 3:20) are in securing their eternal reward in the age to come. Believers should be far more shrewd in preparing for their eternal futures.

THE APPLICATION

"And I say to you, make friends for yourselves by means of the wealth of unrighteousness, so that when it fails, they will receive you into the eternal dwellings. He who is faithful in a very little thing is faithful also in much; and he who is unrighteous in a very little thing is unrighteous also in much. Therefore if you have not

been faithful in the use of unrighteous wealth, who will entrust the true riches to you? And if you have not been faithful in the use of that which is another's, who will give you that which is your own? No servant can serve two masters; for either he will hate the one and love the other, or else he will be devoted to one and despise the other. You cannot serve God and wealth." (16:9–13)

The Lord drew three lessons from the parable concerning believers' attitude toward money: how they view their money in relation to others, themselves, and God.

In relation to others, Jesus exhorted His hearers to **make friends for** themselves **by means of the wealth of unrighteousness,** so called because it belongs to this unrighteous, passing world. Unbelievers, like the unrighteous manager, often use money to buy earthly friends. Believers, on the other hand, are to use their money to evangelize and thus purchase heavenly friends. The **wealth of unrighteousness,** being an element of fallen society's experience, cannot last past this present life (cf. Luke 12:20). When it **fails,** the friends believers have gained through investing in gospel preaching will welcome them **into the eternal dwellings** of heaven. Those friends will be waiting to receive them when they arrive in glory because through their financial sacrifice for reaching the unconverted they heard and believed the gospel.

The Lord calls for Christians to use their money for eternal purposes to produce a heavenly reward. In the familiar words of the Sermon on the Mount, He commanded,

> Do not store up for yourselves treasures on earth, where moth and rust destroy, and where thieves break in and steal. But store up for yourselves treasures in heaven, where neither moth nor rust destroys, and where thieves do not break in or steal; for where your treasure is, there your heart will be also. (Matt. 6:19–21)

Where they invest their money reveals where people's hearts are. Endless personal accumulation is sinful, wasteful, and robs those who pursue it of eternal blessing.

Concerning their attitude toward money as it relates to themselves, Christ exhorted believers to be faithful to make eternal investments. His statement, **He who is faithful in a very little thing is faithful also in much; and he who is unrighteous in a very little thing is unrighteous also in much,** is axiomatic. Some claim that if they had more money, they would give more. But the truth is that character, not circumstances, determines faithfulness. Some, like the poor widow described in Luke 21:1–4, who have nothing give everything; others who have everything give nothing. The issue is not finances, but integrity and spiritual character. Those who are **faithful** with the **very little** they have would be faithful if they had more; those who are **unrighteous**—selfish, proud, indulgent—in the use of what **little** they have would be so if they had much. The determining factor is not how much people possess, but how strong their commitment to the gospel of salvation is.

People's perspective on money and their resulting faithfulness or unfaithfulness has implications for their eternal reward. **If you have not been faithful in the use of unrighteous wealth,** Jesus asked, **who will entrust the true riches to you?** It is foolish to imagine that God will reward those who sinfully waste their opportunity to be **faithful in the use of unrighteous wealth** in this life. Those who fail to invest their wealth in the work of redemption impoverish themselves forever. Eternal reward comes to those who are faithful.

The Lord's question, **If you have not been faithful in the use of that which is another's, who will give you that which is your own?** reveals the importance of stewardship; acknowledging that all we have belongs to God, and we are responsible to manage it to His glory (cf. Matt. 25:14–29).

Finally, Jesus spoke of believers' attitude toward money as it relates to God, using another obvious, common sense example. **No servant can serve two masters;** He warned, **for either he will hate the one and love the other, or else he will be devoted to one and despise the other.** *Douleuō* (**serve**) refers to serving as a slave. Slaves, unlike modern workers, did not have the option of working at a second job for a second employer. They were the property of a master who had singular and absolute control over them. That kind of exclusive service could not be rendered to two masters at the same time.

In the same way, a person **cannot** be both the slave of **God and** of material **wealth.** They cannot be co-rulers in the same heart, for as

John Calvin notes in his commentary on the parallel passage in Matthew 6:24, "Where riches hold the dominion of the heart, God has lost his authority." Conflicting demands will inevitably produce conflicting emotions and attitudes. Those who love money will despise and resent what God demands of them regarding it. But those who love Him will choose to honor Him by not making earthly wealth their master. Instead of using it to selfishly gratify their desires, they will seek to manage the money He has entrusted to them for the salvation of souls to the glory of God.

Why False Teachers Mock the Truth (Luke 16:14–18)

27

Now the Pharisees, who were lovers of money, were listening to all these things and were scoffing at Him. And He said to them, "You are those who justify yourselves in the sight of men, but God knows your hearts; for that which is highly esteemed among men is detestable in the sight of God. The Law and the Prophets were proclaimed until John; since that time the gospel of the kingdom of God has been preached, and everyone is forcing his way into it. But it is easier for heaven and earth to pass away than for one stroke of a letter of the Law to fail. Everyone who divorces his wife and marries another commits adultery, and he who marries one who is divorced from a husband commits adultery." (16:14–18)

It is a paradoxical truth that those who are the most dangerous enemies of God are not the ones who openly oppose Him, but rather those who outwardly appear the most devoted to Him. Many assume that such seemingly pious people, especially those who identify themselves with the God of Scripture, must surely have His approval, when in reality, false forms of worship directed at the God of the Bible are hated by Him. Apostate Judaism and false Christianity, along with all their deceiving teachers, are haters of divine truth and of God.

God's harshest condemnations were reserved not for irreligious fools who deny His existence (Ps. 14:1; 53:1) but for those who professed to be His people and to worship Him. Isaiah's prophecy records God's rejection of even Israel's apostate form of false worship:

> "What are your multiplied sacrifices to Me?" says the Lord. "I have had enough of burnt offerings of rams and the fat of fed cattle; and I take no pleasure in the blood of bulls, lambs or goats. When you come to appear before Me, who requires of you this trampling of My courts? Bring your worthless offerings no longer, incense is an abomination to Me. New moon and sabbath, the calling of assemblies—I cannot endure iniquity and the solemn assembly. I hate your new moon festivals and your appointed feasts, they have become a burden to Me; I am weary of bearing them. So when you spread out your hands in prayer, I will hide My eyes from you; yes, even though you multiply prayers, I will not listen. Your hands are covered with blood. Wash yourselves, make yourselves clean; remove the evil of your deeds from My sight." (1:11–16)

Amos records a similar condemnation:

> "I hate, I reject your festivals, nor do I delight in your solemn assemblies. Even though you offer up to Me burnt offerings and your grain offerings, I will not accept them; and I will not even look at the peace offerings of your fatlings. Take away from Me the noise of your songs; I will not even listen to the sound of your harps." (5:21–23)

In Isaiah 29:13 the Lord condemned those Jewish hypocrites who "draw near with their words and honor Me with their lip service, but they remove their hearts far from Me, and their reverence for Me consists of tradition learned by rote," while in Isaiah 48:1 He denounced those "who swear by the name of the Lord and invoke the God of Israel, but not in truth nor in righteousness."

Jeremiah delivered God's strongly-worded rebuke of the false religionists of his day:

> "Do not trust in deceptive words, saying, 'This is the temple of the Lord, the temple of the Lord, the temple of the Lord.' . . . Behold, you are

> trusting in deceptive words to no avail. Will you steal, murder, and commit adultery and swear falsely, and offer sacrifices to Baal and walk after other gods that you have not known, then come and stand before Me in this house, which is called by My name, and say, 'We are delivered!'—that you may do all these abominations? Has this house, which is called by My name, become a den of robbers in your sight? Behold, I, even I, have seen it," declares the Lord. (7:4, 8–11)

Incredibly, God instructed Jeremiah not even to pray for those false religionists: "As for you, do not pray for this people, and do not lift up cry or prayer for them, and do not intercede with Me; for I do not hear you." (7:16). The Lord then explained the reason for that shocking command:

> "Do you not see what they are doing in the cities of Judah and in the streets of Jerusalem? The children gather wood, and the fathers kindle the fire, and the women knead dough to make cakes for the queen of heaven [cf. 44:17–19, 25]; and they pour out drink offerings to other gods in order to spite Me. Do they spite Me?" declares the Lord. "Is it not themselves they spite, to their own shame?" Therefore thus says the Lord God, "Behold, My anger and My wrath will be poured out on this place, on man and on beast and on the trees of the field and on the fruit of the ground; and it will burn and not be quenched." (vv. 17–20)

In today's society, with its postmodern denial of absolute truth and emphasis on tolerance, many—including some who claim to be evangelicals—teach that God accepts people of any religion. But Scripture teaches just the opposite: "The perverse in heart are an abomination to the Lord" (Prov. 11:20). "The sacrifice of the wicked is an abomination to the Lord" (Prov. 15:8). "The way of the wicked is an abomination to the Lord" (Prov. 15:9). "He who turns away his ear from listening to the law, even his prayer is an abomination" (Prov. 28:9).

Those who deny the gospel are God's enemies, no matter how outwardly religious they may appear to be. They have—wittingly or unwittingly—taken their place with Satan in attacking God and the advance of His kingdom, and will receive from Him the severest judgment. Those who reject Jesus Christ are damned to hell (cf. 1 Cor. 16:22).

Collectively the Pharisees, the religious leaders of Israel in Jesus' day, fit into that category. They were studiously devoted to interpreting and applying the Old Testament law and fastidiously observed Mosaic rituals and ceremonies. They gave every outward indication of being devoted worshipers of the true God of Israel. Yet they were fiercely hostile to and hateful of the Lord Jesus Christ, God incarnate. Initially they had been curious about Him and His teaching, even inviting Him into their homes to learn more about Him (Luke 7:36–50; 11:37–54; 14:1–24), but even in those gatherings there was an undercurrent of animosity that sought to trap and discredit Him. Eventually, that animosity hardened into the vicious rejection that led to bloodthirsty demands for their Messiah's murder.

A comparison of the present passage with the previous chapter of Luke's gospel reveals the escalating hostility of the Pharisees toward Christ. In Luke 15:2 "both the Pharisees and the scribes began to grumble, saying, 'This man receives sinners and eats with them.'" They saw Jesus' associating with the riffraff of Jewish society as proof that He was not sent from God, since He fellowshiped and ate with those whom they deemed to be Satan's people. In the current passage, they moved beyond grumbling to scoffing at and mocking Jesus—just as their ancestors had done to God's prophets (e.g., 2 Kings 2:23; Jer. 20:7–8) and the Old Testament had predicted would be done to the Messiah (Ps. 22:7–8; Isa. 53:3).

The Lord's reply to them reveals seven reasons or motives for the Pharisee's hostility toward the truth: they had corrupt motives, they were antagonistic to God's demands, they were self-justifying, they sought human approval, they were evil at heart, they rejected the gospel of the kingdom, and they had no category for grace. Since those same features still motivate false teachers today, they provide a model to identify them in any era.

They Had Corrupt Motives

Now the Pharisees, who were lovers of money, (16:14a)

The Pharisees were motivated by greed, avarice, and covetousness—the same things that motivated Judas to become a follower of Christ (cf. John 12:5–6). The adjective *philarguros* derives from two words: *phileō*, "to love," or "to have affection for," and *arguros*, "silver." Fallen, sinful people greedily desire to satisfy their needs: thus many are "lovers of money" in addition to being "lovers of self" (2 Tim. 3:2).

Greed is especially a driving force within false teachers. The Bible calls them greedy dogs (Isa. 56:11), "greedy for gain" (Jer. 6:13; 8:10), and says of them, "When they have something to bite with their teeth, they cry, 'Peace,' But against him who puts nothing in their mouths they declare holy war" (Mic. 3:5). Paul warned of those who "are enemies of the cross of Christ, whose end is destruction, whose god is their appetite, and whose glory is in their shame, who set their minds on earthly things" (Phil. 3:18–19), as did Peter, who cautioned his readers that "in their greed [false teachers] will exploit you with false words" (2 Peter 2:3), because they have "a heart trained in greed" (v. 14). Therefore an elder or spiritual leader in the church must be "free from the love of money" (1 Tim. 3:3) and not "shepherd the flock of God ... for sordid gain" (1 Peter 5:2).

Like all false teachers, the Pharisees' motives were corrupt and impure. They had no real love for people, but were obsessed with riches and wealth; they were "full of robbery and wickedness" (Luke 11:39), even stooping so low as to devour widows' houses (Luke 20:47). Even their charitable giving was merely an ostentatious show seeking honor from men (Matt. 6:2). Rather than help their own parents when they had a need, the Pharisees would just as likely say to them cynically, "Whatever I have that would help you is Corban (that is to say, given to God)" (Mark 7:11). In short, the Pharisees operated out of impure, corrupt, self-aggrandizing, greedy motives.

They Were Antagonistic to God's Demands

were listening to all these things and were scoffing at Him. (16:14*b*)

While the Pharisees **were listening to all these things** Jesus was saying, what triggered their scorn was His teaching concerning the proper use of money (vv. 1–13). The Lord's teaching that people are to invest in the kingdom of God to reap spiritual dividends in heaven, and to serve God, not money, indicted the money-loving Pharisees. And those obsessed with obtaining riches responded to the teaching that they did not want to hear by ridiculing and mocking Jesus, the teacher.

Their aggressive, hostile reaction signified that they were false worshipers, with no capacity to receive and respond to the truth. They were spiritually blind (2 Cor. 4:4), dead in their sins (Eph. 2:1), and unable to understand and accept the things of God (1 Cor. 2:14). "This is the judgment," Jesus declared, "that the Light has come into the world, and men loved the darkness rather than the Light, for their deeds were evil" (John 3:19). They are "unwilling to come to [Christ] so that [they] may have life" (John 5:40). Such people may even call Jesus Lord, but they have no capacity to obey Him (Luke 6:46). As a result, their spiritual life has no foundation, and they will be swept away by the torrent of divine judgment (v. 49; cf. John 12:47–48). The redeemed, on the other hand, are those "who hear the word of God and do it" (Luke 8:21; cf. 11:28), and as a result have "eternal life, and [do] not come into judgment, but [have] passed out of death into life" (John 5:24). The evidence that they "have come to know Him" is that they "keep His commandments" (1 John 2:3).

THEY WERE SELF-JUSTIFYING

And He said to them, "You are those who justify yourselves (16:15*a*)

This indictment of the Pharisees is a succinct summary of all false religion. Pharisaic Judaism was a system of works righteousness; of self-justification; of trying to make oneself acceptable to God, earning salvation through good works, maintaining certain ethical and legal standards, and performing religious rituals and ceremonies. There is no doubt that they had a zeal for the idea of God (Rom. 10:2). But zeal divorced from knowledge of the truth is useless. Like all false religious systems, that of the Pharisees was doomed to fail, as the zealous Pharisee Saul of Tarsus eventually realized (cf. Phil. 3:2–12). All of the religious fervor and legalistic efforts that made him a rising star in first-century Judaism (Gal. 1:14) and a persecutor of the church (1 Cor. 15:9; Gal. 1:23) he later acknowledged to be worthless rubbish (Phil. 3:8).

The biblical teaching on salvation is clear and unmistakable: "the righteous will live by his faith" (Hab. 2:4; cf. Rom. 1:17; Gal. 3:11; Heb. 10:38). That truth permeates the New Testament, and only the willfully blind could miss it: "By the works of the Law no flesh will be justified in His sight" (Rom. 3:20); "being justified as a gift by His grace through the redemption which is in Christ Jesus" (v. 24); God is "just and the justifier of the one who has faith in Jesus" (v. 26); "For we maintain that a man is justified by faith apart from works of the Law" (v. 28); "But to the one who does not work, but believes in Him who justifies the ungodly, his faith is credited as righteousness" (4:5); "Therefore, having been justified by faith, we have peace with God through our Lord Jesus Christ" (5:1); "nevertheless knowing that a man is not justified by the works of the Law but through faith in Christ Jesus, even we have believed in Christ Jesus, so that we may be justified by faith in Christ and not by the works of the Law; since by the works of the Law no flesh will be justified" (Gal. 2:16); "The Scripture, foreseeing that God would justify the Gentiles by faith" (3:8); "Now that no one is justified by the Law before God is evident; for, 'The righteous man shall live by faith'" (v. 11); "Therefore the Law has become our tutor to lead us to Christ, so that we may be justified by faith" (v. 24); "For by grace you have been saved through faith; and that not of yourselves, it is the gift of God; not as a result of works, so that no one may boast" (Eph. 2:8–9).

The tragic reality was that the Pharisees had led the people in the direction of hell. They were "blind guides of the blind" (Matt. 15:14), leading the spiritually blind "lost sheep of the house of Israel" (Matt. 10:6) into the pit of hell (Matt. 23:15). Their fatal mistake was that "not knowing about God's righteousness and seeking to establish their own, they did not subject themselves to the righteousness of God" (Rom. 10:3). Seeking to establish their own righteousness and save themselves required them to downplay God's righteousness to make that goal achievable. But doing so overlooked the clear Old Testament teaching regarding God's absolute holiness (Lev. 11:44–45; 19:2; 20:26; Ps. 99:5, 9; Isa. 6:3) and salvation by faith (Hab. 2:4). Through their futile efforts to earn their way into the kingdom they barred the door of salvation for everyone else (Matt. 23:13).

They Sought Human Approval

in the sight of men (16:15*b*)

The Pharisees were like those whom Paul warned the Galatians, "desire to make a good showing in the flesh" (Gal. 6:12). They wanted the adulation and respect of people, and tried to appear noble and virtuous. Jesus rebuked them because they "like[d] to walk around in long robes, and like[d] respectful greetings in the market places" (Mark 12:38), and because "they [did] all their deeds to be noticed by men; for they broaden[ed] their phylacteries and lengthen[ed] the tassels of their garments. They love[d] the place of honor at banquets and the chief seats in the synagogues, and respectful greetings in the market places, and being called Rabbi by men" (Matt. 23:5–7). The only reward for those who parade their self-righteousness is the honor they receive from men; they will receive nothing from God (Matt. 6:1–2, 5, 16).

They Were Evil at Heart

but God knows your hearts; for that which is highly esteemed among men is detestable in the sight of God. (16:15*c*)

The Pharisees' external façade of piety and holiness may have deceived men, but **God** in His omniscience knew what was in their **hearts.** "Woe to you, scribes and Pharisees, hypocrites!" Jesus warned, "For you are like whitewashed tombs which on the outside appear beautiful, but inside they are full of dead men's bones and all uncleanness. So you, too, outwardly appear righteous to men, but inwardly you are full of hypocrisy and lawlessness" (Matt. 23:27–28). In 1 Samuel 16:7 God reminded Samuel that He "sees not as man sees, for man looks at the outward appearance, but the Lord looks at the heart," since He "alone know[s] the hearts of all the sons of men" (1 Kings 8:39; cf. 1 Chron. 28:9; Ps. 44:21; 139:2; Jer. 17:10; 20:12; Rom. 8:27; Rev. 2:23) and "sees what is done in secret" (Matt. 6:18). Jesus "did not need anyone to testify concerning man, for He Himself knew what was in man" (John 2:25).

God not only knew what was in their hearts, but disapproved of it, **for that which is highly esteemed among men is detestable in the sight of God.** God finds all false forms of religion exalted among men **detestable** (the Greek word can refer to something that stinks; that is abominable, disgusting, revolting); that is, not at all a sufficient offering to satisfy Him. The world's religious wisdom is mere foolishness in God's sight (cf. Rom. 1:22; 1 Cor. 1:20).

THEY REJECTED THE GOSPEL OF THE KINGDOM

The Law and the Prophets were proclaimed until John; since that time the gospel of the kingdom of God has been preached, and everyone is forcing his way into it. (16:16)

Anyone makes himself detestable in God's sight by rejecting the gospel of the kingdom, even the most zealous religionists. The phrase **the Law and the Prophets** refers to the Old Testament (cf. 24:27, 44; Matt. 5:17; 7:12; 22:40; John 1:45; Acts 13:15; 24:14; 28:23; Rom. 3:21). The Old Testament era, the era of promise, concluded with the ministry of **John** the Baptist, the last of the Old Testament prophets. In addition to being the final representative of the Old Testament era of promise, John was also the first representative of the New Testament era of fulfillment; his ministry bridged the two eras. He not only predicted Messiah's appearance, but also witnessed it. Because of his unique position and his privilege to be Messiah's forerunner, Jesus declared John to have been the greatest person who had ever lived up until his day (Matt. 11:11). In his outpouring of praise to God, John's father, Zacharias, had noted the fulfillment of the Old Testament promises in the coming of the Messiah (Luke 1:67–79). John's ministry reached its climax when he baptized Jesus the Messiah. The transition from John to Jesus, from the Old Testament era of promise to the New Testament era of fulfillment was complete. "He must increase," John said of Jesus, "but I must decrease" (John 3:30). Not long afterward, John was imprisoned and executed by being beheaded (Matt. 14:3–12).

The phrase **since that time** and similar phrases are important time markers in Luke's gospel, denoting turning points (cf. 1:48; 5:10;

12:52; 22:18,69). After the conclusion of John's ministry, Jesus became the focal point; the fulfillment of the Old Testament promises (cf. 24:27, 44; John 1:45; 5:39; Acts 4:12; Rom. 1:1–3).

That people were **forcing** their **way into it** is another reminder that entering the kingdom is a hard, difficult struggle. While salvation is by no means a purely human effort, true repentance nevertheless involves the will acting in self-denial. "If anyone wishes to come after Me," Jesus solemnly declared, "he must deny himself, and take up his cross daily and follow Me" (Luke 9:23; cf. 14:26–27), since "whoever wishes to save his life will lose it, but whoever loses his life for My sake, he is the one who will save it" (Luke 9:24). There is a monumental struggle in the sinful human soul to crush pride and self-will and come to total penitence.

THEY HAD NO CATEGORY FOR GRACE

But it is easier for heaven and earth to pass away than for one stroke of a letter of the Law to fail. Everyone who divorces his wife and marries another commits adultery, and he who marries one who is divorced from a husband commits adultery." (16:17–18)

At first glance, these two verses appear to have no connection to the preceding ones. They are not random statements tacked on here for no apparent reason, however, but actually do fit logically into the Lord's flow of thought. The Pharisees were offended by Jesus' relationships with tax collectors and other despised sinners (Luke 15:1–2). It was an outrage that offended their spiritual sensibilities that He would mingle with people whom they viewed as the corrupt dregs of Jewish society. In response to that outrage, Jesus had told three parables emphasizing God's joy when sinners repent and embrace salvation (15:3–32). There was no place in the Pharisees' thinking for the joy that comes from that kind of grace and forgiveness. On the contrary, they believed that by preaching grace and forgiveness Jesus was assaulting the law and undermining their entire system of salvation by human achievement, further strengthening their conviction that Jesus was from Satan, not God.

This was their confidence despite the fact that the Lord had said, in His teaching in the Sermon on the Mount, that far from depreciating the law He upheld it down to the minutest detail, actually raising the standard far above where they placed it. The Pharisees were concerned merely with external observance, but He focused on internal obedience from the heart (Matt. 5:17–48).

His declaration that **it is easier for heaven and earth to pass away than for one stroke of a letter of the Law to fail** expresses Christ's absolute confirmation of the permanence of God's law. The Bible reveals that **heaven and earth** will indeed **pass away** (Ps. 102:25–26; Isa. 51:6; Matt. 24:35; 2 Peter 3:7, 10). But it would be easier for that to happen—for the entire created universe to go out of existence—than for the smallest, seemingly most insignificant detail of the law to fail. Not only will the smallest letter of the law (in Hebrew the letter *yodh*, which looks like an apostrophe) not pass away (Matt. 5:18), not even **one stroke of a letter of the Law** will **fail. A stroke** was a minuscule mark that differentiated two Hebrew letters, like the small mark that distinguishes a capital F from a capital E, or a capital R from a capital B in English.

This statement and the similar ones in Matthew 5:18 and 24:35 are probably the clearest internal defense of the verbal inspiration of Scripture. Jesus emphasized that the words of Scripture—down to the smallest part of a letter—are divinely inspired (cf. 2 Sam. 23:1–2; 1 Cor. 2:13).

Despite their professed devotion to the law, it was clear that the Pharisees depreciated it. If they truly believed that all of God's promises would be fulfilled, they would have acknowledged the overwhelming evidence that Jesus was the Messiah. Instead, they rejected Him. Neither did they uphold the law's unchanging moral standards, as Jesus demonstrated by pointing out a command that they ignored.

The Old Testament taught that **everyone who divorces his wife and marries another commits adultery, and he who marries one who is divorced from a husband commits adultery.** The Pharisees did not, of course, openly condone adultery. Instead, they simply divorced their wives and married a woman they preferred. They justified that action by misinterpreting Moses' teaching in Deuteronomy 24:1–4 as condoning divorce on the grounds of "uncleanness" (v. 1 NKJV). That uncleanness was not a reference to adultery, since the death penalty for adultery was in effect (Deut. 22:22), but rather to something else that a woman did that her husband might find shameful. Some Pharisees, and others following their example, seized on that statement and saw in it a blanket permission to divorce their wives for any reason. Needless to say, they interpreted uncleanness in the broadest possible terms, and in practical usage it came to mean whatever a man decided he did not like about his wife. (Some of the reasons on record were being a poor cook, being disrespectful to her mother-in-law, failing to give her husband a son, being less beautiful than another woman, etc.)

But the Old Testament text was neither condoning nor commending divorce, much less commanding it. It was merely acknowledging that divorce happened and there was a need for divinely regulating it. The text was actually a warning from God that if a man divorced his wife without just cause, and she remarried, if her second husband died, or divorced her, the first could not remarry her. Since there was no biblical grounds for the divorce and thus the remarriage was wrong, both she and her second husband would be guilty of adultery, and remarrying again her first husband would make him guilty of marrying an adulteress. Illegitimate, unrestricted divorce and remarriage would result in the proliferation of adultery, which would be "an abomination before the Lord" and "bring sin on the land" (v. 4). The point of Deuteronomy 24:1–4 was to prevent divorce and remarriage. The Pharisees had turned it on its head to give them freedom to divorce their wives for any reason.

Jesus did allow divorce in the case of persistent, unrepentant, hard-hearted adultery (Matt. 5:31–32; 19:1–9). Since God in His common grace had allowed the death penalty for adultery to disappear, that concession was an act of mercy toward the innocent parties, ensuring that an adulterer could be divorced (rather than executed) so that the spouse would not permanently be held in the grip of a spouse's wretched, sinful, unchaste behavior. The apostle Paul gives the word of the Spirit that a believer can also be divorced and remarried if an unbelieving spouse leaves (1 Cor. 7:15).

The Lord's words regarding divorce are an illustration designed to expose the Pharisees' blatant hypocrisy. Despite their professed devotion to the law, they in fact were gross violators of it. And they collectively stood condemned as adulterers through their proliferation of divorces.

The conflict between those who faithfully proclaim the Word of

God and false teachers has not changed. The leader of the conflict, Satan, hasn't changed. His emissaries, both human and demonic, still purvey the doctrines of demons that have been developed and propagated since the fall.

The issue is truth. False religion damns. It does not save, and must be exposed for what it is and its followers warned of damnation and challenged to adhere to a true understanding of God's word. Telling the truth about deceiving liars is the only merciful, compassionate and loving thing that one can do. Jesus confronted those of His day so that they could repent, and so that the people who followed them would see them for who they really were. That is still the responsibility of those whose eyes have been opened to understand the glory of divine truth (cf. Luke 20:45–47).

A Testimony of One Surprised to Be in Hell

(Luke 16:19–31)

28

"Now there was a rich man, and he habitually dressed in purple and fine linen, joyously living in splendor every day. And a poor man named Lazarus was laid at his gate, covered with sores, and longing to be fed with the crumbs which were falling from the rich man's table; besides, even the dogs were coming and licking his sores. Now the poor man died and was carried away by the angels to Abraham's bosom; and the rich man also died and was buried. In Hades he lifted up his eyes, being in torment, and saw Abraham far away and Lazarus in his bosom. And he cried out and said, 'Father Abraham, have mercy on me, and send Lazarus so that he may dip the tip of his finger in water and cool off my tongue, for I am in agony in this flame.' But Abraham said, 'Child, remember that during your life you received your good things, and likewise Lazarus bad things; but now he is being comforted here, and you are in agony. And besides all this, between us and you there is a great chasm fixed, so that those who wish to come over from here to you will not be able, and that none may cross

over from there to us.' And he said, 'Then I beg you, father, that
you send him to my father's house—for I have five brothers—in
order that he may warn them, so that they will not also come to
this place of torment.' But Abraham said, 'They have Moses and
the Prophets; let them hear them.' But he said, 'No, father Abraham, but if someone goes to them from the dead, they will
repent!' But he said to him, 'If they do not listen to Moses and the
Prophets, they will not be persuaded even if someone rises from
the dead.'" (16:19–31)

> C.S. Lewis once observed that

> the dullest and most uninteresting person you talk to may one day be
> a creature which, if you saw it now, you would be strongly tempted to
> worship, or else a horror and a corruption such as you now meet, if at
> all, only in a nightmare. ... There are no *ordinary* people ... It is immor-
> tals whom we joke with, work with, marry, snub and exploit—immortal
> horrors or everlasting splendours. (*The Weight of Glory* [New York:
> Macmillian, 1949], 15. Italics in original.)

His point was that all the divergent paths people travel in life narrow to
just two at death, after which everyone becomes either a glorious being
in heaven, or a wretched being in hell.

No one who takes the Bible seriously doubts the existence of
heaven. But hell is denied by many, and preached by few. Many who profess to believe in the authority of Scripture avoid speaking about hell,
express doubts that any more than a few colossal sinners will go there, or
even deny its existence altogether—in direct contradiction to the teaching of the Lord Jesus Christ. He said more about hell than anyone else,
and solemnly affirmed its existence as the place of eternal, conscious
torment for most people (cf. Matt. 5:22, 29, 30; 7:19; 8:12; 10:28; 13:40, 42, 50;
18:8–9; 22:13; 23:15, 33; 24:51; 25:30, 41; Mark 9:43, 45, 47, 48; Luke 12:5;
13:28; John 15:6). Robert L. Thomas summarizes the Lord's teaching on
hell:

> Throughout His ministry Jesus taught that the lost would depart into
> eternal fire prepared for the devil and his angels and eternal punish-
> ment. In other words, they will suffer endless, conscious agony away
> from the presence of God and His Son. None of the other options that

confuse the evangelical spectrum are viable in light of Jesus' view of eternal punishment. ("Jesus View of Eternal Punishment," *The Master's Seminary Journal* vol. 9, no. 2 [Fall 1998], 167)

Some think that the idea of hell is cruel, unkind, unfair. What kind of a God, they ask, would send people into everlasting punishment? But God is never in the position of defending Himself regarding the truths He reveals in Scripture. His nature, works, and revelation define what is true, just, and righteous. The purpose of the divine revelation of hell's horror is to warn sinners of its reality and the terrifying fate that awaits them there so as to motivate them to repent of their sins and embrace salvation in Christ.

The biblical revelation regarding hell should motivate believers to defend the clear teaching of our Lord and the rest of Scripture. It should also infuse them with a sense of urgency in evangelizing the lost. "Neither a cavalier attitude toward the lost nor a compassionate compromise are appropriate for a subject of such grave import" (Richard L. Mayhue, "Hell: Never, Forever, or Just for Awhile?" *The Master's Seminary Journal* vol. 9, no. 2 [Fall 1998], 131). To warn sinners of the fearful fate that awaits them is an act of sympathy and compassion. But in its zeal to find pragmatic new methods of evangelism, the church has too often abandoned its message. That message must include the bad news of what happens to those who reject the good news of the gospel.

The tragic truth is that most people who end up in hell will be shocked to find themselves there (cf. Matt. 7:22–23; 25:44; Luke 13:25–27). A recent survey revealed that virtually all the people who believe in heaven also believe they will go there (Gallup poll survey, 10–13 May 2007). Such was the case with the rich man in this story. Both to himself and to others, he would have seemed like a lock for heaven. The Jews believed that riches were a sure sign of God's blessing. Therefore the more money a man had the greater his blessing from God. When Jesus said to the disciples, "How hard it will be for those who are wealthy to enter the kingdom of God!" (Mark 10:23), "the disciples were amazed at His words" (v. 24). And when the Lord "answered again and said to them, 'Children, how hard it is to enter the kingdom of God! It is easier for a camel to go through the eye of a needle than for a rich man to enter the kingdom of God'" (vv. 24–25) "they were even more astonished and said to Him, 'Then who can be saved?'" (v. 26), if not the rich.

The disciples' response reflected the common belief of the Jewish people—especially the money-loving (Luke 16:14) Pharisees to whom Jesus directed this story. The rich man symbolizes them, both in their love of money, and in their assumption that their wealth was a sign of God's favor. Like him (vv. 27–30), the Pharisees demanded signs from Jesus before they would believe. And like him, they would one day be shocked to find themselves in hell. They are tragic examples of those who gained the world, but lost their souls (Mark 8:36).

The question arises as to whether this story told by our Lord was an account of an actual event, or a parable. Those who argue that this is a real story do so because none of the individuals in any of the Lord's other parables are ever given a name. But there is nothing inherent in the concept of a parable that would prohibit naming an individual, for ease of identification in the story (especially reasonable since the names Abraham and Moses are also used). And as will be seen, there is an important reason why Jesus gave Lazarus his name. On the other hand, the story's opening words, **Now there was a rich man,** are consistent with the language with which Jesus often began His parables (cf. 10:30; 14:16; 15:11; 19:12). Further, the circumstances depicted in the story cannot be literally true. There is nothing in the Bible that suggests that those in hell can see into heaven and converse with those who are there. Nor is the angels' carrying the poor man's body to heaven the normal experience of believers at death. It is best, therefore, to view this as a parable, a story created by the Lord to convey vital spiritual truth.

The parable may be viewed from two perspectives: the contrasts between the two men, and the lessons the Lord intended the parable to teach.

THE CONTRASTS

"Now there was a rich man, and he habitually dressed in purple and fine linen, joyously living in splendor every day. And a poor man named Lazarus was laid at his gate, covered with sores, and longing to be fed with the crumbs which were falling from the

rich man's table; besides, even the dogs were coming and licking his sores. Now the poor man died and was carried away by the angels to Abraham's bosom; and the rich man also died and was buried. In Hades he lifted up his eyes, being in torment, and saw Abraham far away and Lazarus in his bosom. And he cried out and said, 'Father Abraham, have mercy on me, and send Lazarus so that he may dip the tip of his finger in water and cool off my tongue, for I am in agony in this flame.' But Abraham said, 'Child, remember that during your life you received your good things, and likewise Lazarus bad things; but now he is being comforted here, and you are in agony. And besides all this, between us and you there is a great chasm fixed, so that those who wish to come over from here to you will not be able, and that none may cross over from there to us.' (16:19–26)

The story of these two men is marked by extreme contrasts in life and shocking reversals after death. In life, one was enormously wealthy, the other an impoverished beggar. The rich man was inside the house, the poor man outside. The poor man had no food, the rich man had all the food he could eat. The poor man had needs, the rich man had none. The poor man desired everything, the rich man desired nothing. The poor man suffered, the rich man was satisfied. The poor man was tormented, the rich man was happy. The poor man was humiliated, the rich man was honored. The poor man sought crumbs, the rich man feasted. The poor man needed help, the rich man gave him none. The poor man was a nobody, the rich man was well-known. The poor man had no dig - nity in death, not even a burial, the rich man had dignity in death and a lavish funeral. The poor man possessed no hope, the rich man possessed all hope.

After death, however, the situations of the two were completely reversed. The rich man became poorer than the poor man had ever been, while the poor man became richer than the rich man could have ever imagined. The poor man was on the inside (heaven), while the rich man was on the outside (hell). The poor man enjoyed the great heavenly banquet, while the rich man was totally deprived. The poor man needed nothing, while the rich man lacked everything. The poor man had all his desires fulfilled, while the rich man's desires would go eternally unful-filled.The poor man was satisfied, while the rich man suffered.The poor man was happy, while the rich man was tormented. The poor man was honored, while the rich man was humiliated. The poor man enjoyed a lavish feast, while the rich man longed for a drop of water.The rich man desperately sought help, while the poor man was unable to provide it. The poor man had a name, while the rich man did not. The poor man had dignity, while the rich man had none. All of the poor man's hopes were realized beyond what he could have imagined, while the rich man's hopes vanished forever.

The rich man is the main character in the story. The poor man never speaks; his role is primarily to serve as the contrast to the rich man. The rich man's words give the only testimony from hell found anywhere in the Bible.

The stark differences between these two men can be grouped into three segments: life, death, and life after death.

LIFE

"Now there was a rich man, and he habitually dressed in purple and fine linen, joyously living in splendor every day. And a poor man named Lazarus was laid at his gate, covered with sores, and longing to be fed with the crumbs which were falling from the rich man's table; besides, even the dogs were coming and licking his sores. (16:19–21)

Jesus made the most obvious contrast in the earthly lives of the two men their economic status.The **rich man** He portrayed as extremely wealthy, one who **habitually** (on a daily basis) **dressed in purple and fine linen.** That he was **dressed in purple** means that his outer gar-ment had been dyed with a Tyrian purple dye, which was extracted from sea snails. Because it was very labor intensive to produce, the purple dye was extremely expensive, and only the rich could afford fabrics or gar-ments dyed with it. Lydia, the wealthy woman in whose home the believ-ers in Philippi met (Acts 16:40), was a dealer in such fabrics (v. 14). That he wore an inner garment of **fine linen** made from expensive Egyptian cotton further demonstrates his wealth. Like the rich man in another of Christ's parables whose motto in life was, "Take your ease, eat, drink and be merry" (Luke 12:19), this man was **joyously living in splendor every day.** His lifestyle was a lavish one of self-indulgence and ostentatious display.

In stark contrast to his extravagant lifestyle was the desperate situation of the **poor man.** *Ptōchos* (**poor**) describes a person in the state of most extreme poverty (e.g., Mark 12:42–44). In Galatians 4:9 it is translated "worthless." Jesus created this man as having nothing; he was destitute. In addition to his poverty, he was **covered with** ulcerous **sores;** oozing, open lesions (cf. Rev. 16:2, 11). He had been **laid** (lit., "thrown," or "cast") **at** the rich man's **gate** (probably the entrance to the courtyard of his house). The man evidently was paralyzed, and had been abandoned by those who could no longer care for him in hopes that the rich man would.

Unfortunately the rich man, consumed with his opulent, self-gratifying lifestyle, took no notice of him. Like the priest and the Levite in the parable of the Good Samaritan (Luke 10:30–32), the rich man in Jesus' story ignored someone who urgently needed help. Despite being outwardly religious, he disregarded the second most important commandment of the law, "You shall love your neighbor as yourself" (Lev. 19:18; cf. Matt. 22:34–40). But though he passed the poor man every time he went through his gate, he did nothing to relieve his suffering. His indifference is designed to mirror the disdain with which the Pharisees treated the outcasts of their society.

The name Jesus gave the poor man, **Lazarus,** is significant. It is the same as the brother of Mary and Martha, but used of a fictional person in this case. Lazarus is the Greek translation of the common Hebrew name Eleazar, which means, "whom God has helped." It is an appropriate name, because it symbolizes the only way he was able to enter heaven— God gave him the help essential to receive eternal life. To the rich man and Jewish society he was nameless and insignificant, but Jesus gave him a name that described what God did for him. By giving him a name, Jesus also made it clear that the rich man's brothers would have recognized him as the same man who lay at their gate had he been sent back to warn them (v. 27). In contrast the rich man, who would have been widely known, is given no name. Later tradition calls him Dives, which is not a proper name, but merely the Latin word for rich.

Adding to his misery, the poor man was starving, **longing** intensely **to be fed with the crumbs which were falling from the rich man's table.** The **crumbs** were pieces of stale bread used by the dinner guests to clean their hands, and then tossed under the table for dogs to eat (cf. Matt. 15:26–27). Those same **dogs were coming and licking** the poor man's **sores.** Dogs in biblical times were not domesticated pets, but semi-wild scavengers (cf. Ex. 22:31; 1 Kings 14:11; 16:4; 21:23–24), and are consistently presented in Scripture in a negative light (e.g., 1 Sam. 17:43; 24:14; Ps. 22:16; Prov. 26:11; Phil. 3:2; 2 Peter 2:22; Rev. 22:15).

DEATH

Now the poor man died and was carried away by the angels to Abraham's bosom; and the rich man also died and was buried. (16:22)

The extreme contrast between the two men in life continued in death. While they were alive, the rich man had treated the poor, suffering, man who lay at his gate as if he were already dead. But then everything changed. The **poor man died,** diseased, destitute, and starving. There was no burial, funeral, or earthly honor in death, but honor came from heaven as his body **was carried away by the angels to Abraham's bosom** (see the discussion below). There would not have been one in any case; his body would have been thrown onto the dump with those of the rest of society's outcasts. The **rich man also died,** but unlike the poor man, he **was buried** and no doubt such a man would have been honored with an elaborate funeral. All his resources, money, friends, privilege, and prestige could not buy him another day of life; his riches could not prevent the inevitability of death. And no angels arrived to carry him to heaven.

LIFE AFTER DEATH

In Hades he lifted up his eyes, being in torment, and saw Abraham far away and Lazarus in his bosom. And he cried out and said, 'Father Abraham, have mercy on me, and send Lazarus so that he may dip the tip of his finger in water and cool off my tongue, for I am in agony in this flame.' But Abraham said, 'Child, remember that during your life you received your good things, and likewise Lazarus bad things; but now he is being comforted here, and you are in agony. And besides all this, between us and you there is a great chasm fixed, so that those who wish to come over from here to you will not be able, and that none may cross over from there to us.' (16:23–26)

The dissimilarity between the rich man and Lazarus in life continued through the transition of death and became magnified to the extreme in eternity. In the Lord's story He depicts Lazarus dramatically being carried to heaven by holy angels when he died. This suits the story, but while angels minister to the saints (e.g., Matt. 18:10; Heb. 1:14), there is no biblical precedent for them carrying a believer bodily to heaven at death. The phrase **Abraham's bosom** appears only here in the Bible. It is not, as some believe, a technical term for the abode of the Old Testament saints until after Christ's death made atonement for their sins. It merely indicates that when the poor man died, he went immediately to the side of Abraham in the abode of the righteous.

That angels would minister to a person the Pharisees viewed as an outcast would have shocked them. The belief that disease and poverty signified God's curse on a person was deeply ingrained in their thinking. Job's three friends insisted that his suffering was the result of his sin. Even the disciples asked Jesus regarding a man born blind, "Rabbi, who sinned, this man or his parents, that he would be born blind?" (John 9:2). That such a lowlife as Lazarus was taken to heaven by angels would have been a greater shock for the Pharisees. But not only was he taken to heaven, he was also given the place of honor and intimate fellowship at the side of Abraham, the friend of God (2 Chron. 20:7; James 2:23), the father of the Jewish race and of the faithful (Gen. 15:5), the greatest figure in Jewish history. To the Pharisees, this would have been stunning, incomprehensible, a direct frontal assault on their theological assumptions. This man who was humiliated on earth, a man whom no self-respecting Pharisee would have had anything to do with, was honored in heaven because the Lord helped him and had the angels deliver him.

The rich man's body was honorably buried, with full treatment given to his corpse. His eternal soul, however, went to **Hades.** In the Old Testament Sheol, the equivalent of the New Testament term Hades, was used in a general sense to refer to the realm of the dead (though it was occasionally contrasted with heaven [e.g., Ps. 139:8; Isa. 7:11; Amos 9:2]). In the New Testament, **Hades** refers to the abode of the damned prior to their judgment and sentencing to the final phase of hell—the lake of fire (cf. 10:15; Rev. 1:18; 20:13–14).

The phrase **he lifted up his eyes** indicates that he was fully aware of his surroundings and in conscious **torment.** His soul was not asleep, nor did he go out of existence. Just as Lazarus illustrated that at death the redeemed go immediately into the conscious enjoyment of the bliss of heaven, so the rich man shows that the unredeemed go immediately into conscious torment in hell. For the sake of the point in the story he was allowed to see **Abraham far away and Lazarus in his bosom,** though as noted above that cannot happen in reality. Upon seeing them **he cried out,** addressing Abraham as **Father Abraham,** basing his ensuing plea on his Jewish heritage and descent from Abraham, the father of the Jewish people.

His plea for **mercy**—something he had likely never asked for in life—was an acknowledgment of his guilt and that his punishment was deserved. He did not protest his innocence, or question the severity of his punishment, but merely sought some temporary relief. His plea for Abraham to **send Lazarus** indicates that his view of the beggar had not changed. He still saw Lazarus as someone so lowly and insignificant that if someone were selected to leave heaven and come to hell it should be him. His unchanged, unrepentant attitude illustrates the reality that hell is not remedial, but punitive. That the rich man appealed to Abraham, showing no interest in God the Father or the Lord Jesus Christ, further supports that truth. Those who rejected God in life will not suddenly desire to love and serve Him when they find themselves in hell. One reason hell is forever is that sinful attitudes continue forever, thus the punishment cannot end.

Seeking mercy at the hands of the one to whom he had shown no mercy, the rich man begged Abraham to send lowly Lazarus **so that he** might **dip the tip of his finger in water and cool off** his **tongue,** because he was **in agony in** the **flame** (cf. Matt. 3:12; 5:22; 7:19; 13:40, 42, 50; 18:8, 9; 25:41; Mark 9:43; John 15:6; Jude 7; Rev. 14:10; 19:20; 20:10, 14–15; 21:8). His accusing conscience gave him no hope that he would ever be released from hell. Instead, he sought temporary relief; a drop of water from the finger of the one to whom he would not give a crumb. He was desperate for just the briefest moment of relief in the unending horror of hell.

But Abraham's reply dashed his hopes. He called him **child,** acknowledging that in a racial sense he was his descendant. But his Abrahamic heritage did not keep him out of hell, nor would it mitigate hell's torments for him. Abraham called on him to **remember that during** his **life** he had **received** his **good things, and likewise Lazarus bad things.** But death completely reversed their situations, and **now** Lazarus was **being comforted** in heaven, **and** he was **in agony** in hell. He had chosen a life of proud self-righteousness, including materialistic pleasures and comforts apart from the true righteousness of God, and was enduring the eternal consequences of his choice.

Nor was there any way to send him help. **Besides all this,** Abraham reminded him, **between us and you there is a great chasm fixed, so that those who wish to come over from here to you will not be able, and that none may cross over from there to us.** Our Lord was revealing that death permanently fixes everyone's destiny; no one will escape hell, nor will anyone in heaven visit hell.

The rich man's experience of torment (v. 23) and agony (vv. 24, 25) typifies the sinner's experience in hell. As noted above, hell's torment is frequently described with the words fire, fiery, or flame. Mark 9:48 describes it as a place "where their worm does not die" (cf. Isa. 66:24). The "worm" most likely symbolizes the fully informed, accusing conscience and the gnawing, nagging, relentless guilt it presses upon the soul tortured in hell. Daniel 12:2 speaks of the "disgrace and everlasting contempt" and its accompanying self-hate and loathing that those in hell will experience. Like David (Ps. 51:3), their guilt will continually be before them. Jesus described hell as the "outer darkness" (Matt. 8:12; 22:13; 25:30), a picture of abandonment and banishment, of being cast away permanently from God's presence (cf. 2 Thess. 1:9). Hell's torment makes it a place where "there will be weeping and gnashing of teeth" (Matt. 13:42, 50; 22:13; 24:51; 25:30; Luke 13:28).

Worst of all, there is no hope of relief for hell's inhabitants, who "have no rest day and night" (Rev. 14:11; cf. 20:10). Their sentence is eternal; their punishment never ending. The fire of hell is unquenchable and will never cease to burn (Matt. 3:12; Mark 9:43), since it is everlasting (Matt. 18:8; 25:41; Jude 7). Hence the destruction of the wicked in hell is eternal and never comes to an end (2 Thess. 1:9). (Some argue that "destroy" in Matthew 10:28 indicates that the ungodly are annihilated and go out of existence. That, obviously, would contradict the passages cited above that teach that the lost suffer conscious torment in hell. Obviously, someone who has gone out of existence would be incapable of suffering. Nor does the Greek word translated "destroy" mean to cease to exist, but rather to be rendered useless, perish, or be lost [it is so used in Matt. 9:17; 10:6, 39; 12:14; Mark 3:6; 4:38; 9:22; Luke 13:33; 15:4, 17; 19:10; John 6:12, 27; Rom. 14:15; 1 Cor. 8:11; etc.].)

THE LESSONS

And he said, 'Then I beg you, father, that you send him to my father's house—for I have five brothers—in order that he may warn them, so that they will not also come to this place of torment.' But Abraham said, 'They have Moses and the Prophets; let them hear them.' But he said, 'No, father Abraham, but if someone goes to them from the dead, they will repent!' But he said to him, 'If they do not listen to Moses and the Prophets, they will not be persuaded even if someone rises from the dead.'" (16:27–31)

Several lessons may be drawn from the concluding dialogue of this compelling and frightening story.

First, this parable answers the question of why sinners end up in hell. The rich man seemed certain to make it to heaven, yet instead found himself in hell. The Lord's hearers, particularly the Pharisees, would have been dumfounded, and at a loss to explain why. It was not because he was not of the right racial stock. The Jews erroneously (cf. Matt. 8:11–12; Luke 3:8; 13:28; John 8:31–58) believed that hell was reserved for Gentiles while most Jews (except tax collectors, irreligious Jews, and those guilty of gross sins) would go to heaven. Therefore one's Abrahamic ancestry essentially guaranteed entrance to heaven. Before his salvation, Paul was confident that he would reach heaven because he was "circumcised the eighth day, of the nation of Israel, of the tribe of Benjamin, a Hebrew of Hebrews; as to the Law, a Pharisee; as to zeal, a persecutor of the church; as to the righteousness which is in the Law, found blameless" (Phil. 3:5–6); after his salvation he realized that those things were nothing but "rubbish" (v. 8).

Lazarus represented the outcasts who came to Jesus and received salvation. The rich man is the Pharisees and all who follow their brand of works religion. The rich man was a descendant of Abraham. He appealed to Abraham as his father, or ancestor, and Abraham acknowledged that by calling him "Child." But race is not a factor in determining a person's eternal destiny. Being a Jew does not guarantee one entrance to heaven any more than being a Gentile guarantees one will be sent to hell.

Nor was it his substance that doomed the rich man to hell. It is true that, as noted earlier in this chapter, riches can make it difficult to enter the kingdom. But wealth is not an absolute barrier to salvation, because God has the power to save whomever He chooses (Matt. 19:26). Abraham himself was very rich (Gen. 13:2), as were Isaac (Gen. 26:13), Jacob (Gen. 32:5), Boaz (Ruth 2:1), Job (Job 1:3; 31:25; 42:10–12), David (1 Chron. 29:28), Solomon (2 Chron. 1:11–12; 9:22), and Joseph of Arimathea (Matt. 27:57).

The rich man was not sent to hell because he was a secular, irreligious Jew. Like the Pharisees, he was outwardly religious by the standards of the day, so much so that he thought his riches were a reward from God; he and his brothers were familiar with **Moses and the Prophets,** and he even understood that they needed to repent **so that they** would **not also come to this place of torment** where he found himself. His acknowledgment that they needed to repent also presupposes a belief in sin, the law, and God as the law giver.

While sin damns all the unredeemed to hell, there is nothing to suggest that he was guilty of any especially heinous sins. Like the Jews, he was religious and well respected and that argues for the fact that he was not in hell because he was guilty of such sins.

Some might think that he wound up in hell because he was self-ish, utterly lacking compassion, love, and concern for the poor beggar who lay at his gate. It is true that his sin sent him to hell, and that selfish-ness is at the heart of all sin. But to say that selfishness condemned the rich man to hell is only partially true. Even if he had been generous, kind, and merciful toward Lazarus, those acts of charity and compassion would not have atoned for his sin. Salvation throughout redemptive his-tory has always been solely by God's grace through faith (see the discus-sion of this truth below).

In the end, there is only one reason that the rich man (and by extension all the unredeemed) ended up in hell: failing to believe in and act on the truth of Scripture. Heaven is for those who believe in what God has revealed in His Word and act on it. Abraham affirmed Scripture's suf-ficiency when he said in response to the rich man's request to send Lazarus to his brothers, **They have Moses and the Prophets; let them hear them.** Revealing his lack of belief in Scripture's sufficiency, the rich man pleaded for a supernatural sign: **No, father Abraham, but if someone goes to them from the dead, they will repent!** This was both a complaint and a request. The implication is that he and his broth-ers had insufficient data; that they lacked a sufficiently convincing sign. The Pharisees did exactly that: they repeatedly demanded a sign from the Lord (Matt. 12:38; 16:1; Luke 11:16; John 2:18), which He refused to give them (Matt. 12:39; 16:4). Emphatically confirming the absolute suffi-ciency of Scripture to bring sinners to salvation, Abraham replied, **If they do not listen to Moses and the Prophets** (i.e., the Old Testament), **they will not be persuaded even if someone rises from the dead,** as the resurrection of a real Lazarus and the Lord Himself proves. Since unbelief is at heart a moral, not an intellectual issue, no amount of evi-dence alone can turn unbelief to faith. The Word of God has the power to do so (Heb. 4:12; 1 Peter 1:23).

That reply raises the question of what people before the cross needed to believe to escape hell. First, they needed to believe the truth about God. The Old Testament reveals Him to be the holy, sovereign Creator, Ruler, and Lawgiver who always judges sin. God judged sin at the fall, to which the repeated refrain in the genealogy recorded in Genesis 5, "and he died," testifies. The catastrophic judgment of the flood gives further evidence that God judges sin. Because He is absolutely holy (Isa. 6:3), God's "eyes are too pure to approve evil, and [He] can not look on wickedness with favor" (Hab. 1:13). Therefore He must punish sin, and as a result, "the soul who sins will die" (Ezek. 18:4).

Second, they needed to believe that sinners must repent. Confronted with an overwhelming display of God's nature and acts that rebuked his inadequate view of Him Job said, "I retract, and I repent in dust and ashes" (Job 42:6). Jonah proclaimed God's impending judgment on Nineveh, and its people repented (Jonah 3:4–10). Through Ezekiel, God called for Israel to repent and turn from their sins (Ezek. 18:30–32). "Let the wicked forsake his way," Isaiah declared, "and the unrighteous man his thoughts; and let him return to the Lord, and He will have compassion on him, and to our God, for He will abundantly pardon" (Isa. 55:7).

Third, they needed to believe that salvation is by God's sovereign grace (cf. Ex. 33:19; 34:6–7; Pss. 41:4; 51:1). The New Covenant, by whose provisions all the redeemed throughout redemptive history are saved, is a gracious covenant (Jer. 31:31–34). Thus, sinners in every age have been saved by grace alone, never by their own merit, works, sacrifices, or performance of rituals and ceremonies.

Fourth, they needed to believe that God forgives the penitent sinner because He is, by nature, a forgiving God. In Exodus 34:6–7 God describes Himself as

> the Lord, the Lord God, compassionate and gracious, slow to anger, and abounding in lovingkindness and truth; who keeps lovingkindness for thousands, who forgives iniquity, transgression and sin; yet He will by no means leave the guilty unpunished, visiting the iniquity of fathers on the children and on the grandchildren to the third and fourth generations.

David, no stranger to God's forgiveness (cf. Pss. 32:1, 5; 51:1–4), wrote,

> He has not dealt with us according to our sins, nor rewarded us according to our iniquities. For as high as the heavens are above the earth, so

great is His lovingkindness toward those who fear Him. As far as the
east is from the west, so far has He removed our transgressions from us.
(Ps. 103:10–12)

Micah exclaimed,

Who is a God like You, who pardons iniquity and passes over the rebellious act of the remnant of His possession? He does not retain His
anger forever, because He delights in unchanging love. He will again
have compassion on us; He will tread our iniquities under foot. Yes, You
will cast all their sins into the depths of the sea. (Mic. 7:18–19)

The Pharisees, who imagined that God was less righteous than He is and
that they were more righteous than they were, saw little need for genuine
repentance. They approached God only to confess their sins superficially,
but more to celebrate their own righteousness:

[Jesus] told this parable to some people who trusted in themselves that
they were righteous, and viewed others with contempt: "Two men went
up into the temple to pray, one a Pharisee and the other a tax collector.
The Pharisee stood and was praying this to himself: 'God, I thank You
that I am not like other people: swindlers, unjust, adulterers, or even like
this tax collector.'" (Luke 18:9–11)

Fifth, they needed to believe that God's gracious salvation and
forgiveness of sin is appropriated by faith alone. Abraham "believed in
the Lord; and He reckoned it to him as righteousness" (Gen. 15:6; cf. Rom.
4:3, 9, 20–22; Gal. 3:6–9). Habakkuk wrote that "the righteous will live by
his faith" (Hab. 2:4; cf. Rom. 1:17; Gal. 3:11; Heb. 10:38).

Sixth, they needed to believe that salvation occurred by the
granting or imputing of an alien righteousness; that is, a righteousness
from outside of them (cf. Phil. 3:9). Righteousness was imputed to Abraham when he believed God (Gen. 15:6; cf. Rom. 4:3; Gal. 3:6; James 2:23).

Seventh, they needed to believe that God's justice was satisfied
by transferring His judgment to a substitute. The millions of animals sacrificed throughout Israel's history taught them that "without shedding of
blood there is no forgiveness" (Heb. 9:22). Those countless sacrifices
could not, however, take away sins (Heb. 10:1–4).

Eighth, they needed to believe that Messiah would come and
redeem them from their sins (Job 19:25) through His substitionary death

on their behalf. He would be the seed of the woman, who crushed Satan's head (Gen. 3:15), the suffering servant of Isaiah 53. He would be both human and divine; both David's descendant and his Lord (Matt. 22:42–45); the one who would be humble (Zech 9:9), and yet the king who will rule the nations with a rod of iron (Ps. 2:6–9; cf. Gen. 49:10).

Finally, they needed to believe that reception of salvation requires the forsaking of all sin, or hope of salvation by any human means. In Psalm 3:8 David wrote, "Salvation belongs to the Lord," and He alone is the Savior (Isa. 43:11; 45:21–22). Isaiah 55:6–7, as noted above, also calls for just such a complete abandonment of any other hope of salvation.

The Old Testament, then, contained all the information necessary to lead the honest seeker to salvation. Paul exhorted Timothy to remember "that from childhood you have known the sacred writings [from his believing mother and grandmother; 2 Tim. 1:5] which are able to give you the wisdom that leads to salvation through faith which is in Christ Jesus" (2 Tim. 3:15). Peter proclaimed to the people of Israel that "the things which God announced beforehand by the mouth of all the prophets, that His Christ would suffer, He has thus fulfilled" (Acts 3:18). Jesus indicted the Jewish leaders for understanding that the Old Testament taught the truth about eternal life, yet being unwilling to believe in Him (John 5:39–40). Paul wrote to the Romans that "now apart from the Law the righteousness of God has been manifested, being witnessed by the Law and the Prophets" (Rom. 3:21), and testified to the Corinthians, "For I delivered to you as of first importance what I also received, that Christ died for our sins according to the Scriptures, and that He was buried, and that He was raised on the third day according to the Scriptures" (1 Cor. 15:3–4).

Like the rich man, as noted above, the Jews demanded signs from the Lord. But they rejected the convincing signs that they did receive (John 12:37)—including the resurrection of a dead person. After the Lord performed the astounding miracle of raising Lazarus from the dead (John 11:1–44), the Pharisees' response was to plot His death (vv. 47–53) and that of Lazarus (John 12:10–11). And when the Lord Jesus Christ Himself rose from the dead, the religious leaders bribed the Roman soldiers who had been guarding the tomb to falsely claim that the disciples had stolen His body (Matt. 28:11–15).

For the rich man, Israel, and all who arrive in hell, the issue is not lack of information, but rejection of the truth: "This is the judgment, that the Light has come into the world, and men loved the darkness rather than the Light, for their deeds were evil" (John 3:19).

Four Hallmarks of Humility (Luke 17:1–10)

29

He said to His disciples, "It is inevitable that stumbling blocks come, but woe to him through whom they come! It would be better for him if a millstone were hung around his neck and he were thrown into the sea, than that he would cause one of these little ones to stumble. Be on your guard! If your brother sins, rebuke him; and if he repents, forgive him. And if he sins against you seven times a day, and returns to you seven times, saying, 'I repent,' forgive him." The apostles said to the Lord, "Increase our faith!" And the Lord said, "If you had faith like a mustard seed, you would say to this mulberry tree, 'Be uprooted and be planted in the sea'; and it would obey you. Which of you, having a slave plowing or tending sheep, will say to him when he has come in from the field, 'Come immediately and sit down to eat'? But will he not say to him, 'Prepare something for me to eat, and properly clothe yourself and serve me while I eat and drink; and afterward you may eat and drink'? He does not thank the slave because he did the things which were commanded, does he? So

you too, when you do all the things which are commanded you, say, 'We are unworthy slaves; we have done only that which we ought to have done.'" (17:1–10)

In a day when the focus is on God's love, it may come as a surprise to many that there are things that God hates. For example, His holiness demands that He hate those who commit sin. David wrote, "You are not a God who takes pleasure in wickedness; no evil dwells with You. The boastful shall not stand before Your eyes; You hate all who do iniquity" (Ps. 5:4–5). That hatred specifically encompasses sinful mistreatment of others, such as by devising evil against them or lying about them (Zech. 8:17), violently abusing them (Ps. 11:5), or divorcing them (Mal. 2:16).

God also hates false religion. Moses warned Israel not to imitate the idolatry of the Canaanites: "You shall not behave thus toward the Lord your God, for every abominable act which the Lord hates they have done for their gods" (Deut. 12:31; cf. 16:22). The glorified Christ said to the church at Ephesus, "Yet this you do have, that you hate the deeds of the Nicolaitans [a hedonistic pseudo-Christian cult], which I also hate" (Rev. 2:6; cf. vv. 14–15). Through the prophet Jeremiah God said to His people regarding their idolatry, "I sent you all My servants the prophets, again and again, saying, 'Oh, do not do this abominable thing which I hate.' But they did not listen or incline their ears to turn from their wickedness, so as not to burn sacrifices to other gods" (Jer. 44:4–5). Amos 5:21–23 records God's rejection of Israel's false worship of Him:

> I hate, I reject your festivals, nor do I delight in your solemn assemblies. Even though you offer up to Me burnt offerings and your grain offerings, I will not accept them; and I will not even look at the peace offerings of your fatlings. Take away from Me the noise of your songs; I will not even listen to the sound of your harps.

At the heart of all sin, whether against God or other people, is pride. Some try to say He only hates the sin, not the sinner, but the sinner is the one punished. Since "everyone who is proud in heart is an abomination to the Lord" (Prov. 16:5), it is not surprising that heading a list of seven things God hates are "haughty eyes," representative of a proud heart (Prov. 6:16–19; cf. 21:4). Because God hates sin, He hates the proud.

Paul wrote to the Christians at Rome, "For through the grace given to me I say to everyone among you not to think more highly of himself than he ought to think" (Rom. 12:3). A few verses later he added, "Be of the same mind toward one another; do not be haughty in mind, but associate with the lowly. Do not be wise in your own estimation" (v. 16).

Pride manifests itself in self-righteousness, like that of the "Pharisee [who] stood and was praying this to himself: 'God, I thank You that I am not like other people: swindlers, unjust, adulterers, or even like this tax collector. I fast twice a week; I pay tithes of all that I get'" (Luke 18:11–12). Pride also reveals itself in spiritual arrogance. Paul warned the Corinthians, "Knowledge makes arrogant, but love edifies" (1 Cor. 8:1). Pride also causes the wicked to reject God (Ps. 10:4) and mistreat other people (Pss. 10:2; 31:18).

It was pride that led to Satan being expelled from heaven and Adam and Eve being banished from the garden of Eden. Pride moved Amaziah of Judah to challenge Jehoash, the king of Israel, to a battle in which Amaziah was defeated (2 Kings 14:8–14). Pride caused Uzziah to attempt to usurp the role of the priests by burning incense on the altar of incense in the temple (2 Chron. 26:16)—an act for which God struck him with leprosy (v. 19). Pride motivated Hezekiah to show envoys from Babylon all the treasures of his kingdom (2 Chron. 32:25–26; cf. v. 31; 2 Kings 20:12–13). The daughters of Zion (Isa. 3:16), Ephraim and Samaria (Isa. 9:9–10; 28:1, 3), Babylon (Isa. 13:19) and its king (Dan. 5:18–20), Moab (Isa. 16:6), Judah and Jerusalem (Jer. 13:9), the Philistines (Zech. 9:6), Assyria (Zech. 10:11), and false teachers (1 Tim. 6:3–4) are further examples of the pride that marks the fallen world (1 John 2:16).

The consequences of pride are devastating. Pride defiles a person (Mark 7:20–22), brings dishonor (Prov. 11:2; 29:23), and causes strife (Prov. 28:25). But most significantly, pride brings God's judgment. David wrote that "the Lord . . . fully recompenses the proud doer" (Ps. 31:23), while in Psalm 94:2 the psalmist called on God, the "Judge of the earth," to "render recompense to the proud." Solomon noted that "everyone who is proud in heart is an abomination to the Lord; assuredly, he will not be unpunished" (Prov. 16:5), while in verse 18 he cautioned, "Pride goes before destruction, and a haughty spirit before stumbling." Isaiah warned that "the Lord of hosts will have a day of reckoning against everyone who is proud and lofty and against everyone who is lifted up, that he may be abased.... The pride of man will be humbled and the loftiness of men will be abased" (Isa. 2:12, 17). Mary, the mother of Jesus Christ, declared that God "has done mighty deeds with His arm; He has scattered those who were proud in the thoughts of their heart" (Luke 1:51). Both James (James 4:6) and Peter (1 Peter 5:5) record the statement from Proverbs 3:34 that "God is opposed to the proud, but gives grace to the humble."

During the final months of His ministry, Jesus narrowed His focus to two groups, directing His teaching to His disciples (10:23; 11:1–2; 12:1, 22; 16:1), and to the scribes and Pharisees (11:39–54; 13:31–33; 14:1–4; 15:2–32). Those two groups were juxtaposed to one another; the Pharisees were the false religionists who provided a contrast with true disciples. Everything they were, He wanted His disciples not to be; everything they were not, He wanted His disciples to become.

Since pride was the defining characteristic of the scribes and Pharisees, the disciples were to be marked by humility, understandably an emphasis in the Lord's evangelistic preaching (cf. 14:11; 18:14; Matt. 5:3; 18:4). Although the term itself does not appear in this section, the theme of the first ten verses of this chapter is clearly humility.

In spite of the Old Testament's emphasis on humility (e.g., Num. 12:3; Deut. 8:2, 16; 2 Chron. 7:14; Job 22:29; Pss. 10:17; 25:9; 37:11; Prov. 11:2; 15:33; 18:12; 22:4; 29:23; Isa. 66:2; Mic. 6:8; Zeph. 2:3), the Pharisees were to a large degree characterized by pride. They were proud of their religious achievements and status. Pride motivated them to love "the place of honor at banquets [cf. Luke 14:7] and the chief seats in the synagogues, and respectful greetings in the market places, and being called Rabbi by men" (Matt. 23:6–7). Arrogance caused them to view those whom they considered to be beneath them with contempt (Luke 18:9–12; John 7:49; 9:34) and to refuse to associate with them (cf. Luke 5:30; 7:34; 15:1–2). Pride also caused them to exalt themselves (Luke 16:15) and seek honor from others (John 5:44).

The Lord's strong warning, **Be on your guard!** or "Beware!" is the key that opens the passage. It is one of several warnings of imminent danger Jesus gave. In Matthew 6:1 He warned against hypocrisy. In Matthew 7:15 He warned of the deadly danger of false teachers, while in Matthew

10:17 He warned His followers that they would be persecuted. In Luke 21:34 Jesus warned against being caught unprepared at His return. But the Lord especially warned of the danger posed by the scribes and Pharisees (Matt. 16:6, 11; Luke 12:1; 20:46), because they led the people astray both through their errant teaching and their hypocritical example.

In this passage Jesus defined the essence of humility without using the word. Truly humble people are restrained from offending others, ready to forgive, marked by recognition of weakness, and characterized by rejection of honor.

Humble People Are Restrained from Offending Others

He said to His disciples, "It is inevitable that stumbling blocks come, but woe to him through whom they come! It would be better for him if a millstone were hung around his neck and he were thrown into the sea, than that he would cause one of these little ones to stumble. (17:1–2)

In a fallen, corrupt, imperfect world **it is inevitable that stumbling blocks come.** *Anendektos* (**inevitable**) appears only here in the New Testament. It refers to something that is a certain way and cannot be otherwise. The phrase in the Greek text literally reads negatively, "It is impossible that stumbling blocks not come." **Stumbling blocks** translates the plural form of the noun *skandalon*, which referred originally to the bait stick in a trap. The world is filled with traps, which can seduce the unwary into error regarding the Scriptures, salvation, and living the Christian life. Those who set them do so by means of direct temptation (1 Thess. 4:6), indirect temptation (Eph. 6:4), sinful example (Rom. 14:13–15; 1 Cor. 8:9–13; Gal. 5:13–15), or by failing to stimulate righteousness (Heb. 10:24–25). Above all, traps are set by the lies of false teachers—particularly in this context the blasphemous lies that the scribes and Pharisees spread about the Lord Jesus Christ (cf. Matt. 9:34; 11:19; 12:24; Luke 5:21; John 8:13, 41, 48, 52, 53). Through those lies they lured people onto the broad road that leads to hell (Matt. 7:13–15; 23:15).

But the inevitability of stumbling blocks does not mitigate the guilt of those who bring them, as Jesus' words **woe to him through whom they come** indicate. So serious a matter is it that **it would be better for him if a millstone** (a massive stone used in grinding grain) **were hung around his neck and he were thrown into the sea, than that he would cause one of these little ones to stumble.** The **little ones** here, as in Matthew 18:6 and 10, are not children, but believers. Matthew 18:17 records the first instruction ever given specifically to the church ("tell it to the church"). Significantly, that instruction was a warning against leading fellow believers into sin. In the present passage, the warning was aimed primarily at the unbelieving Pharisees who, as noted above, caused people to stumble by spreading lies about Jesus. Matthew 18:7–9 indicates that our Lord had the world in mind, and the end of such action was hell. But anyone, even a believer, who leads another believer into sin is guilty before God. So serious a matter is it that Jesus warned that it would be better for that person instead to suffer one of the most horrible deaths imaginable—to have **a millstone . . . hung around his neck and** [be] **thrown into the sea.** That would be far more tolerable than to incur the consequences of his act—more severe punishment in hell for unbelievers; chastening in this life and forfeiture of eternal reward for believers.

Humble believers consider others first out of love and unselfish good will. They passionately pursue the truth of God's Word so that they might not offer false teaching that would put an obstacle or hindrance in someone's spiritual life. For the same reason, they live godly lives, setting an example for others to follow. They also do not abuse their liberty in Christ so as not to cause weaker believers to be offended (Rom. 14; 1 Cor. 8).

HUMBLE PEOPLE ARE READY TO FORGIVE

Be on your guard! If your brother sins, rebuke him; and if he repents, forgive him. And if he sins against you seven times a day, and returns to you seven times, saying, 'I repent,' forgive him." (17:3–4)

The strong position against sin set forth in the previous point must be balanced by a gracious, forgiving attitude toward sinners. Humble believers do not give offense, but neither do they take offense. They avoid sinning against others, but they also do not hold a grudge when others sin against them (cf. Luke 11:4).

But being ready to forgive others does not entail being indifferent to their sin. The Lord's warning to the disciples to **be on your guard** against the influence of the scribes and Pharisees is a caution against acting like unbelievers by both giving offense, and being indifferent to the sins of others.

The first step in leading people out of sin is to **rebuke** them. *Epitimaō* (**rebuke**) is a strong term of disapproval; a censure or reprimand conveying a stern warning or admonishment. Matthew 18:15–17 gives the process for implementing the principle set forth here:

> If your brother sins, go and show him his fault in private; if he listens to you, you have won your brother. But if he does not listen to you, take one or two more with you, so that by the mouth of two or three witnesses every fact may be confirmed. If he refuses to listen to them, tell it to the church; and if he refuses to listen even to the church, let him be to you as a Gentile and a tax collector.

The goal of that four step process is to confront and restore the sinner so as to guard the church's purity. The first step is to oppose the sinning brother's behavior in private. Should he refuse to repent, the second step involves confronting him again with no less than two witnesses present to confirm his response. If he again refuses to repent, the third step is to inform the church, so that the entire fellowship can confront him and lovingly call him to repentance. The final step for a hardened, impenitent sinner is to put him out of the church; to treat him like one of the outcasts of Jewish society, a "Gentile and a tax collector" (cf. 1 Cor. 5:1–13; 2 Cor. 13:1–2; 2 Thess. 3:14–15; Titus 3:10–11) or an unbeliever, which he may well be.

Here the question arises as to whether forgiveness should be withheld until a person repents. There are some sins for which forgiveness is completely unconditional. In Galatians 6:1 Paul wrote, "Brethren, even if anyone is caught in any trespass, you who are spiritual, restore such a one in a spirit of gentleness; each one looking to yourself, so that you too will not be tempted." The idea conveyed by the word "caught" is that the person was caught unawares or trapped by the sin; that it was not premeditated. Jesus had the same kind of sin in mind when He said, "Whenever you stand praying, forgive, if you have anything against anyone, so that your Father who is in heaven will also forgive you your transgressions" (Mark 11:25). There is no mention of seeking out the offending person; the forgiveness is immediate and then prayer can continue. For such unplanned, unintentional lapses into sin the principle that "love covers a multitude of sins" (1 Peter 4:8; cf. Prov. 10:12), because it "does not take into account a wrong suffered" (1 Cor. 13:5), applies.

But there are some sins that are to be forgiven only **if** the sinner **repents.** These are willful, premeditated, habitual sins, sins that have become the pattern and direction of the sinner's life. These are the sins that call for the church discipline set forth in Matthew 18. Yet even these sins, when there is genuine repentance, are to be fully and freely forgiven. **If** a person **sins against you seven times a day,"** Jesus said, **"and returns to you seven times, saying, 'I repent,' forgive him."** In Matthew 18:21 Peter asked Him, "Lord, how often shall my brother sin against me and I forgive him? Up to seven times?" Peter thought he was being magnanimous, since the rabbis, misinterpreting such passages as Amos 1:3, 6, 9, 11, 13, 2:1, 4, 6, taught that God forgave only a maximum of three times. Jesus replied, "I do not say to you, up to seven times, but up to seventy times seven" (v. 22). The point is that just as God freely and completely forgives penitent believers, so also must they fully forgive each other.

The Bible reveals at least ten reasons forgiveness is important. First, forgiveness is the most God-like act a person can do. In the Sermon on the Mount Jesus said, "Love your enemies and pray for those who persecute you, so that you may be sons of your Father who is in heaven; for He causes His sun to rise on the evil and the good, and sends rain on the righteous and the unrighteous" (Matt. 5:44–45). Loving one's enemies, which necessitates forgiving them, makes believers like their Father in heaven, who showers the blessings of common grace on those who do not love Him. Just as the forgiving God (cf. Ex. 34:6–7; Pss. 32:1–2; 85:2; 130:4; Isa. 1:18; 43:25; 55:6–7; Jer. 31:33–34; Mic. 7:18–19) forgave them, so also are believers to imitate Him (Eph. 5:1) by forgiving others. Paul commanded the Ephesians, "Be kind to one another, tender-hearted, forgiving each other, just as God in Christ also has forgiven you" (Eph. 4:32; cf. Col. 3:13).

Second, it is not only murder that is forbidden by the sixth commandment, but also anger, wrath, malice, vengeance, and lack of forgiveness. Jesus explained the true meaning of the sixth commandment in the Sermon on the Mount:

> You have heard that the ancients were told, "You shall not commit murder" and "Whoever commits murder shall be liable to the court." But I say to you that everyone who is angry with his brother shall be guilty before the court; and whoever says to his brother, "You good-for-nothing," shall be guilty before the supreme court; and whoever says, "You fool," shall be guilty enough to go into the fiery hell. (Matt. 5:21–22)

In 1 John 3:15 the apostle John wrote, "Everyone who hates his brother is a murderer; and you know that no murderer has eternal life abiding in him."

Third, Christians need to remember that whoever offends them has offended God more. All sin is ultimately against Him as Psalm 51, rising out of David's horrific sin of adultery and murder, makes clear. On the human level, David's sin affected many people. It affected Bathsheba, her husband Uriah, whom David had killed (2 Sam. 12:9), and the child that resulted from his adultery, who died in infancy. David's own children were also affected by the example he set of adultery and murder (cf. 2 Sam. 12:10). The entire nation of Israel suffered from the civil war that resulted from Absalom's rebellion against David. Yet in his anguished confession of his sin and culpability, David cried out to God, "Against You, You only, I have sinned and done what is evil in Your sight" (Ps. 51:4).

Fourth, it is only reasonable that those forgiven for the greater sins they have committed against God, the most Holy One, forgive the lesser sins committed against them, the sinful ones. Jesus' story of a man who was forgiven a massive, unpayable debt, yet refused to forgive a small debt owed him by another man illustrates that truth (Matt. 18:23–35).

Fifth, those who fail to forgive will not enjoy the love of other Christians. When the man refused to forgive the one who owed him money, "his fellow slaves ... were deeply grieved and came and reported to their lord all that had happened" (Matt. 18:31). He was cut off from fellowship with them.

Sixth, failing to forgive results in divine chastening. Enraged that the one whose massive debt he had forgiven refused to forgive his fellow slave "his lord, moved with anger, handed him over to the torturers until he should repay all that was owed him" (Matt. 18:34). Driving home this point Jesus warned, "My heavenly Father will also do the same to you, if each of you does not forgive his brother from your heart" (v. 35).

A seventh principle follows from that truth; namely that those who fail to forgive others will not be forgiven. Jesus made that clear in His teaching on prayer in the Sermon on the Mount: "For if you forgive others for their transgressions, your heavenly Father will also forgive you," He told His audience. But He went on to warn, "If you do not forgive others, then your Father will not forgive your transgressions" (Matt. 6:14–15).

The Lord was not speaking of the eternal forgiveness believers have through justification, but rather of the temporal or parental forgiveness that is a part of sanctification. Those who are bitter, bear grudges, and withhold forgiveness will receive God's chastening. The emptiness, depression, dullness, and lack of assurance and joy many Christians experience is often due to withheld blessing as a result of chastening for an unforgiving heart.

Eighth, failing to forgive renders a person unfit for worship. In Matthew 5:23–24 Jesus said, "If you are presenting your offering at the altar, and there remember that your brother has something against you, leave your offering there before the altar and go; first be reconciled to your brother, and then come and present your offering." When a believer is aware of a conflict with or a lack of forgiveness toward another person, the situation needs to be resolved before coming to worship God. The sin of failing to reconcile precludes worship, which God will not accept if believers harbor sin in their hearts (Ps. 66:18; Prov. 15:8).

Ninth, failure to forgive usurps God's authority. "Never take your own revenge, beloved," wrote Paul, "but leave room for the wrath of God, for it is written, 'Vengeance is Mine, I will repay,' says the Lord" (Rom. 12:19). By refusing to forgive, those who are not qualified to retaliate against sin usurp God's right to do so. Only He has a perfect understanding of the offenses against believers, has ultimate authority, is impartial, wise, good, and always acts in perfect holiness. And, as noted in point three above, God is the one most offended by sins against believers.

Finally, the offenses against believers are the trials that perfect them. James wrote, "Consider it all joy, my brethren, when you encounter various trials, knowing that the testing of your faith produces endurance. And let endurance have its perfect result, so that you may be perfect and complete, lacking in nothing" (James 1:2–4). Viewing the offenses of others as God's means of perfecting believers puts those offenses in a different light, and enables them to follow the example of Christ, "who committed no sin, nor was any deceit found in His mouth; and while being reviled, He did not revile in return; while suffering, He uttered no threats, but kept entrusting Himself to Him who judges righteously" (1 Peter 2:22–23). (I discuss the importance of forgiveness in detail in my book *The Freedom and Power of Forgiveness* [Wheaton, Ill.: Crossway, 1998].)

HUMBLE PEOPLE ARE
MARKED BY RECOGNITION OF WEAKNESS

The apostles said to the Lord, "Increase our faith!" And the Lord said, "If you had faith like a mustard seed, you would say to this mulberry tree, 'Be uprooted and be planted in the sea'; and it would obey you. (17:5–6)

The seeming disconnect between verses 5–10 and the first four verses of this section has led some to view verses 5–10 as unconnected samplings from the Lord's teaching given on other occasions. But there is nothing in this context to suggest that all ten verses are not part of one connected discourse. As the passage unfolds, the connections between its sections will become clear.

The **apostles** were the twelve selected by the Lord in Luke 6:12–16. They have been absent from Luke's narrative since being sent out to preach in 9:1–10 (apart from an allusion to them in 11:49). These were the men who had the extraordinary privilege of being called personally and sovereignly by the Lord Jesus Christ to be His personal representatives. They became eyewitnesses of the resurrection, and the foundation upon which the church was built (Eph. 2:20), as well as Spirit-inspired authors of most of the New Testament. (For more information on the apostles, see *Luke 6–10*, The MacArthur New Testament Commentary [Chicago: Moody, 2011], chaps. 2–8, and *Twelve Ordinary Men* [Nashville: W Publishing Group, 2002].)

But despite their unparalleled privileges, the apostles proved to be all too human. They observed firsthand the countless miracles Jesus performed, heard His teaching, and were discipled by Him. Yet they struggled with a lack of faith, for which Jesus repeatedly rebuked them (Matt. 8:26; 14:31; 16:8; 17:20). Even now, not long before the cross, their response to the Lord's teaching on humility and forgiveness was to say to Him, **"Increase our faith!"** That, however, was a humble, honest admission of weakness on their part. The Greek verb translated **increase** means "to add to," "supplement," "develop," or "grow." They were not denying that they possessed faith, but doubted that it was sufficiently strong. What Jesus demanded in this context seemed to them to be an impossible standard to live up to. It was completely contrary to what they had been taught by the religious leaders.

Like the apostles, humble people are quick to recognize their own inadequacy. "Who is adequate for these things?" the apostle Paul asked rhetorically (2 Cor. 2:16; cf. 3:5). His adequacy came from a humble dependence on God's all-sufficient grace (2 Cor. 12:9; cf. 4:7–12), which empowered him to "labor, striving according to His power, which mightily work[ed] within [him]" (Col. 1:29; cf. 1 Cor. 2:1–5; 15:10).

Jesus affirmed the validity of their question and replied by way of an analogy that indeed they did need a growing faith: **"If you had faith like a mustard seed, you would say to this mulberry tree, 'Be uprooted and be planted in the sea'; and it would obey you."** As noted in the discussion of Luke 13:19 in chapter 17 of this volume, the **mustard seed** was the smallest seed with which the people of Israel would have been familiar. Jesus' analogy calls for a faith that grows like a tiny mustard seed does into to a large shrub (mustard plants can reach fifteen feet in height).

Those who possess such a faith can do amazing things, which the Lord pictured using another analogy. If the apostles had this type of faith, He told them, they **would say to this mulberry tree, 'Be uprooted and be planted in the sea'; and it would obey** [them]." Mulberry trees have an extensive root system, so uprooting one would be a significant thing to do. But Jesus was not speaking of literally moving a tree; He was speaking metaphorically. The point is that those who trust Him will receive supernatural power to do what they could not do in their own human strength (cf. Matt. 17:20; Mark 11:23; John 14:12–14; 2 Cor. 12:10; Eph. 6:10).

Humble people are powerful people because they understand their weakness and depend completely on "Him who is able to do far more abundantly beyond all that we ask or think, according to the power that works within us" (Eph. 3:20).

HUMBLE PEOPLE ARE
CHARACTERIZED BY REJECTION OF HONOR

Which of you, having a slave plowing or tending sheep, will say to him when he has come in from the field, 'Come immediately and sit down to eat'? But will he not say to him, 'Prepare something for me to eat, and properly clothe yourself and serve me while I eat and drink; and afterward you may eat and drink'? He does not thank the slave because he did the things which were commanded, does he? So you too, when you do all the things which are commanded you, say, 'We are unworthy slaves; we have done only that which we ought to have done.'" (17:7–10)

Although some fail to see the connection, this concluding parable fits in with the overall theme of this section. The scribes and Pharisees were obsessed with being honored. In Matthew 23:5–7 Jesus said of them, "They do all their deeds to be noticed by men; for they broaden their phylacteries and lengthen the tassels of their garments. They love the place of honor at banquets and the chief seats in the synagogues, and respectful greetings in the market places, and being called Rabbi by men" (cf. Luke 20:46–47).

That attitude is not to characterize the true followers of Jesus Christ. There is a danger that as they recognize their weakness, trust in God's power, and are used by Him that they become arrogant and prideful. Lest they forget that everything they have and do is solely by God's grace, Jesus told this parable as a warning against spiritual pride.

Doulos (**slave**) refers to a person bound to an owner. That was a common way in which employment was handled, and could be very beneficial when the master treated his slave fairly and humanely. The New Testament frequently describes Christians as slaves of God and the Lord Christ (e.g., Acts 4:29; Rom. 1:1; Gal. 1:10; Col. 1:7; 4:12; 2 Tim. 2:24; 1 Peter 2:16; Rev. 1:1). Slaves were generally better off than freemen, who tended to be day laborers living from hand to mouth. Slaves had security, since they lived in the master's home and he met their needs.

This parable takes place in a rural, agricultural setting, probably depicting a small farm where the **slave** worked **plowing or tending sheep.** His master would not **say to him when he** came **in from the field, "Come immediately and sit down to eat,"** any more than an employer today would, under normal circumstances, not require an employee to put in a full day's work. Instead his master would **say to him, "Prepare something for me to eat, and properly clothe yourself and serve me while I eat and drink; and afterward you may eat and drink." He does not thank the slave because he did the things which were commanded, does he?** The slave would have understood his master's request as a normal part of his responsibility and would not have expected any special honor merely for fulfilling his full daily duty.

Jesus concluded the story by applying it to His disciples: **So you too, when you do all the things which are commanded you, say, "We are unworthy slaves; we have done only that which we ought to have done."** Humble people reject honor. They understand that nothing they do for God makes Him indebted to them. Their service to Him is their duty, and less than He deserves, and no matter what they do they are **unworthy** of the unmerited eternal blessings He graciously grants them.

But in the future, believers will be honored and rewarded when Jesus Himself serves them at the great heavenly banquet (Luke 12:37). Even that, however, will be the result of His grace. Never, either in this world or in heaven, will believers merit anything God lavishly gives them.

The message of our Lord's teaching in this section may be summed up in His statement, "For everyone who exalts himself will be humbled, and he who humbles himself will be exalted" (14:11; cf. 1:52; 18:14; James 4:10; 1 Peter 5:6).

Ten Men Healed; One Man Saved
(Luke 17:11–19)

30

While He was on the way to Jerusalem, He was passing between Samaria and Galilee. As He entered a village, ten leprous men who stood at a distance met Him; and they raised their voices, saying, "Jesus, Master, have mercy on us!" When He saw them, He said to them, "Go and show yourselves to the priests." And as they were going, they were cleansed. Now one of them, when he saw that he had been healed, turned back, glorifying God with a loud voice, and he fell on his face at His feet, giving thanks to Him. And he was a Samaritan. Then Jesus answered and said, "Were there not ten cleansed? But the nine—where are they? Was no one found who returned to give glory to God, except this foreigner?" And He said to him, "Stand up and go; your faith has made you well." (17:11–19)

Miraculous healing was a constant reality in our Lord's ministry. Matthew 4:23 notes that "Jesus was going throughout all Galilee ... healing every kind of disease and every kind of sickness among the people."

As "the news about Him spread throughout all Syria and they brought to Him all who were ill ... He healed them" (v. 24). At Peter's house in Capernaum, "they brought to Him many who were demon-possessed; and He cast out the spirits with a word, and healed all who were ill" (Matt. 8:16). Matthew 9:35 records that "Jesus was going through all the cities and villages, teaching in their synagogues and proclaiming the gospel of the kingdom, and healing every kind of disease and every kind of sickness." Before feeding the five thousand, Jesus "saw a large crowd, and felt compassion for them and healed their sick" (Matt. 14:14). Similarly, before the feeding of the four thousand, "large crowds came to Him, bringing with them those who were lame, crippled, blind, mute, and many others, and they laid them down at His feet; and He healed them" (Matt. 15:30). East of the Jordan River, "large crowds followed Him, and He healed them there" (Matt. 19:2). During Passion Week, the culmination of Christ's earthly ministry, "the blind and the lame came to Him in the temple, and He healed them" (Matt. 21:14; cf. 12:15; Luke 5:15).

The miracles the divine Lord performed, for which there was never a human explanation, provided incontrovertible evidence of His deity and thus convincing testimony to the truth of the Christian faith. They give evidence of His supernatural power supporting His claim to be God Himself (John 5:36; 10:25, 37–38; 14:11). The astonishing healing recorded here in Luke's gospel is one of the countless healing miracles Jesus performed as He banished illness and disease from Israel during His earthly ministry. It took place during His final journey to Jerusalem, which Luke has been chronicling since verse 51 of chapter 9. This healing is the fourth of five selected and recorded miracles from that journey Luke was inspired to recount (cf. 11:14; 13:10–13; 14:1–4; 18:35–43). The first three involved individuals, while the final one involved two persons (though Luke mentions only one of them). This miracle far surpasses the other four in extent. It is a demonstration of divine power that is unmistakable and undeniable—the simultaneous healing of ten men afflicted with leprosy, the most dreaded disease of that time.

In an earlier volume in this series, I wrote the following description of leprosy:

Like its Old Testament counterpart *lepras* (leprosy) is a general term for a number of skin conditions. The most severe of those was Hansen's disease, which is leprosy as it is known today....

Leprosy, or Hansen's disease, is known from ancient writings (c. 600 B.C.) from China, India, and Egypt, and from mummified remains from Egypt. It was common enough in Israel to warrant extensive regulation in the Mosaic law of those suffering from it and related skin diseases (Lev. 13–14). The disease is caused by the bacterium *Mycobacterium leprae*, discovered by the Norwegian scientist G. H. A. Hansen in 1873 (it was the first bacterium to be identified as the cause of a human disease). The bacterium was communicable through touch and breath.

Leprosy attacks the skin, peripheral nerves (especially near the wrists, elbows, and knees), and mucus membrane. It forms lesions on the skin, and can disfigure the face by collapsing the nose and causing folding of the skin (leading some to call it "lion's disease" due to the resulting lion-like appearance of the face). Contrary to popular belief, leprosy does not eat away the flesh. Due to the loss of feeling (especially in the hands and feet), people with the disease wear away their extremities and faces unknowingly. The horrible disfigurement caused by leprosy made it greatly feared, and caused lepers to be outcasts, cut off from all healthy society, for protection. (*Luke 1–5*, The MacArthur New Testament Commentary [Chicago: Moody, 2009], 313)

Adding to the physical suffering of those afflicted with leprosy was the attendant social stigma. Not only were lepers cut off from family, friends, and banned from the rest of society, their condition was also considered to be divine judgment for their sin (as it was in the case of Gehazi [2 Kings 5:25–27] and Uzziah [2 Chron. 26:16–23]. This was consistent with the traditional Jewish belief that suffering was God's judgment for sin [cf. Job 4:7–9; John 9:1–3]).

Although it describes an actual event this story, like a parable, is rich with spiritual truth. It is an amazing demonstration of divine goodness, tenderness, compassion, and mercy, as well as Christ's divine power to heal many of incurable disease and restore them to full health. It is also a story of gratitude, worship, and salvation, while at the same time a tale of shocking ingratitude. It is the story not only of ten lepers who were healed physically, but also of one man who was healed spiritually and eternally.

THE TEN WHO WERE HEALED

While He was on the way to Jerusalem, He was passing between Samaria and Galilee. As He entered a village, ten leprous men who stood at a distance met Him; and they raised their voices, saying, "Jesus, Master, have mercy on us!" When He saw them, He said to them, "Go and show yourselves to the priests." And as they were going, they were cleansed. (17:11–14)

As noted above, this incident took place while Jesus **was on the way to Jerusalem.** Before arriving there for the final time at the beginning of Passion Week, the Lord made three brief visits to the city and its vicinity. He went there for the Feast of Tabernacles (John 7,8), the Feast of Dedication (John 9, 10), and to Bethany, which was near Jerusalem, where He raised Lazarus from the dead. After performing that miracle, Jesus left the environs of Jerusalem for the village of Ephraim (John 11:54), located in the region described here as **between Samaria and Galilee,** where this incident likely took place.

When Jesus **entered** the unnamed **village,** He was confronted with an all too common scene: **ten leprous men who stood at a distance met Him.** Unlike the leper in Luke 5:12–13, who came close enough to Jesus that He could touch him, these men kept their distance as the law required (cf. Lev. 13:45–46; Num. 5:2–3; 2 Kings 7:3).

> Lepers were strictly forbidden to come near other people (cf. Luke 17:12), or to interact with anyone except other lepers. So great was the fear of contagion that lepers were barred from Jerusalem or any other walled city (cf. 2 Kings 7:3). They were forbidden to come within six feet of a healthy person (one hundred and fifty feet if the wind was blowing from the direction of the leper) and were restricted to a special compartment in the synagogue. One rabbi refused to eat an egg bought on a street where there was a leper. Another advocated throwing stones at lepers to force them to keep their distance. (cf. Alfred Edersheim, *The Life and Times of Jesus the Messiah* [Grand Rapids: Eerdmans, 1974], 1:492–95)

> It is now known that leprosy (Hansen's disease) is not highly contagious, since ninety to ninety-five percent of the human race is immune to it. Exactly how the disease is transmitted is not known for certain, but people living in close contact with those with untreated leprosy had a higher risk of becoming infected. But lepers in biblical times were

isolated not only due to fear of infection, but also because they were ceremonially unclean (Lev. 13:45–46). In rabbinic teaching, leprosy was second only to contact with a dead body in terms of defilement. "Not merely actual contact with the leper, but even his entrance defiled a habitation, and everything in it, to the beams of the roof. . . . If he even put his head into a place, it became unclean." (Edersheim, 1:494, 95). (*Luke 1–5*, 314)

This was a pathetic, lonely group of outcasts, eking out a survival existence on the fringe of society.

Seeing Him approaching, **they raised their voices, saying, "Jesus, Master, have mercy on us!"** *Epistatēs* (**Master**) appears in the New Testament only in Luke's gospel, always in reference to Jesus (cf. 5:5; 8:24, 45; 9:33, 49). This is the only occasion where the term was used by someone other than His disciples. *Epistatēs* denotes someone who possesses notable authority or power. The lepers' use of it to address Jesus indicates that they had knowledge of His miraculous ability to heal, which was widely known from His ministry in Galilee and Samaria. Their plea, **have mercy on us,** was a common expression used by people who asked Jesus in pity and compassion to heal them (e.g., Matt. 9:27; 15:22; 17:15; 20:30–31; Mark 10:47–48). Their disease was incurable; their situation hopeless; their lives miserable. Jesus offered their only chance for deliverance. Mustering what hopeful faith they had, these ten desperate men begged the Healer to heal them.

Their pitiful cries attracted the Lord's attention. Unlike the leper whom He healed earlier in Luke's gospel, Jesus did not lay His hands on all of them (cf. 5:13). He had no reluctance to approach and touch lepers, but on this occasion, **when He saw them,** He did not immediately heal them but **He said to them, "Go and show yourselves to the priests"** so that they could be examined and be declared clean (cf. 5:14). Some may wonder why Jesus did not say, "Be healed" at that moment. No doubt in part He was testing their faith in His ability to heal them in His time. His command would be an affirmation of the validity of the law of God (cf. Matt. 5:17–19). By obeying, these men were demonstrating faith and fulfilling their obligation as the law required. The priests who would receive the ex-lepers functioned as the local health inspectors, and there was an elaborate process, lasting for eight days and involving various examinations, sacrifices and rituals, to determine whether a person was free of leprosy (Lev. 14:1–32).

In the type of stunning understatement that describes most of Christ's miracles, Luke merely notes that **as they were going** to show themselves to the priests as He had commanded, the ten men **were cleansed.** There were no spectacular, dramatic words, special effects, or histrionics, just a complete, instantaneous cleansing of all traces of the disease that had infected and disfigured their bodies.

Ironically, the very priests who vehemently rejected Jesus would have to validate the undeniable fact that the lepers had been healed. They would be forced to confirm His supernatural power and strict adherence to the law, and thus become reluctant witnesses to His deity. And during the eight days that their healing was being validated, the men themselves would be living witnesses to Christ's divinity.

The One Who Was Saved

Now one of them, when he saw that he had been healed, turned back, glorifying God with a loud voice, and he fell on his face at His feet, giving thanks to Him. And he was a Samaritan. Then Jesus answered and said, "Were there not ten cleansed? But the nine—where are they? Was no one found who returned to give glory to God, except this foreigner?" And He said to him, "Stand up and go; your faith has made you well." (17:15–19)

Up to this point, the ten men had acted in unison. All had pled for Jesus to heal them; all had obeyed His command and started on their way to the priests; all had been healed. At that point, the uniformity was broken as **one of them,** surely full of joy, amazement, and wonder **when he saw that he had been healed, turned back** toward Jesus. They were all overjoyed at the prospect of returning to a normal life with family and friends, but only this one soul grasped the profound implications of what had happened to him. Recognizing that he had been in the presence of God incarnate, he wanted more than a mere physical healing; his heart longed for salvation from the divine Healer. The Jews knew that the

Old Testament taught that God was primarily a Redeemer and a Savior (Job 19:25; Ps. 19:14; Is. 41:14; 43:3, 11, 14; 45:15, 21; 49:26; 60:16). He understood the reality of his sinful alienation and need for forgiveness and reconciliation with God.

This man did three things that reveal the longing of his heart for that reconciliation. First, unable to restrain his joyful praise, he began **glorifying God with a loud voice.** Luke used the phrase **loud voice** to convey the idea of strong emotion, such as that displayed by Elizabeth (1:42), the followers of Jesus at the triumphal entry (Luke 19:37), and even demons when they were confronted by the Son of God (4:33; 8:28). This may have been the first time in years that he was able to speak above a rasping whisper, since leprosy sometimes affected the larynx.

Second, **he fell on his face at** Jesus' **feet** in worship. That was an affirmation of Christ's deity, since the Old Testament taught that only God was to be worshiped (Ex. 20:3–5; 34:14; Deut. 5:7–9).

Finally, he gave **thanks** to Jesus. The other nine no doubt intended to worship God in the temple. This man, however, did not worship Him through religious ritual at a temple from which God had long since withdrawn His glory. Instead, recognizing the manifestation of divine power and grace he had witnessed, he worshiped God in Christ, the true temple; the one in whom "all the fullness of Deity dwells in bodily form" (Col. 2:9).

What made his response even more amazing was that this man **was a Samaritan.** The Jews and Samaritans hated each other and, under normal circumstances, had no dealings with each other (John 4:9). It was only because the other lepers were outcasts from Jewish society that he was able to associate with them. The Jews certainly would not have expected God to heal or save a Samaritan. Yet not only did God save many people from a Samaritan village (John 4:39, 41–42), but also the first person to whom Jesus revealed that He was the Messiah was a Samaritan woman (John 4:25–26).

The Lord then asked three rhetorical questions that highlight the ingratitude and indifference of the nine. The Greek form of the first question, **"Were there not ten cleansed?"** expects an affirmative answer, since there were ten lepers and they had all been cleansed. Jesus was in effect saying, "There were ten cleansed, weren't there?" But only one had returned to give praise, worship, and thanks to Jesus, which prompted His second rhetorical question, **"But the nine—where are they?"** No answer is given, but presumably they were hurrying on their way to the priests to begin the procedure for being declared clean. The word translated **where** is at the end of the phrase in the Greek text for emphasis, making the question literally read, "But the nine, they are where?" They also should have been there gratefully worshiping Jesus, but having taken what they were given from Him, they felt no compulsion to remain. Since their interest in Him was only selfish and superficial, they had no desire to worship or even give Him thanks.

Sadly, that reflected the prevailing attitude toward Jesus throughout His ministry. Trusting in their Abrahamic lineage, the Jewish people believed that they were thereby entitled to blessing from God. They had no true sense of sin, remorse, or desperation in the face of judgment and hell. They were righteous in themselves and so not looking for a savior from sin. A political and military Messiah was their expectation; someone who would powerfully deliver them from their enemies, provide them with all they needed, and heal all of their diseases (cf. John 6:14–15, 26).

Unlike the hardhearted, impenitent, self-satisfied nine men, the repentant man knew that he needed a Savior. He recognized that he had come face-to-face with God and his soul was traumatized by an overwhelming sense of his sinfulness. Peter had that same reaction after Jesus demonstrated His deity by providing a miraculous catch of fish. "When Simon Peter saw that, he fell down at Jesus' feet, saying, 'Go away from me Lord, for I am a sinful man, O Lord!'" (Luke 5:8).

Jesus' final rhetorical question, **"Was no one found who re - turned to give glory to God, except this foreigner?"** emphasizes that he was not one of the Jewish people. He was a stranger to the covenants, yet he alone of the ten healed lepers **returned to give glory to God.** Barred from worshiping Him in the inner court of the temple, he humbly worshiped God incarnate in the person of Jesus.

The story reached its wonderful conclusion when the Lord **said to him, "Stand up and go; your faith has made you well."** The phrase **made you well** does not translate the word *katharizō* ("cleansed") from verse 14, or the word *iaomai* ("healed") from verse 15. It is *sōzō*, the familiar New Testament term for being saved from sin (e.g., Matt. 1:21; 10:22; 19:25; 24:13; Luke 7:50; 8:12; 13:23; 19:10; John 3:17; 12:47; Acts 2:21, 47; 4:12;

16:30–31; Rom. 5:9–10; 10:9, 13; 1 Cor. 1:18; 2 Cor. 2:15; Eph. 2:8; 1 Tim. 1:15; 2 Tim. 1:9; Titus 3:5; Heb. 7:25; James 1:21). This man alone out of the ten who were miraculously healed received the second miracle of salvation from sin. His trust, gratitude, humility, commitment, love, praise, and worship mark his faith in Jesus as the faith that saves.

But this incident is not merely the story of ten individuals. The one who was redeemed and the nine who were not are representative of the general attitude toward Jesus. The nine represent unbelieving Israel, who had only a superficial interest in Jesus. The people wanted what they could get from Him—healings, food, deliverance from demons, rescue from the oppression of Roman rule—but refused to acknowledge Him as God and worship Him.

On the other hand the penitent man pictures the believing remnant among the Jews and any non-Jewish repentant sinners who will enter the kingdom of God (Matt. 21:31–32). Both groups enjoyed the benefit of Jesus' power and basked in the wonder of His teaching and miracles. But the majority were content with the superficial, temporal benefits they could get from Him. Only a few humbled themselves, glorified Him as God, worshiped Him, and desired that He transform their hearts.

All people face the same two choices. They can be content with experiencing the common grace of the God who "causes His sun to rise on the evil and the good, and sends rain on the righteous and the unrighteous" (Matt. 5:45). Or they can embrace Jesus Christ as Master and Savior and cry out in penitence, "God, be merciful to me, the sinner!" (Luke 18:13). Only the latter will be justified (v. 14) and enter God's eternal kingdom.

The Invisible Kingdom of God
(Luke 17:20–21)

31

Now having been questioned by the Pharisees as to when the kingdom of God was coming, He answered them and said, "The kingdom of God is not coming with signs to be observed; nor will they say, 'Look, here it is!' or, 'There it is!' For behold, the kingdom of God is in your midst." (17:20–21)

The experience of a kingdom is foreign to most Americans. The United States was born in a revolution against the rule of the British monarch George III, and has never had a king or absolute ruler in its history. Although monarchy was the most common form of government for centuries, few countries now are ruled by a king and those with absolute, unchecked power, privilege, and authority are regularly deposed. In those countries that still recognize monarchs they provide some cultural influence and perform ceremonial duties only, while having little or no actual power.

But it is precisely that unilateral rule and authority which society disdains that God claims for Himself. He is the absolute King (Ps 24:8–10;

47:2; 1 Tim. 6:15) who rules over His kingdom (Ps. 45:6; Matt. 6:33) with sole supremacy, absolute sovereignty, and the unrestrained, free exercise of His will. The apostle Paul closed the eleventh chapter of Romans with a benediction that extols God's absolute sovereignty:

> Oh, the depth of the riches both of the wisdom and knowledge of God! How unsearchable are His judgments and unfathomable His ways! For who has known the mind of the Lord, or who became His counselor? Or who has first given to Him that it might be paid back to him again? For from Him and through Him and to Him are all things. To Him be the glory forever. Amen. (Rom. 11:33–36)

Isaiah asked a series of rhetorical questions that form an Old Testament counterpart to Paul's doxology:

> Who has measured the waters in the hollow of His hand, and marked off the heavens by the span, and calculated the dust of the earth by the measure, and weighed the mountains in a balance and the hills in a pair of scales? Who has directed the Spirit of the Lord, or as His counselor has informed Him? With whom did He consult and who gave Him understanding? And who taught Him in the path of justice and taught Him knowledge and informed Him of the way of understanding? (Isa. 40:12–14)

God has supreme wisdom and knowledge, and makes judgments on the basis of information unknown to man. No one gives Him counsel, nor is He obligated to anyone. Based on His perfect knowledge, wisdom, power, and will, God does exactly what He wants when He wants with whom He wants, and for the purpose that He wants.

Job understood that truth. In Job 42:2 he said to God, "I know that You can do all things, and that no purpose of Yours can be thwarted." In Psalm 33:11 the psalmist declared that "the counsel of the Lord stands forever, the plans of His heart from generation to generation." Isaiah wrote, "For the Lord of hosts has planned, and who can frustrate it? And as for His stretched-out hand, who can turn it back?" (Isa. 14:27). Later in Isaiah's prophecy God declared,

> Remember this, and be assured; recall it to mind, you transgressors. Remember the former things long past, for I am God, and there is no other; I am God, and there is no one like Me, declaring the end from the beginning, and from ancient times things which have not been done,

saying, "My purpose will be established, and I will accomplish all My good pleasure." (Isa. 46:8–10)

In a doxology recorded in 1 Chronicles 29:10–13,

> David said, "Blessed are You, O Lord God of Israel our father, forever and ever. Yours, O Lord, is the greatness and the power and the glory and the victory and the majesty, indeed everything that is in the heavens and the earth; Yours is the dominion, O Lord, and You exalt Yourself as head over all. Both riches and honor come from You, and You rule over all, and in Your hand is power and might; and it lies in Your hand to make great and to strengthen everyone. Now therefore, our God, we thank You, and praise Your glorious name."

The Bible teaches that God's sovereignty extends over both the material kingdom, and the spiritual kingdom. The material kingdom is the external, universal kingdom in which God reigns over everything He created. Psalm 10:16 says that "the Lord is King forever and ever"; Psalm 29:10 that "the Lord sits as King forever"; and Psalm 47:2 that He is "a great King over all the earth." Psalm 103:19 declares that "the Lord has established His throne in the heavens, and His sovereignty rules over all," while Psalm 145:13 adds that His "dominion endures throughout all generations" (cf. Dan. 4:34).

The universal kingdom is suffering the effects of rebellion. It is cursed because of sin, both that of the human race, and of Satan and the demons. That curse has stained it both spiritually and physically. As a result, what scientists call the second law of thermodynamics is operating, and the universe is running down, heading toward its disastrous dissolution when "the heavens will be destroyed by burning, and the elements will melt with intense heat!" (2 Peter 3:12). Spiritually, Satan and his demon hosts, along with the fallen human race, persist in foolishly and futilely attempting to thwart the kingdom purposes of almighty God.

The universal created kingdom is not, however, in view in this passage. The Lord's discussion with the Pharisees on this occasion in - volved His internal, personal, spiritual kingdom. That realm of God's rule, the sphere of salvation, includes all those whom God has redeemed. God reveals His authority over the universal kingdom through the general revelation manifested in creation, in human reason, and in the moral law written in the heart and conscience. He reveals the nature of His rule over the spiritual kingdom through the special revelation of Scripture.

As He does in the universal kingdom, God exercises absolute authority in His spiritual kingdom. He is sovereign over who enters it and how they enter, exercises absolute right, power, and privilege, and does exactly what He wills by the means of His Word. Thus, Jesus Christ is Lord and King over the spiritual kingdom just as He is over the material kingdom; He is sovereign in the universe, and He is sovereign over His people. God's external, universal rule is direct; His internal, personal rule is also direct, through the indwelling Holy Spirit.

In contrast to His rule in the universal kingdom, which is immediate (without a mediator), God mediates His rule over the spiritual kingdom through agents. Through those men He gave the special revelation in Scripture that ushers people into that kingdom. Although angels were involved in mediating the law (Acts 7:53; Gal. 3:19; Heb. 2:2), for the most part God used men, including Adam, Noah, Abraham, Isaac, Jacob, Joseph, Samuel, and Israel's priests, prophets, and kings (e.g., David, Solomon). God channeled His mediation through the nation of Israel, "to whom belongs the adoption as sons, and the glory and the covenants and the giving of the Law and the temple service and the promises, whose are the fathers, and from whom is the Christ according to the flesh, who is over all, God blessed forever. Amen" (Rom. 9:4–5).

But the culminating, unequalled, all-glorious mediator is the Lord Jesus Christ. He is far superior to all other mediators first of all because He is God incarnate; "the radiance of [the Father's] glory and the exact representation of His nature" (Heb. 1:3) and the one in whom "all the fullness of Deity dwells in bodily form" (Col. 2:9; cf. John 1:1, 14; 14:9). Further, Jesus is the ultimate mediator because His sacrificial death on the cross makes all reconciliation possible. Paul wrote, "For there is one God, and one mediator also between God and men, the man Christ Jesus" (1 Tim. 2:5). Before His birth the angel Gabriel told Mary that Jesus "will be great and will be called the Son of the Most High; and the Lord God will give Him the throne of His father David; and He will reign over the house of Jacob forever, and His kingdom will have no end" (Luke 1:32–33). His coming as King was the fulfillment of Israel's hope. Psalm 2:6 speaks prophetically of God's establishing the Messiah as King, while Isaiah wrote of Him,

> For a child will be born to us, a son will be given to us; and the government will rest on His shoulders; and His name will be called Wonderful Counselor, Mighty God, Eternal Father, Prince of Peace. There will be no end to the increase of His government or of peace, on the throne of David and over his kingdom, to establish it and to uphold it with justice and righteousness from then on and forevermore. The zeal of the Lord of hosts will accomplish this. (Isa. 9:6–7; cf. Jer. 23:5)

Jesus did not come into the world to establish the universal kingdom; He was already King over that realm (cf. Eph. 1:20–21), as His power over death, disease, and creation demonstrated. Jesus did come to provide access into His spiritual kingdom for His people. But the Jewish people did not understand that, and were expecting the Messiah to establish the promised temporal, earthly kingdom. In this brief passage, the Pharisees questioned Jesus about the kingdom, and He corrected their misunderstanding regarding it.

THE KINGDOM QUESTIONED

Now having been questioned by the Pharisees as to when the kingdom of God was coming, (17:20*a*)

The kingdom the Jewish people expected Messiah to establish encompassed everything promised in the Abrahamic (Gen. 12), Davidic (2 Sam. 7), and New (Jer. 31) covenants. According to the prophets, it will be marked by a time of unprecedented peace in nature, when predators will no longer harm their prey (Isa. 11:6–7) and children will play in safety near venomous snakes (v. 8). The topography of the planet will be drastically changed; for example, the Mount of Olives will be split in two (Zech. 14:4). Messiah's kingdom will be marked by peace (Isa. 32:17–18; Mic. 4:2–4), joy (Isa. 61:7, 10), comfort (Isa. 40:1–2), prosperity (Amos 9:13–15), health (Isa. 35:5–6), holiness (Isa. 35:8), truth (Isa. 65:16) and Messiah's personal rule (Isa. 9:6–7; 11:1–4, 10).

The nineteenth-century historian Emil Schürer summarized the Jewish people's expectations regarding the coming of Messiah and the establishing of His kingdom as follows: First, the coming of Messiah would be preceded by a time of tribulation. Second, in the midst of the turmoil an Elijah-like prophet would appear heralding Messiah's coming. Third, Messiah would establish His glorious kingdom, and vindicate His people. Fourth, the nations would ally themselves together to fight Messiah. Fifth, Messiah would destroy all those opposing nations. Sixth, Jerusalem would be restored, and made new and glorious. Seventh, the dispersed Jews scattered all over the world would return to Israel. Eighth, Israel would become the center of the world and all the nations would be subjugated to the Messiah. Finally, the Messiah would establish His kingdom, which would be a time of eternal peace, righteousness, and glory (*A History of the Jewish People in the Time of Jesus Christ* [New York: Scribners, 1896], 2:154–178).

Those expectations were drawn from the Old Testament and embellished in the extrabiblical writings. They reveal that the Jews did not see two comings of Messiah. They were not looking for the spiritual kingdom; they were not looking for a Savior who would be the sacrifice for sins, because they regarded themselves as righteous (cf. Luke 18:9–12).

What the people of Israel were eagerly anticipating was the establishment of the earthly kingdom. Luke 19:11 records that "Jesus went on to tell a parable, because He was near Jerusalem, and they supposed that the kingdom of God was going to appear immediately." The frenzied crowds at the triumphal entry shouted, "Hosanna! Blessed is he who comes in the name of the Lord, even the King of Israel" (John 12:13). That misunderstanding of the purpose of His first coming explains why Jesus was **questioned by the Pharisees as to when the kingdom of God was coming** (cf. the disciples' similar question in Luke 17:37). They missed the reality that the kingdom comes first in the hearts of believers before it will be fully realized in its millennial glory (see the exposition of 13:18–21 in chapter 17 of this volume).

Neither Jesus nor the kingdom that was the constant theme of His preaching (cf. 4:43; 6:20; 7:28; 8:1; 9:11, 60, 62; 11:20; 12:31; 13:20, 28–29; 16:16; 18:16–17; Matt. 4:17) met the Pharisees' expectations. Jesus claimed to be a king, but He had no regal coronation or bearing. He was born under the most humble of circumstances, in a stable with a manger as His crib. Instead of royalty, His first visitors were lowly shepherds. Even when the magi (king makers from Persia) arrived, their visit to Him was private. And He grew up in the despised village of Nazareth (John 1:46), which was located in Galilee, a region looked down on by the more sophisticated Judeans.

The Pharisees constantly demanded that Jesus perform the type of spectacular, cataclysmic signs in the heavens and on the earth (cf. Joel 1:15; 2:1, 2, 10, 11, 30–32; 3:1–2, 14–20) that they associated with Messiah's coming (cf. 11:16; Matt. 12:38; 16:1; John 2:18; 4:48; 6:30). When He did not, they refused to believe in Him, slandered Him, and sought to discredit Him. That consistently cynical attitude makes it likely that the questions they addressed to Jesus on this occasion were insincere and intended to mock Him (cf. 16:14).

THE KINGDOM EXPLAINED

He answered them and said, "The kingdom of God is not coming with signs to be observed; nor will they say, 'Look, here it is!' or, 'There it is!' For behold, the kingdom of God is in your midst." (17:20*b*–21)

As He consistently did in His confrontations with the Pharisees, Jesus dismantled their misconceptions. The present form of **the kingdom of God is not coming with signs to be observed,** He told them. Their constant seeking after signs was therefore misguided, based on a misunderstanding of the nature of the spiritual kingdom. There are no visible signs of the coming of that aspect of the kingdom that would lead people to **say, "Look, here it is!" or, "There it is!";** its coming will not be heralded by visible spectacles.

The Pharisees failed to discern the spiritual kingdom because not having experienced the new birth, they were dead and blind. Jesus told the prominent Pharisee Nicodemus, "Truly, truly, I say to you, unless one is born again he cannot see the kingdom of God" (John 3:3; cf. Matt. 13:11–16). As the apostle Paul would later write, "A natural man does not accept the things of the Spirit of God, for they are foolishness to him; and he cannot understand them, because they are spiritually appraised" (1 Cor. 2:14). Those who fail to recognize the King cannot see His kingdom.

But the spiritual kingdom will not always remain invisible. At Christ's second coming, it will be unmistakably visible to all (Rev. 1:7; cf. 19:11–21). Not only will He be revealed in all His glory, but the redeemed will also be unveiled for who they really are (Rom. 8:19–21; 1 John 3:2). But until then the kingdom will continue to expand invisibly as people are added to it by salvation.

Idou (**behold**) introduces the Lord's shocking statement that **"the kingdom of God is in your midst."** *Entos* (**midst**) literally means "inside." In its only other appearance in the New Testament, the word refers to the inside of a cup (Matt. 23:26). Many translators, seeking to avoid the apparent difficulty of Jesus saying that the kingdom was inside the unbelieving Pharisees, translate the phrase in which it appears **in your midst.** However a different phrase, *en mesō,* is regularly used to communicate the idea of "in the midst of," or "among" (e.g., Matt. 10:16; Luke 2:46; 8:7; 10:3; 22:27; 24:36; Acts 1:15; 2:22; Heb. 2:12). The apparent difficulty is easily resolved by understanding **your** in the broadest national sense rather than as a narrow reference to the Pharisees. As was inevitably the case, the crowd listening to the Lord's dialogue with the Pharisees ran the gamut from the outright rejecters to the curious but uncommitted, to the true disciples of Jesus. The Lord was reinforcing the point that the spiritual kingdom is internal and not manifested by observable signs.

The kingdom of which Jesus spoke is, as Paul wrote, marked by "righteousness and peace and joy in the Holy Spirit" (Rom. 14:17). It exists in the hearts of all those in whom the King lives. The wonder of wonders is that the Trinity takes up residence in the hearts of those who embrace Christ and enter the spiritual kingdom. In John 14:17 Jesus promised that the Holy Spirit would indwell believers, while in verse 23 He added, "If anyone loves Me, he will keep My word; and My Father will love him, and We will come to him and make Our abode with him."

Entering the spiritual kingdom by the gospel became the message of the early church. During the forty days between His resurrection and His ascension, Jesus prepared them to preach that message by "speaking of the things concerning the kingdom of God" (Acts 1:3). Philip the evangelist's ministry involved "preaching the good news about the kingdom of God" (Acts 8:12). The apostle Paul "strengthen[ed] the souls of the disciples, encouraging them to continue in the faith, and saying, 'Through many tribulations we must enter the kingdom of God'" (Acts 14:22). In Ephesus "he entered the synagogue and continued speaking out boldly for three months, reasoning and persuading them about the kingdom of God" (Acts 19:8). When he met with the leaders of the Jewish community at Rome Paul "was explaining to them by solemnly testifying about the kingdom of God and trying to persuade them concerning Jesus, from both the Law of Moses and from the Prophets, from morning until evening" (Acts 28:23). He told the Corinthians that "the kingdom of God does not consist in words but in power" (1 Cor. 4:20), and warned them that "the unrighteous will not inherit the kingdom of God" (6:9; cf. Gal. 5:21; Eph. 5:5). So central was the kingdom to Paul's ministry that he described himself as a worker for the kingdom of God (Col. 4:11).

The prophesied signs concerning the future earthly kingdom that the Pharisees demanded from Jesus will be manifested when that kingdom is established at the second coming. Our Lord's return to judge unbelievers and establish His earthly kingdom is the subject of the next section of Luke's gospel.

Seven Characteristics of the King's Coming (Luke 17:22–37)

32

And He said to the disciples, "The days will come when you will long to see one of the days of the Son of Man, and you will not see it. They will say to you, 'Look there! Look here!' Do not go away, and do not run after them. For just like the lightning, when it flashes out of one part of the sky, shines to the other part of the sky, so will the Son of Man be in His day. But first He must suffer many things and be rejected by this generation. And just as it happened in the days of Noah, so it will be also in the days of the Son of Man: they were eating, they were drinking, they were marrying, they were being given in marriage, until the day that Noah entered the ark, and the flood came and destroyed them all. It was the same as happened in the days of Lot: they were eating, they were drinking, they were buying, they were selling, they were planting, they were building; but on the day that Lot went out from Sodom it rained fire and brimstone from heaven and destroyed them all. It will be just the same on the day that the Son of Man is revealed. On that day, the one who is on the housetop

and whose goods are in the house must not go down to take them out; and likewise the one who is in the field must not turn back. Remember Lot's wife. Whoever seeks to keep his life will lose it, and whoever loses his life will preserve it. I tell you, on that night there will be two in one bed; one will be taken and the other will be left. There will be two women grinding at the same place; one will be taken and the other will be left. Two men will be in the field; one will be taken and the other will be left." And answering they said to Him, "Where, Lord?" And He said to them, "Where the body is, there also the vultures will be gathered." (17:22–37)

All true Christians who understand Scripture, love the Lord Jesus Christ, and are concerned about His glory desire His return. They desire to see Him set aside His long humiliation and return in majesty and glory to reign. Like the Thessalonians, they eagerly "wait for [God's] Son from heaven, whom He raised from the dead, that is Jesus" (1 Thess. 1:10) and are "looking for the blessed hope and the appearing of the glory of our great God and Savior, Christ Jesus" (Titus 2:13). Paul referred to Christians as those "who have loved [Christ's] appearing" (2 Tim. 4:8). At the close of the book of Revelation, the apostle John responded to Christ's promise, "Yes, I am coming quickly" by saying, "Amen. Come, Lord Jesus" (Rev. 22:20).

It is a characteristic of the spiritually mature that they long for the second coming not for personal gain, but for the glory of Christ. They desire to see Jesus vindicated and exalted (cf. John 17:24), instead of reviled and dishonored. On the other hand, those who care little about Christ's honor and God's glory, who view Jesus as the means to their own personal fulfillment, have little interest in the second coming. Contemporary evangelism encourages that self-centered perspective. It makes the salvation of sinners the goal and relegates God to being merely the means to accomplishing that goal. But that is the opposite of what Scripture teaches. The glory of God is the goal of redemption, and the salvation of sinners is a means of accomplishing that goal.

Scoffers have always denied that Jesus Christ will return literally and bodily to establish and reign over His earthly kingdom. "Know this first of all," Peter wrote, "that in the last days mockers will come with their mocking, following after their own lusts, and saying, 'Where is the promise of His coming? For ever since the fathers fell asleep, all continues just as it was from the beginning of creation'" (2 Peter 3:3–4). If the universe is a closed, naturalistic system of cause and effect, then divine intervention—including the return of Christ—is ruled out *a priori.* In modern times that view became known as uniformitarianism, and was popularized in geology by Charles Lyell, a contemporary of Charles Darwin. Uniformitarianism denies God's interventions in the world's history, in particular His creation of the universe in six days and the worldwide flood of Noah's day.

Uniformity as a natural principle is beneficial, and expresses God's sustained, predictable, consistent design for His creation. If the natural laws and processes built into the universe at its creation did not normally function in a systematic and stable manner, there would be chaos. Thus, the Bible teaches the truth that the universe and our world function as the uniform operation of natural causes in an open system, but in which the Creator can (and does) supernaturally intervene. To advocate uniformitarianism as an inviolable law so rigid that it denies the possibility of God acting in history is to believe a foolish and damning lie.

The Bible teaches the reality of Christ's second coming just as certainly as it does that of His first coming. But just as the Old Testament prophets could not fully understand all that was involved in Christ's first coming before it happened (1 Peter 1:10–11), so also His second coming is shrouded in mystery. The basic outline of the events surrounding the second coming is clear. The rapture of the church will be followed by the seven-year tribulation, at the end of which Christ will return in judgment and establish His thousand-year earthly kingdom. After a final rebellion led by Satan is crushed, the current heaven and earth will be destroyed, the Great White Throne judgment will take place, and a new heaven and new earth will be created for all the righteous, which will last forever. Because no prophetic sign is necessary before the Rapture, the next event on the prophetic horizon, every generation of Christians lives in the anticipation of Christ's imminent coming for His church (1 John 3:1–3).

The return of the Lord Jesus Christ is essential for the following reasons.

First, the promise of God demands the second coming. Of the

more than three hundred prophecies in the Old Testament related to the coming of Christ, only about a third of them were fulfilled at His first coming. That leaves about two thirds—more than two hundred—prophecies yet to be fulfilled at His return.

Second, the teaching of Jesus Christ demands the second coming. The Lord repeatedly spoke of His return (v. 30; 12:40; 18:8; 21:27; Matt. 16:27–28; 24:27, 30, 37, 39, 44; 25:31; 26:64; Rev. 3:11), and His trustworthiness demands that those predictions be fulfilled.

Third, the revelation by the Holy Spirit demands the second coming. He is the one who inspired the Bible and every prophecy of the second coming it contains. His trustworthiness mandates their fulfillment.

Fourth, God's plan for the church demands the second coming. In John 14:3 Jesus promised, "If I go and prepare a place for you, I will come again and receive you to Myself, that where I am, there you may be also." Paul described that same event, the rapture of the church, in 1 Thessalonians 4:14–17:

> For if we believe that Jesus died and rose again, even so God will bring with Him those who have fallen asleep in Jesus. For this we say to you by the word of the Lord, that we who are alive and remain until the coming of the Lord, will not precede those who have fallen asleep. For the Lord Himself will descend from heaven with a shout, with the voice of the archangel and with the trumpet of God, and the dead in Christ will rise first. Then we who are alive and remain will be caught up together with them in the clouds to meet the Lord in the air, and so we shall always be with the Lord. (cf. 1 Cor. 15:51–52)

Having been taken to heaven in the rapture, the church will return with Christ at His second coming (Rev. 19:14). The fulfillment of those passages necessitates Christ's return.

Fifth, the future of Israel demands the second coming. Zechariah's prophecy records God's promise of Israel's salvation:

> I will pour out on the house of David and on the inhabitants of Jerusalem, the Spirit of grace and of supplication, so that they will look on Me whom they have pierced; and they will mourn for Him, as one mourns for an only son, and they will weep bitterly over Him like the bitter weeping over a firstborn. (12:10)

> In that day a fountain will be opened for the house of David and for the inhabitants of Jerusalem, for sin and for impurity. (13:1)

It is after Israel's repentance and salvation that the second coming and the establishment of the promised kingdom takes place (14:4–9). Thus, Israel's hope is inextricably linked to the Lord's return.

Sixth, the corruption of the world demands the second coming. The present sin-cursed, Satan-dominated world cannot be the final chapter of redemptive history. Therefore,

> the Lord Jesus will be revealed from heaven with His mighty angels in flaming fire, dealing out retribution to those who do not know God and to those who do not obey the gospel of our Lord Jesus. These will pay the penalty of eternal destruction, away from the presence of the Lord and from the glory of His power. (2 Thess. 1:7–9)

Seventh, the exaltation of Jesus Christ demands the second coming. The last view of Him that the world sees cannot be of Him hanging on a cross between two thieves. He will return in glory when

> immediately after the tribulation of those days the sun will be darkened, and the moon will not give its light, and the stars will fall from the sky, and the powers of the heavens will be shaken. And then the sign of the Son of Man will appear in the sky, and then all the tribes of the earth will mourn, and they will see the Son of Man coming on the clouds of the sky with power and great glory. And He will send forth His angels with a great trumpet and they will gather together His elect from the four winds, from one end of the sky to the other. (Matt. 24:29–31; cf. 25:31–32; Rev. 5:1–14)

Eighth, the destruction of Satan (Gen. 3:15) demands the second coming. When the Lord Jesus Christ returns, Satan will be bound and sentenced to the abyss (the bottomless pit) for a thousand years (Rev. 20:1–3), and ultimately sentenced to the lake of fire (v. 10).

Finally, as noted above, the hope of the church demands the second coming (1 Thess. 1:10; Titus 2:13).

As discussed in the previous chapter of this volume, the Jewish people failed to understand that there are two aspects of the kingdom: the visible earthly kingdom, and the invisible spiritual kingdom. The promised earthly kingdom that they were eagerly anticipating at Christ's first coming will be established at His second coming. But only those who are part of the spiritual kingdom will enter the earthly kingdom.

Having discussed the present spiritual kingdom in verses 20–21, the Lord in this section turned to the future earthly kingdom. Unlike the spiritual kingdom, the coming of the earthly kingdom will be manifest to all, being inaugurated by the literal return of the Lord Jesus Christ. In this passage, Jesus detailed seven features of His coming. It will be desired by believers, visible globally, delayed by rejection, unexpected in its timing, revealing in its nature, divisive in its effect, and permanent in its fatality.

JESUS' COMING WILL BE DESIRED BY BELIEVERS

And He said to the disciples, "The days will come when you will long to see one of the days of the Son of Man, and you will not see it. (17:22)

As was usually the case, the crowd listening to Jesus consisted of both the hostile Pharisees and His **disciples.** Having addressed the Pharisees in the preceding section (verses 20–21), the Lord now instructed His true disciples, those who are in the kingdom, about His return.

Son of Man is a messianic term connected with the coming of Messiah to establish His kingdom. In Daniel 7:13–14 Daniel

> kept looking in the night visions, and behold, with the clouds of heaven One like a Son of Man was coming, and He came up to the Ancient of Days and was presented before Him. And to Him was given dominion, glory and a kingdom, that all the peoples, nations and men of every language might serve Him. His dominion is an everlasting dominion which will not pass away; and His kingdom is one which will not be destroyed.

The title Son of Man, which emphasizes His humanity, was the Lord's favorite designation of Himself, appearing eighty-four times in the Gospels. **Long** translates a form of the verb *epithumeō*, which signifies a strong, driving, consuming passion, whether for evil (e.g., Matt. 5:28) or as in this case, for the greatest good (cf. Matt. 13:17).

The singular "day" (vv. 24, 30) refers to the epoch of Christ's return, while the plural **days,** as it does in v. 26, refers to the sequence of events within that epoch (cf. Amos 8:11, 13). The time will come when believers will passionately yearn for the Lord to return, like the tribulation martyrs who cried out, "How long, O Lord, holy and true, will You refrain from judging and avenging our blood on those who dwell on the earth?" (Rev. 6:10). Like the apostle John they will say, "Amen. Come, Lord Jesus" (Rev. 22:20). What will prompt those exclamations will not merely be their desire for relief, but that Christ would be glorified. Like David, who said, "Zeal for Your house has consumed me, and the reproaches of those who reproach You have fallen on me" (Ps. 69:9), believers will not be able to bear seeing Christ dishonored.

But despite their desperate longing for the Son of Man's return, it will be delayed and they **will not see it.** It will come in God's perfect timing and until then believers must "be patient ... until the coming of the Lord" and "strengthen [their] hearts" (James 5:7–8).

JESUS' COMING WILL BE VISIBLE GLOBALLY

They will say to you, 'Look there! Look here!' Do not go away, and do not run after them. For just like the lightning, when it flashes out of one part of the sky, shines to the other part of the sky, so will the Son of Man be in His day. (17:23–24)

The first coming of the Son of God was quiet and private. He was born in obscurity when His parents visited the small village of Bethlehem in Judea and lived His first thirty years in an obscure town in Galilee. Apart from His parents and the shepherds, none were aware of His birth. His return, on the other hand, the whole world will see.

Ever eager to corrupt the truth, satanic false teachers will try to deceive believers by enticing them to **look there** or **look here** for Christ. They will claim that He has returned in secret and revealed Himself only to insiders. But such people will be false christs; charlatans and deceivers of whom the Lord warned, "See to it that you are not misled; for many will come in My name, saying, 'I am He,' and, 'The time is near.' Do not go after them" (Luke 21:8). His return will be obvious to all, just as **lightning, when it flashes out of one part of the sky, shines to the other part of the sky.** Like a flash of lightning, His appearance will be sudden, unmistakable, and visible. There also will be dramatic changes in the heavenly bodies:

> the sun will be darkened, and the moon will not give its light, and the stars will fall from the sky, and the powers of the heavens will be shaken. And then the sign of the Son of Man will appear in the sky, and then all the tribes of the earth will mourn, and they will see the Son of Man coming on the clouds of the sky with power and great glory. (Matt. 24:29–30)

Jesus will appear in blazing glory, like a conquering general, mounted on a white horse and accompanied by the armies of heaven (Rev. 19:11–14). As a result, "every eye will see Him" (Rev. 1:7). This is a spectacle that no one will miss.

JESUS' COMING WILL BE DELAYED BY REJECTION

But first He must suffer many things and be rejected by this generation. (17:25)

Before the Lord Jesus Christ could return in glory **He** had to first **suffer many things,** both from the nation, and from God. Without His sacrificial, substitutionary death to redeem His people, there could be no internal or external kingdom. The Lord constantly taught that He would suffer both by suffering death under God's wrath as a substitute for sinners while also being **rejected by this** unbelieving, perverted (Luke 9:41), wicked (Luke 11:29), murderous (Luke 11:50–51) **generation** (Luke 9:22,44; 12:50; 13:33; 18:31–33; 24:26–27; cf. Acts 17:2–3).

Jesus will not return to reign until Israel's rejection ends. After indicting the people of Israel for rejecting their Messiah (Acts 3:12–15), Peter exhorted them,

> Therefore repent and return, so that your sins may be wiped away, in order that times of refreshing may come from the presence of the Lord;

and that He may send Jesus, the Christ appointed for you, whom heaven must receive until the period of restoration of all things about which God spoke by the mouth of His holy prophets from ancient time. (vv. 19–21)

It is only after they repent and return to God and have their sins forgiven that the kingdom (the "times of refreshing" and the "period of restoration of all things" [Acts 3:19–21]) will come, just as "God spoke by the mouth of His holy prophets from ancient time" in the Old Testament prophecies of the kingdom.

God had promised Abraham that He would bless Israel and through them the world (Gen. 12:1–3). Even though they rejected and killed their Messiah (Acts 2:23), God's irrevocable, unconditional covenant with them remained in force. They were still "the sons of the prophets and of the covenant which God made with [their] fathers, saying to Abraham, 'And in your seed all the families of the earth shall be blessed,'" because for them "first, God raised up His Servant and sent Him to bless [them] by turning every one of [them] from [their] wicked ways" (Acts 3:25–26). The opportunity for salvation was still there.

When the future salvation of Israel depicted in Zechariah 12:10–13:1 (cf. Jer. 31:31–34; Ezek. 36:24–27) and Romans 11:25–27 takes place and the believing remnant is redeemed, Christ will return and set up His kingdom (Zech. 14:4–9).

JESUS' COMING WILL BE
UNEXPECTED IN ITS TIMING

And just as it happened in the days of Noah, so it will be also in the days of the Son of Man: they were eating, they were drinking, they were marrying, they were being given in marriage, until the day that Noah entered the ark, and the flood came and destroyed them all. It was the same as happened in the days of Lot: they were eating, they were drinking, they were buying, they were selling, they were planting, they were building; but on the day that Lot went out from Sodom it rained fire and brimstone from

heaven and destroyed them all. It will be just the same on the day that the Son of Man is revealed. (17:26–30)

Jesus offered two historical parallels to what life will be like **in the days of the Son of Man.** As noted above, **days** refers to the sequence of events involved in Christ's return to judge the wicked and set up His kingdom. During the time of tribulation (Matt. 24:21, 29; Rev. 7:14) immediately preceding His return, life will be much like it was immediately before two significant Old Testament judgments.

The **days of Noah** and the **days of Lot** were marked first of all by indifference. People **were eating, they were drinking, they were marrying, they were being given in marriage . . . they were buying, they were selling, they were planting,** and **they were building** right up to the moment that judgment fell; **until the day that Noah entered the ark** and **the day that Lot went out from Sodom.**

The days of Noah and Lot were also two of the most wretched, vile, evil periods in human history. Wickedness was rampant. In Noah's day "the wickedness of man was great on the earth, and . . . every intent of the thoughts of his heart was only evil continually" (Gen. 6:5). It was a time of widespread demonic activity, as demon-possessed men ravaged women (v. 2). Sodom in Lot's day was also marked by sexual perversion, so much so that the city's name came to refer to homosexual sin. So vile were its inhabitants that they attempted to rape the two angels sent to rescue Lot and his family from Sodom's imminent judgment (Gen. 19:4–11).

The days of the tribulation under divine judgment leading up to the Lord's return will also be a time of unprecedented wickedness. Satan's puppet, the Antichrist, will rule the world. Some of the most wicked, vile, and perverted demons, who had been incarcerated in the abyss (the bottomless pit), will be released to run amuck over the earth (Rev. 9:1–11). Most significantly the Holy Spirit, who heretofore had restrained evil, will no longer do so, allowing wickedness to reach its maximum level (2 Thess. 2:6–7).

As will be the case **on the day that the Son of Man is re - vealed,** devastating judgment came suddenly and inescapably in the days of Noah and Lot. After Noah and his family entered the ark, it came about after the seven days, that the water of the flood came upon the earth. In the six hundredth year of Noah's life, in the second month, on the seventeenth day of the month, on the same day all the fountains of the great deep burst open, and the floodgates of the sky were opened. The rain fell upon the earth for forty days and forty nights. (Gen. 7:10–12)

As a result,

All flesh that moved on the earth perished, birds and cattle and beasts and every swarming thing that swarms upon the earth, and all mankind; of all that was on the dry land, all in whose nostrils was the breath of the spirit of life, died. Thus [God] blotted out every living thing that was upon the face of the land, from man to animals to creeping things and to birds of the sky, and they were blotted out from the earth; and only Noah was left, together with those that were with him in the ark. (vv. 21–23)

After Lot, his wife, and his daughters were taken out of Sodom by the angels (Gen. 19:16), "the Lord rained on Sodom and Gomorrah brimstone and fire from the Lord out of heaven, and He overthrew those cities, and all the valley, and all the inhabitants of the cities, and what grew on the ground" (vv. 24–25).

In another parallel between the days of Noah and Lot and the return of Christ, both Noah and his family and Lot and his family were taken away to safety before judgment fell. That pictures the rapture of the church before the tribulation and God's preservation from His wrath of those converted during the tribulation. Significantly, because the event is for the church, none of the passages describing the rapture (John 14:1–3; 1 Cor. 15:51–52; 1 Thess. 4:13–18) mention judgment.

The judgments in the days of Noah and Lot were preceded by warnings. Noah was "a preacher of righteousness" (2 Peter 2:5) during the 120 years before the flood (Gen. 6:3; 1 Peter 3:20). Lot also was a righteous man, who was grieved by the unrighteousness that surrounded him (2 Peter 2:7–8) and undoubtedly confronted it. Though the day or hour cannot be known (Matt. 24:36), the rapture of the church, the devastating judgments, the preaching of the 144,000 Jewish evangelists, the two witnesses, and an angel from heaven will give ample warning that Christ's return is near and the ultimate judgment is about to fall.

But instead of repenting, unbelievers during the tribulation will continue to reject all the warning signs that judgment is near (Rev. 9:20–21). In fact, they will revile and curse God for causing them to suffer (Rev. 16:9, 11, 21). It seems incredible that in the midst of the devastation of the planet, people will remain indifferent, and attempt to carry on life as usual. But those who reject the truth of Scripture will not be persuaded by any signs and wonders, no matter how spectacular (Luke 16:31; John 12:37).

JESUS' COMING WILL BE REVEALING IN NATURE

On that day, the one who is on the housetop and whose goods are in the house must not go down to take them out; and likewise the one who is in the field must not turn back. Remember Lot's wife. Whoever seeks to keep his life will lose it, and whoever loses his life will preserve it. (17:31–33)

The Lord's return will disclose people's hearts and reveal what they love. Jesus' words in these verses stand as a warning against preferring the things of this world to Him. When the judgments that will culminate with the return of Christ (triggered by Antichrist's desecration of the temple [Matt. 24:15–18]) begin, **the one who is on the housetop and whose goods are in the house must not go down to take them out; and likewise the one who is in the field must not turn back.** With judgment about to fall, there will be no need to save anything; nothing of the past needs to be taken into the glory of the kingdom. People who do turn back for their possessions demonstrate that their hearts are fixed on the things of this world (1 John 2:15–17); they will be guilty of failing to heed Jesus' warning to **remember Lot's wife.** After the angels led Lot, his wife, and his two daughters out of Sodom, one urgently warned them, "Escape for your life! Do not look behind you, and do not stay anywhere in the valley; escape to the mountains, or you will be swept away" (Gen. 19:17). Ignoring that warning, Lot's "wife, from behind him, looked back, and she became a pillar of salt" (v. 26). Unable to fully let go of the world, she was destroyed on the brink of safety. Like the weeds in the weedy soil, love of the world's riches choked out her faith. She is a tragic illustration of those who come to the edge of salvation but turn back, and of the principle that whoever seeks to keep his life will lose it, and **whoever loses his life will preserve it** (cf. 9:23–25; Matt. 10:39; John 12:25).

JESUS' COMING WILL BE DIVISIVE IN ITS EFFECT

I tell you, on that night there will be two in one bed; one will be taken and the other will be left. There will be two women grinding at the same place; one will be taken and the other will be left. Two men will be in the field; one will be taken and the other will be left." (17:34–36)

Jesus Christ inevitably brings division, sometimes even within families. In Matthew 10:35–37 Jesus declared,

> For I came to set a man against his father, and a daughter against her mother, and a daughter-in-law against her mother-in-law; and a man's enemies will be the members of his household. He who loves father or mother more than Me is not worthy of Me; and he who loves son or daughter more than Me is not worthy of Me. (cf. the exposition of Luke 14:26 in chapter 23 of this volume)

In this passage Jesus described the ultimate and permanent division that will take place when He returns. **On that night there will be two in one bed** and on the part of the globe where it is day, **there will be two women** (possibly a mother and daughter, two sisters, or two friends) **grinding at the same place.** (Verse 36, which records a third example, is not found in the earliest and most reliable Greek manuscripts of Luke. It was copied by a scribe from Matt. 24:40.) In each case, whether sleeping or awake, **one will be taken and the other will be left.** And that separation will occur over the whole world.

The question arises as to what it means to be **taken** and **left.** Some have related this to the rapture, but a comparison with Matthew 24:37–41 and its illustration of God taking people away in the flood makes it clear this is judgment. In both cases then, the one **taken** is destroyed in judgment, while the one left behind, obviously a true believer in Jesus

Christ, escapes judgment to enter the kingdom. The Lord illustrated this same principle in the parable of the wheat and tares (Matt. 13:24–30) and the analogy of the sheep and goat judgment (Matt. 25:31–46).

JESUS' COMING WILL BE PERMANENT IN ITS FATALITY

And answering they said to Him, "Where, Lord?" And He said to them, "Where the body is, there also the vultures will be gathered." (17:37)

Unable to grasp the scope of the judgment Jesus described, the disciples **said to Him, "Where, Lord?"** Failing to comprehend that the Lord's coming would trigger a worldwide judgment, they wanted to know the specific location of this event. The Lord's enigmatic reply, **"Where the body is, there also the vultures will be gathered,"** was possibly a Jewish proverb. **Vultures** are scavengers, and will feed on the corpses of those killed in the judgments associated with the second coming. Wherever in the world the bodies of the unregenerate lie and the vultures gather will be where Christ has been in judgment.

Those who fail to heed the warnings of imminent judgment and reject the Son of Man will be caught in that judgment and will not enter the millennial or the eternal kingdom. Jude warns that the Lord will come "with many thousands of His holy ones, to execute judgment upon all, and to convict all the ungodly of all their ungodly deeds which they have done in an ungodly way, and of all the harsh things which ungodly sinners have spoken against Him" (Jude 14–15).

As is the case with all biblical truth, the sobering realities expressed in this passage demand self-examination and action. "Since all these things are to be destroyed in this way," Peter wrote, "what sort of people ought you to be in holy conduct and godliness?" (2 Peter 3:11). Only those who come to Christ before it is too late can eagerly watch "for the blessed hope and the appearing of the glory of our great God and Savior, Christ Jesus" (Titus 2:13) instead of "shrink[ing] away from Him in shame at His coming" (1 John 2:28).

Bibliography

Bock, Darrell L. *Luke 1:1–9:50*. Baker Exegetical Commentary on the New Testament. Grand Rapids: Baker, 1994.

Bruce, Alexander B. "The Synoptic Gospels," in W. Robertson Nicoll, ed. *The Expositor's Greek Testament*. Vol. 1. Reprint. Peabody, Mass.: Hendrickson, 2002.

Carson, D. A., Douglas J. Moo, and Leon Morris. *An Introduction to the New Testament*. Grand Rapids: Zondervan, 1992.

Ellis, E. Earle. *The Gospel of Luke*. The New Century Bible Commentary. Grand Rapids: Eerdmans, 1974.

Gooding, David. *According to Luke*. Grand Rapids: Eerdmans, 1987.

Guthrie, Donald. *New Testament Introduction*. Revised edition. Downers Grove, Ill.: InterVarsity, 1990.

Hendriksen, William. *Exposition of the Gospel According to Luke*. New Testament Commentary. Grand Rapids: Baker, 1978.

Hiebert, D. Edmond. *An Introduction to the New Testament*. Vol. 1, *The Gospels and Acts*. Chicago: Moody, 1975.

Lenski, R. C. H. *The Interpretation of St. Luke's Gospel.* Minneapolis: Augsburg, 1961.

Liefeld, Walter L., and David W. Pao. "Luke," in Tremper Longman III and David E. Garland, eds. *The Expositor's Bible Commentary.* Vol. 10. Revised edition. Grand Rapids: Zondervan, 2007.

Marshall, I. Howard. *The Gospel of Luke.* The New International Greek Testament Commentary. Grand Rapids: Eerdmans, 1978.

Morris, Leon. *The Gospel According to St. Luke.* The Tyndale New Testament Commentaries. Grand Rapids: Eerdmans, 1975.

Plummer, Alfred. *The Gospel According to St. Luke.* The International Critical Commentary. Edinburgh: T. & T. Clark, 1969.

Stein, Robert H. *Luke.* The New American Commentary. Nashville: Broadman & Holman, 1992.

Indexes

Index of Greek Words and Phrases

abba, 12
aganakteō, 202
agōnizomai, 219
anendektos, 377
anomia, 38
aphōn, 134
aphrones, 99
apotassō, 285
archisunagōgos, 199
arguros, 345
astheneia, 200

bios, 133

diaballō, 335
diaskorpizō, 310
douleuō, 321, 339
doulos, 386
doxazō, 15

ekteleō, 286
en mesō, 404
entos, 404
epilambanomai, 260
epistatēs, 391
epitimaō, 379
epizēteō, 144
eudokeō, 146
eulogeō, 15

genea, 82

hagiazō, 15
hamartia, 38
harpagēs, 99
homologeō, 120
huios, 322
hupokritēs, 112
hupsoō, 15

iaomai, 394
idou, 404

kai idou, 200
kataskēnoō, 209
katharizō, 394
katoikeō, 76
klēronomia, 308
kollaō, 311

mathētēs, 116, 279

orate, 132
ousias, 308

parabasis, 38
paraptōma, 38
patēr, 12
perisseuō, 133
philarguros, 344
phileō, 345

philos, 53
phortia, 104
phronimos, 162
phronimōs, 337
phulassō, 132
pistos, 162
pleonexia, 132
ponēria, 99
ptōchos, 361

skandalon, 377
skopeō, 90
sōzōs, 394
sunagō, 309
sunechomai, 171

teknon, 322
trechō, 315

zēteō, 144
zōē, 133

Index of Scripture

Genesis		20:7	2	20:8–11	15
1:1	17	24:12–14	6	20:9	130
3:15	371, 411	25:21	2	20:12	283
5	369	26:13	128	20:15	130, 333
6:3	177, 221, 417	29:9	296	22:25	130
6:5	416	29:31	283	22:28	230
7–12	417	30:43	128	22:31	362
7:13	218	31:39	297	23:7	37
12	248	32:5	367	33:13	6
12:1–3	415	32:6	367	33:18	16
12:10	310			33:19	236, 369
13:2	128	**Exodus**		34:6	183, 235
15:6	84, 370	3:1	296	34:6–7	369, 380
18:1–8	54	8:19	66		
18:25	41	12:11	158	**Leviticus**	
19:8	54	16:1–3	240	2:13	288
19:16	218, 417	19:10–11	231	11:13–15	140
19:17	418	19:12	5	11:44–45	347

13–14	389	32:9–11	237	18:46	158
13:45–46	391	32:22	170	19:9–10	7
14:1–32	392			21:17–22	230
15:1–3	258	**Joshua**			
19:3	308	7:1–25	129	**2 Kings**	
19:13	312	21:43–45	248	2:23	344
19:18	361			4:29	158
24:14–16	239	**Judges**		4:33	2
27:30–33	101	16:4–6	129	5:25–27	389
		16:27–30	129	6:25–29	310
Numbers				7:3	390
5:2–3	390	**Ruth**		13:23	236
11:1–3	240	1:1	310	14:8–14	375
12:3	376	2:1	128, 367	14:25	85
14:1–38	240			17:7–17	240–41
14:13–19	2	**1 Samuel**		19:15–19	2
18:19	288	1:10–12	2	20:20	187
19:11–22	102	4:21	242	21:16	231
20:12	15	6:7	34		
22–24	129	8:7	11	**1 Chronicles**	
23:19	154	15:16–19	230	5:20	2
27:1–11	131	16:7	100, 348	16:27	292
31:8	129	17:34–35	297	28:9	348
		17:43	362		
Deuteronomy		28:24	317	**2 Chronicles**	
4:37	245			1:11–12	367
7:6–8	245	**2 Samuel**		7:14	6
8:11–14	130	7	401	13:5	288
8:17–18	333	7:12–17	248	20:7	363
8:18	128	7:18–29	2	24:20–22	108, 231
9:24	20	12:9	381	26:16–23	389
12:31	374	21:1	310	36:15–16	236
13:3	48	23:1–2	351		
13:5	255			**Ezra**	
15:4–6	129	**1 Kings**		6:9–10	288
21:15–17	131, 283	2:28–34	108	9:5–15	2
21:17	308	8:22–53	2	9:6	313
22:22	351	8:46	37, 181		
24:1–4	351, 352	9:6–7	243	**Nehemiah**	
24:5	272	10:23	128	1:2–3	51
24:14–15	312	17:21	2	1:4	51
30:3	237	18:1–2	310	1:4–11	2
31:27	20	18:18	230	5:7	333
32:6	11	18:44–45	175	9:17–38	236

9:26	106	25:12	14	102:13	237
9:26–27	248	27:7	52	102:15	16
		29:2	15	102:25–26	351
Job		29:10	399	103:12	269–370
1:3	128	32:1	41,369	103:19	10,24
2:7	201	32:5	313	104:27	141
4:7	183	33:11	398	105:43	292
4:7–9	389	33:18–19	35	115:1	15
5:7	180	34	145	118:26	246
8:13	13	34:8–10	145	119:5	6
13:24	180	34:10	141	119:18	91
14:1	180	34:15	145	139:7–12	14
19:25	370,393	34:19	145	139:8	364
23:10	47	36:9	88	141:8	47
31:24–25	130	37:2	145	143:1	52
31:24–28	333	37:3–5	145	145:18	5
34:22	117	37:9	145		
38:3	158	37:11	145	**Proverbs**	
38:41	141	37:18–19	35	6:1–5	130
42:2	51,398	37:21	130	6:6–8	140
42:6	369	37:25	35,141,145	6:16–19	374
		44:21	181	10:4	131
Psalms		50:15	5	11:20	343
2	210	50:21	10	11:24	131
2:6–9	154,207	51	38,39,41,381	14:23	131,332
2:7–8	21	51:1	236	15:8	2
3:8	371	51:2	2	15:9	343
5:3	7	51:4	43,381	16:5	264,375
5:4–5	374	51:5	37	17:15	37
6:8	222	55:1–2	52	20:4	141
7:17	5	61:1	52	20:9	37
9:1	6	62:8	7	21:5	131
10:4	375	63:5	8	21:17	131
14:1	134,342	65:2	2	21:20	130,332
16:8	16	66:18	2,46,382	23:4–5	129
17:1	52	69:9	413	23:17	119
18:6	5	72:7	169	23:18	13
22:1	180	72:19	15	25:6–7	262
22:3	6	75:6–7	264	27:23–24	130,332
22:6–8	232	78:38	236	28:9	2,343
22:7–8	344	84:11	57	28:19	131
23	299	86:5	37	28:25	375
23:1	141	96:8	16	30:7–9	33
24:8–10	397	102:1–2	52	30:8–9	129

Ecclesiastes
2:18–19 135
5:10 129, 133
7:20 37
12:14 117

Song of Solomon
2:15 230

Isaiah
1:11–16 342
1:23 230
2:2–4 224
2:12 376
3:9 101
5:1–2 190
5:1–7 242
5:3–4 190
9:6 18, 169
9:6–7 154, 401
13:19 375
14:27 398
25:6–9 269
29:13 295, 342
30:9 20
30:18 236
33:13–16 146
38:17 39
40:1–2 401
40:3–4 220
42:8 15
45:17 217
46:8–10 399
48:1 342
53 232, 329
53:1–12 246
53:6 40
53:10 146, 234
54:3 210
54:10 249
55:1 218
55:6 178, 191
55:7 369
55:12 169

56:6–7 217
56:10–12 102
56:11 254
57:19 169
59:2 37
61:1–3 58
62:5 292
63:10 20
64:6 71
65:5 113
65:17 151
66:24 365

Jeremiah
1:17 158
6:13 345
7:4 342–43
7:8–11 343
7:16 343
7:31 118
13:16 238
13:23 72
14:13 255
20:18 180
23:3 218
23:5 154, 401
23:5–6 249
26:20–23 231
31 401
31:31–34 369
31:35–37 249
32:37, 41 292
42:19–22 115
44:4–5 374

Lamentations
2:14 255
3:22–23 236

Ezekiel
2:5 20
4:9 34
8:1 199
18:4 369

18:30–32 369
18:31 320
20:33–38 249
22:27 230
31:3–6 212
33:31–32 114
34:25 169, 415
36:25–27 58
36:26 105
37 155
37:26 169
43:23–24 288

Daniel
2:22 88
4:10–12 211
4:34 399
4:37 264
5:26 22
7:13–14 412
7:25 157
9:3 7
9:24–27 156
12:2 365

Hosea
2:19 250
3:4–5 249
7:3–7 230
8:1 20
9:7 254

Joel
1:15 403
2:12–13 71
2:13 236

Amos
1:3 380
5:21–23 342, 374
8:5 333
8:11 413
9:2 364

Jonah		**Malachi**		6:12	38,42	
1–3	224	1:2–3	283	6:14–15	382	
1:1–2	85	1:6	14	6:16	113,125	
2:1–9	2,7	3:8	130	6:18	348	
3–4	183			6:19–20	135	
3:4	87	**Matthew**		6:19–21	139,147,228	
3:4–10	369	1:21	394	6:24	139,148,340	
		2:16	194	6:25	138	
Micah		3:2	188,250,274	6:25–33	33	
2:12–13	210	3:7	190	6:25–34	119,130	
3:5	131,345	3:12	365,366	6:26	140	
4:1–8	210	3:17	120	6:27	142	
4:3	154	4:17	23,24,	6:30	143	
5:2	210,226		188,216,402	6:33	146	
7:6	173	4:23	217,387	7:4–5	113	
7:18–19	39,370	5:3–5	264	7:7–8	13,34	
7:19	42,236	5:3–6	83	7:9	56	
		5:11–12	239	7:11	57	
Nahum		5:13–14	73	7:13–14	25,95,220	
1:3	37	5:14	77	7:13–15	254,377	
		5:16	16	7:14	281	
Habakkuk		5:17	170	7:15	95	
1:13	41,369	5:17–19	391	7:21	11,25,281	
2:4	347,370	5:17–48	351	7:21–22	121	
		5:18	351	7:21–23	94,282	
Zephaniah		5:20	43,84,103,256	7:22	221	
3:14–17	293	5:21–22	381	7:22–23	357	
		5:22	99,118,356	7:23	121,222	
Haggai		5:23–24	45	7:24	77	
1:1–11	141	5:28	412	7:28	81,176	
2:8	333	5:31–32	352	8:11	23	
		5:44–45	43,380	8:11–12	223,367	
Zechariah		5:45	395	8:12	223	
1:1	108	5:48	38	8:26	384	
2:10–12	211	6:1–2	348	9:10–11	257	
8:17	374	6:1–5	256	9:11	194	
8:20–23	211	6:2	113,125,175,195	9:13	170,320	
8:22–23	217	6:2–3	333	9:27	391	
12:9–10	250	6:2–4	334	9:32–33	194	
12:10	155,177,	6:5	4,113,125	9:33	62	
	246,410	6:6	4,6,118	9:34	206	
13:1	250,411	6:7	4,5	10:1	75	
14:4	156	6:8	11	10:6	347	
14:4–9	154,415	6:9–13	3	10:21	174	

10:27	284	15:7	96	23:15	99, 112, 280
10:28	366	15:14	89, 256, 347	23:25	73
10:34	173	15:26–27	362	23:25–28	99
10:34–36	283	15:36	3	23:26	404
11:11	349	16:6	116, 213	23:28	320
11:15	289	16:24	284	23:29–30	106
11:20	188, 202	16:27	117	23:32	108
11:25	10	17:20	385	23:33	71
11:27	219	18:7–9	378	23:34	11
11:28–30	67, 87, 105	18:10	300, 363	23:35	108
12:1	82	18:15–17	379	23:39	173
12:1–14	197	18:17	378	24:15–18	418
12:7	259	18:21	380	24:21	416
12:11	203	18:23–35	43, 381	24:27	154
12:22–30	61	18:25	44	24:29–30	414
12:24	61, 81, 259	18:26	44, 312	24:29–31	411
12:31	123	18:27	44	24:30	155
12:31–32	62	18:28	44	24:34	151, 152
12:34	82	18:30	44	24:36	157, 417
12:38	368, 403	18:31	381	24:37–41	419
12:39	238, 368	18:34	382	24:42–44	157
12:39–40	85	19:13	3	24:44–51	162
12:43–45	74	19:21	128, 147	24:45–51	114, 154
12:44	75	19:22	128	24:51	164
13	207	19:29	94, 174	25:1–12	159, 276
13:10–11	216	20:13–14	312	25:14–29	339
13:10–13	264	21:31–32	395	25:21	147, 293
13:11–16	403	21:38	308	25:24	310
13:13–15	90, 304	22:1–14	250, 270	25:27	130
13:17	412	22:2–4	159, 317	25:31–46	156
13:20–22	287	22:19–21	113	25:34	23
13:24–30	420	22:34–40	361	26:14–16	129
13:32	208, 209	22:38	73	26:24	129, 168
13:39–42	120	23	71, 114	26:25	279
13:44–46	26, 140, 281	23–25	154	26:26–27	3
14:1–2	229	23:2	104	26:28	40
14:3–12	107, 349	23:4	202	26:36–44	3
14:5	228	23:5	113	26:37–38	268
14:9–10	229	23:5–7	385	26:39	27
14:14	388	23:6	101, 113, 262	26:39–44	51
14:19	3	23:7	101, 113	26:41	2, 30
14:23	3	23:8–12	102	26:56	30
14:31	260	23:12	264	26:58–75	30
15:1–2	98	23:13	254, 347	26:59–61	109

27:24	227	13:32	153	7:13	237
27:27–31	227	14:1	274,329	7:18–24	4
27:46	3,181	14:25	23	7:36–50	257,344
27:57	128			8:1	205
28:11–14	202	**Luke**		8:3	207
28:11–15	84,86,371	1:31–33	247	8:10	289
28:16–17	207	1:32–33	400	8:14–15	2
28:19	72,216	1:67–79	349	8:21	77,346
		1:78	88	8:37	171
Mark		1:79	169	9:9	229
1:14–15	199,205	2:1–4	52	9:11	2
1:15	165,285	2:14	169	9:17	133
1:23–26	201	2:34	194	9:18	3
1:35	3	2:37	2	9:22	414
1:40	237	3:3–9	313	9:23	25,140,219,
2:16	257	3:4–5	220		278,281,350
3:2	258	3:21	2	9:23–24	25,120
3:5	260,268	4:1–13	194	9:23–25	419
3:22	194	4:16	198	9:23–26	161
3:35	27	4:16–30	194	9:28–29	3
4:19	130	4:18	83,176,226	9:51–19:27	217
4:23	289	4:27–28	51	10:9	23
5:22	199	4:28–30	176,200	10:16	122
6:12	216,313	4:33–35	61	10:21	3
6:14–16	229	4:43	23	10:22	116
6:17–18	228	5:5	391	10:25–37	198
6:19	228	5:8	394	10:30	358
6:34	298	5:12–13	390	10:30–32	361
7:1	103	5:15	388	11:1–2*a*	1
7:3	104	5:17	103	11:1–2*d*	19
7:8–13	255	5:21	37,80	11:1–4	8,51
8:36	358	5:27–29	83	11:1*b*	3
8:38	238	5:29–32	80	11:2*b*	5
9:19	239	5:32	71,123,280	11:2*b, c*	9
9:48	365	5:33	4	11:3	31,32
10:1	227	6:5	80,197,259	11:3–4	31
10:17–22	219	6:6–11	80,258	11:4	379
10:23	357	6:12–13	3	11:4*a*	36
10:38	171	6:12–16	383	11:4*b*	46
11:25	380	6:20	205	11:5	2
12:7	308	6:36	45	11:5–8	8,53
12:15	113	6:39	105	11:5–13	49
12:38	101	6:46	25	11:8	273
12:42–44	361	7:8	120	11:9–10	8,55

11:11–12	55	12:1–12	111, 112	13:3*b*	187
11:11–13	8	12:1–13:9	139, 282	13:4–5*a*	187
11:13	56	12:2–7	117	13:6–9	188–89
11:13–16	65	12:5	29, 273	13:10	198
11:14–23	59	12:8–9	119–120	13:10–17	193–94
11:15	81, 115, 123	12:10–12	121	13:11–13	113, 200
11:16	81	12:13–21	127, 139	13:14–17	201
11:17–18	64	12:15	29, 132	13:15	260
11:17–23	63	12:16–20	133	13:15–16	114
11:19	65	12:19	361	13:17	260
11:20	206, 208	12:20	100, 221, 338	13:18–19	208
11:20–23	66	12:21	135	13:18–21	205
11:23	60, 74	12:22–23	139	13:19	384
11:24–26	75	12:22–34	137, 138	13:20–21	212
11:24–28	69	12:24	140, 143	13:22–30	213
11:27–28	76	12:25–26	141	13:23*b*–24	218
11:29	61, 63, 81	12:27–29	142	13:24	255
11:29*a*	82	12:30–31	143	13:24–28	282
11:29*b*–30	85	12:32	218	13:25*a*	220
11:29–32	82	12:32–34	146	13:25*b*–27	222
11:29–36	79, 80	12:34	128	13:28–29	23
11:31–32	86	12:35*a*	158	13:28–30	160, 223
11:33	88	12:35*b*	158	13:31*a*	227
11:33–36	87	12:35–40	157–58	13:31*b*	228
11:34	89	12:35–48	149, 150	13:31–33	225
11:35	90	12:36–38	159	13:32–33	229
11:36	90	12:37	386	13:34	237–38
11:37–38	80	12:39–40	160		274, 299
11:37–54	94	12:40	157, 221	13:34–35	190, 235, 280
11:38	98	12:41	184	13:35	274
11:38–44	97	12:41–48	161–62, 173	13:35*a*	241
11:39	83, 345	12:42–44	162	13:35*b*	244
11:39–40	256	12:45–48	163	14:1–14	253, 254
11:40–41	99	12:49–50	170	14:1*a*	257
11:42	100	12:49–59	167–68, 168	14:1*b*–2	258
11:43	262	12:51–53	172–73	14:3–6	259
11:43–44	101	12:54–56	175	14:7	376
11:45–54	103	12:54–57	113	14:7–10	261
11:46	104	12:54–59	174, 283	14:11	264
11:47–51	105	12:57–59	177	14:12–14	261
11:52–54	108	13:1–3*a*	184	14:15–24	250, 267–68
11:53–54	116	13:1–5	165, 184	14:16	22
12	157	13:1–9	179, 221	14:16–17	270
12:1	189, 377	13:3	221	14:18–20	271

14:21–23	272	16:16	25, 281, 349	19:10	87, 170,
14:24	273	16:17–18	350		280, 295, 320
14:25–27	282	16:19–21	360	19:11	402
14:25–35	277–78	16:19–26	359	19:26	273
14:26	25, 219, 419	16:19–31	355–56	19:37	393
14:27	25	16:22	362	19:41	268
14:28–32	286	16:23–26	363	19:41–44	177, 238
14:33	25, 147,	16:27–31	266	19:43	171
	219, 282	17:1–2	377	20:9–16	232
14:34–35	288	17:1–10	373, 374	20:20	115
15	329	17:3–4	378	20:26	260
15:1–2	257, 305, 350	17:4	44	20:45–47	353
15:1–3	335	17:5–6	383	20:46	262
15:1–10	291–92	17:7–10	385	20:46–47	385
15:2	244	17:11–14	390	20:47	34
15:3–7	295–96	17:11–19	387	21:1–4	339
15:3–32	350	17:15–19	392	21:8	414
15:7	273, 321	17:20*a*	401	21:12–13	124
15:8–10	299	17:20*b*–21	403	21:19	124
15:11–12	307	17:20–21	209, 397	22:29–30	224
15:11–19	306–7	17:21	23	22:42	172
15:11–32	301, 303–4	17:22	412	22:63	171
15:13	335	17:22–37	407–8	22:65	195
15:13–16	309	17:23–24	413	23:13	233
15:17–19	311–12	17:26	22	24:27	109
15:20–24	313–14	17:26–30	415–16	24:30	3
15:20–32	43	17:29	12	24:47	188
15:22	316	17:31–35	418	24:50–51	3
15:23–24	317	17:34–36	419		
15:25–30	83, 318–19	17:37	402, 420	**John**	
15:25–32	318	18:1	2, 29	1:9	88
15:31–32	322	18:2–5	29	1:11	176, 194, 242
16:1	328	18:9	263	1:12	12, 147
16:1–8	334	18:9–11	370	1:29	17, 206
16:1–13	331–32	18:11	375	1:38	103
16:5	376	18:11–12	263	1:45	350
16:9–13	337–38	18:13	39, 395	1:48	189
16:14	131, 298, 328,	18:14	263	2:13–17	226
	335, 345, 358	18:18–23	285	2:18	195
16:14*a*	344	18:18–27	83	2:20	124
16:14–18	341	18:21	321	2:25	64, 348
16:15*a*	346	18:22	140	2:27	124
16:15*b*	348	19:8	128	3:3	403
16:15*c*	348	19:9	128, 203	3:7–8	123

3:15	12, 43	9:39	171	14:27	169
3:19	372	10:8	254	15:6	288, 356
3:19–20	89	10:10	170	15:14	25
3:30	349	10:11	296, 298	15:18–19	281
3:36	165, 274	10:12–13	296	15:18–20	195
4:9	393	10:25	63, 176, 259	15:24	81, 84
4:25–26	393	10:31	176	15:26	123
4:34	27, 231	10:40–42	227	16:8	39, 58, 123
5:17	11	11:1–45	190	16:13	57
5:18	11, 227	11:35	268	16:28	170
5:22	132	11:41–42	3	17:5	172
5:23	120, 122	11:47	62	17:6	16
5:24	178, 280	11:47–50	233	17:15	47
5:25–29	154	11:47–53	81	17:24	408
5:28–29	264	11:53	94, 274	18:36	207
5:36	89, 388	11:54	390	18:37	170
5:43	170	12:2	96	18:38	185
5:44	262, 376	12:5–6	344	19:1–16	63
6:14–15	218, 394	12:10–11	371	19:30	172
6:37	178	12:25	219, 284	20:17	12
6:38	170	12:26	125		
6:44	219	12:27	15	**Acts**	
6:59	199	12:28	3	1:3	23, 206, 404
6:60	279	12:31	95, 155	1:8	58
7:28–49	80	12:35	176	1:11	152, 153
7:33	191	12:36	337	1:14	2, 7
7:43	173	12:37	86, 418	1:15	404
7:49	96, 102, 202, 256	12:37–40	164	1:24	2
7:52	187	12:46	170	2:1–13	195
8:12	81, 88, 91	13:1–5	160	2:21	394
8:13	80, 377	13:6	41	2:22	329
8:21	191	14:1–3	156, 417	2:22–23	233
8:33–59	269	14:2	154	2:23	234
8:37	176	14:2–3	145	2:37	336
8:42	96, 122	14:3	156	2:41	177
8:44	66, 95, 144	14:6	122	3:12–15	414–15
8:46	176	14:9	400	3:14	242
8:48	80	14:13	10	3:14–15	245
8:58–59	80	14:15	25, 77	3:18	371
9:1–3	389	14:17	154	3:19–21	415
9:2	363	14:21	25	4:1–3	107
9:7	187	14:23	25	4:27	234
9:15–16	257	14:24	25	4:29	386
9:16	198, 259	14:26	57	5:1–2	129

5:1–11	114	
5:5	129	
5:17–42	195	
5:18–41	107	
5:34–40	97	
5:41	182	
7:53	400	
7:58–60	107	
8:1	107,240	
9:4	239	
11:18	131	
11:26	279	
12:1–2	107	
12:1–19	195	
12:21–23	186	
15:10	104	
16:19	260	
16:40	360	
17:16–34	196	
17:30	219	
17:31	250	
18:8	199	
18:18	285	
19:8	405	
19:11–12	65	
19:13–16	65	
20:29–30	255	
20:30	110	
20:35	130	
23:6	100	
23:6–8	256	
24:15	264	
26:10	107	
26:11	275	
26:18	77,281	
27:10	104	
28:8	2	

Romans

1:10	2	
1:16	73,244,275	
1:18–23	95	
1:18–32	74,163	
1:21	90	
1:24	221,242	
1:25	133	
2:4	13	
2:16	117	
2:19–20	174	
2:20	100	
2:29	100	
3:10	37	
3:10–12	72	
3:20	347	
3:21	349,371	
3:22	83	
3:23	37,181	
3:25	172	
3:26	178	
4:3	40	
4:5	316	
5:5	58	
5:6	38	
5:9	217	
8:8	77,83,105	
8:9	57	
8:17	147	
8:18–21	213	
8:18–22	156	
8:19–21	404	
8:28	183,234	
9:4–5	190,274,400	
9:13	283	
9:32	245	
10:2	346	
10:9	120,173	
10:9–10	175	
10:17	122	
10:21	241	
11:25–26	248,250	
11:25–27	415	
11:26	155	
11:33–36	398	
12:3	375	
12:12	2,30	
12:14	196	
12:19	46,382	
13:1–4	32	
13:6–7	333	
13:11–14	159	
14:1	378	
14:17	26,147,293,404	
15:6	10,17	
15:13	13	
16:17	110	
16:20	119	

1 Corinthians

1:4	154	
1:7	154	
1:18	395	
1:20	349	
2:8	234	
2:9	276	
2:14	403	
3:1	280	
3:10–15	156	
4:5	87,117	
4:12	196	
4:20	405	
5	45	
5:1–13	379	
7:5	47	
7:14	212	
7:15	352	
9:24	315	
9:25–27	142	
10:31	72	
11:29–30	142	
12:3	58,122	
15:3–4	371	
15:12	152	
15:20–23	152	
15:33	116	
15:35–38	208	
15:36	100	
15:51–52	410	
16:22	73,343	

2 Corinthians

1:4	182	

1:6	182–83	**Ephesians**		1:13	22,281	
1:8–9	182	1:7	40	1:13–14	67	
2:13	285	1:11	10,27	1:14	37	
2:15	395	1:20–21	401	1:16	24	
2:16	171,384	2:1	37,38,83,	1:27	13	
2:17	254		105,144,346	1:29	219,384	
3:6	123	2:1–3	301	2:9	393	
4:4	47,109,346	2:1–10	210	2:13–14	40	
4:6	88	2:8	284	3:1–2	144	
4:17–18	182	2:8–9	172	4:2	2	
4:41	89	2:12	144	4:11	405	
5:9	77	2:17	169	4:14	61	
5:14	171	2:20	383			
5:16	246	3:20	58	**1 Thessalonians**		
5:17	77	4:18	144	1:9–10	188	
5:18–20	71,173,178	4:27	119	1:10	178,408,411	
5:20	90,329	4:32	381	4:6	377	
5:21	30,40	5:1	380	4:14–17	410	
6:2	90,165,191	5:5	133	4:15	157	
6:14	73	5:8	91,337	4:16–17	151	
7:9–11	313	5:13	87	4:17	156	
8:8	334	5:17	100	5:2–4	161	
9:7	333	5:25	283	5:17	2	
11:2	154	6:11	118			
11:13	115	6:18	2,31	**2 Thessalonians**		
11:14–15	64			1:6–9	275	
11:32–33	196	**Philippians**		1:7–9	411	
12:10	46	1:23	172	1:9	366	
		2:10–11	21	2:3	21	
Galatians		3:2	254	2:6–7	416	
1:3–4	231	3:2–12	346	3:10	332	
1:14	83,346	3:5–6	367	3:10–12	36	
2:16	104,347	3:8	265,347			
2:20	120,222	3:9	370	**1 Timothy**		
3:13	171	3:10	50	1:9	21	
3:24	175	3:18–19	254	1:11	301	
3:28	224,244	3:20	337	1:12–16	265	
4:9	361	4:4	293	2:1	24	
4:22–31	12	4:6	12	2:5	400	
5:13–15	377	4:16	333	4:1	47	
5:21	405	4:19	14,140,144	4:2	112	
5:22	293			4:7–8	142	
6:1	379	**Colossians**		4:8	71	
6:12	348	1:5	13	4:10	219	

5:24–25	117	10:25	157	2:22–23	46, 383
6:3–4	375	10:26	124	2:24	40
6:4	254	10:26–31	84, 165,	2:24–25	298
6:8	140		168, 269	2:25	296
6:10	129, 333	10:27	124, 170	3:15	16
6:12	219	10:28	124	4:8	380
6:15	398	10:29	124	4:12–14	124
6:17	128, 129, 333	10:29–31	109	4:14	74
		10:30–31	124	5:6	264
2 Timothy		11:25	310	5:7	34, 140
1:5	371	12:2	146, 172, 292	5:10	4
1:15–16	196	13:20	296		
2:12	163			**2 Peter**	
2:15	vii	**James**		1:4	12
2:18	152	1:2–4	46, 182, 383	1:20–21	154
2:26	74	1:6–8	143	1:21	122
3:2	345	1:13	46	2:3	345
3:6	95	1:14–15	48	2:7–8	417
3:12	222	1:22	77	3:3–4	409
4:8	155, 408	2:13	45	3:7	250
		2:14–26	287	3:9	183, 186
Titus		2:23	40, 363	3:10	156, 161
1:2	154	3:15	47	3:11	420
2:4	283	3:17	163	3:12	26, 399
2:8	196	4:6	299, 376	3:14	161
2:13	155, 408,	4:7–10	264–65	3:15–16	108
	411, 420	4:10	386		
3:10–11	379	4:13–16	134	**1 John**	
		4:14	153	1:5	88
Hebrews		5:4	333	1:5–7	91
1:2	154	5:7–8	413	1:9	39
1:3	400	5:11	236	2:13	50
2:2–4	123	5:16	30	2:15	22
2:12	404			2:15–17	418
2:14	67, 172	**1 Peter**		2:19	287
6:4–6	62, 123	1:5–7	124	2:23	122
6:4–8	164	1:6–7	181	2:28	420
9:12	172	1:7	155	3:1–3	409
9:22	370	1:10–11	409	3:4	38
9:27	178, 188	1:13	158	3:8	67
10	123	1:23	123, 368	3:10	12, 120
10:1–4	370	2:1	114	3:17	130, 333
10:10–18	40	2:9	91	4:2–3	122
10:24–25	377	2:15	100	4:4	118

2 John		3:11	410	19:14	156, 410
7	254	3:14	17	20:1–6	26
9	122	4:8–11	300	20:2	155
12	293	6–19	151, 156	20:4	156
		9:1–11	416	20:4–6	207
3 John		9:20–21	418	20:10	118
2	2	11:15	22	20:10–15	275
		12–22	157	20:11–15	156, 178
Jude		14:10	365	21	151
4	254	14:11	366	22	151
7	366	16:2	361	22:7	154
14–15	420	19:6–9	154	22:15	362
		19:7	156	22:17	329
Revelation		19:9	269	22:18–19	151
1:7	404, 414	19:11–15	209	22:20	26, 408, 413
1:18	364	19:11–21	156		
3:3	160	19:13	18		

Index of Subjects

Abel, 108

Abraham
descendants' salvation and, 223, 264, 367
in rich man and Lazarus parable, 362–65, 368
wealth and, 128

Abrahamic Covenant, 236, 248, 415

Absolute truth. *See* Truth

Achan, 129, 333

Adultery, 351–52

Agur, 32–33, 129

Altar call, 216

Amos, 342

Ananias and Sapphira, 114, 129, 333

Anti-Semitism, 243–44

Antiochus Epiphanes, 97

Anxiety, 138–39
See also Worry

"Anxious bench," 216

Apocalypse, 152

Apostasy, 164

Apostles, 383–84

Armageddon, 152–53

Arrogance, 375, 376

Austria, 244

Bacterium, 389

Balaam, 129, 333

Banquets, 270–75

Baptism, 171

Beelzebul, 61–65

Believers, 42, 46, 48, 162–63

Bethlehem, 226

Birds, 140–41, 211, 212

Black Death, 244

Blasphemy, 62–67, 80, 123–24, 239

Blessing and cursing, 240, 247

Blindness. *See* Spiritual blindness

Bock, Darrell L., 118, 284

Bodily resurrection. *See* Resurrection, Second coming

Boettner, Loraine, 248

Boldness, in prayer, 53–55, 58

Brooks, Thomas, 8

Cain, 108
Calvin, John, 340
Casting out demons, 61–65
Catholic Church. *See* Roman Catholic
    Church
Chiasm, 324
Children of Abraham, 223
Christianity Lite, 278–79
Church
    consumer mindset and, 278–79
    God's program for, 154
    persecution of, 195, 197
    Second coming and, 410, 417
    spiritual kingdom and, 404
Church discipline, 45
Cleansing of temple, 226
Clothing, 15, 142–43
Coins, 299–300
Committment, 288
Compassion
    God's comfort and, 182
    of Jesus, 260, 388
    lack of, 113
    Old Testament descriptions, 235–37
Consumer mindset, 278–79
Covenant theology, 247
Creation, groaning of, 156
Cultural morality, 69–74
Cultural settings, 293
Cursing and blessing, 240, 247

Daniel, 211–12
Darkness, 89, 90, 91
David, 35
Days, 412, 413, 416
Death, 359–60, 362–66
Debts, 44
Decius, 197
Decretive will of God, 28
Delilah, 129
Demons, 61–65, 75, 76
Depravity, 56–57
Diocletian, 197
Disasters, 180, 186

Discernment
    lack of, 113, 174–75
    of need for judgment, 178–79
    of the time, 175–77, 191
Disciples, 207, 279, 280, 285
Discipleship
    change in meaning of, 279
    committment needed, 282–84
    cost of, 284–88
    salvation and, 280–81
Disobedience, 240–43
Distressed, 171–72
Divided kingdoms, 64
Divorce, 351–52
Dogs, 262
Domitian, 197
Dreyfus, Alfred, 244
Dropsy (edema), 258

Earthly kingdom, 209–12, 411, 412
Eleazar, 361
Elijah, 226
Elisha, 226
Elliot, Jim, 148, 187
England, 243, 244
Essenes, 96, 255, 256
Eternal future, 337, 338
Eternal punishment, 124, 125, 223, 255,
    366
    See also Hell
Evangelism methodology, 216, 224,
    278–79, 281–83
Excuses, 271–72, 274
External religion. *See* False religion
Extrabiblical regulations/traditions,
    98, 101, 198, 259
Ezekiel, 212

Faith
    divine righteousness and, 83
    Holy Spirit and, 202
    justification by, 347
    lack of, 143, 384
    non-saving, 287

saving, 220
testing of, 124, 181
Word of God and, 368
False religion/religionists
  God's hatred of, 374
  hypocrisy and, 95–96
  man-made regulations and, 101
  prophetic rebukes of, 342–43
  spiritual qualities lacking in, 103–10, 256
  symbolism and, 98, 99
  Word Faith movement, 9–10
False teachers, 95, 96, 109–10, 254–55, 343–44
Family division, 173–74, 283–84
Famine, 310
Fatherhood of God, 11–14, 56, 57
Fear of God, 118–19
Fig trees, 189–90
First World War, 152
Food diversity/variety, 34
Forgiveness
  apart from works, 315–16
  by believers, 42, 46
  importance of, 381–83
  judicial, 39, 40
  Pharisees and, 350
  relational, 41, 42
  of sin, 39–41, 236
  unlimited, 43, 44
Foxes, 229–30
France, 244
Friends, 53, 54, 56, 183, 310, 363

Galilee, 228
Gehenna, 118
Gentiles, 223–24
George III (king), 397
Giving, 100, 333–34
Glorifying God, 15
God
  attributes of, 292
  authority of, 46, 382
  divine compassion of, 236–39

existence of, 13–14
fear of, 118–19
forgiveness of, 369–70
glory of, 32
grace of, 326
joy of, 292–301
love for Israel, 245
mankind's conception of, 50
names of, 16–18
promises regarding Israel, 248–50
providential care of, 32–36, 140–41
as sacred, 14–18
as Savior, 37–46
as shelter, 46–48
sovereignty of, 22–24, 51–52, 234, 398–99
as supreme, 27–30
will/purpose of, 27–30
wisdom/knowledge of, 398
wrath of, 74
See also Fatherhood of God; God the Father; Sovereignty of God
God the Father
  giving the kingdom, 146–48
  honoring, 116–19
  provision of, 143–46
  sovereignty of, 234
Gomorrah, 417
Gospel invitation, 275
Grace, 326, 347, 350, 369
Greed, 131–35, 344–45
  See also Materialism
Guyana, 255

Hades, 364
Hallowed, 15, 16
Hamilton, Floyd, 24
Hand washing, 9
Hansen's disease (leprosy), 389–91
Hasidim, 97
Healings, 257–60, 387–95
Health, 141–42
"Health and Wealth" movement, 8, 94, 95

Heart, 100, 348, 404
Heaven, 121, 357–60, 364–65, 367
Heavenly reward, 337, 338
Hell
  as believers' motivation, 367
  Christ's teaching on, 356–57
  degrees of punishment in, 164–65
  fear of God and, 118–19
  reality of, 223
  torment of, 365–66
  unbelief and, 124, 368
Henley, William Ernest, 19
Heraclius (Byzantine emperor), 243
Herod Antipas, 227–30, 232
Herod Archelaus, 228
Herod the Great, 226
Herodias, 228
Hidden will of God, 28
Hired men, 312
Hitler, Adolf, 244
Holocaust, 244
Holy Spirit
  actions of, 58
  blasphemy against, 123–24
  gift of, 57
  honoring, 121–25
  second coming and, 410
  testimony of, 154
Honor, 385–86
Hope, 13, 155, 182, 371
Hospitality, 54
Humble people
  forgiving others and, 379–83
  recognition of weakness in, 383–85
  rejection of honor by, 385–86
  stumbling blocks and, 377–78
Humility, 264, 265, 315, 376–86
Hyperpreterism, 151, 152
Hypocrisy
  avoiding, 116–25
  evidence and, 176
  exposure of, 117
  of false religionists, 95–96
  in Israel's history, 114

New Testament instances, 115
  Pharisees and, 96, 131, 257–65
Hypocrites, 96, 112–13, 201–3

Idolatry, 133
Inclusiveness, 73
Indulgences, 202
Inner rooms, 117–18
"Invictus" (Henley), 19–20
Isaiah, 246, 342
Islam, 244
Israel
  anti-Semitism and, 243–44
  covenant theology and, 247
  disobedience of, 240–43
  future of, 154–55, 190
  God's compassion for, 236–39, 245
  God's mediation through, 400
  hypocrisy and, 114
  remnant of, 218
  salvation of, 410–11

Jehoiakim, 231
Jeremiah, 342–43
Jerusalem, 107, 177, 239, 243, 251
Jesus Christ
  attempts on life of, 225–27
  compassion of, 237–38, 260, 388
  conflict/opposition and, 80–82, 176,
    194–203, 206–7, 305
  first coming, 413
  hell, teaching on, 356–57
  honoring/confessing, 119–22
  judgment declarations, 101, 102,
    106, 108
  prayer and, 2–3
  relationship with, 222
  salvation, teaching on, 67, 216–24
  suffering of, 414
  ultimate mediator, 400
  washing the disciples' feet, 41–42
  See also Resurrection, Second com-
    ing
Jewish leaders

extrabiblical regulations of, 198, 259
hostility/opposition to Jesus, 80–81,
176, 194, 206–7
murder of Jesus and, 226–27
See also Essenes; Pharisees; Scribes
and Pharisees; Zealots
Jewish people, 227, 232, 233, 393–94
Job, 129–30, 180, 363
John the Baptist, 4, 107, 219, 228, 229,
349
Jonah, 85–86, 87
Jones, Jim, 255
Jonestown incident, 255
Josephus, 243, 256
Joy, 7–8, 292–301, 306
Judaism, 194, 197
Judas Iscariot, 129, 168, 333
Judgment
Christ's declarations of, 101, 102,
106, 108
inevitability of, 187–88
on pride, 375–76
as punishment for sin, 13, 369
reality of, 2, 82
of Satan, 155
second coming and, 420
self-assessment and, 178
unbelief and, 274–75, 419–20
Judicial forgiveness, 39, 40
Justification, 347

Khayyam, Omar
"The Rubaiyat," 28–29
Kingdom of God
aspects of, 24–26, 64, 139
Christ's emphasis on, 205–6
cultural morality and, 72
entering, 199–200
external power of, 208–12
future form of, 23
internal influence of, 212–13
Paul's ministry and, 404–5
questioned, 401
seeking, 144–45

small beginnings of, 207
as spiritual, 403–5
Kings, 397

Lamps, 159
Lawlessness, 21
The Law, 104, 351
Lawyers, 108
See also Scribes
Lazarus (in parable), 359–65, 367
Lazarus (Mary and Martha's brother),
371
Leaven, 212–13
Legalism, 321
See also Self-righteousness
Leprosy. *See* Hansen's disease
Lewis, C.S., 356
Mere Christianity, 60
Licinius, 197
Life, 133
Lifespan, 141–42
Light, 87–91, 159
Lord's Prayer
God's person and, 11–18
God's promises in, 49–58
God's provision and, 31–48
God's purpose and, 20–30
as model prayer, 1–8
See also Prayer
Lot, 416, 417, 418
Lot's wife, 418
Luther, Martin, 202
Lyell, Charles, 409

MacArthur, John
The Murder of Jesus, 233, 234
A Tale of Two Sons, 322
Why Government Can't Save You, 70
Man of lawlessness, 21
Management, of money, 334–37
Manasseh (king), 231
Materialism, 131, 134, 135
See also Greed
Mere Christianity (Lewis), 60, 217

Messianic kingdom, 207, 209–13
Micah, 210
Millennial kingdom, 23–24, 26–27
Miracles, 388
Miraculous healing, 387–95
Mockers, 408–9
Mohler, Albert, 70
Monarchies, 397
Money
  love of, 129, 130, 340, 344–45
  management of, 333–37
  obtaining, 332–33
  wealth and, 129
Moralism, 69–74, 76, 77
Morality, 83, 84
Morris, Leon, 104–5
Moses, 15, 104, 245
Mulberry trees, 384–85
Murder, 43
The Murder of Jesus. See John
  MacArthur
Mustard seeds, 208–9, 211, 384
Mycobacterium leprae. See Hansen's
  disease

Nazareth, 226
Needs, 14, 32–36, 48
Nero, 197
New Covenant, 369
Nineveh, 85, 87
Noah, 416, 417

Obedience, 16, 128, 182, 240, 247
Old Testament prayers, 2, 5–6
Ostentation, 101–2

Parables, 189, 261, 293, 294
Paul, 195–96, 404–5
Peace, 169
Penitence. *See* Repentance
People of the Land, 294–95
People's Temple. *See* Jim Jones
Perea, 227, 228, 231
Perfection, 383

Persecution, 195–97
Peter, 29, 30, 41, 195, 197
Pharisees
  evil influence of, 102
  extrabiblical traditions of, 98, 101
  false religionism of, 99, 100, 103–10,
    255, 343–44
  healing on the Sabbath and, 257–60
  hostility/opposition to Jesus, 80,
    227, 345–46
  hypocrisy and, 96, 131, 257–65
  Jesus' indictment of, 300
  moralism and, 71, 73
  origin of, 97
  outcasts and, 363
  Prodigal Son parable and, 328–29
  a sign and, 81
  social reciprocity and, 263
  theology of, 256
Pharisees and scribes, 256–57, 295,
  300
Philip the Tetrarch (son of Herod the
  Great), 228
Physical needs, 32–34, 36
Pilate. *See* Pontius Pilate
Piper, John, 122
Places of honor, 262, 263
Pods, 311
Pompeii's destruction, 186
Pontius Pilate, 184–85, 227
Poverty, 32–33
Prayer
  attitude for, 6–8
  boldness in, 53–55, 58
  effectiveness in, 30
  false religions and, 9–10
  God's glory and, 10–11
  importance of, 1–2, 8
  New Testament examples, 2–3
  Old Testament examples, 2, 5–6
  traditional/customary, 4
  See also Lord's Prayer
Preceptive will of God, 28
Preparedness, 157–65

Preterism, 151–52
Pride, 264, 265, 375–76
Priests, 391–92
Prodigal, 307
Prodigal Son parable, 305–28
Profession of faith, 124
Prophecies
    of Israel's future, 247
    of Messiah's earthly kingdom, 209–
        12
    of second coming, 153–54, 409–10
Prophets, 106, 107, 230–32, 239–40
Providence, 140–41
Provision, 32–36, 143–46
Purple dye, 360

Queen of Sheba, 86–87

Rabbis, 101, 103, 131, 279
The Rapture, 153, 156–57, 410, 417
Ravens, 140–41
Readiness, 157–65
Rebellion, 20, 21, 240–41, 309–11
Reciprocity, social, 272–73, 363, 373
Reconciliation, 392–93
Redemption, 24–26, 339
Redemptive kingdom, 24–26
    See also Kingdom of God
The Reformation, 202
Regeneration, 77
Rejoicing, 317
    See also Joy
Relational forgiveness, 41, 42
Repentance
    elements involved in, 188, 220, 350
    God's patience and, 183
    necessity of, 219
    responsibility and, 219, 284–85
    salvation and, 224, 369
    sin and, 313
Resources (natural), 34–36
Resurrection, 86, 268, 269, 151–52, 269
    See also Second coming
Rich man (in parable), 359–68

Rich young ruler, 128, 147, 285
Riches, 32–33, 357, 367
    See also Wealth
Righteousness, 347, 370
    See also Self-righteousness; Works-
        righteousness
Rings, 316, 317
Robes, 316, 317
Roman Catholic Church, 197, 202
Roman soldiers, 233
Romans, 196–97
Russia, 244

Sabbath, 197–98, 201–3, 257–60
Sacredness of God. *See* God
Sadducees, 80, 96, 97, 255, 256
Salt, 288
Salt and light, 72–73
Salvation
    Christ's perspective of, 67, 216–24
    commitment to gospel of, 339
    hope and, 371
    humility and, 264, 265
    of Israel, 410–11
    as kingdom banquet, 273
    missing opportunity for, 221
    the New Covenant and, 369
    reconciliation in, 392–93
    redemptive kingdom and, 24–26
    refusal to accept, 250–51
    repentance and, 224, 369
    roadblocks to, 147–48
Salvation message, 71
Salvation truth, 95
Samaritans, 392, 393
Sanctification, 161
Sandals, 316
Sanhedrin, 195
Satan
    agents of, 66
    as Beelzebul, 62
    Christ's power and, 218
    destruction of, 411
    fearing, 118–19

Jesus' confrontation with, 194
judgment of, 155
opposition to truth, 95
powerlessness of, 67
woman with sickness and, 200–201
Saul of Tarsus, 195
Saving gospel, 70–72
Scoffers, 408–9
Scribes, 103, 104, 257, 258
Scribes and Pharisees
Jesus' denunciations of, 71, 114, 115
opposition to Jesus, 81–82, 305
the prophets and, 106
self-righteousness of, 109, 320–22
See also Pharisees; Scribes
Second coming
believers' desire for, 412–13
the church and, 410, 417
date setting regarding, 153, 157
denying, 151–52, 153
divisiveness of, 419–20
doctrine of, 150–51
events surrounding, 409
judgment and, 420
necessity of, 409–11
praying for, 26, 27
preterism and, 151–52
prophecies of, 153–54, 409–10
readiness for, 157–65
reasons for, 153–56
timing of, 413–18
See also Resurrection
Second World War, 152
Self-assessment, 178
Self-denial, 25, 219, 278, 281, 284, 350
Self-reformation, 76
Self-righteousness, 84, 101, 320–22,
326–27, 348
Shamefulness, 311–13, 318–22
Shamelessness, 307–11, 316–18
Sheep, 296–98
Shepherds, 206, 294, 296–99, 402
Shinners, J.H., 208–9
Sight, 88–91

Signs, 81, 84–86, 371, 404, 418
Siloam, pool of, 187
Siloam, tower in, 187
Sin
confession of, 39
against God, 381
God's forgiveness of, 39–41, 236
judgment for, 13, 369
leading others out of, 379
New Testament words for, 38
repentance and, 313
selfishness and, 368
temptation and, 46–48
universal nature of, 37
the unpardonable, 62
unrepentant, 311
Sire, James W., 14
Slaves, 386
Social reciprocity, 263, 272–73, 336
Social stigma, 389
Societal morality, 69–72
Sodom, 416, 417
Solomon, 86–87
Son of Man, 86, 123, 161, 412, 416
Sovereign will, 28
Sovereignty of God, 22–24, 28, 51–52,
234, 398–99
Spiritual blindness, 81, 89
Spiritual kingdom, 39, 399, 400, 404,
412
See also Kingdom of God
Spiritual obstacles, 377–78
Spiritual truth, 108, 110
Spiritual warfare, 73
Sproul, R.C., 28
Stalin, Josef, 244
Status, 101
Stephen, 195
Stewardship, 334–39
Stoning, 239
Stories, 306–7
See also Parables
Stumbling blocks, 377–78

Substitutionary atonement doctrine, 40
Suffering, 180, 181, 414
Swine, 311
Symbolism, 98, 99
Synagogues, 198–200

A Tale of Two Sons. See John MacArthur
Teachers of the law. *See* Lawyers; Scribes
Temple, 195, 199, 226, 242, 243
Temporal desperation, 220–21
Temptation, 46–48
Testing, 48
   See also Trials
Tetzel, Johan, 202
"The Rubaiyat" (Khayam), 28–29
Theodosius (Byzantine emperor), 243
Theology, 247, 248, 256
Thomas, Robert L., 356
"Thou Art Coming, O My Saviour" (Havergal), 21
Tiberius, 228
Torment, 365, 366
   See also Hell
Total depravity, 56–57
Tozer, A.W., 18, 50
Traditions, 4
Treasure in heaven, 135, 139
Trials, 46, 124, 181, 182, 383, 391
   See also Testing
The tribulation, 153, 156, 157
Trinity, 121
Truth
   absolute, 60, 343
   Christ's application of, 273
   false teachers and, 353–54, 413
   receiving of, 346, 372
   salvation, 95
   spiritual, 95, 304
Tsar Alexander II, 244

Tyrian purple dye, 360

Unbelief, 274–75, 368, 418–20
Unclean spirits, 76
   See also Demons
Uniformitarianism, 409
Universal kingdom, 24, 399–401
   See also Kingdom of God
Unlimited forgiveness, 43, 44
Unpardonable sin, 62
The unregenerate, 144
Urban II (pope), 243

Vultures, 420

Washing the disciples' feet, 41–42
Watchfulness, 157–65
Watson, Thomas, 5
Wealth, 128, 129, 339, 340, 357–61, 367
Wedding feasts, 262
Wickedness, 82, 83
Will of disposition (God's), 28
Woe (declaration of judgment), 101, 102, 106, 108
Word Faith movement, 9–10, 32
Word of Truth, vii
Works-righteousness, 346
World War I, 152
World War II, 152
Worry
   absence of, 140
   divine preference and, 142–43
   God's provision and, 140–41
   God's sovereignty and, 142
   salvation and, 147–48
Worship, 45, 382
Wrath of God. *See* God

Zaccheus, 128
Zealots, 96, 255, 256
Zechariah (the prophet), 107, 211, 231
Zephaniah, 292–93

The MacArthur New Testament Commentary series includes:

Matthew 1–7

Matthew 8–15

Matthew 16–23

Matthew 24–28

Mark 1–8

Mark 9–16

Luke 1–5

Luke 6–10

Luke 11–17

Luke 18–24

John 1–11

John 12–21

Acts 1–12

Acts 13–28

Romans 1–8

Romans 9–16

First Corinthians

Second Corinthians

Galatians

Ephesians

Philippians

Colossians & Philemon

First & Second Thessalonians

First Timothy

Second Timothy

Titus

Hebrews

James

First Peter

Second Peter & Jude

First–Third John

Revelation 1–11

Revelation 12–22

www.MoodyPublishers.com | 1-800-678-6928